angel Trains

BRITISH RAILWAYS

LOCOMOTIVES & COACHING STOCK

2007

The Complete Guide to all Locomotives & Coaching Stock which operate on National Rail & Eurotunnel

Robert Pritchard, Peter Fox & Peter Hall

ISBN 978 1 902 336 55 8

© 2007. Platform 5 Publishing Ltd., 3 Wyvern House, Sark Road, Sheffield, S2 4HG, England.

CONTENTS

Updates 4
Provision of Information 5
Acknowledgements 5
Britain's Railway System 6

SECTION 1 – LOCOMOTIVES

Introduction 10
General Information 12
1.1. Diesel Locomotives.................................... 17
1.2. Electric & Electro-Diesel Locomotives 81
1.3. Eurotunnel Locomotives 89
1.4 Former BR main line locos in industrial service 92

SECTION 2 – LOCO-HAULED PASSENGER COACHING STOCK

Introduction 94
The development of BR Standard Coaches 98
2.1. BR Number Series Stock 100
2.2. High Speed Train Trailer Cars 134
2.3. Saloons 161
2.4. Pullman Car Company Series 165
2.5. Passenger Coaching Stock Awaiting Disposal 168
2.6. 99xxx Range Number Conversion Table 169
2.7. Preserved Locomotive Support Coaches Table 169
2.8 Mark 4 fixed formation sets 170

SECTION 3 – DIESEL MULTIPLE UNITS

Introduction 172
General Information 173
3.1. Diesel Mechanical & Diesel Hydraulic Units 175
    3.1.1. First Generation Units 175
    3.1.2. Second Generation Units 176
3.2. Diesel-Electric DMUs 227
3.3. Service DMUs 233
3.4. DMUs Awaiting Disposal 237

SECTION 4 – ELECTRIC MULTIPLE UNITS

Introduction 238
General Information 239
4.1. 25 kV AC 50 Hz Overhead & Dual-Voltage Units 241
4.2. 750 V DC Third Rail Units 284
4.3. Eurostar Units 322

CONTENTS

4.4. Service/Internal Use EMUs 324
4.5. EMUs Awaiting Disposal 324

SECTION 5 – NON PASSENGER COACHING STOCK

5.1. Non Passenger-Carrying Coaching Stock 326
5.2. NPCCS Awaiting Disposal 335

SECTION 6 – SERVICE STOCK

6.1. Service Stock.. 336
6.2. Service Stock Awaiting Disposal 344

SECTION 7 – UK Light Rail & Metro Systems

7.1. Blackpool & Fleetwood Tramway 346
7.2. Sheffield Supertram 350
7.3. Docklands Light Railway 351
7.4. Croydon Tramlink 352
7.5. Greater Manchester Metrolink............................. 353
7.6. Nottingham Express Transit............................... 355
7.7. Midland Metro 356
7.8. Tyne & Wear Metro 356

SECTION 8 – CODES

8.1. Livery Codes 360
8.2. Owner Codes.. 366
8.3. Locomotive Pool Codes 370
8.4. Operator Codes 374
8.5. Allocation & Location Codes 376
8.6. Abbreviations 380
8.7. Builder Details 381

COVER PHOTOGRAPHS

Front Cover: 67008 slows for the speed restriction over Allt Coire Achaladair bridge at Achallader with the 04.50 Edinburgh–Fort William Sleeper portion on 10 June 2006. This was the first time a Class 67 had worked this train, having replaced Class 37/4s. **Jonathan Allen**

Rear Cover: Tyne & Wear Metro cars 4085, in the standard red livery, and 4042 in a colourful advertising livery for Metro Radio pause at West Jesmond with a service to Park Lane (Sunderland) on 7 October 2006. **Robert Pritchard**

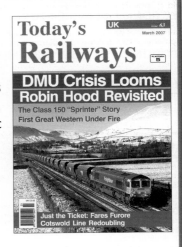

PROVISION OF INFORMATION

This book has been compiled with care to be as accurate as possible, but in some cases official information is not available and the publisher cannot be held responsible for any errors or omissions. We would like to thank the companies and individuals which have been co-operative in supplying information to us. The authors of this book will be pleased to receive notification of any inaccuracies readers may find in the series, and also any additional information to supplement our records and thus enhance future editions. Please send comments to:

Robert Pritchard, Platform 5 Publishing Ltd., 3 Wyvern House, Sark Road, Sheffield, S2 4HG, England.

Tel: 0114 255 2625 **Fax:** 0114 255 2471
e-mail: robert@platform5.com

This book is updated to January 2007.

ACKNOWLEDGEMENTS

The author would like to thank all Train Operating Companies, Freight Companies and Leasing Companies that have helped with the compilation of this book.

Thanks are also due to those who sent reports of changes observed during 2006 for the **Today's Railways UK** magazine "Stock Changes" column and for corrections given to the 2007 "pocket book" series. In particular we are indebted to:

Brian Loughlin, Tony Russell, Nick Lawford, John Hall, Brian Aylott, Martin Haywood, Brian Ovington, Mark Beal, Colin Marsden, Mike Stone, Brian Garvin, Rowland Pittard, John Atkinson, Michael Hunt and many others.

UK LIGHT RAIL SYSTEMS

From this edition we are pleased to be able to include a new section listing the rolling stock of the UK's Light Rail and Metro Systems (excluding the London and Glasgow Underground systems, although we hope to include the Glasgow system at a later date). This was previously listed in this book and as part of the Platform 5 Diesel Multiple Unit pocket book until 2001, but in future will appear as part of this book and also in the EMU pocket book.

BRITAIN'S RAILWAY SYSTEM

INFRASTRUCTURE & OPERATION

Britain's national railway infrastructure is owned by a "not for dividend" company, Network Rail. Many stations and maintenance depots are leased to and operated by Train Operating Companies (TOCs), but some larger stations remain under Network Rail control. The only exception is the infrastructure on the Isle of Wight, which is nationally owned and is leased to the Island Line franchisee.

Trains are operated by TOCs over Network Rail, regulated by access agreements between the parties involved. In general, TOCs are responsible for the provision and maintenance of the locomotives, rolling stock and staff necessary for the direct operation of services, whilst Network Rail is responsible for the provision and maintenance of the infrastructure and also for staff needed to regulate the operation of services.

DOMESTIC PASSENGER TRAIN OPERATORS

The large majority of passenger trains are operated by the TOCs on fixed term franchises. Franchise expiry dates are shown in parentheses in the list of franchisees below:

Franchise	Franchisee	Trading Name
Central Trains[1]	National Express Group plc (until 11 November 2007)	Central Trains
Chiltern Railways	M40 Trains Ltd. (until 21 July 2021)	Chiltern Railways
Cross-Country[2]	Virgin Rail Group Ltd. (until 11 November 2007)	Virgin Trains
Gatwick Express[3]	National Express Group plc (until 1 May 2011)	Gatwick Express
Greater Western[4]	First Group plc (until 1 April 2013)	First Great Western
Greater Anglia[5]	National Express Group plc (until 1 April 2011)	"One"
Integrated Kent[6]	GoVia Ltd. (Go-Ahead/Keolis) (until 1 April 2012)	Southeastern
InterCity East Coast[7]	GNER Holdings Ltd.	Great North Eastern Railway
InterCity West Coast	Virgin Rail Group Ltd. (until 9 March 2012)	Virgin Trains
Island Line[8]	Stagecoach Holdings plc (until 4 February 2007)	Island Line
LTS Rail	National Express Group plc (until 29 May 2011)	c2c
Merseyrail Electrics[9]	Serco/NedRail (until 20 July 2028)	Merseyrail Electrics

Midland Main Line[10]	National Express Group plc (until 11 November 2007)	Midland Mainline
North London Railways[11]	National Express Group plc (until 11 November 2007)	Silverlink Train Services
Northern Rail[12]	Serco/NedRail (until 12 September 2013)	Northern
ScotRail	First Group plc (until 17 October 2011)	First ScotRail
South Central	GoVia Ltd. (Go-Ahead/Keolis) (until 31 December 2009)	Southern
South Western[8]	Stagecoach Holdings plc (until 4 February 2007)	South West Trains
Thameslink/Great Northern[13]	First Group plc (until 1 April 2012)	First Capital Connect
Trans-Pennine Express	First Group/Keolis (until 1 February 2012)	First Trans-Pennine Express
Wales & Borders	Arriva Trains Ltd. (until 7 December 2018)	Arriva Trains Wales

Notes:

[1] Due to be abolished on expiry. Services to be split between the new East Midlands franchise (also incorporating the existing Midland Mainline franchise and part of Cross-Country) and West Midlands franchises (including all existing West Midlands area Central Trains and Silverlink services). Chiltern Railways have been asked to submit a separate proposal to operate the existing Birmingham Snow Hill Central Trains services.

[2] A new expanded Cross-Country franchise will be created from November 2007, also including the existing Central Trains Birmingham–Stansted Airport and Nottingham–Hereford/Cardiff services.

[3] Gatwick Express has been proposed for possible absorption by Southern as part of the DfT's Brighton Main Line Route Utilisation Strategy. This could take place before the expiry of the current Gatwick Express franchise.

[4] The new Greater Western franchise started on 1 April 2006 and incorporates the former Great Western, Wessex Trains and Thames Trains franchises. Awarded for seven years to 2013 with a possible extension by a further three if performance targets are met.

[5] Incorporates the former Anglia and Great Eastern franchises and the West Anglia half of West Anglia Great Northern. Awarded for seven years with a likely extension for a further three.

[6] The new Integrated Kent franchise started on 1 April 2006 for an initial period of six years to 2012, to be extended by a further two if performance targets are met.

[7] The new East Coast franchise started on 1 May 2005 and was intended to last for an initial period of seven years, to be extended by a further three if performance targets were met. However, the recent financial difficulties of GNER's holding company Sea Containers have led to a decision by the Department for Transport to relet the franchise. The new operator is expected to assume responsibility between late 2007 and mid-2008. Until that time GNER will maintain services under a temporary "Management Agreement".

[8] These two franchises will be combined to form the new South Western franchise on 4 February 2007, held by Stagecoach Holdings. The new franchise will be in place by the time this publication goes on sale.

[9] Now under control of Merseytravel PTE instead of the DfT. Franchise due to be reviewed after seven years and then every five years to fit in with Merseyside Local Transport Plan.

[10] Due to be replaced by the new East Midlands franchise, incorporating all existing Midland Mainline and East Midlands area Central Trains services.

[11] Due to be abolished on expiry. Services to be split between a new London Rail franchise (control of which will be transferred to Transport for London) and the new West Midlands franchise.

[12] Urban and rural services previously run by Arriva Trains Northern and First North Western were transferred to the new Northern franchise on 12 December 2004. Trans-Pennine services formerly run by these operators were taken over by the new Trans-Pennine Express franchise on 1 February 2004. The Northern franchise runs for up to 8¾ years.

[13] Incorporates the former Thameslink franchise and Great Northern half of the former West Anglia Great Northern franchise. Runs for six years to 2012 with a possible extension for up to three years depending on performance targets.

All new franchises officially start at 02.00 on the first day. Because of this the finishing date of an old franchise and the start date of its successor are the same.

A major reorganisation of franchises is under way. See **Today's Railways UK** magazine for developments.

The following operators run non-franchised services only:

Operator	Trading Name	Route
BAA	Heathrow Express	London Paddington–Heathrow Airport
Hull Trains §	Hull Trains	London King's Cross–Hull
West Coast Railway	West Coast Railway Company	Birmingham–Stratford-on-Avon Fort William–Mallaig* York–Scarborough*

* Special summer-dated services only.
§ Owned by First Group.

INTERNATIONAL PASSENGER OPERATIONS

Eurostar (UK) operates international passenger-only services between the United Kingdom and continental Europe, jointly with French National Railways (SNCF) and Belgian National Railways (SNCB/NMBS). Eurostar (UK) is a subsidiary of London & Continental Railways, which is jointly owned by National Express Group plc and British Airways.

In addition, a service for the conveyance of accompanied road vehicles through the Channel Tunnel is provided by the tunnel operating company, Eurotunnel.

FREIGHT TRAIN OPERATIONS

The following operators operate freight train services under "Open Access" arrangements:

English Welsh & Scottish Railway Ltd (EWS).
GB Railfreight Ltd. (owned by First Group)
Direct Rail Services Ltd.
Freightliner Ltd.
Fastline
Victa Westlink Rail (formerly FM Rail)
Advenza (Cotswold Rail)

1. LOCOMOTIVES

INTRODUCTION

SCOPE

This section contains details of all locomotives which can run on Britain's national railway network, plus those of Eurotunnel. Locomotives which are owned by, for example, EWS and Freightliner which have been withdrawn from service and awaiting disposal are now listed in the main list, as are those owned by companies such as Harry Needle and DRS which are awaiting possible restoration to service. Only preserved locomotives which are currently used on the National Rail network are included. Others, which may be Network Rail registered but not at present certified for use, are not included, but will be found in the Platform 5 book, "Preserved Locomotives and Multiple Units". Locos already at scrapyards are not generally included, unless they are there for storage purposes and not for disposal.

LOCO CLASSES

Loco classes are listed in numerical order of class. Principal details and dimensions are quoted for each class in metric and/or imperial units as considered appropriate bearing in mind common UK usage.

Builders: These are shown in class headings. Abbreviations used are found in section 8.8.

All dimensions and weights are quoted for locomotives in an "as new" condition with all necessary supplies (e.g. oil, water and sand) on board. Dimensions are quoted in the order length x width. Lengths quoted are over buffers or couplers as appropriate. All widths quoted are maxima. Where two different wheel diameter dimensions are shown, the first refers to powered wheels and the second refers to non-powered wheels.

NUMERICAL LISTINGS

Locomotives are listed in numerical order. Where numbers actually carried are different from those officially allocated, these are noted in class headings where appropriate. Where locomotives have been recently renumbered, the most immediate previous number is shown in parentheses. Each locomotive entry is laid out as in the following example:

RSL No.	Detail	Livery	Owner	Pool	Allocn.	Name
47813	+m **CD**	CD	CD	CRRH	GL	John Peel

Detail Differences. Only detail differences which currently affect the areas and types of train which locomotives may work are shown. All other detail differences are specifically excluded. Where such differences occur within a class or part class, they are shown in the "Detail" column alongside the individual locomotive number.

Standard abbreviations used are:

a	Train air brake equipment only.
b	Drophead buckeye couplers.
c	Scharfenberg couplers.
d	Fitted with retractable Dellner couplers.
k	Fitted with Swinghead Automatic "buckeye" combination couplers.
p	Train air, vacuum and electro-pneumatic brakes.
r	RETB fitted
s	Slow Speed Control equipment.
v	Train vacuum brake only.
x	Train air and vacuum brakes ("Dual brakes").
+	Additional fuel tank capacity.
§	Sandite laying equipment.

In all cases use of the above abbreviations indicates the equipment indicated is normally operable. Meaning of non-standard abbreviations and symbols is detailed in individual class headings.

Codes. Codes are used to denote the livery, owner, pool and depot of each locomotive. Details of these will be found in section 8 of this book.

Names. Only names carried with official sanction are listed. As far as possible names are shown in UPPER/lower case characters as actually shown on the name carried on the locomotive.

GENERAL INFORMATION

CLASSIFICATION AND NUMBERING

All locomotives are classified and allocated numbers by the Rolling Stock Library under the TOPS numbering system, introduced in 1972. This comprises a two-digit class number followed by a three-digit serial number. Where the actual number carried by a locomotive differs from the allocated number, or where an additional number is carried to the allocated number, this is shown by a note in the class heading.

For diesel locomotives, class numbers offer an indication of engine horsepower as shown in the table below.

Class No. Range	Engine h.p.
01–14	0–799
15–20	800–1000
21–31	1001–1499
32–39	1500–1999
40–54, 57	2000–2999
55–56, 58–69	3000+

For electric locomotives class numbers are allocated in ascending numerical order under the following scheme:

Class 70–80	direct current and DC/diesel dual system locomotives.
Class 81 onwards	alternating current and AC/DC dual system locos.

Numbers in the 89xxx series are allocated by the Rolling Stock Library to locomotives which have been de-registered but subsequently re-registered for use on the Network Rail network and whose original number has already been re-used. 89xxx numbers are normally only carried inside locomotive cabs and are not carried externally in normal circumstances.

WHEEL ARRANGEMENT

For main line locomotives the number of driven axles on a bogie or frame is denoted by a letter (A = 1, B = 2, C = 3 etc.) and the number of non-powered axles is denoted by a number. The use of the letter "o" after a letter indicates each axle is individually powered, whilst the "+" symbol indicates bogies are inter-coupled.

For shunting locomotives, the Whyte notation is used. In this notation the number of leading wheels are given, followed by the number of driving wheels and then the trailing wheels.

HAULAGE CAPABILITY OF DIESEL LOCOMOTIVES

The haulage capability of a diesel locomotive depends upon three basic factors:

1. Adhesive weight. The greater the weight on the driving wheels, the greater the adhesion and more tractive power can be applied before wheelslip occurs.

2. The characteristics of its transmission. To start a train the locomotive has to exert a pull at standstill. A direct drive diesel engine cannot do this, hence the need for transmission. This may be mechanical, hydraulic or electric. The present British Standard for locomotives is electric transmission. Here the diesel engine drives a generator or alternator and the current produced is fed to the traction motors. The force produced by each driven wheel depends on the current in its traction motor. In other words, the larger the current, the harder it pulls. As the locomotive speed increases, the current in the traction motor falls, hence the *Maximum Tractive Effort* is the maximum force at its wheels the locomotive can exert at a standstill. The electrical equipment cannot take such high currents for long without overheating. Hence the *Continuous Tractive Effort* is quoted which represents the current which the equipment can take continuously.

3. The power of its engine. Not all power reaches the rail, as electrical machines are approximately 90% efficient. As the electrical energy passes through two such machines (the generator or alternator and the traction motors), the *Power at Rail* is approximately 81% (90% of 90%) of the engine power, less a further amount used for auxiliary equipment such as radiator fans, traction motor blowers, air compressors, battery charging, cab heating, Electric Train Supply (ETS) etc. The power of the locomotive is proportional to the tractive effort times the speed. Hence when on full power there is a speed corresponding to the continuous tractive effort.

HAULAGE CAPABILITY OF ELECTRIC LOCOMOTIVES

Unlike a diesel locomotive, an electric locomotive does not develop its power on board and its performance is determined only by two factors, namely its weight and the characteristics of its electrical equipment. Whereas a diesel locomotive tends to be a constant power machine, the power of an electric locomotive varies considerably. Up to a certain speed it can produce virtually a constant tractive effort. Hence power rises with speed according to the formula given in section three above, until a maximum speed is reached at which tractive effort falls, such that the power also falls. Hence the power at the speed corresponding to the maximum tractive effort is lower than the maximum speed.

BRAKE FORCE

The brake force is a measure of the braking power of a locomotive. This is shown on the locomotive data panels so operating staff can ensure sufficient brake power is available on freight trains.

ELECTRIC TRAIN SUPPLY (ETS)

A number of locomotives are equipped to provide a supply of electricity to the train being hauled to power auxiliaries such as heating, cooling fans, air conditioning and kitchen equipment. ETS is provided from the locomotive by means of a separate alternator (except Class 33 locos, which have a DC generator). The ETS index of a locomotive is a measure of the electrical power available for train supply.

Similarly, most loco-hauled coaches also have an ETS index, which in this case is a measure of the power required to operate equipment mounted in the coach. The sum of the ETS indices of all the hauled vehicles in a train must not exceed the ETS index of the locomotive.

ETS is commonly (but incorrectly) known as ETH (Electric Train Heating), which is a throwback to the days before loco-hauled coaches were equipped with electrically powered auxiliary equipment other than for train heating.

ROUTE AVAILABILITY (RA)

This is a measure of a railway vehicle's axle load. The higher the axle load of a vehicle, the higher the RA number on a scale from 1 to 10. Each Network Rail route has a RA number and in general no vehicle with a higher RA number may travel on that route without special clearance.

MULTIPLE & PUSH-PULL WORKING

Multiple working between vehicles (i.e. two or more powered vehicles being driven from one cab) is facilitated by jumper cables connecting the vehicles. However, not all types are compatible with each other, and a number of different systems are in use, each system being incompatible with any other.

Association of American Railroads (AAR) System: Classes 59, 66, and 67.
Blue Star Coupling Code: Classes 20, 25, 31, 33, 37 40 and 73.
DRS System: Classes 20/3, 37 and 47.
Green Circle Coupling Code: Class 47 (not all equipped).
Orange Square Coupling Code: Class 50.
Red Diamond Coupling Code: Classes 56 and 58.
SR System: Classes 33/1, 73 and various electric multiple units.
Within Own Class only: Classes 43 and 60.

Many locomotives use a time-division multiplex (TDM) system for push-pull and multiple working which utilises the existing RCH jumper cables fitted to coaching stock vehicles. Previously these cables had only been used to control train lighting and public address systems.

Class 47 locos 47701–47717 were equipped with an older non-standard TDM system.

1. DIESEL LOCOMOTIVES

CLASS 08   BR/ENGLISH ELECTRIC   0-6-0

Built: 1955–1962 by BR at Crewe, Darlington, Derby Locomotive, Doncaster or Horwich Works.
Engine: English Electric 6KT of 298 kW (400 h.p.) at 680 r.p.m.
Main Generator: English Electric 801.
Traction Motors: Two English Electric 506.
Maximum Tractive Effort: 156 kN (35000 lbf).
Continuous Tractive Effort: 49 kN (11100 lbf) at 8.8 m.p.h.
Power At Rail: 194 kW (260 h.p.).   **Train Brakes:** Air & vacuum.
Brake Force: 19 t.   **Dimensions:** 8.92 x 2.59 m.
Weight: 49.6–50.4 t.   **Wheel Diameter:** 1372 mm.
Design Speed: 20 m.p.h.   **Maximum Speed:** 15 m.p.h.
Fuel Capacity: 3037 litres.   **RA:** 5.
Train Supply: Not equipped.
Multiple Working: m Equipped for multiple working. All others not equipped.

Notes: † – Equipped with remote control (Hima Sella system) for working at Celsa (formerly Allied Steel & Wire), Cardiff.

§ – Equipped with remote control (Cattron system) for evaluation purposes.

Actual locations for operational shunters are given where known, apart from EWS and Freightliner-operated locos which move about on a regular basis.

Non-standard liveries/numbering:

08350 Carries number D3420.
08414 As **DG**, but with BR & Railfreight Distribution logos and large bodyside numbers. Carries number D3529.
08442 Dark grey lower bodyside with light grey upper bodyside.
08460 Light grey with black underframe, cab doors, window surrounds & roof. Carries number D3575.
08480 Yellow with a red bodyside band. Carries number "TOTON No 1".
08499 Pullman Rail blue & white.
08568 and 08730 Alstom (Springburn) livery. Dark grey lower bodyside with light grey upper bodyside. Red solebar stripe.
08613 Blue with a white bodyside stripe & BOMBARDIER TRANSPORTATION branding.
08616 Carries number 3783.
08629 Red with italic numbers.
08648 Yellow with black cabsides & roof.
08649 Grey with blue, white & red stripes & Alstom logo. Carries number D3816.
08682 Dark blue with a grey roof.
08699 All-over mid blue.
08701 Carries number "Tyne 100".
08715 "Day-glo" orange.
08721 As **B**, but with a black roof & "Express parcels" branding with red & yellow stripe.

08824 Carries number "IEMD01".
08883 Caledonian Railway style blue.
08911 Royal blue with a grey roof.
08928 As **FO** with large bodyside numbers & light blue solebar.

Originally numbered in series D3000–D4192.

Class 08/0. Standard Design.

08077	**FL**	P	DFLS	FD	
08308 a	**CS**	RT	MOLO	IS	
08331	**GN**	RT	MOLS	ZB	
08350	**G**	LW	MBDL	CP	
08375 a	**RT**	RT	MOLO	ZB	
08389 a	**E**	E	WSWM	BS	
08393 a	**E**	E	WSEM	TO	
08397 a	**E**	E	WZTS	AN	
08401 a	**DG**	E	WZTS	IM	
08402 a	**E**	E	WNXX	ML	
08405 a	**E**	E	WSWR	OC	
08410 a	**GL**	FG	EFSH	PZ	
08411 a	**B**	E	WNYX	AN	
08414 a	**O**	E	WNYX	TT	
08417 a	**SB**	SO	CDJD	ZA	
08418 a	**E**	E	WZTS	BS	
08428 a	**B**	E	WSEM	TO	
08441 a	**E**	E	WNYX	ML	
08442 a	**O**	E	WSXX	EH	RICHARD J. WENHAM EASTLEIGH DEPOT DECEMBER 1989–JULY 1999
08451	**GB**	VW	ATXX	MA	
08454	**K**	VW	ATLO	WB	
08460 a	**O**	E	WZTS	AN	
08466 a†	**E**	E	WSAW	MG	
08472	**WA**	WA	RFSH	EC	
08480 a	**O**	E	WSXX	TO	
08482 a	**E**	E	WRLN	TD	
08483	**GL**	FG	EFSH	OO	DUSTY Driver David Miller
08485 a	**B**	E	WZTS	CU	
08489 a	**E**	E	WZTS	MH	
08492 a	**B**	HN	HNRL	BH	
08493 a	**B**	RT	MOLS	DW	
08495	**E**	E	WSNE	TE	NOEL KIRTON OBE
08499 a	**O**	E	WSXX	CF	
08500	**E**	E	WSSC	ML	
08506 a	**B**	E	WNXX	OC	
08507 a	**HN**	HN	HNRL	CZ	
08509 a	**F**	E	WNYX	IM	
08510 a	**B**	E	WZTS	EH	
08511 a	**E**	E	WNYX	AY	
08512 a	**E**	E	WSEM	TO	
08514 a	**E**	E	WSNE	TE	
08516 a	**E**	E	WSXX	BK	

08523	ML	RT	MOLO	SB	
08525	MA	MA	HISL	NL	
08526	E	E	WNTS	MG	
08527	F	HN	HNRL	BH	
08528	DG	E	WNTS	BS	
08529	B	RT	MOLS	DW	
08530	FL	P	DFLS	FD	
08531 a	DG	P	DFLS	FD	
08535	DG	RT	MOLS	CP	
08536	B	MA	HISE	DY (S)	
08538	DG	E	WRWM	BS	
08540	E	E	WNTR	TO	
08541	DG	HN	HNRS	OC	
08543	DG	E	WNYX	BS	
08561	B	E	WNXX	DR	
08567	E	E	WNYX	DR	
08568 a	O	AM	ARZH	ZH	St. Rollox
08569	E	E	WNYX	DR	
08571 a	WA	WA	HBSH	BN	
08573	RT	RT	MOLO	WR	
08575	FL	P	DFLS	FD	
08577	E	E	WNTR	BS	
08578	E	E	WSWM	BS	
08580	E	E	WNYX	BS	
08582 a	DG	E	WNYX	DR	
08585	FL	P	DFLS	FD	Vicky
08587	E	E	WNXX	MG	
08588	RT	RT	MOLO	ZI	
08593	E	E	WSWM	BS	
08596 a†	WA	WA	RFSH	ZB	
08597	E	E	WNTR	TE	
08599	E	E	WNTR	IM	
08605	E	E	WSSC	ML	
08611	V	VW	ATXX	LL	Downside C.S.
08613	O	RT	KCSI	ZI	
08615	WA	WA	RFSH	EC	
08616	GW	MA	HGSS	TS	COOKIE
08617	VP	VW	ATLO	WB	
08623	E	E	WNTR	TO	
08624	FL	P	DFLS	FD	
08629	O	AM	ARZN	ZN	
08630	E	E	WSGW	MG	
08631	N	PO	SDFR	DF (S)	EAGLE
08632	E	E	WSWM	BS	
08633	E	E	WSEM	TO	
08635	B	E	WNYX	TT	
08641	FB	FG	EFSH	LA	
08644	GL	FG	EFSH	LA	
08645	GL	FG	EFSH	LA	
08646	F	E	WNXX	MG	
08648	O	RT	MOLO	NW	

08649		**0**	AM	ARZN	ZN	G.H. Stratton
08651	a	**DG**	E	WNYX	BS	
08653		**E**	E	WRWM	BS	
08662		**E**	E	WSNE	TE	
08663	a	**GL**	FG	EFSH	PM	
08664		**E**	E	WSLS	OC	DON GATES 1952-2000
08665		**E**	E	WNYX	HM	
08669	a	**WA**	WA	RFSH	ZB	
08670	a	**E**	E	WNYX	ML	
08676		**E**	E	WSWR	OC	
08682		**0**	BT	KDSD	ZF	Lionheart
08683		**E**	E	WNXX	TT	
08685		**E**	E	WSNE	TE	
08689	a	**E**	E	WSWR	OC	
08690		**MA**	MA	HISE	NL	
08691		**FL**	WA	DFLS	FD	Terri
08694	a	**E**	E	WNXX	OC	
08695	a	**E**	E	WNYX	AY	
08696	a	**G**	VW	ATLO	MA	LONGSIGHT TMD
08697		**B**	MA	HISE	DY (S)	
08698	a	**E**	E	WNTS	TE	
08699		**0**	CD	CROL	AS	
08701	a	**RX**	E	WSXX	Ford, Bridgend	
08703	a	**E**	E	WSEM	TO	
08706		**E**	E	WSWM	BS	
08709		**E**	E	WSWM	BS	MOLLY'S DAY
08711	k	**RX**	E	WSEM	TO	
08714		**E**	E	WSGW	MG	Cambridge
08715	v	**0**	E	WNXX	CU	
08720	a	**E**	E	WNYX	ML	
08721		**0**	VW	ATLO	MA	STARLET
08724		**WA**	WA	HBSH	NL	
08730		**0**	AM	ARZH	ZH	The Caley
08735		**E**	E	WSEM	TO	
08737	a	**E**	E	WSWM	BS	
08738	m	**ECR**	E	WNXX	TO	
08742		**RX**	E	WNXX	BS	
08745		**FE**	P	DHLT	SZ	
08750	a	**RT**	RT	MOLO	WR	
08752	†	**E**	E	WSAW	MG	
08754		**FL**	RT	MOLO	MY	
08756		**DG**	RT	MOLO	ZB (S)	
08757		**RG**	E	WSWR	OC	
08762		**RT**	RT	MOLO	ZB	
08765		**E**	E	WSLS	OC	
08770	a	**DG**	E	WNTR	Onllwyn	
08775		**E**	E	WSWM	BS	
08776	a	**DG**	E	WNTR	DR	
08780		**RV**	RV	RTSO	CP	
08782	a†	**CU**	E	WRWM	BS	CASTLETON WORKS
08783		**E**	E	WRWM	BS	

08784		E	E	WSEM	TO
08785 a	FL	P	DFLS	FD
08786 a	DG	E	WSLN	TD
08788	RT	RT	MOLO	IS
08790	B	VW	ATLO	MA	M.A. Smith
08792	F	E	WNXX	BS
08795	GL	FG	EFSH	LE
08798	E	E	WSSC	ML
08799 a	E	E	WSNE	TE	ANDY BOWER
08802	RX	E	WNTS	AN
08804	E	E	WSWR	OC
08805	B	MA	HGSS	SI
08807	BR	E	WNYX	ML
08809	AR	CD	CREL	AS (S)
08810 a	AR	LW	MBDL	CP
08813 a	DG	HN	HNRS	LM
08818	HN	HN	HNRL	LM	MOLLY
08819	DG	RT	MOLS	DW
08822	GL	FG	EFSH	LE
08824 ak	K	E	WSXX	CE
08827 a	B	HN	HNRS	LM
08828 a	E	E	WSXX	BS
08830	LW	AW	MBDL	ZB
08834	DR	DR	XHSH	KM
08836	GL	FG	EFSH	PM
08842	E	E	WSWM	BS
08844	E	E	WRWM	BS	CHRIS WREN 1955–2002
08847	CD	CD	CREL	NC
08853 a	B	WA	RFSH	BN
08854 †	E	E	WRLS	OC
08856	B	E	WNXX	DC
08865	E	E	WSWR	OC
08866	E	E	WSSC	ML
08868	B	HN	HNRL	CP
08869	G	HN	HNRS	LM
08871	CD	CD	CREL	NC
08872	E	E	WZTS	IM	TONY LONG STRATFORD DEPOT 1971–2002
08874	SL	RT	MOLO	BY	Catherine
08877	DG	E	WSXX	SP
08879	E	E	WSLS	OC
08881	DG	E	WZTS	ML
08883	O	E	WNYX	ML
08884	B	E	WZTS	BS
08885	GB	RT	MOLO	MY
08886 §	E	E	WSAW	MG
08887 a	VP	VW	ATXX	MA
08888	E	E	WNTS	TE
08890	DG	E	WNYX	EH
08891	FL	P	DFLS	FD	J.R 1951–2005
08892	DR	DR	XHSH	KM
08894	B	E	WNYX	AN

08896		E	E	WNXX	TT	
08897		E	E	WSWM	BS	
08899		MA	MA	HISE	DY	
08900		DG	E	WNTS	MG	
08902		B	E	WNYX	AN	
08904		E	E	WSLN	TD	
08905		E	E	WNTS	BS	
08907		E	E	WRWM	BS	
08908		MM	MA	HISL	DY	
08909		E	E	WREM	TO	
08910		B	E	WNYX	TT	
08911		0	NM	MBDL	YK	MATEY
08912		B	E	WNYX	TT	
08913		E	E	WNXX	ML	
08915		F	E	WNXX	TO	
08918		DG	E	WNTS	OC	
08919		RX	E	WNYX	OC	
08920		F	E	WNXX	BS	
08921	†	E	E	WSAW	MG	
08922		DG	E	WRSC	ML	
08924		E	E	WNTS	ML	
08925		B	E	WNXX	DR	
08926		B	E	WNYX	AN	
08927		B	E	WNTS	ML	
08928		0	HN	HNRS	LM	
08933		E	E	WRLS	OC	
08934	a	VP	VW	ATXX	WB	
08936		HN	HN	CREL	GL (S)	
08939	m	ECR	E	WRWR	OC	
08941		E	E	WSAW	MG	
08942		B	E	WNYX	TT	
08946		FE	E	WNYX	AN	
08947		B	E	WNXX	WY	
08948	c	EP	EU	GPSS	NP	
08950		MA	MA	HISL	NL	
08951	†	E	E	WNTS	AN	FRED
08953	a	DG	E	WNXX	DR	
08954		F	E	WNXX	AN	
08955		F	E	WNXX	BS	
08956		SB	SO	CDJD	ZA	

Class 08/9. Reduced height cab. Converted 1985–1987 by BR at Landore T&RSMD.

08993		E	E	WNTR	DR
08994	a	E	E	WSEM	TO
08995	a	E	E	WNTR	DR

CLASS 09   BR/ENGLISH ELECTRIC   0-6-0

Built: 1959–1962 by BR at Darlington or Horwich Works.
Engine: English Electric 6KT of 298 kW (400 h.p.) at 680 r.p.m.
Main Generator: English Electric 801.
Traction Motors: English Electric 506.
Maximum Tractive Effort: 111 kN (25000 lbf).
Continuous Tractive Effort: 39 kN (8800 lbf) at 11.6 m.p.h.
Power At Rail: 201 kW (269 h.p.).   **Train Brakes:** Air & vacuum.
Brake Force: 19 t.   **Dimensions:** 8.92 x 2.59 m.
Weight: 49 t.   **Wheel Diameter:** 1372 mm.
Design Speed: 27 m.p.h.   **Maximum Speed:** 27 m.p.h.
Fuel Capacity: 3037 litres.   **RA:** 5.
Train Supply: Not equipped.   **Multiple Working:** Not equipped.

Class 09/0 were originally numbered D3665–D3671, D3719–3721, D4099–D4114.

Class 09/0. Built as Class 09.

09001	**E**	E	WSGW	MG	
09003	**E**	E	WSWR	OC	
09005 k	**E**	E	WRLS	OC	
09006	**E**	E	WSLS	OC	
09007	**ML**	E	WNTS	Worksop	
09008	**E**	E	WNTR	BS	
09009	**E**	E	WNXX	SL	Three Bridges C.E.D.
09010	**DG**	E	WNTR	HG	
09011	**DG**	E	WNTS	MG	
09012	**DG**	E	WNXX	HG	
09013	**DG**	E	WSGW	MG	
09014	**DG**	E	WSNE	TE	
09015	**E**	E	WSGW	MG	
09016	**E**	E	WNXX	BZ	
09017	**E**	E	WSGW	MG	
09018	**E**	E	WNXX	HG	
09019	**ML**	E	WSWR	OC	
09020	**E**	E	WSGW	MG	
09021	**E**	E	WNXX	IM	
09022 a	**E**	E	WSWM	BS	
09023 a	**E**	E	WSEM	TO	
09024	**ML**	E	WSLS	OC	
09026	**G**	SN	HWSU	BI	Cedric Wares

Class 09/1. Converted from Class 08. 110 V electrical equipment.
Converted: 1992–1993 by RFS Industries, Kilnhurst.

09101	(08833)	**DG**	E	WSGW	MG
09102	(08832)	**DG**	E	WNTS	MG
09103	(08766)	**DG**	E	WSSC	ML
09104	(08749)	**DG**	E	WNXX	TE
09105	(08835)	**DG**	E	WSGW	MG
09106	(08759)	**DG**	E	WSEM	TO
09107	(08845)	**DG**	E	WRSC	ML

Class 09/2. Converted from Class 08. 90 V electrical equipment.
Converted: 1992 by RFS Industries, Kilnhurst.

09201	(08421)	ak	**DG**	E	WSNE	TE
09202	(08732)		**DG**	E	WNYX	DR
09203	(08781)		**DG**	E	WNYX	CE
09204	(08717)		**DG**	E	WNXX	TY
09205	(08620)		**DG**	E	WSNE	TE

CLASS 20   ENGLISH ELECTRIC   Bo-Bo

Built: 1957–1968 by English Electric Company at Vulcan Foundry, Newton le
Willows or by Robert Stephenson & Hawthorn at Darlington.
Engine: English Electric 8SVT Mk. II of 746 kW (1000 h.p.) at 850 r.p.m.
Main Generator: English Electric 819/3C.
Traction Motors: English Electric 526/5D or 526/8D.
Maximum Tractive Effort: 187 kN (42000 lbf).
Continuous Tractive Effort: 111 kN (25000 lbf) at 11 m.p.h.
Power At Rail: 574 kW (770 h.p.).   **Train Brakes:** Air & vacuum.
Brake Force: 35 t.   **Dimensions:** 14.25 x 2.67 m.
Weight: 73.4–73.5 t.   **Wheel Diameter:** 1092 mm.
Design Speed: 75 m.p.h.   **Maximum Speed:** 75 m.p.h.
Fuel Capacity: 1727 litres.   **RA:** 5.
Train Supply: Not equipped.   **Multiple Working:** Blue Star.

Non-standard liveries/numbering:

20088 RFS grey.
20092 BR Central Services red & grey.
20132 Carries number D8132.
20138 and 20215 As **F0** but with a red solebar stripe.
20906 Carries no number.

Originally numbered in series D8007–D8190, D8315–D8325.

Class 20/0. Standard Design.

20016	**B**	HN	HNRS	LM	
20032	**B**	HN	HNRS	LM	
20057	**B**	HN	HNRS	LM	
20072	**B**	HN	HNRS	LM	
20081	**B**	HN	HNRS	LM	
20088	**0**	HN	HNRS	LM	
20092	**0**	HN	HNRS	BH	
20096	**F**	HN	HNRL	BH	
20121	**B**	HN	HNRS	BH	
20132	**G**	HN	HNRS	BH	
20138	**0**	HN	HNRS	LM	
20215	**0**	HN	HNRS	LM	

Class 20/3. Direct Rail Services refurbished locos. Details as Class 20/0 except:

Refurbished: 1995–1996 by Brush Traction at Loughborough (20301–20305) or 1997–1998 by RFS(E) at Doncaster (20306–20315). Disc indicators or headcode panels removed.

Train Brakes: Air.	**Maximum Speed:** 75 m.p.h.	
Weight: 76 t.	**Fuel Capacity:** 2900 (+ 4909) litres.	
Brake Force: 35 t.	**RA:** 6.	

Multiple Working: DRS system.

20301	(20047)	+	**DR**	DR XHNC	KM	Max Joule 1958–1999
20302	(20084)		**DR**	DR XHNC	KM	
20303	(20127)	+	**DR**	DR XHNC	KM	
20304	(20120)		**DR**	DR XHNC	KM	
20305	(20095)		**DR**	DR XHNC	KM	
20306	(20131)	+	**DR**	DR XHNC	KM	
20307	(20128)	+	**DR**	DR XHNC	KM	
20308	(20187)	+	**DR**	DR XHNC	KM	
20309	(20075)	+	**DR**	DR XHNC	KM	
20310	(20190)	+	**DR**	DR XHNC	KM	
20311	(20102)	+	**DR**	DR XHMW	ZH	
20312	(20042)	+	**DR**	DR XHNC	KM	
20313	(20194)	+	**DR**	DR XHNC	KM	
20314	(20117)	+	**DR**	DR XHNC	KM	
20315	(20104)	+	**DR**	DR XHNC	KM	

Class 20/9. Harry Needle Railroad Company (former Hunslet-Barclay/DRS) locos.

Details as Class 20/0 except:

Refurbished: 1989 by Hunslet-Barclay at Kilmarnock.

Train Brakes: Air.   **Fuel Capacity:** 1727 (+ 4727) litres.

20901	(20101)		**DR**	HN HNRL	BH
20902	(20060)	+	**DR**	HN HNRS	LM
20903	(20083)	+	**DR**	HN HNRS	ZH
20904	(20041)		**DR**	HN HNRL	BH
20905	(20225)	+	**F**	HN HNRL	BH
20906	(20219)		**DR**	HN HNRS	CP

CLASS 31 BRUSH/ENGLISH ELECTRIC A1A-A1A

Built: 1958–1962 by Brush Traction at Loughborough.
Engine: English Electric 12SVT of 1100 kW (1470 h.p.) at 850 r.p.m.
Main Generator: Brush TG160-48.   **Traction Motors:** Brush TM73-68.
Maximum Tractive Effort: 160 kN (35900 lbf).
Continuous Tractive Effort: 83 kN (18700 lbf) at 23.5 m.p.h.
Power At Rail: 872 kW (1170 h.p.).   **Train Brakes:** Air & vacuum.
Brake Force: 49 t.   **Dimensions:** 17.30 x 2.67 m.
Weight: 106.7–111 t.   **Wheel Diameter:** 1092/1003 mm.
Design Speed: 90 m.p.h.   **Maximum Speed:** 90 m.p.h.
Fuel Capacity: 2409 litres.   **RA:** 5 or 6.
Train Supply: Not equipped.   **Multiple Working:** Blue Star.

Originally numbered D5520–D5699, D5800–D5862 (not in order).

Non-standard livery/numbering:

31190 Also carries number D5613.
31301 As **F0** but with a red solebar stripe.

Class 31/1. Standard Design. RA: 5.

31102	**CE**	NR	QETS	TH	
31105	**Y**	NR	QADD	DF	
31106	**FR**	HJ	RVLO	DF	SPALDING TOWN
31107	**K**	NR	QETS	DF	
31128	**FR**	PO	SDPP	DF	CHARYBDIS
31190	**G**	PO	RVLO	DF	
31200	**F**	NR	QETS	TH	
31233 a	**Y**	NR	QADD	DF	
31285	**Y**	NR	QADD	DF	
31301	**0**	FM	SDXL	MQ	
31319	**F**	NR	QETS	TH	

Class 31/4. Electric Train Supply equipment. RA: 6.
Train Supply: Electric, index 66.

31415	**B**	FM	SDXL	MQ	
31420	**IM**	E	WNXX	OC	
31422	**IM**	PO	MBDL	TM (S)	
31423	**IM**	PO	MBDL	MQ (S)	
31427	**B**	E	WNXX	OC	
31437	**CE**	FM	SDXL	MQ	
31439	**RR**	FM	SDXL	MQ	
31452	**FR**	CD	CRRH	GL	MINOTAUR
31454	**IC**	FM	SDPP	DF	THE HEART OF WESSEX
31459	**K**	RE	RVLO	DF	CERBERUS
31461	**DG**	CD	CREL	DF (S)	
31466 a	**E**	E	WNXX	OC	
31468	**FR**	FM	SDPP	DF	HYDRA

Class 31/6. ETS through wiring and controls. RA: 5.

31601 (31186)	**WX**	FM	SDPP	DF	GAUGE 'O' GUILD 1956–2006
31602 (31191)	**FR**	FM	SDPP	DF	CHIMAERA

CLASS 33   BRCW/SULZER   Bo-Bo

Built: 1960–1962 by the Birmingham Railway Carriage & Wagon Company at Smethwick.
Engine: Sulzer 8LDA28 of 1160 kW (1550 h.p.) at 750 r.p.m.
Main Generator: Crompton Parkinson CG391B1.
Traction Motors: Crompton Parkinson C171C2.
Maximum Tractive Effort: 200 kN (45000 lbf).
Continuous Tractive Effort: 116 kN (26000 lbf) at 17.5 m.p.h.
Power At Rail: 906 kW (1215 h.p.)   **Train Brakes:** Air & vacuum.
Brake Force: 35 t.   **Dimensions:** 15.47 x 2.82 (2.64 m. 33/2).
Weight: 76-78 t.   **Wheel Diameter:** 1092 mm.
Design Speed: 85 m.p.h.   **Maximum Speed:** 85 m.p.h.
Fuel Capacity: 3410 litres.   **RA:** 6.
Train Supply: Electric, index 48 (750 V DC only).
Multiple Working: Blue Star.

Originally numbered in series D6500–D6597 but not in order.

Non-standard liveries/numbering:

33046 All over mid-blue. Carries no number.
33109 Carries number D6525.

Class 33/0. Standard Design.

33021	**FR**	FM	SDFR	DF (S)	Eastleigh
33025	**WS**	WC	MBDL	CS	Glen Falloch
33029	**WS**	WC	MBDL	CS	Glen Loy
33030	**DR**	WC	MBDL	CS (S)	
33046	**0**	PO	SDXL	DF	

Class 33/1. Fitted with Buckeye Couplings & SR Multiple Working Equipment for use with SR EMUs, TC stock & Class 73s. Also fitted with flashing light adaptor for use on Weymouth Quay line.

33103 b	**FR**	CM	SDFR	DF	SWORDFISH
33109 b	**B**	FM	SDXL	CP	

Class 33/2. Built to former Loading Gauge of Tonbridge–Battle Line.
All equipped with slow speed control.

33202	**FR**	CD	CRRH	GL	METEOR
33207	**WS**	WC	MBDL	CS	Jim Martin

CLASS 37   ENGLISH ELECTRIC   Co-Co

Built: 1960–1965 by English Electric Company at Vulcan Foundry, Newton le Willows or by Robert Stephenson & Hawthorn at Darlington.
Engine: English Electric 12CSVT of 1300 kW (1750 h.p.) at 850 r.p.m.
Main Generator: English Electric 822/10G.
Traction Motors: English Electric 538/A.
Maximum Tractive Effort: 245 kN (55500 lbf).
Continuous Tractive Effort: 156 kN (35000 lbf) at 13.6 m.p.h.
Power At Rail: 932 kW (1250 h.p.).   **Train Brakes:** Air & vacuum.
Brake Force: 50 t.   **Dimensions:** 18.75 x 2.74 m.
Weight: 102.8–108.4 t.   **Wheel Diameter:** 1092 mm.
Design Speed: 90 m.p.h.   **Maximum Speed:** 80 m.p.h.
Fuel Capacity: 4046 (+ 7678) litres.   **RA:** 5 (§ 6).
Train Supply: Not equipped.
Multiple Working: Blue Star († DRS system).

Originally numbered D6600–D6608, D6700–D6999 (not in order).

Non-standard liveries/numbering:

37351 Carries number 37002 on one side only.
37402 Light grey lower bodyside & dark grey upper bodyside.
37403 Also carries number D6607.
37411 Also carries number D6990.

Class 37/0. Standard Design. Details as above.

37010	a	**CE**	HN	HNRS	LM
37023		**ML**	DR	XHSS	LB
37029	§	**DR**	DR	XHSS	KM
37038	†	**DR**	DR	XHNC	KM
37042	+	**E**	E	WNTR	DR
37046	a	**CE**	E	WZKF	TY
37047	+	**ML**	E	WNTA	HG
37051		**E**	DR	XHSS	LB
37055	+	**ML**	E	WNXX	TE
37057	+	**E**	E	WNTA	HM
37058	a+	**CE**	E	WZKF	TY
37059	a+†	**DR**	DR	XHNC	KM
37065	+	**ML**	E	WNTR	TT
37069	a+†	**DR**	DR	XHNC	KM
37077	a	**ML**	E	WZKF	BK
37087	a	**DR**	DR	XHNC	KM
37100	a	**F**	HN	HNRS	BH
37108	+	**WS**	TT	TTTC	CS (S)
37109		**E**	E	WNTA	HG
37114	r+	**E**	E	WNTA	BS	City of Worcester
37116	+	**B**	E	WNYX	EH
37146	a	**CE**	E	WNXX	TY
37158		**WS**	WC	MBDL	CS (S)
37165	a+	**CE**	TT	MBDL	CS (S)
37170	a	**CE**	HN	HNRS	LM

37174 a	**E**	E	WNTS	BS	
37178 +	**F**	HN	HNRS	BH	
37194	**DR**	DR	XHNC	KM	
37196 a	**CE**	E	WZKF	TY	
37197	**DR**	DR	XHMW	ZH	
37203	**ML**	E	WNTR	BS	
37214	**WS**	WC	MBDL	CS	Loch Laidon
37216 a	**ML**	E	WNTR	ML	
37217 +	**B**	HN	HNRS	AY	
37218 †	**DR**	DR	XHNC	KM	
37220 +	**F**	HN	HNRS	LM	
37221 a	**F**	E	WZKF	TY	
37222	**F**	HN	HNRS	CS	
37229 §	**DR**	DR	XHNC	KM	Jonty Jarvis 8-12-1998 to 18-3-2005
37235	**F**	WC	MBDL	CS (S)	
37238 a+	**F**	E	WZKF	TY	
37248 +	**WS**	TT	MBDL	CS	Loch Arkaig
37250 a+	**F**	E	WZKF	TY	
37259 †	**DR**	DR	XHNC	KM	
37261 a+	**DR**	DR	XHNC	KM	
37293 a+	**ML**	E	WZKF	TY	
37294 a+	**CE**	E	WNXX	CD	
37308 +	**B**	E	WNTR	TT	

Class 37/3. Re-geared (CP7) bogies. Details as Class 37/0 except:

Maximum Tractive Effort: 250 kN (56180 lbf).
Continuous Tractive Effort: 184 kN (41250 lbf) at 11.4 m.p.h.
Design Speed: 80 m.p.h.

37351 +	**CE**	E	WNXX	CD	
37372	**ML**	E	WNTA	ML	
37375 a+	**ML**	E	WNTS	TO	
37377 +	**U**	E	WZKF	BK	
37379 a	**ML**	E	WNXX	BK	
37383 +	**ML**	RV	RTLS	CP	

Class 37/4. Refurbished with electric train supply equipment. Main generator replaced by alternator. Re-geared (CP7) bogies. Details as Class 37/0 except:
Main Alternator: Brush BA1005A.   **Power At Rail:** 935 kW (1254 h.p.).
Traction Motors: English Electric 538/5A.
Maximum Tractive Effort: 256 kN (57440 lbf).
Continuous Tractive Effort: 184 kN (41250 lbf) at 11.4 m.p.h.
Weight: 107 t.
Design Speed: 80 m.p.h.
Fuel Capacity: 7678 litres.
Train Supply: Electric, index 30.

37401 r	**GS**	E	WNTR	ML	
37402	**O**	E	WNTR	TO	Bont Y Bermo
37403 a	**G**	E	WNYX	MG	
37405 r	**E**	E	WKBN	TO	
37406 r	**E**	E	WKBN	TO	The Saltire Society
37407	**F**	E	WNYX	MO	

37408		E	E	WNYX	TO	
37409		F	E	WNXX	ML	
37410	r	E	E	WKCN	TO	
37411		G	E	WNTS	MG	CAERPHILLY CASTLE/CASTELL CAERFFILI
37412		F	E	WNXX	MG	Driver John Elliott
37413		E	E	WNXX	MG	
37415		E	E	WNXX	MG	
37416		GS	E	WNTS	ML	
37417	ra	E	E	WKBN	TO	Richard Trevithick
37418	r	E	E	WNTR	TT	
37419		E	E	WNTR	OC	
37420		RR	E	WNXX	CD	
37421	r	E	E	WNTR	ML	
37422		E	E	WNTR	EH	Cardiff Canton
37423		F	DR	XHSS	LB	
37424		F	E	WNYX	ML	
37425		BL	E	WNTR	MG	Pride of the Valleys/
						Balchder y Cymoedd
37426		E	E	WNXX	CD	
37427	r	E	E	WNTR	ML	
37428		GS	E	WNXX	MG	
37429		RR	E	WNXX	TT	
37430	a	F	E	WNYX	ML	

Class 37/5. Refurbished without train supply equipment. Main generator replaced by alternator. Re-geared (CP7) bogies. Details as Class 37/4 except:
Maximum Tractive Effort: 248 kN (55590 lbf).
Weight: 106.1–110.0 t.

37503	r§	E	E	WNTA	DR	
37505	a§	F	E	WZKF	AY	
37510	a	DR	DR	XHNC	KM	
37513	as§	LH	E	WNXX	OC	
37515	as	DR	DR	XHNC	KM	
37516	s§	LH	E	WNTA	DR	
37517	as§	LH	E	WNTA	HM	
37518	a§	F	E	WZKF	AY	
37519		F	E	WZKF	EH	
37520	r§	E	E	WNXX	CD	
37521	r§	E	E	WNTA	DR	English China Clays

Class 37/6. Originally refurbished for Nightstar services. Main generator replaced by alternator. UIC jumpers. Details as Class 37/5 except:
Maximum Speed: 90 m.p.h.   **Train Brake:** Air.
Train Supply: Not equipped, but electric through wired.
Multiple Working: Blue Star († DRS system).

37601		EP	EU	GPSV	NP	
37602	†	DR	DR	XHNC	KM	
37603		EP	EU	GPSV	NP	
37604		EP	EU	GPSV	NP	
37605	†	DR	DR	XHNC	KM	
37606	†	DR	DR	XHNC	KM	

37607	†	**DR**	DR	XHNC	KM	
37608	†	**DR**	DR	XHNC	KM	
37609	†	**DR**	DR	XHNC	KM	
37610	†	**DR**	DR	XHNC	KM	
37611	†	**DR**	DR	XHNC	KM	The MALCOLM Group
37612	†	**DR**	DR	XHNC	KM	

Class 37/5 continued.

37667	rs	**DR**	DR	XHSS	BH	
37668	s§	**E**	E	WNTA	HM	
37669	r	**E**	E	WNTR	MG	
37670	r	**E**	E	WNTR	MG	St. Blazey T&RS Depot
37671	a	**F**	E	WZKF	TY	
37672	as	**F**	HN	HNRS	BH	
37673	§	**F**	E	WNXX	TE	
37674	§	**F**	E	WNTA	ML	Saint Blaise Church 1445–1995
37675	as§	**F**	E	WNTA	MG	Margam TMD
37676	a§	**F**	E	WNTA	HM	
37677	a§	**F**	E	WNXX	IM	
37678	a§	**F**	E	WNXX	BS	
37679	a§	**F**	E	WZKF	AY	
37680	a§	**F**	HN	HNRS	Hope	
37682	r§	**E**	E	WNTA	HM	
37683	a	**F**	E	WNXX	TE	
37684	ar§	**E**	E	WNTA	MG	Peak National Park
37685	a§	**IC**	E	WNTA	HM	
37688		**DR**	DR	XHSS	LB	
37689	a§	**F**	E	WNTA	HM	
37692	s§	**F**	E	WNTA	MG	Didcot Depot
37693	as	**F**	E	WZKF	TY	
37694	§	**E**	E	WNTR	OC	
37695	s§	**E**	E	WNTR	HM	
37696	as	**F**	E	WZKF	BK	
37698	a§	**LH**	E	WNTA	MG	

Class 37/7. Refurbished locos. Main generator replaced by alternator. Re-geared (CP7) bogies. Ballast weights added. Details as Class 37/5 except:
Main Alternator: GEC G564AZ (37796–803) Brush BA1005A (others).
Maximum Tractive Effort: 276 kN (62000 lbf).
Weight: 120 t. **RA:** 7.

37701	as	**F**	E	WZKF	OC	
37702	s	**GIF**	E	WZKS	ES (S)	
37703		**GIF**	E	WZKS	ES	
37704	s	**E**	HN	HNRS	MG	
37705		**F**	E	WZKF	ML	
37706		**E**	E	WNTA	HM	
37707		**E**	E	WNTA	BS	
37708	a	**F**	E	WNXX	HM	
37709		**F**	E	WNTA	MH	
37710		**LH**	E	WNTA	HM	
37712	a	**E**	E	WNTA	HM	

37713	**LH**	HN	HNRS	CD	
37714 a	**GIF**	E	WZKS	ES	
37716	**GIF**	E	WZKS	ES	
37717	**E**	E	WNTA	HM	
37718	**GIF**	E	WZKS	ES	
37719 a	**F**	E	WZKF	OC	
37796 as	**F**	E	WZKF	TY	
37798	**ML**	E	WNTA	MG	
37799 as	**GIF**	E	WZKS	ES	
37800 a	**GIF**	E	WZKS	ES	
37801 s	**GIF**	E	WZKS	ES	
37803 a	**ML**	E	WNXX	TY	
37883	**GIF**	E	WZKS	ES	
37884	**GIF**	E	WZKS	ES	
37886	**E**	E	WNTA	MH	Sir Dyfed/County of Dyfed
37887 s	**F**	E	WZKF	IM	
37888	**GIF**	E	WZKS	ES (S)	
37890 a	**F**	E	WNTA	MG	
37891 a	**F**	E	WZKF	TY	
37892	**F**	E	WZKF	OC	
37893	**E**	E	WNTA	BS	
37894 as	**F**	E	WZKF	TY	
37895 s	**E**	E	WNTA	BS	
37896 s	**F**	E	WNTA	MG	
37897 s	**F**	HN	HNRS	BS	
37898 s	**F**	HN	HNRS	MG	

CLASS 40   ENGLISH ELECTRIC   1Co-Co1

Built: 1958–1962 by the English Electric Co. at Vulcan Foundry, Newton le Willows.
Engine: English Electric 16SVT Mk2 of 1490 kW (2000 h.p.) at 850 r.p.m.
Main Generator: English Electric 822/4C.
Traction Motors: English Electric 526/5D or EE526/7D.
Maximum Tractive Effort: 231 kN (52000 lbf).
Continuous Tractive Effort: 137 kN (30900 lbf) at 18.8 m.p.h.

Power At Rail: 1160 kW (1550 h.p.).	**Train Brakes:** Air & vacuum.
Brake Force: 51 t.	**Dimensions:** 21.18 x 2.78 m.
Weight: 132 t.	**Wheel Diameter:** 914/1143 mm.
Design Speed: 90 m.p.h.	**Maximum Speed:** 90 m.p.h.
Fuel Capacity: 3250 litres.	**RA:** 6.
Train Supply: Steam.	**Multiple Working:** Blue Star.

| 40145 | **B** | 40 | ELRD | BQ |

CLASS 43   BREL/PAXMAN   Bo-Bo

Built: 1976–1982 by BREL at Crewe Works.
Engine: Paxman Valenta 12RP200L of 1680 kW (2250 h.p.) at 1500 r.p.m.
(* Paxman 12VP185 of 1565 kW (2100 h.p.) at 1500 r.p.m.).
(m MTU 16V4000 R41R of 1680kW (2250 h.p.) at 1500 r.p.m.). Being fitted to the
entire First Great Western and GNER fleets.
Main Alternator: Brush BA1001B.
Traction Motors: Brush TMH68–46 or GEC G417AZ, frame mounted.
Maximum Tractive Effort: 80 kN (17980 lbf).
Continuous Tractive Effort: 46 kN (10340 lbf) at 64.5 m.p.h.
Power At Rail: 1320 kW (1770 h.p.).   **Train Brakes:** Air.
Brake Force: 35 t.   **Dimensions:** 17.79 x 2.71 m.
Weight: 70.25 t.   **Wheel Diameter:** 1020 mm.
Design Speed: 125 m.p.h.   **Maximum Speed:** 125 m.p.h.
Fuel Capacity: 4500 litres.   **RA:** 5.
Train Supply: Three-phase electric.
Multiple Working: Within class, jumpers at non-driving end only.

Notes: † Buffer fitted.

43013, 43014 and 43062 are fitted with measuring apparatus & front-end cameras.

+ Allocated for transfer to GNER.

Non-standard livery: 43101 All over black with a red cab.

Advertising livery: 43087 Hornby red with yellow decals.

43002	**FG**	A	EFPC	PM	TECHNIQUEST
43003	**FG**	A	EFPC	PM	ISAMBARD KINGDOM BRUNEL
43004 m	**FB**	A	EFPC	PM	First for the future/
					First ar gyfer y dyfodol
43005	**FG**	A	EFPC	PM	
43006	**GN**	A	IECP	EC	Kingdom of Fife
43007	**MN**	A	IMLP	NL	
43008	**GN**	A	IECP	EC	
43009 m	**FB**	A	EFPC	PM	First transforming travel
43010	**FG**	A	EFPC	PM	
43012	**FG**	A	EFPC	PM	
43013 †	**Y**	P	QCAR	EC	
43014 †	**Y**	P	QCAR	EC	
43015	**FG**	A	EFPC	PM	
43016	**FG**	A	EFPC	PM	Peninsula Medical School
43017	**FG**	A	EFPC	PM	
43018	**FG**	A	EFPC	LA	
43020	**FG**	A	EFPC	LA	John Grooms
43021 m	**FB**	A	EFPC	LA	David Austin – Cartoonist
43022	**FG**	A	EFPC	LA	
43023 m	**FB**	A	EFPC	LA	
43024	**FG**	A	EFPC	LA	
43025 m	**FB**	A	EFPC	LA	
43026 m	**FB**	A	EFPC	LA	

43027		**FG**	A	EFPC	LA		Glorious Devon
43028		**FG**	A	EFPC	LA		
43029		**FG**	A	EFPC	LA		
43030		**FG**	A	EFPC	PM		Christian Lewis Trust
43031		**FG**	A	EFPC	PM		
43032		**FG**	A	EFPC	PM		The Royal Regiment of Wales
43033		**FG**	A	EFPC	PM		Driver Brian Cooper
							15 June 1947–5 October 1999
43034		**FG**	A	EFPC	PM		The Black Horse
43035		**FG**	A	EFPC	PM		
43036		**FG**	A	EFPC	PM		
43037		**FG**	A	EFPC	PM		PENYDARREN
43038		**GN**	A	IECP	EC		City of Dundee
43039		**GN**	A	IECP	EC		
43040		**FG**	A	EFPC	PM		Bristol St. Philip's Marsh
43041		**FG**	A	EFPC	PM		City of Discovery
43042		**FG**	A	EFPC	PM		
43043	*	**MN**	P	IMLP	NL		
43044	*	**MN**	P	IMLP	NL		
43045	*	**MN**	P	IMLP	NL		
43046		**MN**	P	IMLP	NL		
43047	*	**MN**	P	IMLP	NL		
43048	*	**MN**	P	IMLP	NL		
43049	*	**MN**	P	IMLP	NL		Neville Hill
43050	*	**MN**	P	IMLP	NL		
43051		**MN**	P	IMLP	NL	(S)+	
43052	*	**MN**	P	IMLP	NL		
43053		**MN**	P	IMLP	NL	(S)+	
43054		**MN**	P	IMLP	NL		
43055	*	**MN**	P	IMLP	NL		
43056		**MN**	P	IMLP	NL	(S)+	
43057		**MN**	P	IMLP	NL	(S)+	
43058		**MN**	P	IMLP	NL		
43059	*	**MN**	P	IMLP	NL		
43060	*	**MN**	P	IMLP	NL		
43061	*	**MN**	P	IMLP	NL		
43062		**Y**	P	QCAR	EC		
43063		**FG**	P	EFPC	LA		
43064		**MN**	P	IMLP	NL	(S)	
43065	†	**V**	P	SBXL	DP		
43066		**MN**	P	IMLP	NL		
43067	†	**Y**	P	SBXL	DP		
43068	†	**V**	P	SBXL	DP		
43069		**MN**	P	EFPC	LA	(S)	Rio Enterprise
43070		**CD**	P	EFPC	LA	(S)	
43071		**FG**	P	EFPC	LA		
43072	*	**MN**	P	IMLP	NL		Derby Etches Park
43073	*	**MN**	P	IMLP	NL		
43074	*	**MN**	P	IMLP	NL		
43075	*	**MN**	P	IMLP	NL		
43076	*	**MN**	P	IMLP	NL		

43077		**MN**	P	IMLP	NL (S)+	
43078		**GN**	P	EFPC	LB (S)	
43079		**FG**	P	EFPC	LA	
43080	†	**GN**	P	SBXL	DP	
43081		**MN**	P	IMLP	NL	
43082	*	**MN**	P	IMLP	NL	
43083		**MN**	P	IMLP	NL	
43084	†	**V**	P	SBXL	DP	
43085		**MN**	P	IMLP	NL	
43086		**MN**	P	EFPC	LA (S)	
43087		**AL**	P	EFPC	LA (S)	
43088		**FG**	P	EFPC	LA	
43089		**Y**	P	QCAR	LB (S)	
43091		**FG**	P	EFPC	LA	
43092	m	**FB**	FG	EFPC	LE	
43093	m	**FB**	FG	EFPC	LE	
43094	m	**FB**	FG	EFPC	LE	
43095		**GN**	A	IECP	EC	Perth
43096		**GN**	A	IECP	EC	Stirling Castle
43097	m	**FB**	FG	EFPC	LE	Environment Agency
43098	m	**FB**	FG	EFPC	LE	
43099		**GN**	P	IECP	EC	
43101		**O**	P	SBXL	LB	
43102		**GN**	P	IECP	EC	Diocese of Newcastle
43103		**V**	P	SBXL	LM	
43104		**MN**	A	IMLP	NL	
43105		**GN**	A	IECP	EC	City of Inverness
43107		**GN**	A	IECP	EC	Tayside
43108		**GN**	A	IECP	EC	Old Course St Andrews
43109		**GN**	A	IECP	EC	Leeds International Film Festival
43110		**GN**	A	IECP	EC	Stirlingshire
43111		**GN**	A	IECP	EC	
43112		**GN**	A	IECP	EC	Doncaster
43113		**GN**	A	IECP	EC	The Highlands
43115		**GN**	A	IECP	EC	Aberdeenshire
43116		**GN**	A	IECP	EC	The Black Dyke Band
43117		**GN**	A	IECP	EC	Bonnie Prince Charlie
43118		**GN**	A	IECP	EC	City of Kingston upon Hull
43119		**GN**	A	IECP	EC	Harrogate Spa
43121		**V**	P	SBXL	ZB	
43122		**V**	FG	EFPC	LB (S)	
43123	†	**V**	P	SBXL	DP	
43124		**FG**	A	EFPC	LE	
43125	m	**FB**	A	EFPC	LE	
43126		**FG**	A	EFPC	LE	City of Bristol
43127		**FG**	A	EFPC	LE	Sir Peter Parker 1924–2002
						Cotswold Line 150
43128		**FG**	A	EFPC	LE	
43129	m	**FB**	A	EFPC	LE	
43130	m	**FB**	A	EFPC	LE	
43131		**FG**	A	EFPC	LE	Sir Felix Pole

43132		**FG**	A	EFPC	LE	
43133	m	**FB**	A	EFPC	LE	
43134		**FG**	A	EFPC	LE	County of Somerset
43135	m	**FB**	A	EFPC	LE	
43136		**FG**	A	EFPC	LE	
43137		**FG**	A	EFPC	LE	Newton Abbot 150
43138		**FG**	A	EFPC	LE	
43139		**FG**	A	EFPC	LE	Driver Stan Martin
						25 June 1960 – 6 November 2004
43140		**FG**	A	EFPC	LE	
43141	m	**FB**	A	EFPC	LE	
43142		**FG**	A	EFPC	LE	
43143		**FG**	A	EFPC	LE	Stroud 700
43144		**FG**	A	EFPC	LE	
43145		**FG**	A	EFPC	LE	
43146		**FG**	A	EFPC	LE	
43147	m	**FB**	A	EFPC	LE	
43148		**FG**	A	EFPC	LE	
43149		**FG**	A	EFPC	LE	BBC Wales Today
43150		**FG**	A	EFPC	LE	Bristol Evening Post
43151		**FG**	A	EFPC	LE	
43152		**FG**	A	EFPC	LE	
43153	m	**FB**	FG	EFPC	LE	
43154	m	**FB**	FG	EFPC	LE	
43155	m	**FB**	FG	EFPC	LE	
43156		**FG**	P	EFPC	LA	
43157		**V**	P	SBXL	ZB	
43158	m	**FB**	FG	EFPC	LE	
43159		**MN**	P	EFPC	LA (S)	
43160		**V**	P	QCAR	LB (S)	
43161		**FG**	P	EFPC	LA	
43162		**FG**	P	EFPC	LA	
43163	m	**FB**	A	EFPC	LA	
43164	m	**FB**	A	EFPC	LA	
43165	m	**FB**	A	EFPC	LA	Prince Michael of Kent
43166		**MN**	A	IMLP	NL	
43167		**GN**	A	IECP	EC	DELTIC 50 1955–2005
43168	m	**FB**	A	EFPC	LA	
43169	*	**FG**	A	EFPC	LA	THE NATIONAL TRUST
43170	*	**FG**	A	EFPC	LA	Edward Paxman
43171		**FG**	A	EFPC	LA	
43172		**FG**	A	EFPC	LA	
43174		**FG**	A	EFPC	LA	Bristol–Bordeaux
43175	m	**FB**	A	EFPC	LA	
43176	m	**FB**	A	EFPC	LA	
43177	m	**FB**	A	EFPC	LA	
43178		**MN**	A	IMLP	NL	
43179	*	**FG**	A	EFPC	LA	Pride of Laira
43180		**FG**	P	EFPC	LA	
43181		**FG**	A	EFPC	LA	Devonport Royal Dockyard 1693–1993
43182		**FG**	A	EFPC	LA	

43183	m	**FB**	A	EFPC	LA	
43184		**MN**	A	IMLP	NL	
43185		**FG**	A	EFPC	LA	Great Western
43186		**FG**	A	EFPC	LA	Sir Francis Drake
43187		**FG**	A	EFPC	LA	
43188		**FG**	A	EFPC	LA	City of Plymouth
43189		**FG**	A	EFPC	LA	RAILWAY HERITAGE TRUST
43190		**FG**	A	EFPC	LA	
43191	*	**FG**	A	EFPC	LA	Seahawk
43192		**FG**	A	EFPC	LA	City of Truro
43193		**MN**	P	EFPC	LA (S)	
43194		**V**	FG	EFPC	LB (S)	
43195		**FG**	P	EFPC	LA	
43196		**Y**	P	EFPC	LA (S)	
43197		**GN**	P	EFPC	LB (S)	
43198	m	**FB**	FG	EFPC	LE	

Class 43/2. New numbering series for GNER power cars when rebuilt with new MTU engines. Power cars are being renumbered by adding 200 to their original number. The following power cars are confirmed for renumbering, more are expected to follow.

43206	(43006)					
43208	(43008)					
43238	(43038)					
43239	(43039)					
43290	(43090)	m	**GN**	P	IECP	EC	
43295	(43095)					
43296	(43096)					
43300	(43100)	m	**GN**	P	IECP	EC	Craigentinny
43305	(43105)					
43306	(43106)	m	**GN**	A			Fountains Abbey
43307	(43107)					
43308	(43108)					
43309	(43109)					
43310	(43110)					
43311	(43111)					
43312	(43112)					
43313	(43113)					
43314	(43114)	m	**GN**	A			East Riding of Yorkshire
43315	(43115)					
43316	(43116)					
43317	(43117)					
43318	(43118)					
43319	(43119)					
43320	(43120)	m	**GN**	A	IECP	EC	National Galleries of Scotland
43367	(43167)					

CLASS 45   BR/SULZER   1Co-Co1

Built: 1963 by BR at Derby Locomotive Works.
Engine: Sulzer 12LDA28B of 1860 kW (2500 h.p.) at 750 r.p.m.
Main Generator: Crompton-Parkinson CG426 A1.
Traction Motors: Crompton-Parkinson C172 A1.
Maximum Tractive Effort: 245 kN (55000 lbf).
Continuous Tractive Effort: 134 kN (31600 lbf) at 22.3 m.p.h.

Power At Rail: 1490 kW (2000 h.p.).	**Train Brakes:** Air & vacuum.
Brake Force: 63 t.	**Dimensions:** 20.70 x 2.78 m.
Weight: 136 t.	**Wheel Diameter:** 914/1143 mm.
Design Speed: 90 m.p.h.	**Maximum Speed:** 90 m.p.h.
Fuel Capacity: 3591 litres.	**RA:** 6.
Train Supply: Electric, index 66.	**Multiple Working:** Not equipped.

Originally numbered D61.

45112   **B**   PO   SDMS   DF   THE ROYAL ARMY ORDNANCE CORPS

CLASS 47   BR/BRUSH/SULZER   Co-Co

Built: 1963–1967 by Brush Traction, at Loughborough or by BR at Crewe Works.
Engine: Sulzer 12LDA28C of 1920 kW (2580 h.p.) at 750 r.p.m.
Main Generator: Brush TG160-60 Mk4 or TM172-50 Mk1.
Traction Motors: Brush TM64-68 Mk1 or Mk1A.
Maximum Tractive Effort: 267 kN (60000 lbf).
Continuous Tractive Effort: 133 kN (30000 lbf) at 26 m.p.h.

Power At Rail: 1550 kW (2080 h.p.).	**Train Brakes:** Air.
Brake Force: 61 t.	**Dimensions:** 19.38 x 2.79 m.
Weight: 111.5–120.6 t.	**Wheel Diameter:** 1143 mm.

Design Speed: 95 m.p.h.
Maximum Speed: 95 m.p.h. (* 75 m.p.h.).
Fuel Capacity: 3273 (+ 5550).   **RA:** 6 or 7.
Train Supply: Not equipped.
Multiple Working: † DRS system, m Green Circle (operational locos only).

Originally numbered in series D1100–D1111, D1500–D1999 but not in order.

Non-standard liveries/numbering:

47033 Carries no number.
47145 Dark blue with Railfreight Distribution logos.
47812 Carries number D1916.
47815 Also carries number D1748.
47829 "Police" livery of white with a broad red band outlined in yellow.
47851 Also carries number D1648.
47853 "XP64 blue" with red cabside panels. Also carries number D1733.
47972 BR Central Services red & grey.

Class 47/0 (Dual-braked locos) or Class 47/2 (Air-braked locos). Standard Design. Details as above.

47033	**CD**	CD	CROL	GL	
47053 +	**FE**	FM	SDXL	BH	
47145 +m	**0**	FM	SDFL	DF	MYRDDIN EMRYS
47150 *+	**FL**	FL	DFLH	FD	
47186 +	**FE**	FM	SDXL	KT	
47194	**F**	WC	MBDL	CS (S)	
47197 *	**FF**	P	DHLT	BA	
47200 +m	**CD**	CD	CRRH	GL	The Fosse Way
47201 +	**FE**	FM	SDXL	KT	
47219 +	**FE**	FM	SDXL	KT	
47224 x*	**F**	P	DHLT	CP	
47226 +	**F**	FM	SDXL	KT	
47228 +	**F**	FM	SDXL	KT	
47236 +	**FE**	WC	MBDL	CS (S)	
47237 +†	**DR**	DR	XHNC	KM	
47245 +m	**WS**	WC	MBDL	CS	
47270 *	**FL**	P	DHLT	BA	Cory Brothers 1842–1992
47279 *+	**FL**	P	DHLT	BA	
47280 +	**F**	FM	SDXL	KT	
47289 *+	**FF**	P	DHLT	BA	
47292 *+	**FL**	P	DHLT	BA	
47293 +	**FE**	FM	SDXL	KT	
47298 +†	**DR**	DR	XHSS	BH	

Class 47/3 (Dual-braked locos) or Class 47/2 (Air-braked locos).
Details as Class 47/0 except: **Weight:** 113.7 t.

47302 +	**FF**	FL	DHLT	BA	
47303 *+	**FF**	P	DHLT	BA	Freightliner Cleveland
47306 +	**FE**	HN	HNRS	BZ	The Sapper
47307 +	**FE**	FM	SDXL	KT	
47309 *+	**FF**	FL	DHLT	SZ	European Rail Operator of The Year
47313 +	**F**	FM	SDXL	KT	
47314 +	**F**	FM	SDXL	KT	
47316 +m	**CD**	CD	CRRH	OY	(S) Cam Peak
47335 +	**F**	FM	SDXL	KT	
47338 +	**FE**	CD	CROL	DW	
47355 m	**K**	FM	SDFL	DF	(S)AVOCET
47358 *+	**FF**	P	DHLT	SZ	IVANHOE
47360 +	**FE**	FM	SDXL	KT	
47363	**F**	FM	SDXL	CS	
47368 x	**F**	FM	SDXL	CS	
47370 *+	**FF**	P	DHLT	IP	
47375 +	**K**	FM	SDFL	DF (S)	

Class 47/4. Electric Train Supply equipment.
Details as Class 47/0 except:

Weight: 120.4–125.1 t.   **Fuel Capacity:** 3273 (+ 5887) litres.
Train Supply: Electric. ETH 66.   **RA:** 7.

47475	x	**RX**	HN	HNRS	HM
47488	x	**GG**	FM	SDFR	BH (S)
47489	x	**RG**	FM	SDXL	CS
47492	x	**RX**	GD	MBDL	CS (S)
47501	x†	**DR**	DR	XHNC	KM
47525	x	**FE**	FM	SDXL	CS
47526	x	**BL**	FM	SDXL	CS
47528	x	**IM**	CD	CRUR	DW
47550	x	**IM**	PO	SDXL	IR
47575	x	**RG**	RV	RTLS	BQ
47635	x	**BL**	E	WNTR	OC

Class 47/7. Previously fitted with an older form of TDM.

Details as Class 47/4 except:
Weight: 118.7 t.   **Fuel Capacity:** 5887 litres.
Maximum Speed: 100 m.p.h.

47701	x	**FR**	WF	MBDL	LM (S)	Waverley
47703	x	**FR**	CD	CRRH	GL	HERMES
47707	x	**RX**	FM	SDXL	BH	
47709	x	**BP**	FM	SDFR	DF	DIONYSOS
47710	x	**FR**	FM	SDFR	DF (S)	
47712	x	**BP**	FM	SDFR	DF	ARTEMIS
47714	xm	**AR**	CD	CRRH	GL	
47715		**FR**	FM	SDXL	YK	POSEIDON
47717	x	**RG**	FM	SDXL	BH	

Class 47/7. Former Railnet dedicated locos. All have twin fuel tanks and are fitted with RCH jumper cables for operation with Propelling Control Vehicles (PCVs).

47721		**RX**	E	WNXX	TT	Saint Bede
47722		**V**	E	WNXX	TT	
47726		**RX**	E	WNXX	TT	Manchester Airport Progress
47727		**E**	E	WNTR	WN	Castell Caerffili/Caerphilly Castle
47732	x	**RX**	E	WNTR	HM	
47733		**RX**	E	WNTR	HM	
47734		**RX**	E	WNTR	HM	
47736		**RX**	E	WNXX	CD	
47737		**RX**	E	WNSS	HM	
47739		**RX**	E	WNSS	ML	
47741		**V**	E	WNXX	TT	
47742		**RX**	E	WNXX	TT	The Enterprising Scot
47744		**E**	FM	SDXL	BH	
47746		**RX**	E	WNTR	CD	
47747		**E**	E	WNTR	MH	Florence Nightingale
47749		**RX**	E	WNXX	HM	
47750		**V**	E	WNXX	HM	
47758	x	**E**	E	WNXX	TT	

47759	**RX**	E	WNXX	CD	
47760	**E**	E	WNTR	HM	
47761	**RX**	E	WNTR	MG	
47767	**E**	FM	SDXL	AS	
47769	**V**	RV	RTLO	CP	Resolve
47770	**RX**	E	WNXX	BS	Reserved
47772 x	**RX**	E	WNTR	MG	
47773	**E**	E	WNXX	HM	
47776 x	**RX**	E	WNXX	HM	
47781	**RX**	E	WNXX	TT	Isle of Iona
47782	**RX**	E	WNXX	OC	
47783	**RX**	E	WNXX	CD	
47784	**RX**	E	WNXX	CD	
47785	**E**	E	WNTR	ML	
47786	**E**	E	WNXX	HM	
47787	**E**	E	WNXX	HM	
47789	**RX**	E	WNSS	TT	
47790	**E**	E	WNTR	HM	
47791	**RX**	E	WNXX	SY	
47792	**E**	E	WNTR	HM	
47793	**E**	E	WNTR	HM	

Class 47/4 continued. RA6. Most fitted with extended-range fuel tanks (+).

47836 to be renumbered from 47780 in early 2007.

47798	**RP**	NM	MBDL	CS (S)	Prince William
47799	**RP**	E	WNXX	FB	Prince Henry
47802 +†	**DR**	DR	XHNC	KM	
47805 +m	**RV**	RV	RTLO	CP	TALISMAN
47810 +	**CD**	CD	CRRH	GL	Captain Sensible
47811 +	**GL**	FL	DFLH	FD	
47812 +m	**GG**	RV	RTLO	CP	
47813 +m	**CD**	CD	CRRH	GL	John Peel
47815 +m	**GG**	RV	RTLO	CP	GREAT WESTERN
47816 +	**GL**	FL	DFLH	FD	
47818 +	**1**	CD	CRRH	GL	
47826 +	**IC**	WC	MBDL	CS	Springburn
47828 +m	**CD**	CD	CRRH	GL	Joe Strummer
47829 +	**0**	RV	RTLS	CD	
47830 +	**GL**	FL	DFLH	FD	
47832 +m	**FM**	FM	SDFR	DF	DRIVER TOM CLARK O.B.E.
47836 +	**RX**	CD	CROL	BH	
47839 +m	**RV**	RV	RTLO	CP	PEGASUS
47840 +	**B**	P	SBXL	CE	NORTH STAR
47841 +	**V**	FL	DFLH	FD	
47843 +m	**RV**	RV	RTLO	CP	VULCAN
47847 +m	**BL**	RV	RTLO	CP	
47848 +m	**RV**	RV	RTLO	CP	TITAN STAR
47851 +	**GG**	WC	MBDL	CS	Traction Magazine
47853 +m	**0**	RV	RTLO	CP	RAIL EXPRESS
47854 +	**WS**	WC	MBDL	CS	
47972	**0**	FM	SDXL	CS	

CLASS 50   ENGLISH ELECTRIC   Co-Co

Built: 1967–1968 by English Electric at Vulcan Foundry, Newton-le-Willows.
Engine: English Electric 16CVST of 2010 kW (2700 h.p.) at 850 r.p.m.
Main Generator: English Electric 840/4B.
Traction Motors: English Electric 538/5A.
Maximum Tractive Effort: 216 kN (48500 lbf).
Continuous Tractive Effort: 147 kN (33000 lbf) at 23.5 m.p.h.

Power At Rail: 1540 kW (2070 h.p.).	**Train Brakes:** Air & vacuum.
Brake Force: 59 t.	**Dimensions:** 20.88 x 2.78 m.
Weight: 116.9 t.	**Wheel Diameter:** 1092 mm.
Design Speed: 105 m.p.h.	**Maximum Speed:** 90 m.p.h.
Fuel Capacity: 4796 litres.	**RA:** 6.
Train Supply: Electric, index 61.	**Multiple Working:** Orange Square.

Originally numbered D431 and D449. 50044 carries number D444.

50031	**BL**	PO	CFOL	KR	Hood
50044	**GG**	50	CFOL	KR	EXETER
50049	**BL**	50	CFOL	KR	Defiance

CLASS 52   BR/MAYBACH   C-C

Built: 1961–1964 Swindon Works.
Engine: Two Maybach MD655 of 1007 kW (1350 h.p) at 1500 r.p.m.
Transmission: Hydraulic. Voith L630rV.
Maximum Tractive Effort: 297 kN (66700 lbf).
Continuous Tractive Effort: 201 kN (45200 lbf) at 14.5 m.p.h.

Power At Rail: 1490 kW (2000 h.p.).	**Train Brakes:** Air & vacuum.
Brake Force: 83 t.	**Dimensions:** 20.7 m x 2.78 m.
Weight: 110 t.	**Wheel Diameter:** 1092 mm.
Design Speed: 90 m.p.h.	**Maximum Speed:** 90 m.p.h.
Fuel Capacity: 3900 litres.	**RA:** 6.
Train Supply: Steam.	**Multiple Working:** Not equipped.

Never allocated a number in the 1972 number series.

Registered on TOPS as No. 89416.

D1015	**M**	DT	MBDL	OC	WESTERN CHAMPION

CLASS 55   ENGLISH ELECTRIC   Co-Co

Built: 1961 by English Electric at Vulcan Foundry, Newton-le-Willows.
Engine: Two Napier-Deltic D18-25 of 1230 kW (1650 h.p.) each at 1500 r.p.m.
Main Generators: Two English Electric 829/1A.
Traction Motors: English Electric 538/A.
Maximum Tractive Effort: 222 kN (50000 lbf).
Continuous Tractive Effort: 136 kN (30500 lbf) at 32.5 m.p.h.

Power At Rail: 1969 kW (2640 h.p.).	**Train Brakes:** Air & vacuum.
Brake Force: 51 t.	**Dimensions:** 21.18 x 2.68 m.
Weight: 100 t.	**Wheel Diameter:** 1092 mm.

Design Speed: 105 m.p.h.
Fuel Capacity: 3755 litres.
Train Supply: Electric, index 66.

Maximum Speed: 100 m.p.h.
RA: 5.
Multiple Working: Not equipped.

Originally numbered D9000.

Registered on TOPS as No. 89500.

55022	**B**	MW ELRD	BQ	ROYAL SCOTS GREY

CLASS 56   BRUSH/BR/RUSTON   Co-Co

Built: 1976–1984 by Electroputere at Craiova, Romania (as sub contractors for Brush) or BREL at Doncaster or Crewe Works.
Engine: Ruston Paxman 16RK3CT of 2460 kW (3250 h.p.) at 900 r.p.m.
Main Alternator: Brush BA1101A.
Traction Motors: Brush TM73-62.
Maximum Tractive Effort: 275 kN (61800 lbf).
Continuous Tractive Effort: 240 kN (53950 lbf) at 16.8 m.p.h.
Power At Rail: 1790 kW (2400 h.p.).   **Train Brakes:** Air.
Brake Force: 60 t.   **Dimensions:** 19.36 x 2.79 m.
Weight: 126 t.   **Wheel Diameter:** 1143 mm.
Design Speed: 80 m.p.h.   **Maximum Speed:** 80 m.p.h.
Fuel Capacity: 5228 litres.   **RA:** 7.
Train Supply: Not equipped.   **Multiple Working:** Red Diamond.

Note: All equipped with Slow Speed Control.

Non-standard liveries:

56063 As **F**, but with the light grey replaced by a darker grey.
56027 and 56109 Are **LH** but with the Loadhaul branding on one side only.

56006	**B**	E	WNSS	BH
56007	**FER**	E	WZGF	OC
56011	**E**	FM	SDXL	CV
56018	**FER**	E	WZGF	WB
56021	**LH**	FM	SDXL	CV
56022	**F**	FM	SDXL	IR
56025	**F**	E	WNXX	IM
56027	**LH**	E	WNXX	IM
56029	**F**	J	RCJA	LB (S)
56031	**FER**	E	WZGF	WB
56032	**FER**	E	WZGF	OC
56033	**F**	E	WNXX	HM
56034	**LH**	J	RCJA	LB (S)
56037	**E**	E	WZTS	OC
56038	**FER**	E	WZGF	DM
56041	**E**	E	WNXX	HM
56043	**F**	E	WNXX	IM
56044	**F**	X	WNSO	LB
56046	**CE**	E	WNXX	TO
56048	**CE**	E	WZTS	HM
56049	**FER**	E	WZGF	OC
56051	**FER**	E	WZGF	OC

56052	**F**	E	WNXX	IM
56053	**F**	E	WNXX	HM
56054	**F**	E	WNXX	FB
56055	**LH**	E	WNXX	HM
56056	**F**	E	WNTR	HM
56058	**FER**	E	WZGF	OC
56059	**FER**	E	WZGF	OC
56060	**FER**	E	WZGF	OC
56062	**E**	E	WNSS	MG
56063	**0**	X	WNSO	LB
56064	**F**	E	WNXX	IM
56065	**FER**	E	WZGF	WB
56067	**E**	E	WNXX	FB
56068	**E**	E	WNXX	HM
56069	**FER**	E	WZGF	WB
56070	**F**	E	WNTR	OC
56071	**FER**	E	WZGF	OC
56072	**F**	E	WNSS	HM
56073	**F**	E	WNXX	TO
56074	**FER**	E	WZGF	OC
56076	**F**	E	WNXX	IM
56077	**LH**	E	WNXX	CD
56078	**FER**	E	WZGF	FN
56079	**F**	E	WNXX	HM
56081	**FER**	E	WZGF	OC
56082	**F**	E	WNXX	IM
56083	**LH**	E	WNXX	FB
56084	**LH**	E	WNXX	IM
56085	**LH**	E	WNXX	TE
56086	**F**	E	WNXX	IM
56087	**FER**	E	WZGF	WB
56088	**E**	E	WNSS	TE
56089	**E**	E	WNXX	IM
56090	**FER**	E	WZGF	OC
56091	**FER**	E	WZGF	DM
56093	**F**	E	WNXX	HM
56094	**FER**	E	WZGF	WB
56095	**FER**	E	WZGF	WB
56096	**FER**	E	WZGF	OC
56099	**F**	E	WNXX	HM
56100	**LH**	E	WNXX	MG
56101	**F**	E	WNXX	IM
56102	**LH**	E	WNXX	TE
56103	**FER**	E	WZGF	OC
56104	**FER**	E	WZGF	WB
56105	**FER**	E	WZGF	WB
56106	**FER**	E	WZGF	FN
56107	**LH**	E	WNTR	FB
56108	**F**	E	WNXX	TE
56109	**LH**	E	WNXX	FB
56110	**LH**	E	WNXX	HM

56111	**LH**	E	WNXX	TE		
56112	**LH**	E	WNXX	OC		
56113	**FER**	E	WZGF	OC		
56114	**E**	E	WNTR	IM		
56115	**FER**	E	WZGF	WB		
56116	**LH**	E	WNXX	HM		
56117	**FER**	E	WZGF	WB		
56118	**FER**	E	WZGF	OC		
56119	**E**	E	WNTR	HM		
56120	**E**	E	WNXX	FB		
56127	**F**	E	WNXX	TE		
56128	**F**	HN	HNRS	LM		
56129	**F**	E	WNXX	TE		
56131	**F**	X	WNSO	LB		
56133	**F**	E	WZTS	OC		
56134	**F**	E	WZTS	HM		
56301	(56045)	**FA**	J	RCJA	RR	
56302	(56124)	**FA**	J	RCJA	RR	
56303	(56125)	**FA**	RE	RCJA	RR	

CLASS 57   BRUSH/GM   Co-Co

Built: 1964–1965 by Brush Traction at Loughborough or BR at Crewe Works as Class 47. Rebuilt 1997–2004 by Brush Traction at Loughborough.
Engine: General Motors 12 645 E3 of 1860 kW (2500 h.p.) at 904 r.p.m.
Main Alternator: Brush BA1101D.
Traction Motors: Brush TM64-68 Mark 1 or Mark 1a.
Maximum Tractive Effort: 244.5 kN (55000 lbf).
Continuous Tractive Effort: 140 kN (31500 lbf) at ?? m.p.h.
Power at Rail: 1507 kW (2025 h.p.).   **Train Brakes:** Air.
Brake Force: 80 t.   **Dimensions:** 19.38 x 2.79 m.
Weight: 120.6 t.   **Wheel Diameter:** 1143 mm.
Design Speed: 75 m.p.h.   **Maximum Speed:** 75 m.p.h.
Fuel Capacity: 5550 litres.   **RA:** 6
Train Supply: Not equipped.   **Multiple Working:** Not equipped.

Class 57/0. No Train Supply Equipment. Rebuilt 1998–2000.

57001	(47356)	**FL**	P	DFTZ	FD	Freightliner Pioneer
57002	(47322)	**FL**	P	DFTZ	FD	Freightliner Phoenix
57003	(47317)	**FL**	P	DFTZ	FD	Freightliner Evolution
57004	(47347)	**FL**	P	DFTZ	FD	Freightliner Quality
57005	(47350)	**FL**	P	DFTZ	FD	Freightliner Excellence
57006	(47187)	**FL**	P	DFTZ	FD	Freightliner Reliance
57007	(47332)	**FL**	P	DFTZ	FD	Freightliner Bond
57008	(47060)	**FL**	P	DFTZ	FD	Freightliner Explorer
57009	(47079)	**FL**	P	DFTZ	FD	Freightliner Venturer
57010	(47231)	**FL**	P	DFTZ	FD	Freightliner Crusader
57011	(47329)	**FL**	P	DFTZ	FD	Freightliner Challenger
57012	(47204)	**FL**	P	DFTZ	FD	Freightliner Envoy

Class 57/3. Electric Train Supply Equipment. Virgin Trains locos. Rebuilt 2002–2004. Details as Class 57/0 except:

Engine: General Motors 12645F3B of 2050 kW (2750 h.p.) at 954 r.p.m.
Main Alternator: Brush BA1101F (recovered from a Class 56) or Brush BA1101G.
Fuel Capacity: 5887 litres.   **Train Supply:** Electric, index 100.
Design Speed: 95 m.p.h.   **Maximum Speed:** 95 m.p.h.
Brake Force: 60 t.   **Weight:** 117 t.

57301	(47845)	d	**VT**	P	ATTB	MA	SCOTT TRACY
57302	(47827)	d	**VT**	P	ATTB	MA	VIRGIL TRACY
57303	(47705)	d	**VT**	P	ATTB	MA	ALAN TRACY
57304	(47807)	d	**VT**	P	ATTB	MA	GORDON TRACY
57305	(47822)	d	**VT**	P	ATTB	MA	JOHN TRACY
57306	(47814)	d	**VT**	P	ATTB	MA	JEFF TRACY
57307	(47225)	d	**VT**	P	ATTB	MA	LADY PENELOPE
57308	(47846)	d	**VT**	P	ATTB	MA	TIN TIN
57309	(47806)	d	**VT**	P	ATTB	MA	BRAINS
57310	(47831)	d	**VT**	P	ATTB	MA	KYRANO
57311	(47817)	d	**VT**	P	ATTB	MA	PARKER
57312	(47330)	d	**VT**	P	ATTB	MA	THE HOOD
57313	(47371)	d	**VT**	P	ATTB	MA	TRACY ISLAND
57314	(47372)	d	**VT**	P	ATTB	MA	FIREFLY
57315	(47234)	d	**VT**	P	ATTB	MA	THE MOLE
57316	(47290)	d	**VT**	P	ATTB	MA	FAB 1

Class 57/6. Electric Train Supply Equipment. Prototype ETS loco. Rebuilt 2001. Details as Class 57/0 except:

Main Alternator: Brush BA1101E.   **Fuel Capacity:** 3273 litres.
Train Supply: Electric, index 100.   **Weight:** 113 t.
Design Speed: 95 m.p.h.   **Maximum Speed:** 95 m.p.h.
Brake Force: 60 t.

57601	(47825)	**WC**	WC MBDL	CS	

Class 57/6. Electric Train Supply Equipment. First Great Western locos. Rebuilt 2004. Details as Class 57/3.

57602	(47337)	**GL**	P	EFOO	OO	Restormel Castle
57603	(47349)	**GL**	P	EFOO	OO	Tintagel Castle
57604	(47209)	**GL**	P	EFOO	OO	Pendennis Castle
57605	(47206)	**GL**	P	EFOO	OO	Totnes Castle

CLASS 58   BREL/RUSTON   Co-Co

Built: 1983–1987 by BREL at Doncaster Works.
Engine: Ruston Paxman 12RK3ACT of 2460 kW (3300 h.p.) at 1000 r.p.m.
Main Alternator: Brush BA1101B.   **Traction Motors:** Brush TM73-62.
Maximum Tractive Effort: 275 kN (61800 lbf).
Continuous Tractive Effort: 240 kN (53950 lbf) at 17.4 m.p.h.
Power At Rail: 1780 kW (2387 h.p.).   **Train Brakes:** Air.
Brake Force: 60 t.   **Dimensions:** 19.13 x 2.72 m.
Weight: 130 t.   **Wheel Diameter:** 1120 mm.

Design Speed: 80 m.p.h.
Fuel Capacity: 4214 litres.
Train Supply: Not equipped.
Maximum Speed: 80 m.p.h.
RA: 7.
Multiple Working: Red Diamond.

Notes: All equipped with Slow Speed Control.

Locos in use in The Netherlands currently carry the following numbers: 58039; 5811, 58044; 5812 and 58038; 5814.

Non-standard liveries:

58001 As **FO** but with a red solebar stripe.
58038 Vos Logistics (black with a broad orange stripe).

58001	**O**	E	WNXX	BH	
58002	**ML**	E	WNXX	EH	
58003	**F**	E	WNXX	TO	Markham Colliery
58004	**FER**	E	WZFF	EH	
58005	**ML**	E	WZTS	TO	
58006	**F**	E	WZTS	EH	
58007	**SCO**	E	WZFF	EH	
58008	**ML**	E	WNXX	TT	
58009	**SCO**	E	WZFF	WB	
58010	**FER**	E	WZFF	EH	
58011	**FER**	E	WZFF	EH	
58012	**F**	E	WNXX	TT	
58013	**ML**	E	WZTS	EH	
58014	**ML**	E	WNXX	TT	
58015	**FER**	E	WZFF	EH	
58016	**FER**	E	WZFF	OC	
58017	**F**	E	WZTS	EH	
58018	**FER**	E	WZFF	EH	
58019	**F**	E	WNXX	TO	Shirebrook Colliery
58020	**GIF**	E	WZFS	ES	
58021	**FER**	E	WZFF	EH	
58022	**F**	E	WNXX	CD	
58023	**ML**	E	WNXX	TT	
58024	**GIF**	E	WZFS	ES	
58025	**GIF**	E	WZFS	ES	
58026	**F**	E	WZTS	EH	
58027	**SCO**	E	WZFF	EH	
58028	**F**	E	WNXX	TT	
58029	**GIF**	E	WZFS	ES	
58030	**GIF**	E	WZFS	ES	
58031	**GIF**	E	WZFS	ES	
58032	**FER**	E	WZFF	DM	
58033	**TSO**	E	WZFF	EH	
58034	**FER**	E	WZFF	EH	
58035	**FER**	E	WZFF	FN	
58036	**ML**	E	WZFH	TT	
58037	**E**	E	WNXX	EH	
58038	**O**	E	WZFH	TB	
58039	**ACT**	E	WZFH	TB	
58040	**SCO**	E	WZFF	EH	

58041	**GIF**	E	WZFS	ES
58042	**ML**	E	WNXX	EH
58043	**GIF**	E	WZFS	ES
58044	**ACT**	E	WZFH	TB
58045	**F**	E	WNXX	OC
58046	**FER**	E	WZFF	DM
58047	**TSO**	E	WZFF	EH
58048	**E**	E	WNXX	OC
58049	**TSO**	E	WZFF	EH
58050	**TSO**	E	WZFF	EH

CLASS 59   GENERAL MOTORS   Co-Co

Built: 1985 (59001/59002/59004) or 1989 (59005) by General Motors, La Grange, Illinois, USA or 1990 (59101–59104), 1994 (59201) and 1995 (59202–59206) by General Motors, London, Ontario, Canada.
Engine: General Motors 16-645E3C two stroke of 2460 kW (3300 h.p.) at 904 r.p.m.
Main Alternator: General Motors AR11 MLD-D14A.
Traction Motors: General Motors D77B.
Maximum Tractive Effort: 506 kN (113 550 lbf).
Continuous Tractive Effort: 291 kN (65 300 lbf) at 14.3 m.p.h.
Power At Rail: 1889 kW (2533 h.p.).   **Train Brakes:** Air.
Brake Force: 69 t.   **Dimensions:** 21.35 x 2.65 m.
Weight: 121 t.   **Wheel Diameter:** 1067 mm.
Design Speed: 60 (* 75) m.p.h.   **Maximum Speed:** 60 (* 75) m.p.h.
Fuel Capacity: 4546 litres.   **RA:** 7.
Train Supply: Not equipped.   **Multiple Working:** AAR System.

Class 59/0. Owned by Foster-Yeoman.

59001	**FY**	FY	XYPO	MD	YEOMAN ENDEAVOUR
59002	**FY**	FY	XYPO	MD	ALAN J DAY
59004	**FY**	FY	XYPO	MD	PAUL A HAMMOND
59005	**FY**	FY	XYPO	MD	KENNETH J PAINTER

Class 59/1. Owned by Hanson Quarry Products.

59101	**HA**	HA	XYPA	MD	Village of Whatley
59102	**HA**	HA	XYPA	MD	Village of Chantry
59103	**HA**	HA	XYPA	MD	Village of Mells
59104	**HA**	HA	XYPA	MD	Village of Great Elm

Class 59/2. Owned by EWS.

59201	*	**E**	E	WDAK	TO	Vale of York
59202	*	**E**	E	WDAK	TO	Vale of White Horse
59203	*	**E**	E	WDAK	TO	Vale of Pickering
59204	*	**E**	E	WDAK	TO	Vale of Glamorgan
59205	*b	**E**	E	WDAK	TO	L. Keith McNair
59206	*b	**E**	E	WDAK	TO	Pride of Ferrybridge

CLASS 60   BRUSH/MIRRLEES   Co-Co

Built: 1989–1993 by Brush Traction at Loughborough.
Engine: Mirrlees 8MB275T of 2310 kW (3100 h.p.) at 1000 r.p.m.
Main Alternator: Brush BA1006A.
Traction Motors: Brush TM2161A.
Maximum Tractive Effort: 500 kN (106500 lbf).
Continuous Tractive Effort: 336 kN (71570 lbf) at 17.4 m.p.h.
Power At Rail: 1800 kW (2415 h.p.).   **Train Brakes:** Air.
Brake Force: 74 (+ 62) t.   **Dimensions:** 21.34 x 2.64 m.
Weight: 129 (+ 131) t.   **Wheel Diameter:** 1118 mm.
Design Speed: 62 m.p.h.   **Maximum Speed:** 60 m.p.h.
Fuel Capacity: 4546 (+ 5225) litres.   **RA:** 7.
Train Supply: Not equipped.   **Multiple Working:** Within class.

Notes: All equipped with Slow Speed Control.

60034, 60061, 60064, 60066, 60072, 60073, 60077, 60079, 60082, 60084, 60088 and 60090 carry their names on one side only.

60500 used to carry the number 60016.

60007, 60044 and 60078 carry EWS logos on their **LH** or **ML** liveries.

60001	**E**	E	WNTS	TO	The Railway Observer
60002 +	**E**	E	WCBI	TO	High Peak
60003 +	**E**	E	WNTR	TO	FREIGHT TRANSPORT ASSOCIATION
60004 +	**E**	E	WNTR	IM	
60005 +	**E**	E	WNTS	TO	BP Gas Avonmouth
60006	**CU**	E	WNTS	TO	Scunthorpe Ironmaster
60007 +	**LH**	E	WCBK	TO	
60008	**E**	E	WCAI	TO	Sir William McAlpine
60009 +	**E**	E	WCBI	TO	
60010 +	**E**	E	WCBI	TO	
60011	**ML**	E	WNTR	TO	
60012 +	**E**	E	WNTS	TE	
60013	**EG**	E	WCAM	TO	Robert Boyle
60014	**EG**	E	WNTR	TE	Alexander Fleming
60015 +	**EG**	E	WCBK	TO	Bow Fell
60017 +	**E**	E	WCBI	TO	Shotton Works Centenary Year 1996
60018	**E**	E	WNTR	TO	
60019	**E**	E	WCAI	TO	PATHFINDER TOURS 30 YEARS OF RAILTOURING 1973–2003
60020 +	**E**	E	WCBK	TO	
60021 +	**E**	E	WCBK	TO	Star of the East
60022 +	**E**	E	WCBK	TO	
60023 +	**E**	E	WNTR	TE	
60024	**E**	E	WCAM	TO	
60025 +	**E**	E	WCBI	TO	Caledonian Paper
60026 +	**E**	E	WCBI	TO	
60027 +	**E**	E	WNTR	MG	
60028 +	**EG**	E	WCBI	TO	John Flamsteed
60029	**E**	E	WCAI	TO	Clitheroe Castle

PLATFORM 5 MAIL ORDER

PRESERVED LOCOMOTIVES OF BRITISH RAILWAYS

A new 12th edition of Preserved Locomotives is currently in preparation and will be published in summer 2007. It contains full details of all ex-British Railways and constituent companies' steam, diesel & electric locomotives and diesel & electric multiple units that are still in existence. Includes technical details for each class of vehicle including builder, year of manufacture, wheel arrangement and tractive effort. Further details of numbers carried, names and locations are provided for each individual vehicle, plus a full list of preservation sites and industrial locations. Also includes details of locomotives and multiple units formerly owned by London Underground Limited and its predecessors, plus locomotives once owned by the British Military.

If you would like to be notified when this new edition is available, please contact our Mail Order Department.

Telephone, fax or send your order to the Platform 5 Mail Order Department. See page 384 of this book for details.

60030	+	E	E	WCBI	TO	
60031		E	E	WNTR	IM	ABP Connect
60032		F	E	WNTR	TO	William Booth
60033	+	CU	E	WNTR	MG	Tees Steel Express
60034		EG	E	WCAM	TO	Carnedd Llewelyn
60035		E	E	WCAI	TO	
60036		E	E	WCAN	TO	GEFCO
60037	+	E	E	WNTS	MG	Aberddawan/Aberthaw
60038	+	E	E	WCBI	TO	AvestaPolarit
60039		E	E	WNTR	MG	
60040		E	E	WNTR	TE	
60041	+	E	E	WNTR	IM	
60042		E	E	WCAI	TO	The Hundred of Hoo
60043		E	E	WCAI	TO	
60044		ML	E	WNTR	MG	
60045		E	E	WCAM	TO	The Permanent Way Institution
60046	+	EG	E	WCBI	TO	William Wilberforce
60047		E	E	WNTR	TO	
60048		E	E	WNTR	IM	EASTERN
60049		E	E	WNTR	TE	
60050		E	E	WNTS	TE	
60051	+	E	E	WNTR	IM	
60052	+	E	E	WCBI	TO	Glofa Twr – The last deep mine in Wales – Tower Colliery
60053		E	E	WCAI	TO	NORDIC TERMINAL
60054	+	F	E	WCBI	TO	Charles Babbage
60055	+	EG	E	WCBI	TO	Thomas Barnardo
60056	+	EG	E	WCBM	TO	William Beveridge
60057		EG	E	WNTR	TO	Adam Smith
60058	+	E	E	WNTR	IM	
60059	+	LH	E	WCBK	TO	Swinden Dalesman
60060		EG	E	WNTR	IM	James Watt
60061		F	E	WCAM	TO	Alexander Graham Bell
60062		E	E	WCAI	TO	
60063		EG	E	WCAM	TO	James Murray
60064	+	EG	E	WNTS	IM	Back Tor
60065		E	E	WNTR	TE	Spirit of JAGUAR
60066		EG	E	WCAI	TO	John Logie Baird
60067		EG	E	WNTR	MG	James Clerk-Maxwell
60068		EG	E	WCAM	TO	Charles Darwin
60069		E	E	WNTR	TO	Slioch
60070	+	F	E	WNTS	IM	John Loudon McAdam
60071	+	E	E	WCBI	TO	Ribblehead Viaduct
60072		EG	E	WCAI	TO	Cairn Toul
60073		EG	E	WCAI	TO	Cairn Gorm
60074		EG	E	WCAI	TO	
60075		E	E	WNTR	TE	
60076		EG	E	WCAI	TO	
60077	+	EG	E	WNTS	TO	Canisp
60078		ML	E	WNTR	MG	
60079		EG	E	WNTR	IM	Foinaven

60080	+	E	E	WNTR	TO	
60081	+	GW	E	WNTS	TO	ISAMBARD KINGDOM BRUNEL
60082		EG	E	WCAK	TO	Mam Tor
60083		E	E	WCAM	TO	Mountsorrel
60084		F	E	WNTR	TE	Cross Fell
60085		E	E	WNTR	IM	MINI Pride of Oxford
60086		EG	E	WNTS	TO	Schiehallion
60087		E	E	WNTS	TO	Barry Needham
60088		F	E	WNTS	TO	Buachaille Etive Mor
60089	+	E	E	WNTS	TO	THE RAILWAY HORSE
60090	+	EG	E	WCBK	TO	Quinag
60091	+	EG	E	WNTR	IM	An Teallach
60092	+	EG	E	WCBI	TO	Reginald Munns
60093		E	E	WNTR	IM	
60094		E	E	WNTR	IM	Rugby Flyer
60095		EG	E	WCAK	TO	
60096	+	E	E	WCBK	TO	
60097	+	E	E	WCBK	TO	ABP Port of Grimsby & Immingham
60098	+	E	E	WNTS	IM	Charles Francis Brush
60099		EG	E	WCAK	TO	Ben More Assynt
60100		E	E	WCAK	TO	Pride of Acton
60500		E	E	WCAI	TO	RAIL Magazine

CLASS 66   GENERAL MOTORS/EMD   Co-Co

Built: 1998–2007 by General Motors/EMD, London, Ontario, Canada (Model JT42CWR (low emission locos Model JT42CWRM)).
Engine: General Motors 12N-710G3B-EC two stroke of 2385 kW (3200 h.p.) at 904 r.p.m.
Main Alternator: General Motors AR8/CA6.
Traction Motors: General Motors D43TR.
Maximum Tractive Effort: 409 kN (92000 lbf).
Continuous Tractive Effort: 260 kN (58390 lbf) at 15.9 m.p.h.

Power At Rail: 1850 kW (2480 h.p.).	**Train Brakes:** Air.
Brake Force: 68 t.	**Dimensions:** 21.35 x 2.64 m.
Weight: 127 t.	**Wheel Diameter:** 1120 mm.
Design Speed: 87.5 m.p.h.	**Maximum Speed:** 75 m.p.h.
Fuel Capacity: 6550 litres.	**RA:** 7.
Train Supply: Not equipped.	**Multiple Working:** AAR System.

Notes: All equipped with Slow Speed Control.

Class 66 delivery dates. The Class 66 design has evolved over a ten year period with over 400 of these locos now in use in the UK. For clarity the delivery dates (by year) for each batch of locos delivered to the UK is as follows:

66001–66250	EWS. 1998–2000
66401–66410	DRS. 2003
66411–66420	DRS. 2006
66501–66505	Freightliner. 1999
66506–66520	Freightliner. 2000
66521–66525	Freightliner. 2000 (66521 since scrapped).

66526–66531	Freightliner. 2001
66532–66537	Freightliner. 2001
66538–66543	Freightliner. 2001
66544–66553	Freightliner. 2001
66554	Freightliner. 2002*
66555–66566	Freightliner. 2002
66567–66574	Freightliner. 2003
66575–66577	Freightliner. 2004
66578–66581	Freightliner. 2005
66582–66592	Freightliner. Due 2007
66601–66606	Freightliner. 2000
66607–66612	Freightliner. 2002
66613–66618	Freightliner. 2003
66619–66622	Freightliner. 2005
66623–66627	Freightliner. Due 2007
66701–66707	GB Railfreight. 2001
66708–66712	GB Railfreight. 2002
66713–66717	GB Railfreight. 2003
66718–66722	GB Railfreight. 2006
66723–66727	GB Railfreight. 2006
66951–66952	Freightliner. 2004

* Replacement for 66521, written off in the Great Heck accident in 2001.

Class 66/0. EWS-operated locomotives.

All fitted with Swinghead Automatic "Buckeye" Combination Couplers except 66001 and 66002.

66001	E	A	WBAN	TO	
66002	E	A	WBAN	TO	
66003	E	A	WBAI	TO	Lafarge Quorn
66004	E	A	WBAN	TO	
66005	E	A	WBAM	TO	
66006	E	A	WBAN	TO	
66007	E	A	WBAK	TO	
66008	E	A	WBAM	TO	
66009	E	A	WBAM	TO	
66010	E	A	WBEN	FN	
66011	E	A	WBEN	TO	
66012	E	A	WBAI	TO	
66013	E	A	WBAN	TO	
66014	E	A	WBAN	TO	
66015	E	A	WBAI	TO	
66016	E	A	WBAM	TO	
66017	E	A	WBAM	TO	
66018	E	A	WBAM	TO	
66019	E	A	WBAM	TO	
66020	E	A	WBAI	TO	
66021	E	A	WBAM	TO	
66022	E	A	WBEN	FN	
66023	E	A	WBAI	TO	
66024	E	A	WBAN	TO	

66025	E	A	WBAN	TO
66026	E	A	WBEN	TO
66027	E	A	WBAN	TO
66028	E	A	WBEN	FN
66029	E	A	WBEN	FN
66030	E	A	WBAN	TO
66031	E	A	WBAM	TO
66032	E	A	WBEN	FN
66033	E	A	WBAM	TO
66034	E	A	WBAN	TO
66035	E	A	WBAN	TO
66036	E	A	WBEN	FN
66037	E	A	WBAM	TO
66038	E	A	WBEN	FN
66039	E	A	WBAI	TO
66040	E	A	WBAM	TO
66041	E	A	WBAN	TO
66042	E	A	WBEN	FN
66043	E	A	WBAI	TO
66044	E	A	WBAM	TO
66045	E	A	WBEN	FN
66046	E	A	WBAN	TO
66047	E	A	WBAN	TO
66048	E	A	WBAN	TO
66049	E	A	WBEN	FN
66050	E	A	WBAM	TO
66051	E	A	WBAI	TO
66052	E	A	WBEN	FN
66053	E	A	WBAN	TO
66054	E	A	WBAN	TO
66055	E	A	WBLI	TO
66056	E	A	WBLI	TO
66057	E	A	WBLI	TO
66058	E	A	WBLI	TO
66059	E	A	WBLI	TO
66060	E	A	WBAM	TO
66061	E	A	WBAM	TO
66062	E	A	WBEN	FN
66063	E	A	WBAM	TO
66064	E	A	WBEN	FN
66065	E	A	WBAM	TO
66066	E	A	WBAK	TO
66067	E	A	WBAN	TO
66068	E	A	WBAM	TO
66069	E	A	WBAM	TO
66070	E	A	WBAN	TO
66071	E	A	WBEN	FN
66072	E	A	WBAM	TO
66073	E	A	WBEN	TO
66074	E	A	WBAI	TO
66075	E	A	WBAI	TO

66076	**E**	A	WBAN	TO	
66077	**E**	A	WBAM	TO	Benjamin Gimbert G.C.
66078	**E**	A	WBAI	TO	
66079	**E**	A	WBAK	TO	James Nightall G.C.
66080	**E**	A	WBAM	TO	
66081	**E**	A	WBAN	TO	
66082	**E**	A	WBAM	TO	
66083	**E**	A	WBAM	TO	
66084	**E**	A	WBAM	TO	
66085	**E**	A	WBAM	TO	
66086	**E**	A	WBAN	TO	
66087	**E**	A	WBAN	TO	
66088	**E**	A	WBAN	TO	
66089	**E**	A	WBAN	TO	
66090	**E**	A	WBAK	TO	
66091	**E**	A	WBAM	TO	
66092	**E**	A	WBAN	TO	
66093	**E**	A	WBAM	TO	
66094	**E**	A	WBAM	TO	
66095	**E**	A	WBAN	TO	
66096	**E**	A	WBAM	TO	
66097	**E**	A	WBAK	TO	
66098	**E**	A	WBAN	TO	
66099 r	**E**	A	WBBN	TO	
66100 r	**E**	A	WBBM	TO	
66101 r	**E**	A	WBBM	TO	
66102 r	**E**	A	WBBM	TO	
66103 r	**E**	A	WBBM	TO	
66104 r	**E**	A	WBBN	TO	
66105 r	**E**	A	WBBM	TO	
66106 r	**E**	A	WBBN	TO	
66107 r	**E**	A	WBBN	TO	
66108 r	**E**	A	WBBM	TO	
66109	**E**	A	WBAN	TO	
66110 r	**E**	A	WBBM	TO	
66111 r	**E**	A	WBBN	TO	
66112 r	**E**	A	WBBM	TO	
66113 r	**E**	A	WBBM	TO	
66114 r	**E**	A	WBBK	TO	
66115	**E**	A	WBAK	TO	
66116	**E**	A	WBAN	TO	
66117	**E**	A	WBAK	TO	
66118	**E**	A	WBAM	TO	
66119	**E**	A	WBAN	TO	
66120	**E**	A	WBAN	TO	
66121	**E**	A	WBAM	TO	
66122	**E**	A	WBAM	TO	
66123	**E**	A	WBEN	TO	
66124	**E**	A	WBAK	TO	
66125	**E**	A	WBAM	TO	
66126	**E**	A	WBAN	TO	

66127	E	A	WBAN	TO	
66128	E	A	WBAM	TO	
66129	E	A	WBAI	TO	
66130	E	A	WBAI	TO	
66131	E	A	WBAM	TO	
66132	E	A	WBAM	TO	
66133	E	A	WBAN	TO	
66134	E	A	WBAM	TO	
66135	E	A	WBAN	TO	
66136	E	A	WBAM	TO	
66137	E	A	WBAN	TO	
66138	E	A	WBAN	TO	
66139	E	A	WBAN	TO	
66140	E	A	WBAM	TO	
66141	E	A	WBAK	TO	
66142	E	A	WBAM	TO	
66143	E	A	WBAN	TO	
66144	E	A	WBAK	TO	
66145	E	A	WBAM	TO	
66146	E	A	WBAN	TO	
66147	E	A	WBAM	TO	
66148	E	A	WBAN	TO	
66149	E	A	WBAM	TO	
66150	E	A	WBAI	TO	
66151	E	A	WBAN	TO	
66152	E	A	WBAK	TO	
66153	E	A	WBAN	TO	
66154	E	A	WBAI	TO	
66155	E	A	WBAN	TO	
66156	E	A	WBAK	TO	
66157	E	A	WBAI	TO	
66158	E	A	WBAM	TO	
66159	E	A	WBAK	TO	
66160	E	A	WBAI	TO	
66161	E	A	WBAK	TO	
66162	E	A	WBAM	TO	
66163	E	A	WBAN	TO	
66164	E	A	WBAM	TO	
66165	E	A	WBAM	TO	
66166	E	A	WBAI	TO	
66167	E	A	WBAN	TO	
66168	E	A	WBAI	TO	
66169	E	A	WBAI	TO	
66170	E	A	WBAN	TO	
66171	E	A	WBAN	TO	
66172	E	A	WBAK	TO	PAUL MELLENEY
66173	E	A	WBAN	TO	
66174	E	A	WBAI	TO	
66175	E	A	WBAN	TO	
66176	E	A	WBAN	TO	
66177	E	A	WBAK	TO	

66178	E	A	WBAN	TO	
66179	E	A	WBAM	TO	
66180	E	A	WBAN	TO	
66181	E	A	WBAM	TO	
66182	E	A	WBAK	TO	
66183	E	A	WBAM	TO	
66184	E	A	WBAN	TO	
66185	E	A	WBAN	TO	
66186	E	A	WBAM	TO	
66187	E	A	WBAN	TO	
66188	E	A	WBAK	TO	
66189	E	A	WBAI	TO	
66190	E	A	WBAK	TO	
66191	E	A	WBAM	TO	
66192	E	A	WBAK	TO	
66193	E	A	WBAN	TO	
66194	E	A	WBAM	TO	
66195	E	A	WBAM	TO	
66196	E	A	WBAI	TO	
66197	E	A	WBAN	TO	
66198	E	A	WBAM	TO	
66199	E	A	WBAN	TO	
66200	E	A	WBAM	TO	RAILWAY HERITAGE COMMITTEE
66201	E	A	WBAI	TO	
66202	E	A	WBAM	TO	
66203	E	A	WBAM	TO	
66204	E	A	WBAN	TO	
66205	E	A	WBAN	TO	
66206	E	A	WBAN	TO	
66207	E	A	WBAK	TO	
66208	E	A	WBAN	TO	
66209	E	A	WBAM	TO	
66210	E	A	WBAN	TO	
66211	E	A	WBAM	TO	
66212	E	A	WBAM	TO	
66213	E	A	WBAM	TO	
66214	E	A	WBAM	TO	
66215	E	A	WBEN	FN	
66216	E	A	WBAN	TO	
66217	E	A	WBAN	TO	
66218	E	A	WBAN	TO	
66219	E	A	WBAI	TO	
66220	E	A	WBAM	TO	
66221	E	A	WBAK	TO	
66222	E	A	WBAM	TO	
66223	E	A	WBAN	TO	
66224	E	A	WBAN	TO	
66225	E	A	WBAK	TO	
66226	E	A	WBAM	TO	
66227	E	A	WBAK	TO	
66228	E	A	WBAN	TO	

66229	E	A	WBEN	TO
66230	E	A	WBAN	TO
66231	E	A	WBAI	TO
66232	E	A	WBAI	TO
66233	E	A	WBAM	TO
66234	E	A	WBEN	TO
66235	E	A	WBAN	TO
66236	E	A	WBAM	TO
66237	E	A	WBAN	TO
66238	E	A	WBAM	TO
66239	E	A	WBAI	TO
66240	E	A	WBAM	TO
66241	E	A	WBEN	TO
66242	E	A	WBAM	TO
66243	E	A	WBAM	TO
66244	E	A	WBAM	TO
66245	E	A	WBAI	TO
66246	E	A	WBEN	TO
66247	E	A	WBAM	TO
66248	E	A	WBAI	TO
66249	E	A	WBEN	TO
66250	E	A	WBAN	TO

Class 66/4. Direct Rail Services-operated locomotives.
66401–66410. Porterbrook locos. Details as Class 66/0.

Advertising livery: 66405 WH Malcolm (DRS Blue with WH Malcolm logos).

66401	DS	P	XHIM	KM
66402	DS	P	XHIM	KM
66403	DS	P	XHIM	KM
66404	DS	P	XHIM	KM
66405	AL	P	XHIM	KM
66406	DS	P	XHIM	KM
66407	DS	P	XHIM	KM
66408	DS	P	XHIM	KM
66409	DS	P	XHIM	KM
66410	DS	P	XHIM	KM

66411–66420. Low emission. HBOS-owned. Details as Class 66/0 except:

Engine: EMD 12N-710G3B-U2 two stroke of 2420 kW (3245 h.p.) at 904 r.p.m.
Traction Motors: General Motors D43TRC.
Fuel Capacity: 5150 litres.

Advertising livery: 66411 Eddie Stobart Rail (two tone blue & white).

66411	AL	HX	XHIM	KM
66412	DS	HX	XHIM	KM
66413	DS	HX	XHIM	KM
66414	DS	HX	XHIM	KM
66415	DS	HX	XHIM	KM
66416	DS	HX	XHIM	KM
66417	DS	HX	XHIM	KM
66418	DS	HX	XHIM	KM

| 66419 | **DS** | HX | XHIM | KM |
| 66420 | **DS** | HX | XHIM | KM |

Class 66/5. Freightliner-operated locomotives. Details as Class 66/0.

Advertising livery: 66522 Shanks Waste (one half of loco Freightliner green and one half of Shanks' Waste light green).

66501	**FL**	P	DFGM	FD	Japan 2001
66502	**FL**	P	DFGM	FD	Basford Hall Centenary 2001
66503	**FL**	P	DFGM	FD	The RAILWAY MAGAZINE
66504	**FL**	P	DFGM	FD	
66505	**FL**	P	DFGM	FD	
66506	**FL**	H	DFHH	FD	Crewe Regeneration
66507	**FL**	H	DFRT	FD	
66508	**FL**	H	DFHH	FD	
66509	**FL**	H	DFHH	FD	
66510	**FL**	H	DFRT	FD	
66511	**FL**	H	DFRT	FD	
66512	**FL**	H	DFHH	FD	
66513	**FL**	H	DFHH	FD	
66514	**FL**	H	DFRT	FD	
66515	**FL**	H	DFRT	FD	
66516	**FL**	H	DFGM	FD	
66517	**FL**	H	DFGM	FD	
66518	**FL**	H	DFRT	FD	
66519	**FL**	H	DFHH	FD	
66520	**FL**	H	DFRT	FD	
66522	**AL**	H	DFRT	LD	
66523	**FL**	H	DFRT	FD	
66524	**FL**	H	DFHH	LD	
66525	**FL**	H	DFHH	FD	
66526	**FL**	P	DFRT	LD	Driver Steve Dunn (George)
66527	**FL**	P	DFRT	LD	Don Raider
66528	**FL**	P	DFHH	FD	
66529	**FL**	P	DFHH	FD	
66530	**FL**	P	DFHH	LD	
66531	**FL**	P	DFHH	FD	
66532	**FL**	P	DFGM	FD	P&O Nedlloyd Atlas
66533	**FL**	P	DFGM	FD	Hanjin Express/Senator Express
66534	**FL**	P	DFGM	FD	OOCL Express
66535	**FL**	P	DFGM	FD	
66536	**FL**	P	DFGM	FD	
66537	**FL**	P	DFGM	FD	
66538	**FL**	H	DFIM	FD	
66539	**FL**	H	DFIM	FD	

66540	**FL**	H	DFIM	FD	Ruby
66541	**FL**	H	DFIM	FD	
66542	**FL**	H	DFIM	FD	
66543	**FL**	H	DFIM	FD	
66544	**FL**	P	DFHG	LD	
66545	**FL**	P	DFHG	FD	
66546	**FL**	P	DFNR	FD	
66547	**FL**	P	DFNR	LD	
66548	**FL**	P	DFHG	LD	
66549	**FL**	P	DFHG	LD	
66550	**FL**	P	DFHG	LD	
66551	**FL**	P	DFHG	LD	
66552	**FL**	P	DFHG	LD	Maltby Raider
66553	**FL**	P	DFHG	LD	
66554	**FL**	H	DFHG	LD	
66555	**FL**	H	DFHG	LD	
66556	**FL**	H	DFHG	LD	
66557	**FL**	H	DFHG	FD	
66558	**FL**	H	DFHG	FD	
66559	**FL**	H	DFNR	LD	
66560	**FL**	H	DFHG	FD	
66561	**FL**	H	DFHG	FD	
66562	**FL**	H	DFHG	LD	
66563	**FL**	H	DFHG	FD	
66564	**FL**	H	DFHG	LD	
66565	**FL**	H	DFHG	LD	
66566	**FL**	H	DFHG	LD	
66567	**FL**	H	DFIM	FD	
66568	**FL**	H	DFIM	FD	
66569	**FL**	H	DFIM	FD	
66570	**FL**	H	DFIM	FD	
66571	**FL**	H	DFIM	FD	
66572	**FL**	H	DFIM	FD	
66573	**FL**	H	DFIM	FD	
66574	**FL**	H	DFIM	FD	
66575	**FL**	H	DFIM	FD	
66576	**FL**	H	DFIM	FD	Hamburg Sud Advantage
66577	**FL**	H	DFIM	FD	
66578	**FL**	H	DFIM	FD	
66579	**FL**	H	DFIM	FD	
66580	**FL**	H	DFIM	FD	
66581	**FL**	H	DFHG	FD	Sophie

Class 66/5. Freightliner-operated low emission locos. On order. Details as Class 66/0 except:
Engine: EMD 12N-710G3B-U2 two stroke of 2420 kW (3245 h.p.) at 904 r.p.m.
Traction Motors: General Motors D43TRC.
Fuel Capacity: 5150 litres.

66582
66583
66584

66585
66586
66587
66588
66589
66590
66591
66592

Class 66/6. Freightliner-operated locomotives with modified gear ratios. Details as Class 66/0 except:

Maximum Tractive Effort: 467 kN (105080 lbf).
Continuous Tractive Effort: 296 kN (66630 lbf) at 14.0 m.p.h.
Design Speed: 65 m.p.h.   **Maximum Speed:** 65 m.p.h.

66601	**FL**	P	DFHH	FD	The Hope Valley
66602	**FL**	P	DFRT	FD	
66603	**FL**	P	DFRT	FD	
66604	**FL**	P	DFRT	FD	
66605	**FL**	P	DFRT	FD	
66606	**FL**	P	DFRT	FD	
66607	**FL**	P	DFHG	FD	
66608	**FL**	P	DFHG	FD	
66609	**FL**	P	DFHG	FD	
66610	**FL**	P	DFHG	FD	
66611	**FL**	P	DFHG	FD	
66612	**FL**	P	DFHG	FD	Forth Raider
66613	**FL**	H	DFHG	FD	
66614	**FL**	H	DFHG	FD	
66615	**FL**	H	DFHG	FD	
66616	**FL**	H	DFHG	FD	
66617	**FL**	H	DFHG	FD	
66618	**FL**	H	DFHG	FD	Railways Illustrated Annual Photographic Awards Alan Barnes Derek W. Johnson MBE
66619	**FL**	H	DFHG	FD	
66620	**FL**	H	DFHG	FD	
66621	**FL**	H	DFHG	FD	
66622	**FL**	H	DFHG	FD	

Class 66/6. Freightliner-operated low emission locos with modified gear ratios. On order.
Fuel Capacity: 5150 litres.

Advertising livery: 66623 Bardon Aggregates (blue).

66623	**AL**	HX
66624	**FL**	HX
66625		
66626		
66627		

Class 66/7. GB Railfreight-operated locomotives. Details as Class 66/0.

Non-standard/Advertising liveries:

66705 **GB** livery but with the addition of "Union Jack" bodyside vinyls.
66709 Black & orange with MEDITE branding.

66701	**GB**	H	GBRT	WN	Whitemoor
66702	**GB**	H	GBRT	WN	Blue Lightning
66703	**GB**	H	GBRT	WN	Doncaster PSB 1981–2002
66704	**GB**	H	GBRT	WN	Colchester Power Signalbox
66705	**GB**	H	GBRT	WN	Golden Jubilee
66706	**GB**	H	GBRT	WN	Nene Valley
66707	**GB**	H	GBRT	WN	Sir Sam Fay GREAT CENTRAL RAILWAY
66708	**GB**	H	GBCM	WN	
66709	**AL**	H	GBCM	WN	Joseph Arnold Davies
66710	**GB**	H	GBCM	WN	
66711	**GB**	H	GBCM	WN	
66712	**GB**	H	GBCM	WN	Peterborough Power Signalbox
66713	**GB**	H	GBCM	WN	Forest City
66714	**GB**	H	GBCM	WN	Cromer Lifeboat
66715	**GB**	H	GBCM	WN	VALOUR – IN MEMORY OF ALL RAILWAY EMPLOYEES WHO GAVE THEIR LIVES FOR THEIR COUNTRY
66716	**GB**	H	GBCM	WN	Willesden Traincare Centre
66717	**GB**	H	GBCM	WN	Good Old Boy

66718–66727. Low emission. Details as Class 66/0 except:

Engine: EMD 12N-710G3B-U2 two stroke of 2420 kW (3245 h.p.) at 904 r.p.m.
Traction Motors: General Motors D43TRC.
Fuel Capacity: 5546 litres (66718–722) or 5150 litres (66723–727).

66718	**MT**	H	GBCM	WN	Gwyneth Dunwoody
66719	**MT**	H	GBCM	WN	METRO-LAND
66720	**MT**	H	GBCM	WN	Metronet Pathfinder
66721	**MT**	H	GBCM	WN	Harry Beck
66722	**MT**	H	GBCM	WN	Sir Edward Watkin
66723	**GF**	H	GBCM	WN	
66724	**GF**	H	GBCM	WN	
66725	**GF**	H	GBCM	WN	
66726	**GF**	H	GBCM	WN	
66727	**GF**	H	GBCM	WN	

Class 66/9. Freightliner locos. Low emission "demonstrator" locos. Details as Class 66/0 except:

Engine: EMD 12N-710G3B-U2 two stroke of 2420 kW (3245 h.p.) at 904 r.p.m.
Traction Motors: General Motors D43TRC.
Fuel Capacity: 5905/5150 litres.

66951	**FL**	H	DFHG	FD
66952	**FL**	H	DFHG	FD

CLASS 67 ALSTOM/GENERAL MOTORS EMD Bo-Bo

Built: 1999–2000 by Alstom at Valencia, Spain, as sub-contractors for General Motors (General Motors model JT42 HW-HS).
Engine: General Motors 12N-710G3B-EC two stroke of 2385 kW (3200 h.p.) at 904 r.p.m.
Main Alternator: General Motors AR9A/HEP7/CA6C.
Traction Motors: General Motors D43FM.
Maximum Tractive Effort: 141 kN (31770 lbf).
Continuous Tractive Effort: 90 kN (20200 lbf) at 46.5 m.p.h.
Power At Rail: 1860 kW.
Brake Force: 78 t.
Weight: 90 t.
Design Speed: 125 m.p.h.
Fuel Capacity: 4927 litres.
Train Supply: Electric, index 66.
Train Brakes: Air.
Dimensions: 19.74 x 2.72 m.
Wheel Diameter: 965 mm.
Maximum Speed: 125 m.p.h.
RA: 8.
Multiple Working: AAR System.

Note: All equipped with Slow Speed Control and Swinghead Automatic "Buckeye" Combination Couplers.

Non-standard livery: 67029 All over silver with EWS logos (EWS "Special Train").

67001		**E**	A	WAAN	TO	
67002		**E**	A	WAAN	TO	
67003		**E**	A	WAAN	TO	
67004	r	**E**	A	WABN	TO	Post Haste
67005		**RZ**	A	WAAN	TO	Queen's Messenger
67006		**RZ**	A	WAAN	TO	Royal Sovereign
67007	r	**E**	A	WABN	TO	
67008		**E**	A	WNTR	TO	
67009	r	**E**	A	WABN	TO	
67010		**E**	A	WNTS	TO	Unicorn
67011	r	**E**	A	WABN	TO	
67012		**E**	A	WAAN	TO	
67013		**E**	A	WNTR	BK	
67014		**E**	A	WAAN	TO	
67015		**E**	A	WAAN	TO	
67016		**E**	A	WAAN	TO	
67017		**E**	A	WAAN	TO	Arrow
67018		**E**	A	WAAN	TO	Rapid
67019		**E**	A	WAAN	TO	
67020		**E**	A	WAAN	TO	
67021		**E**	A	WAAN	TO	
67022		**E**	A	WAAN	TO	
67023		**E**	A	WAAN	TO	
67024		**E**	A	WNTS	TO	
67025		**E**	A	WAAN	TO	Western Star
67026		**E**	A	WAAN	TO	
67027		**E**	A	WAAN	TO	Rising Star
67028		**E**	A	WAAN	TO	
67029		**0**	A	WAAN	TO	
67030	r	**E**	A	WABN	TO	

PLATFORM 5 MAIL ORDER

RAILWAYS RESTORED 2007

Ian Allan

Fully revised and updated edition of the definitive guide to heritage
railways, railway museums and preservation centres in the British
Isles. Contains essential opening and operating information for over
180 heritage locations, plus details of on-site facilities, disabled
access, special events and other useful information. Also includes a
locomotive stocklist for most locations and 2007 timetables for over
60 operating railways. Well illustrated. 224 pages. **£14.99.**

RAIL ATLAS OF GREAT BRITAIN & IRELAND
11th edition

Oxford Publishing Company

Fully revised and updated edition of the definitive UK railway atlas.
Shows all lines with multiple/single track distinction and colours used
to denote municipal/urban railways, preserved lines and freight only
lines. Also shows all stations, junctions, freight terminals, depots,
works and marshalling yards. Includes many enlargements of
complicated layouts, plus an index map and a full index to locations.
128 pages. Hardback. **£14.99.**

**Telephone, fax or send your order to the Platform 5 Mail Order
Department. See page 384 of this book for details.**

▲ Freightliner-liveried 08691 "Terri" awaits its next turn of duty at Felixstowe North Terminal on 25/05/05. **Chris Booth**

▼ EWS-liveried 09022 shunts in Rugby Yard on 14/05/05. **Mark Beal**

DRS-liveried 20307 and 20309 are seen heading south on the West Coast Main Line at Red Bank with 6K73 15.38 Sellafield–Crewe Nuclear Flasks on 30/05/06. **Paul Senior**

▲ Inter-City-liveried 31454 "HEART OF WESSEX" leads a 5Z33 09.42 Oxley–Barrow Hill (via Derby) stock movement at Chesterfield on 06/07/06. 47145 was on the rear. **Robert Pritchard**

▼ West Coast Railway Company-liveried 33207 "Jim Martin" found use at the Bo'ness & Kinneil diesel gala on 29/04/06. Here it is seen near Birkhill with an afternoon service from Bo'ness. **Ian Lothian**

37612 and 37218 storm through Lichfield Trent Valley with 4L46 11.18 Ditton–Purfleet DRS Intermodal on 08/06/06.

Chris Booth

BR Blue-liveried 40145 passes Diggle with a Pathfinder railtour from Crewe to Whitby on 03/06/06. **Gavin Morrison**

▲ Carrying the new First Group "Dynamic Lights" livery 43009 "First transforming travel" leads 43126 at Duffryn with an unidentified e.c.s. working to Cardiff Central on 20/05/06. **John Catterson**

▼ A GNER HST set led by 43119 "Harrogate Spa" forms the 07.00 Edinburgh–London King's Cross at Eaton Lane Crossing near Retford on 14/07/06. **Andrew Wills**

FM Rail's 47145 "MYRDDIN EMRYS" is seen working 6Z59 11.00 York North Yard–Coalville wagon movement at Milford, Derbyshire on 12/07/06.

Mick Tindall

Revised BR Blue-liveried 50049 "Defiance" passes Ponthir, just north of Newport, with 1Z47 16.20 Cardiff–Crewe additional service for Arriva Trains Wales on 14/04/06.
Andrew Mist

▲ Fastline's three Class 56s entered service in 2006. On 12/06/06 56301 passes Slitting Mill, north of Chesterfield on the Midland "Old Road" with 4O90 11.01 Doncaster–Thamesport Intermodal, conveying just flat wagons. **Andrew Wills**

▼ Freightliner's 57004 "Freightliner Quality" heads 4O51 10.03 Cardiff Wentloog–Southampton Freightliner at Battledown, west of Basingstoke, on 01/03/06. **Brian Denton**

EWS-liveried 59205 "L. Keith McNair" passes Crofton with 7A09 06.56 Merehead–Acton loaded stone on 30/08/06.

Ron Westwater

60021 "Star of the East" is seen at Ribblehead with 6E13 12.40 Newbiggin–Knottingley empty gypsum containers on 08/09/05. **Rodney Lissenden**

▲ 66240 passes Toton on 07/06/05 with an emty coal train from Ratcliffe Power Station. **Paul Shannon**

▼ GBRf Metronet-liveried 66722 is seen at Norton Hammer, just south of Sheffield, with a returning Hertfordshire Railtours charter from Deepcar to Ealing Broadway on 10/06/06. **Gavin Morrison**

▲ Special EWS Silver-liveried 67029 propells the EWS Company Train at Acton Turvill on 08/06/05. The train was running as a 12.56 Bath–Bath circular.

John Chalcraft

▼ GBRf-liveried 73209 "Alison" leads 73136 in BR Blue livery with 6G10 15.00 Purley–Eastleigh engineers' train at Worting on 19/08/06. 73204 and 73208 were on the rear.

Chris Wilson

Freightliner-liveried 86621 and 86604 cross Float Viaduct south of Carstairs with 4M74 14.10 Coatbridge–Crewe Freightliner on 03/02/06.

Ian Lothian

▲ In unbranded DRS blue livery 87022 heads north at Hanslope Junction with 1S96 16.26 Willesden–Shieldmuir Mail (325 units) on 20/06/06. Since this photo was taken this loco has been renamed "Cock o' the North". **Dave Gommersall**

▼ Ex-works in First Group livery 90024 stands outside Toton depot on 10 August. After release from Toton the loco was used to haul First ScotRail's Caledonian Sleeper services. **Richard Tuplin**

▲ 91125 "Berwick-upon-Tweed" storms north at Eaton Lane with the 08.35 King's Cross–Leeds on 14/07/06. **Andrew Wills**

▼ In EPS two tone grey livery with EWS vinyls 92024 "J. S. Bach" passes Longport with 4069 14.01 Trafford Park–Dollands Moor Intermodal on 30/05/06.
Cliff Beeton

2. ELECTRO-DIESEL & ELECTRIC LOCOMOTIVES

CLASS 73   BR/ENGLISH ELECTRIC   Bo-Bo

Electro-diesel locomotives which can operate either from a DC supply or using power from a diesel engine.

Built: 1965–1967 by English Electric Co. at Vulcan Foundry, Newton le Willows.
Engine: English Electric 4SRKT of 447 kW (600 h.p.) at 850 r.p.m.
Main Generator: English Electric 824/5D.
Electric Supply System: 750 V DC from third rail.
Traction Motors: English Electric 546/1B.
Maximum Tractive Effort (Electric): 179 kN (40000 lbf).
Maximum Tractive Effort (Diesel): 160 kN (36000 lbf).
Continuous Rating (Electric): 1060 kW (1420 h.p.) giving a tractive effort of 35 kN (7800 lbf) at 68 m.p.h.
Continuous Tractive Effort (Diesel): 60 kN (13600 lbf) at 11.5 m.p.h.
Maximum Rail Power (Electric): 2350 kW (3150 h.p.) at 42 m.p.h.
Train Brakes: Air, vacuum & electro-pneumatic († Air & electro-pneumatic).
Brake Force: 31 t.   **Dimensions:** 16.36 x 2.64 m.
Weight: 77 t.   **Wheel Diameter:** 1016 mm.
Design Speed: 90 m.p.h.   **Maximum Speed:** 90 m.p.h.
Fuel Capacity: 1409 litres.   **RA:** 6.
Train Supply: Electric, index 66 (on electric power only).
Multiple Working: SR 27-way System & Blue Star.

Formerly numbered E6001–E6020/E6022–E6026/E6028–E6049 (not in order).

Note: Locomotives numbered in the 732xx series are classed as 73/2 and were originally dedicated to Gatwick Express services.

Non-standard numbering: 73136 Also carries number D6043.

73103	**IM**	FM	SDXL	MQ	
73107	**K**	FM	SDED	DF	SPITFIRE
73109	**SD**	SW	HYWD	WD	Battle of Britain 50th Anniversary
73117	**IM**	FM	SDXL	MQ	
73118 †c	**EP**	EU	GPSN	NP	
73130 †c	**EP**	EU	GPSN	NP	
73136	**B**	73	CSPC	SL	Perseverance
73141	**IM**	NR	QAED	ZR (S)	
73201 †	**SD**	P	HYWD	WD	
73202 †	**GX**	P	IVGA	SL (S)	Dave Berry
73203 †	**GX**	GB	GBZZ	SE	
73204 †	**GB**	GB	GBED	DF	Janice
73205 †	**GB**	GB	GBED	DF	Jeanette
73206 †	**GB**	GB	GBED	DF	Lisa
73207 †	**GX**	GB	GBZZ	TN	
73208 †	**B**	GB	GBED	DF	Kirsten

73209 †	**GB**	GB	GBED	DF	Alison
73212 †	**Y**	NR	QAED	DF	
73213 †	**Y**	NR	QAED	DF	
73235 †	**SD**	P	HYWD	WD	

CLASS 86   BR/ENGLISH ELECTRIC   Bo-Bo

Built: 1965–1966 by English Electric Co. at Vulcan Foundry, Newton le Willows or by BR at Doncaster Works.
Electric Supply System: 25 kV AC 50 Hz overhead.
Train Brakes: Air.   **Brake Force:** 40 t.
Dimensions: 17.83 x 2.65 m.   **Weight:** 83–86.8 t.
RA: 6.   **Multiple Working:** TDM system.
Train Supply: Electric, index 66.

Formerly numbered E3101–E3200 (not in order).

Class 86/1. Class 87-type bogies & motors.

Details as above except:
Traction Motors: GEC 412AZ frame mounted.
Maximum Tractive Effort: 258 kN (58000 lbf).
Continuous Rating: 3730 kW (5000 h.p.) giving a tractive effort of 95 kN (21300 lbf) at 87 m.p.h.
Maximum Rail Power: 5860 kW (7860 h.p.) at 50.8 m.p.h.
Wheel Diameter: 1150 mm.   **Weight:** 86.8 t.
Design Speed: 110 m.p.h.   **Maximum Speed:** 110 m.p.h.

| 86101 | **B** | AC | ACXX | BH | Sir William A Stanier FRS |

Class 86/2. Standard design rebuilt with resilient wheels and Flexicoil suspension.

Traction Motors: AEI 282BZ axle hung.
Maximum Tractive Effort: 207 kN (46500 lbf).
Continuous Rating: 3010 kW (4040 h.p.) giving a tractive effort of 85 kN (19200 lbf) at 77.5 m.p.h.
Maximum Rail Power: 4550 kW (6100 h.p.) at 49.5 m.p.h.
Wheel Diameter: 1156 mm.   **Weight:** 85–86.2 t.
Design Speed: 125 m.p.h.   **Maximum Speed:** 100 m.p.h.

Non-standard livery/numbering: 86233 and 86259 BR "Electric blue" livery.
86233 Also carries number E3172.
86259 Also carries number E3137.

86205	**V**	H	SAXL	LM	
86212	**V**	H	SAXL	EM	
86215	**AR**	H	SAXL	SN	
86217	**AR**	H	SAXL	LM	
86218	**AR**	H	SAXL	KM	
86223	**AR**	H	SAXL	OY	Norwich Union
86226	**V**	H	SAXL	LM	
86228	**IC**	H	SAXL	LM	Vulcan Heritage
86229	**V**	H	SAXL	LM	

86230	**AR**	H	SAXL	SN	
86231	**V**	H	SAXL	LM	
86232	**AR**	H	SAXL	KM	
86233	**O**	H	SAXL	OY	
86234	**AR**	H	SAXL	LM	
86235	**AR**	H	SAXL	DF	
86242	**AR**	H	SAXL	SN	
86245	**V**	H	SAXL	LM	
86246	**AR**	H	SAXL	LM	
86247	**V**	H	SAXL	LM	
86248	**V**	H	SAXL	LM	Sir Clwyd/County of Clwyd
86250	**AR**	H	SAXL	LM	
86251	**V**	H	SAXL	LM	
86258	**V**	H	SAXL	LB	
86259	**O**	PO	MBDL	TM	Les Ross
86260	**AR**	H	SAXL	LM	

Class 86/4.

Traction Motors: AEI 282AZ axle hung.
Maximum Tractive Effort: 258 kN (58000 lbf).
Continuous Rating: 2680 kW (3600 h.p.) giving a tractive effort of 89 kN (20000 lbf) at 67 m.p.h.
Maximum Rail Power: 4400 kW (5900 h.p.) at 38 m.p.h.
Wheel Diameter: 1156 mm. **Weight:** 83–83.9 t.
Design Speed: 100 m.p.h. **Maximum Speed:** 100 m.p.h.

| 86401 | **N** | AC | ACAC | LM | Northampton Town |
| 86424 | **RX** | NR | SDXL | CP | |

Class 86/5. Regeared locomotive operated by Freightliner.

Details as Class 86/4 except:

Continuous Rating: 2680 kW (3600 h.p.) giving a tractive effort of 117 kN (26300 lbf) at 67 m.p.h.
Maximum Speed: 75 m.p.h. **Train Supply:** Electric, isolated.

| 86501 (86608) | **FL** | FL | DFGC | FE | |

Class 86/6. Freightliner-operated locomotives.

Details as Class 86/4 except:

Maximum Speed: 75 m.p.h. **Train Supply:** Electric, isolated.

86602	**FL**	FL	DHLT	BA	
86604	**FL**	FL	DFNC	FE	
86605	**FL**	FL	DFNC	FE	
86606	**FF**	FL	DHLT	CE	
86607	**FL**	FL	DFNC	FE	
86609	**FL**	FL	DFNC	FE	
86610	**FL**	FL	DFNC	FE	
86612	**FL**	P	DFNC	FE	
86613	**FL**	P	DFNC	FE	
86614	**FF**	P	DFNC	FE	

86615	**FL**	P	DHLT	CE	Rotary International
86620	**FL**	P	DHLT	CE	Philip G Walton
86621	**FL**	P	DFNC	FE	
86622	**FF**	P	DFNC	FE	
86623	**FF**	P	DHLT	BA	
86627	**FL**	P	DFNC	FE	
86628	**FL**	P	DFNC	FE	
86632	**FL**	P	DFNC	FE	
86633	**FF**	P	DHLT	BA	
86635	**FL**	P	DHLT	BA	
86637	**FF**	P	DFNC	FE	
86638	**FL**	P	DFNC	FE	
86639	**FL**	P	DFNC	FE	

Class 86/9. Network Rail-owned locomotives. Rebuilt for use as Mobile Load Bank test locos to test Overhead Line Equipment, initially on the WCML. No. 1 end Traction Motors isolated. Can still move under own power.

Maximum Speed: 60 m.p.h.   **Train Supply:** Electric, isolated.

| 86901 | **Y** | NR | QACL | RU | CHIEF ENGINEER |
| 86902 | **Y** | NR | QACL | RU | RAIL VEHICLE ENGINEERING |

CLASS 87   BREL/GEC   Bo-Bo

Built: 1973–1975 by BREL at Crewe Works.
Electric Supply System: 25 kV AC 50 Hz overhead.
Traction Motors: GEC G412AZ frame mounted.
Maximum Tractive Effort: 258 kN (58000 lbf).
Continuous Rating: 3730 kW (5000 h.p.) giving a tractive effort of 95 kN (21300 lbf) at 87 m.p.h.
Maximum Rail Power: 5860 kW (7860 h.p.) at 50.8 m.p.h.
Train Brakes: Air.   **Brake Force:** 40 t.
Dimensions: 17.83 x 2.65 m.   **Weight:** 83.3 t.
Wheel Diameter: 1150 mm.   **Design Speed:** 110 m.p.h.
Maximum Speed: 110 m.p.h.   **Train Supply:** Electric, index 95.
RA: 6.   **Multiple Working:** TDM system.

87002	**P**	P	SBXL	WB	The AC Locomotive Group
87003	**V**	P	SBXL	LM	
87004	**V**	P	SBXL	LM	
87006	**DR**	P	SBXL	WB	
87007	**CD**	P	SBXL	WB	
87008	**CD**	P	SBXL	WB	
87009	**V**	P	SBXL	LM	
87010	**V**	P	SBXL	LM	
87011	**V**	P	SBXL	LM	
87013	**V**	P	SBXL	LM	
87014	**V**	P	SBXL	LM	
87017	**V**	P	SBXL	LM	
87018	**V**	P	SBXL	LM	
87020	**V**	P	SBXL	LM	

87021	V	P	SBXL	LM	
87022	DR	P	GBAC	WB	Cock o' the North
87023	V	P	SBXL	LM	
87025	V	P	SBXL	LM	
87026	V	P	SBXL	WB	
87027	V	P	SBXL	LM	
87028	DR	P	GBAC	WB	Lord President
87029	V	P	SBXL	LM	
87030	V	P	SBXL	LM	
87032	V	P	SBXL	LM	
87033	V	P	SBXL	LM	
87034	V	P	SBXL	LM	

CLASS 90   GEC   Bo-Bo

Built: 1987–1990 by BREL at Crewe Works (as sub contractors for GEC).
Electric Supply System: 25 kV AC 50 Hz overhead.
Traction Motors: GEC G412CY frame mounted.
Maximum Tractive Effort: 258 kN (58000 lbf).
Continuous Rating: 3730 kW (5000 h.p.) giving a tractive effort of 95 kN
(21300 lbf) at 87 m.p.h.
Maximum Rail Power: 5860 kW (7860 h.p.) at 68.3 m.p.h.
Train Brakes: Air.
Brake Force: 40 t.
Weight: 84.5 t.
Design Speed: 110 m.p.h.
Train Supply: Electric, index 95.
Multiple Working: TDM system.

Dimensions: 18.80 x 2.74 m.
Wheel Diameter: 1150 mm.
Maximum Speed: 110 m.p.h.
RA: 7.

Non-standard livery: 90036 As **FE** but with a yellow roof. EWS stickers.

90001	b	1	P	IANA	NC	
90002	b	1	P	IANA	NC	
90003	b	1	P	IANA	NC	Raedwald of East Anglia
90004	b	1	P	IANA	NC	
90005	b	1	P	IANA	NC	Vice-Admiral Lord Nelson
90006	b	1	P	IANA	NC	Modern Railways Magazine/
						Roger Ford
90007	b	1	P	IANA	NC	Sir John Betjeman
90008	b	1	P	IANA	NC	
90009	b	1	P	IANA	NC	
90010	b	1	P	IANA	NC	
90011	b	1	P	IANA	NC	Let's Go East of England
90012	b	1	P	IANA	NC	
90013	b	1	P	IANA	NC	
90014	b	1	P	IANA	NC	Norfolk and Norwich Festival
90015	b	1	P	IANA	NC	
90016		FL	P	DFLC	FE	
90017	b	E	E	WNTR	CE	
90018	b	E	E	WEFE	CE	
90019	b	FS	E	WEFE	CE	

90020 b	E	E	WEFE	CE	Collingwood
90021	FE	E	WNTS	CE	
90022	EG	E	WNTR	CE	Freightconnection
90023	E	E	WNTR	CE	
90024	FS	E	WEFE	CE	
90025	F	E	WNTR	CE	
90026	E	E	WEFE	CE	
90027	F	E	WEFE	CE	Allerton T&RS Depot
90028	E	E	WEFE	CE	Hertfordshire Rail Tours
90029	E	E	WNTR	CE	The Institution of Civil Engineers
90030	E	E	WNTS	CE	Crewe Locomotive Works
90031	E	E	WEFE	CE	The Railway Children Partnership Working For Street Children Worldwide
90032	E	E	WNTR	CE	
90033	FE	E	WNTS	CE	
90034	E	E	WEFE	CE	
90035	E	E	WEFE	CE	
90036	0	E	WEFE	CE	
90037	E	E	WNTS	CE	Spirit of Dagenham
90038	FE	E	WNTR	CE	
90039	E	E	WEFE	CE	
90040	E	E	WNTS	CE	The Railway Mission
90041	FL	P	DFLC	FE	
90042	FF	P	DFLC	FE	
90043	FF	P	DFLC	FE	Freightliner Coatbridge
90044	FF	P	DFLC	FE	
90045	FF	P	DFLC	FE	
90046	FL	P	DFLC	FE	
90047	FF	P	DFLC	FE	
90048	FF	P	DFLC	FE	
90049	FF	P	DFLC	FE	
90050	FF	E	WNTS	CE	

CLASS 91   GEC   Bo-Bo

Built: 1988–1991 by BREL at Crewe Works (as sub contractors for GEC).
Electric Supply System: 25 kV AC 50 Hz overhead.
Traction Motors: GEC G426AZ.
Maximum Tractive Effort: 190 kN (43 000 lbf).
Continuous Rating: 4540 kW (6090 h.p.) giving a tractive effort of 170 kN at 96 m.p.h.
Maximum Rail Power: 4700 kW (6300 h.p.) at ?? m.p.h.
Train Brakes: Air.
Brake Force: 45 t.
Weight: 84 t.
Design Speed: 140 m.p.h.
Train Supply: Electric, index 95.
Multiple Working: TDM system.

Dimensions: 19.41 x 2.74 m.
Wheel Diameter: 1000 mm.
Maximum Speed: 125 m.p.h.
RA: 7.

Note: Locos originally numbered in the 910xx series, but renumbered upon completion of overhauls at Bombardier, Doncaster by the addition of 100 to their original number. The exception to this rule was 91023 which was renumbered 91132.

91101	**GN**	H	IECA	BN	City of London
91102	**GN**	H	IECA	BN	Durham Cathedral
91103	**GN**	H	IECA	BN	County of Lincolnshire
91104	**GN**	H	IECA	BN	Grantham
91105	**GN**	H	IECA	BN	County Durham
91106	**GN**	H	IECA	BN	East Lothian
91107	**GN**	H	IECA	BN	Newark on Trent
91108	**GN**	H	IECA	BN	City of Leeds
91109	**GN**	H	IECA	BN	The Samaritans
91110	**GN**	H	IECA	BN	David Livingstone
91111	**GN**	H	IECA	BN	Terence Cuneo
91112	**GN**	H	IECA	BN	County of Cambridgeshire
91113	**GN**	H	IECA	BN	County of North Yorkshire
91114	**GN**	H	IECA	BN	St. Mungo Cathedral
91115	**GN**	H	IECA	BN	Holyrood
91116	**GN**	H	IECA	BN	Strathclyde
91117	**GN**	H	IECA	BN	Cancer Research UK
91118	**GN**	H	IECA	BN	Bradford Film Festival
91119	**GN**	H	IECA	BN	County of Tyne & Wear
91120	**GN**	H	IECA	BN	Royal Armouries
91121	**GN**	H	IECA	BN	Archbishop Thomas Cranmer
91122	**GN**	H	IECA	BN	Tam the Gun
91124	**GN**	H	IECA	BN	Reverend W Awdry
91125	**GN**	H	IECA	BN	Berwick-upon-Tweed
91126	**GN**	H	IECA	BN	York Minster
91127	**GN**	H	IECA	BN	Edinburgh Castle
91128	**GN**	H	IECA	BN	Peterborough Cathedral
91129	**GN**	H	IECA	BN	Queen Elizabeth II
91130	**GN**	H	IECA	BN	City of Newcastle
91131	**GN**	H	IECA	BN	County of Northumberland
91132	**GN**	H	IECA	BN	City of Durham

CLASS 92   BRUSH   Co-Co

Built: 1993–1996 by Brush Traction at Loughborough.
Electric Supply System: 25 kV AC 50 Hz overhead or 750 V DC third rail.
Traction Motors: Asea Brown Boveri design. Model 6FRA 7059B (Asynchronous 3-phase induction motors).
Maximum Tractive Effort: 400 kN (90 000 lbf).
Continuous Rating: 5040 kW (6760 h.p.) on AC, 4000 kW (5360 h.p.) on DC.
Maximum Rail Power: **Train Brakes:** Air.
Brake Force: 63 t.   **Dimensions:** 21.34 x 2.67 m.
Weight: 126 t.   **Wheel Diameter:** 1070 mm.
Design Speed: 140 km/h (87 m.p.h.).   **Maximum Speed:** 140 km/h (87 m.p.h.).
Train Supply: Electric, index 108 (AC), 70 (DC).
RA: 7.

92001	E	HX	WTAE	CE	Victor Hugo
92002	EG	HX	WTAE	CE	H.G. Wells
92003	EG	HX	WTAE	CE	Beethoven
92004	EG	HX	WTAE	CE	Jane Austen
92005	EG	HX	WTAE	CE	Mozart
92006	EP	SF	WNWX	CE	Louis Armand
92007	EG	HX	WTAE	CE	Schubert
92008	EG	HX	WNTR	CE	Jules Verne
92009	EG	HX	WTAE	CE	Elgar
92010	EP	SF	WNWX	CE	Molière
92011	EG	HX	WTAE	CE	Handel
92012	EG	HX	WTAE	CE	Thomas Hardy
92013	EG	HX	WTAE	CE	Puccini
92014	EP	SF	WNWX	CE	Emile Zola
92015	EG	HX	WTAE	CE	D.H. Lawrence
92016	EG	HX	WTAE	CE	Brahms
92017	EG	HX	WTAE	CE	Shakespeare
92018	EP	SF	WNWX	CE	Stendhal
92019	EG	HX	WTAE	CE	Wagner
92020	EP	EU	WNWX	CE	Milton
92021	EP	EU	WNWX	CE	Purcell
92022	EG	HX	WTAE	CE	Charles Dickens
92023	EP	SF	WNWX	CE	Ravel
92024	EG	HX	WTAE	CE	J.S. Bach
92025	EG	HX	WTAE	CE	Oscar Wilde
92026	EG	HX	WNTR	CE	Britten
92027	EG	HX	WTAE	CE	George Eliot
92028	EP	SF	WNWX	CE	Saint Saëns
92029	EG	HX	WTAE	CE	Dante
92030	EG	HX	WTAE	CE	Ashford
92031	E	HX	WTAE	CE	The Institute of Logistics and Transport
92032	EP	EU	WNWX	CE	César Franck
92033	EP	SF	WNWX	CE	Berlioz
92034	EG	HX	WTAE	CE	Kipling
92035	EP	HX	WNTS	CE	Mendelssohn
92036	EG	HX	WTAE	CE	Bertolt Brecht
92037	EG	HX	WTAE	CE	Sullivan
92038	EP	SF	WNWX	CE	Voltaire
92039	EG	HX	WTAE	CE	Johann Strauss
92040	EP	EU	WNWX	CE	Goethe
92041	EG	HX	WTAE	CE	Vaughan Williams
92042	EG	HX	WTAE	CE	Honegger
92043	EP	SF	WNWX	CE	Debussy
92044	EP	EU	WNWX	CE	Couperin
92045	EP	EU	WNWX	CE	Chaucer
92046	EP	EU	WNWX	CE	Sweelinck

1.3. EUROTUNNEL LOCOMOTIVES

DIESEL LOCOMOTIVES

0001–0005   MaK   Bo-Bo

Built: 1992–1993 by MaK at Kiel, Germany (Model DE1004).
Engine: MTU 12V 396 Tc of 1180 kW (1580 h.p.) at 1800 rpm.
Main Alternator: BBC.   **Traction Motors:** BBC.
Maximum Tractive Effort: 305 kN (68600 lbf).
Continuous Tractive Effort: 140 kN (31500 lbf) at 20 mph.
Power At Rail: 750 kW (1012 h.p.).
Brake Force: 120 kN.   **Dimensions:** 16.50 x ?? x ?? m.
Weight: 84 t.   **Wheel Diameter:** 1000 mm.
Design Speed: 120 km/h.   **Maximum Speed:** 120 km/h.
Fuel Capacity: **Train Brakes:** Air.
Train Supply: Not equipped.   **Multiple Working:** Within class.

0001	GY	ET	EU
0002	GY	ET	EU
0003	GY	ET	EU
0004	GY	ET	EU
0005	GY	ET	EU

0031–0042   HUNSLET/SCHÖMA   0–4–0

Built: 1989–1990 by Hunslet Engine Company at Leeds as 900 mm. gauge.
Rebuilt: 1993-1994 by Schöma in Germany to 1435 mm. gauge.
Engine: Deutz of 270 kW (200 h.p.) at ???? rpm.
Transmission: Mechanical.   **Maximum Tractive Effort:**
Cont. Tractive Effort: **Power At Rail:**
Brake Force: **Dimensions:**
Weight: **Wheel Diameter:**
Design Speed: 50 km/h.   **Maximum Speed:** 50 km/h.
Fuel Capacity: **Train Brakes:** Air.
Train Supply: Not equipped.   **Multiple Working:** Not equipped.

0031	Y	ET	EU	FRANCES
0032	Y	ET	EU	ELISABETH
0033	Y	ET	EU	SILKE
0034	Y	ET	EU	AMANDA
0035	Y	ET	EU	MARY
0036	Y	ET	EU	LAWRENCE
0037	Y	ET	EU	LYDIE
0038	Y	ET	EU	JENNY
0039	Y	ET	EU	PACITA
0040	Y	ET	EU	JILL
0041	Y	ET	EU	KIM
0042	Y	ET	EU	NICOLE

ELECTRIC LOCOMOTIVES

9001–9838   BRUSH/ABB   Bo-Bo-Bo

Built: 1993–2002 by Brush Traction at Loughborough.
Supply System: 25 kV AC 50 Hz overhead.
Traction Motors: Asea Brown Boveri design. Asynchronous 3-phase motors.
Model 6FHA 7059 (as built). Model 6FHA 7059C (7000 kW rated locos).
Maximum Tractive Effort: 400kN (90 000lbf).
Continuous Rating: Class 9/0 and 9/1: 5760 kW (7725 h.p.). Class 9/7 and 9/8: 7000 kW (9387 h.p.).

Maximum Rail Power:	**Multiple Working:** TDM system.
Brake Force: 50 t.	**Dimensions:** 22.01 x 2.97 x 4.20 m.
Weight: 132 t.	**Wheel Diameter:** 1250 mm.
Design Speed: 100 m.p.h.	**Maximum Speed:** 87 m.p.h.
Train Supply: Electric.	**Train Brakes:** Air.

CLASS 9/0 Original build mixed traffic locos.

9005	**EB**	ET	EU	JESSYE NORMAN
9006	**EB**	ET	EU	REGINE CRESPIN
9007	**EB**	ET	EU	DAME JOAN SUTHERLAND
9011	**EB**	ET	EU	JOSÉ VAN DAM
9013	**EB**	ET	EU	MARIA CALLAS
9015	**EB**	ET	EU	LÖTSCHBERG 1913
9018	**EB**	ET	EU	WILHELMENA FERNANDEZ
9022	**EB**	ET	EU	DAME JANET BAKER
9023	**EB**	ET	EU	DAME ELISABETH LEGGE-SCHWARZKOPF
9024	**EB**	ET	EU	GOTTHARD 1882
9026	**EB**	ET	EU	FURKATUNNEL 1982
9027	**EB**	ET	EU	BARBARA HENDRICKS
9029	**EB**	ET	EU	THOMAS ALLEN
9031	**EB**	ET	EU	
9033	**EB**	ET	EU	MONTSERRAT CABALLE
9036	**EB**	ET	EU	ALAIN FONDARY
9037	**EB**	ET	EU	GABRIEL BACQUIER
9040	**EB**	ET	EU	

CLASS 9/1. Freight Shuttle dedicated locos.

9101	**EB**	ET	EU
9102	**EB**	ET	EU
9103	**EB**	ET	EU
9104	**EB**	ET	EU
9105	**EB**	ET	EU
9106	**EB**	ET	EU
9107	**EB**	ET	EU
9108	**EB**	ET	EU
9109	**EB**	ET	EU
9110	**EB**	ET	EU
9111	**EB**	ET	EU

| 9112 | **EB** | ET | EU |
| 9113 | **EB** | ET | EU |

CLASS 9/7. Later build (2001–2002) increased power freight shuttle locos.

9701	**EB**	ET	EU
9702	**EB**	ET	EU
9703	**EB**	ET	EU
9704	**EB**	ET	EU
9705	**EB**	ET	EU
9706	**EB**	ET	EU
9707	**EB**	ET	EU

CLASS 9/8 Locos rebuilt from Class 9/0 by adding 800 to the loco number. Uprated to 7000 kW. Generally used on freight duties.

9801	**EB**	ET	EU	LESLEY GARRETT
9802	**EB**	ET	EU	STUART BURROWS
9803	**EB**	ET	EU	BENJAMIN LUXON
9804	**EB**	ET	EU	VICTORIA DE LOS ANGELES
9808	**EB**	ET	EU	ELISABETH SODERSTROM
9809	**EB**	ET	EU	FRANÇOIS POLLET
9810	**EB**	ET	EU	JEAN-PHILIPPE COURTIS
9812	**EB**	ET	EU	LUCIANO PAVAROTTI
9814	**EB**	ET	EU	LUCIA POPP
9816	**EB**	ET	EU	WILLARD WHITE
9817	**EB**	ET	EU	JOSÉ CARRERAS
9819	**EB**	ET	EU	MARIA EWING
9820	**EB**	ET	EU	Nicolai Ghiaurov
9821	**EB**	ET	EU	TERESA BERGANZA
9825	**EB**	ET	EU	
9828	**EB**	ET	EU	DAME KIRI TE KANAWA
9832	**EB**	ET	EU	RENATA TEBALDI
9834	**EB**	ET	EU	MIRELLA FRENI
9835	**EB**	ET	EU	Nicolai Gedda
9838	**EB**	ET	EU	HILDEGARD BEHRENS

1.4. FORMER BR MAIN LINE LOCOS IN INDUSTRIAL SERVICE

Former British Rail main line locomotives considered to be in "industrial use" are now listed here. These locomotives do not currently have Network Rail engineering acceptance for operation on the National Rail network.

Number	*Other no./name*	*Location*
Class 11		
12082	01553	St. Modwen Properties, Long Marston
12088		Johnson's (Chopwell), Widdrington Disposal Point
Class 03		
03112		Port of Boston, Boston Docks
03179	CLIVE	First Capital Connect, Hornsey, London
03196	JOYCE/GLYNIS	West Coast Railway Company, Carnforth
D2381		West Coast Railway Company, Carnforth
Class 07		
07001		Creative Logistics, Salford, Manchester
Class 08		
08032		Hanson Aggregates, Whatley Quarry
08054		Tarmac (Northern), Swinden Quarry, Grassington
08113	H017	RMS Locotec, Wakefield
08202		The Potter Group, Knowsley, Merseyside
08296		Hanson Aggregates, Machen Quarry, near Newport
08320	SUSAN	Imerys Clay Company, Blackpool Driers, Burngullow
08345	LOCO 3	Deanside Transit, Hillington, Glasgow
08388		Reliance Ind. Estate, Newton Heath, Manchester
08398	ANNABEL	Imerys Clay Company, Rocks Works, Bugle
08413	H040	RMS Locotec, Wakefield
08423	H011	RMS Locotec, Wakefield
08447		Deanside Transit, Hillington, Glasgow
08484		Felixstowe Dock & Railway Company, Felixstowe
08502	ANGIE	SembCorp Utilities Teesside, Wilton, Middlesbrough
08503		SembCorp Utilities Teesside, Wilton, Middlesbrough
08517		Wabtec Rail, Doncaster (West Yard)
08594		Wabtec Rail, Doncaster (West Yard)
08598	H016	The Potter Group, Knowsley, Merseyside
08600		A. V. Dawson, Middlesbrough
08602	004	Bombardier Transportation, Derby Works
08622	H028 7	Faber Prest Ports, Flixborough Wharf, Scunthorpe
08643		Foster Yeoman Quarries, Merehead Stone Terminal
08650	ISLE OF GRAIN	Foster Yeoman Quarries, Isle of Grain
08652		Hanson Aggregates, Whatley Quarry
08655		LH Group Services, Barton-under-Needwood
08668		Wabtec Rail, Doncaster

08678	ARTILA	West Coast Railway Company, Carnforth
08704		Port of Boston, Boston Docks
08728		Deanside Transit, Hillington, Glasgow
08731		Foster Yeoman Quarries, Merehead Stone Terminal
08736	LOCO 4	Deanside Transit, Hillington, Glasgow
08740		LH Group Services, Barton-under-Needwood
08743	Bryan Turner	SembCorp Utilities Teesside, Wilton, Middlesbrough
08764	003 FLORENCE	Transfesa, Tilbury Riverside Terminal, Tilbury
08774	ARTHUR VERNON	
	DAWSON	A.V. Dawson, Middlesbrough
08826		Foster Yeoman Quarries, Merehead Stone Terminal
08846	003	Bombardier Transportation, Derby Works
08870	H024	Castle Cement, Ketton, Stamford
08873		Manchester Ship Canal Co., Trafford Park, Manchester
08903		SembCorp Utilities Teesside, Wilton, Middlesbrough
08937	BLUEBELL MEL	Wabtec Rail, Doncaster (West Yard)
08943	PET II	Bombardier Transportation, Crewe Works

Class 14

09504		Victa Railfreight, Dagenham
09524	14901	RMS Locotec, Wakefield
09529	14029	Victa Railfreight, Dagenham

Class 20

20056	81	Corus, Appleby-Frodingham Works, Scunthorpe
20066	82	Corus, Appleby-Frodingham Works, Scunthorpe
20168	SIR GEORGE EARLE	Lafarge Blue Circle Cement, Hope

Class 56

56009		Brush Traction, Loughborough Works

NS Class 600

Note: NS Class 600 are of a similar design to BR Class 08 and those now in the UK have been included here for clarity.

625	690	PD Ports, Teesport
627	685	RMS Locotech, Wakefield
632	687	PD Ports, Teesport
649	692	PD Ports, Teesport
653		RMS Locotech, Wakefield

2. LOCO-HAULED PASSENGER COACHING STOCK

INTRODUCTION

LAYOUT OF INFORMATION

Coaches are listed in numerical order of painted number in batches according to type.

Each coach entry is laid out as in the following example (previous number(s) column may be omitted where not applicable):

No.	Prev. No.	Notes	Livery	Owner	Operator	Depot/Location
10229	(11059)	*	1	P	1	NC

Notes:

The owner is the responsible custodian of the coach and this may not always be the owner by law.
The operator is the organisation which facilitates the use of the coach and may not be the actual train operating company which runs the train.

DETAILED INFORMATION & CODES

Under each type heading, the following details are shown:

- "Mark" of coach (see below).
- Descriptive text.
- Number of first class seats, standard class seats, lavatory compartments and wheelchair spaces shown as F/S nT nW respectively.
- Bogie type (see below).
- Additional features.
- ETH Index.

TOPS TYPE CODES

TOPS type codes are allocated to all coaching stock. For vehicles numbered in the passenger stock number series the code consists of:

(1) Two letters denoting the layout of the vehicle as follows:

AA   Gangwayed Corridor
AB   Gangwayed Corridor Brake
AC   Gangwayed Open (2+2 seating)
AD   Gangwayed Open (2+1 seating)
AE   Gangwayed Open Brake

AF   Gangwayed Driving Open Brake
AG   Micro-Buffet
AH   Brake Micro-Buffet
AI   As "AC" but with drop-head buckeye and gangway at one end only
AJ   Restaurant Buffet with Kitchen
AK   Kitchen Car
AL   As "AC" but with disabled person's toilet (Mark 4 only)
AN   Miniature Buffet
AP   Pullman First with Kitchen
AQ   Pullman Parlour First
AR   Pullman Brake First
AS   Sleeping Car
AT   Royal Train Coach
AU   Sleeping Car with Pantry
AV   Mark 4 Barrier Vehicle
AW   EMU Translator vehicle
AX   Generator Van (1000 V DC)
AZ   Special Saloon
GS   HST Barrier Vehicle
NW   Desiro Barrier Vehicle

2) A digit denoting the class of passenger accommodation:

First		4	Unclassified
Standard (formerly second)		5	None
Composite (first & standard)			

3) A suffix relating to the build of coach.

Mark 1	C	Mark 2C	G	Mark 3 or 3A
Mark 2	D	Mark 2D	H	Mark 3B
Mark 2A	E	Mark 2E	J	Mark 4
Mark 2B	F	Mark 2F		

OPERATING CODES

Operating codes used by train company operating staff (and others) to denote vehicle types in general. These are shown in parentheses adjacent to TOPS type codes. Letters used are:

Brake	K Side corridor with lavatory
Composite	O Open
First Class	S Standard Class (formerly second)

Various other letters are in use and the meaning of these can be ascertained by referring to the titles at the head of each type.

Readers should note the distinction between an SO (Open Standard) and a TSO (Tourist Open Standard) The former has 2+1 seating layout, whilst the latter has 2+2.

BOGIE TYPES

BR Mark 1 (BR1). Double bolster leaf spring bogie. Generally 90 m.p.h., but Mark 1 bogies may be permitted to run at 100 m.p.h. with special maintenance. Weight: 6.1 t.

BR Mark 2 (BR2). Single bolster leaf-spring bogie used on certain types of non-passenger stock and suburban stock (all now withdrawn). Weight: 5.3 t.

COMMONWEALTH (C). Heavy, cast steel coil spring bogie. 100 m.p.h. Weight: 6.75 t.

B4. Coil spring fabricated bogie. Generally 100 m.p.h., but B4 bogies may be permitted to run at 110 m.p.h. with special maintenance. Weight: 5.2 t.

B5. Heavy duty version of B4. 100 m.p.h. Weight: 5.3 t.

B5 (SR). A bogie originally used on Southern Region EMUs, similar in design to B5. Now also used on locomotive hauled coaches. 100 m.p.h.

BT10. A fabricated bogie designed for 125 m.p.h. Air suspension.

T4. A 125 m.p.h. bogie designed by BREL (now Bombardier Transportation).

BT41. Fitted to Mark 4 vehicles, designed by SIG in Switzerland. At present limited to 125 m.p.h., but designed for 140 m.p.h.

BRAKES

Air braking is now standard on British main line trains. Vehicles with other equipment are denoted:

v   Vacuum braked.
x   Dual braked (air and vacuum).

HEATING & VENTILATION

Electric heating and ventilation is now standard on British main-line trains. Certain coaches for use on charter services may also have steam heating facilities, or be steam heated only.

PUBLIC ADDRESS

It is assumed all coaches are now fitted with public address equipment, although certain stored vehicles may not have this feature. In addition, it is assumed all vehicles with a conductor's compartment have public address transmission facilities, as have catering vehicles.

COOKING EQUIPMENT

It is assumed that Mark 1 catering vehicles have gas powered cooking equipment, whilst Mark 2, 3 and 4 catering vehicles have electric powered cooking equipment unless stated otherwise.

ADDITIONAL FEATURE CODES

d	Secondary door locking.
dg	Driver–Guard communication equipment.
f	Facelifted or fluorescent lighting.
h	"High density" seating.
k	Composition brake blocks (instead of cast iron).
n	Day/night lighting.
p	Public telephone.
pg	Public address transmission and driver-guard communication.
pt	Public address transmission facility.
q	Catering staff to shore telephone.
w	Wheelchair space.
z	Disabled persons' toilet.
★	Blue star multiple working cables fitted.

Standard class coaches with wheelchair space also have one tip-up seat per space.

NOTES ON ETH INDICES

The sum of ETH indices in a train must not be more than the ETH index of the locomotive. The normal voltage on British trains is 1000 V. Suffix 'X' denotes 600 amp wiring instead of 400 amp. Trains whose ETH index is higher than 66 must be formed completely of 600 amp wired stock. Class 33 and 73 locomotives cannot provide a suitable electric train supply for Mark 2D, Mark 2E, Mark 2F, Mark 3, Mark 3A, Mark 3B or Mark 4 coaches. Class 55 locomotives provide an e.t.s. directly from one of their traction generators into the train line. Consequently voltage fluctuations can result in motor-alternator flashover. Thus these locomotives are not suitable for use with Mark 2D, Mark 2E, Mark 2F, Mark 3, Mark 3A, Mark 3B or Mark 4 coaches unless modified motor-alternators are fitted. Such motor alternators were fitted to Mark 2D and 2F coaches used on the East Coast main line, but few remain fitted.

BUILD DETAILS

Lot Numbers
Vehicles ordered under the auspices of BR were allocated a lot (batch) number when ordered and these are quoted in class headings and sub-headings.

Builders
These are shown for each lot. Abbreviations used are shown in Section 7.6.

Information on sub-contracting works which built parts of vehicles e.g. the underframes etc. is not shown.
In addition to the above, certain vintage Pullman cars were built or rebuilt at the following works:

Metropolitan Carriage & Wagon Company, Birmingham
Midland Carriage & Wagon Company, Birmingham

Pullman Car Company, Preston Park, Brighton
Conversions have also been carried out at the Railway Technical Centre, Derby,
LNWR, Crewe and Blakes Fabrications, Edinburgh.

Vehicle Numbers
Where a coach has been renumbered, the former number is shown in
parentheses. If a coach has been renumbered more than once, the original
number is shown first in parentheses, followed by the most recent previous
number.

Numbering Systems
Seven different numbering systems were in use on BR. These were the BR
series, the four pre-nationalisation companies' series', the Pullman Car
Company's series and the UIC (International Union of Railways) series. BR
number series coaches and former Pullman Car Company series are listed
separately. There is also a separate listing of "Saloon" type vehicles which
are registered and have engineering acceptance to run on the national railway
system. Please note the Mark 2 Pullman vehicles were ordered after the
Pullman Car Company had been nationalised and are therefore numbered in
the BR series.

THE DEVELOPMENT OF BR STANDARD COACHES

The standard BR coach built from 1951 to 1963 was the Mark 1. This type
features a separate underframe and body. The underframe is normally 64 ft.
6 in. long, but certain vehicles were built on shorter (57 ft.) frames. Tungsten
lighting was standard and until 1961, BR Mark 1 bogies were generally
provided. In 1959 Lot No. 30525 (TSO) appeared with fluorescent lighting and
melamine interior panels, and from 1961 onwards Commonwealth bogies
were fitted in an attempt to improve the quality of ride which became very
poor when the tyre profiles on the wheels of the BR1 bogies became worn.
Later batches of TSO and BSO retained the features of Lot No. 30525, but
compartment vehicles – whilst utilising melamine panelling in standard class
– still retained tungsten lighting. Wooden interior finish was retained in first
class vehicles where the only change was to fluorescent lighting in open
vehicles (except Lot No. 30648, which had tungsten lighting). In later years
many Mark 1 coaches had BR 1 bogies replaced by B4.

In 1964, a new prototype train was introduced. Known as "XP64", it featured
new seat designs, pressure heating & ventilation, aluminium compartment
doors and corridor partitions, foot pedal operated toilets and B4 bogies. The
vehicles were built on standard Mark 1 underframes. Folding exterior doors
were fitted, but these proved troublesome and were later replaced with hinged
doors. All XP64 coaches have been withdrawn, but some have been preserved.
The prototype Mark 2 vehicle (W 13252) was produced in 1963. This was an
FK of semi-integral construction and had pressure heating & ventilation,
tungsten lighting, and was mounted on B4 bogies. This vehicle has been
preserved by the National Railway Museum and is currently stored at MoD
Kineton DM. The production build was similar, but wider windows were used.

The TSO and SO vehicles used a new seat design similar to that in the XP64 and fluorescent lighting was provided. Interior finish reverted to wood. Mark 2 vehicles were built from 1964–66.

The Mark 2A design, built 1967–68, incorporated the remainder of the features first used in the XP64 coaches, i.e. foot pedal operated toilets (except BSO), new first class seat design, aluminium compartment doors and partitions together with fluorescent lighting in first class compartments. Folding gangway doors (lime green coloured) were used instead of the traditional one-piece variety.

The following list summarises the changes made in the later Mark 2 variants:

Mark 2B: Wide wrap around doors at vehicle ends, no centre doors, slightly longer body. In standard class, one toilet at each end instead of two at one end as previously. Red folding gangway doors.

Mark 2C: Lowered ceiling with twin strips of fluorescent lighting and ducting for air conditioning, but air conditioning not fitted.

Mark 2D: Air conditioning. No opening top-lights in windows.

Mark 2E: Smaller toilets with luggage racks opposite. Fawn folding gangway doors.

Mark 2F: Plastic interior panels. Inter-City 70 type seats. Modified air conditioning system.

The Mark 3 design has BT10 bogies, is 75 ft. (23 m.) long and is of fully integral construction with Inter-City 70 type seats. Loco-hauled coaches are classified Mark 3A, Mark 3 being reserved for HST trailers. A new batch of FO and BFO, classified Mark 3B, was built in 1985 with Advanced Passenger Train-style seating and revised lighting. The last vehicles in the Mark 3 series were the driving brake vans built for West Coast Main Line services.

The Mark 4 design was built by Metro-Cammell for use on the East Coast Main Line after electrification and features a body profile suitable for tilting trains, although tilt is not fitted, and is not intended to be. This design is suitable for 140 m.p.h. running, although is restricted to 125 m.p.h. because the signalling system on the route is not suitable for the higher speed. The bogies for these coaches were built by SIG in Switzerland and are designated BT41. Power operated sliding plug exterior doors are standard. All Mark 4s were rebuilt with completely new interiors in 2003–05 and are referred to as "Mallard" stock by GNER.

2.1. BR NUMBER SERIES PASSENGER STOCK

AJ11 (RF)   RESTAURANT FIRST

Mark 1. Spent most of its life as a Royal Train vehicle and was numbered 2907 for a time. Built with Commonwealth bogies, but B5 bogies substituted. 24/–. ETH 2.

Lot No. 30633 Swindon 1961. 41 t.

325	**PC**	VS	*VS*	SL

AP1Z (PFK)   PULLMAN FIRST WITH KITCHEN

Mark 2. Pressure Ventilated. Seating removed and replaced with servery. 2T. B5 bogies. ETH 6.

Lot No. 30755 Derby 1966. 40 t.

504	**PC**	WC	*WC*	CS	ULLSWATER
506	**PC**	WC	*WC*	CS	WINDERMERE

AQ1Z (PFP)   PULLMAN PARLOUR FIRST

Mark 2. Pressure Ventilated. 36/– 2T. B4 bogies. ETH 5.

Non-standard livery: 546 is maroon & beige.

Lot No. 30754 Derby 1966. 35 t.

546	**0**	WC		CS	CITY OF MANCHESTER
548	**PC**	WC	*WC*	CS	GRASMERE
549	**PC**	WC	*WC*	CS	BASSENTHWAITE LAKE
550	**PC**	WC	*WC*	CS	RYDAL WATER
551	**PC**	WC	*WC*	CS	BUTTERMERE
552	**PC**	WC	*WC*	CS	ENNERDALE WATER
553	**PC**	WC	*WC*	CS	CRUMMOCK WATER

AR1Z (PFB)   PULLMAN BRAKE FIRST

Mark 2. Pressure Ventilated. 30/– 2T. B4 bogies. ETH 4.

Lot No. 30753 Derby 1966. 35 t.

586	**PC**	WC	*WC*	CS	DERWENTWATER

AJ21 (RG) GRIDDLE CAR

Mark 1. Rebuilt from RF. –/30. B5 bogies. ETH 2.

This vehicle was numbered DB975878 for a time when in departmental service for British Railways.

Lot No. 30013 Doncaster 1952. Rebuilt Wolverton 1965. 40 t.

| 1105 | (302) | v | **G** | MH | *MH* | RL |

AJ1F (RFB) BUFFET OPEN FIRST

Mark 2F. Air conditioned. Converted 1988–9/91 at BREL, Derby from Mark 2F FOs. 1200/1/3/11/14–16/20/21/50/2/5/6/9 have Stones equipment, others have Temperature Ltd. 25/– 1T 1W (except 1253 which is 26/– 1T). B4 bogies. d. ETH 6X.

1200/3/11/14/16/20/52/5/6. Lot No. 30845 Derby 1973. 33 t.
1201/4/5/7/8/10/12/13/15/19/21/50/1/4/8/60. Lot No. 30859 Derby 1973–74. 33 t.
1202/53/9. Lot No. 30873 Derby 1974–75. 33 t.

† Fitted with new m.a. sets.

1200	(3287, 6459)	†	**RV**	H	*RV*	CP
1201	(3361, 6445)		**V**	H		TM
1202	(3436, 6456)	†	**V**	H		KT
1203	(3291)	†		H	*RV*	CP
1204	(3401)	†	**V**	H		SN
1205	(3329, 6438)	†	**Y**	AE		ZA
1207	(3328, 6422)	†	**V**	H		KT
1208	(3393)		**V**	H		KT
1210	(3405, 6462)	†	**FB**	H	*SR*	IS
1211	(3305)			H		LM
1212	(3427, 6453)	†	**V**	H	*RV*	CP
1213	(3419)	†	**V**	DM		MQ
1214	(3317, 6433)		**AR**	H		KT
1215	(3377)		**AR**	H		KT
1216	(3302)	†	**V**	H	*RV*	CP
1219	(3418)		**AR**	H		KT
1220	(3315, 6432)	†	**CS**	H	*SR*	IS
1221	(3371)			H	*VI*	CV
1250	(3372)	†	**V**	H	*RV*	CP
1251	(3383)	†	**V**	H		KT
1252	(3280)	†	**V**	H		KT
1253	(3432)	†	**V**	H		KT
1254	(3391)	†	**V**	H	*VI*	CV
1255	(3284)	†	**V**	H		KT
1256	(3296)	†		H		MQ
1258	(3322)	†	**V**	H	*RV*	CP
1259	(3439)	†	**V**	H		KT
1260	(3378)	†	**V**	H	*RV*	CP

AK51 (RKB)   KITCHEN BUFFET

Mark 1. Built with no seats but three Pullman-style seats now fitted in bar area.
B5 bogies. ETH 1.

Lot No. 30624 Cravens 1960–61. 41 t.

1566   **VN** VS *VS* CP

AJ41 (RBR)   RESTAURANT BUFFET

Mark 1. Built with 23 loose chairs. All remaining vehicles refurbished with 23
fixed polypropylene chairs and fluorescent lighting. ETH 2 (2X*). 1683/92/99
were further refurbished with 21 chairs, wheelchair space and carpets.

s Modified for use as servery vehicle with seating removed.

1651–1699. Lot No. 30628 Pressed Steel 1960–61. Commonwealth bogies. 39 t.
1730. Lot No. 30512 BRCW 1960–61. B5 bogies. 37 t.

Non-standard liveries: 1683 and 1699 Oxford Blue.
1657 Nanking blue.

1651		**CI**	RV	*RV*	CP	1683	s	**O**	RV	*RV*	CP
1657	s	**O**	CD	*CD*	EM	1692	s	**CH**	RV	*RV*	CP
1658		**BG**	E	*E*	OM	1696		**G**	E	*E*	OM
1659	s	**PC**	RA	*WT*	OM	1698	s	**GC**	E	*E*	OM
1671	x*	**M**	E	*E*	OM	1699	s	**O**	RV	*RV*	CP
1679	s	**GC**	E	*E*	OM	1730	x	**M**	BK	*BK*	BT
1680	s*	**GC**	E	*E*	OM						

AN2F (RSS)   SELF-SERVICE BUFFET CAR

Mark 2F. Air conditioned. Temperature Ltd. equipment. Inter-City 70 seats.
Converted 1974 from a Mark 2F TSO as a prototype self-service buffet for APT-
P. Sold to Northern Ireland Railways 1983 and regauged to 5'3". Since withdrawn,
repatriated to Great Britain and converted back to standard gauge. –/24. B5
bogies. ETH 12X.

Lot No. 30860 Derby 1973–74. 33 t.

1800   (5970, NIR546)   **PC** WT *WT* OM

AN21 (RMB)   MINIATURE BUFFET CAR

Mark 1. –/44 2T. These vehicles are basically an open standard with two full
window spaces removed to accommodate a buffet counter, and four seats
removed to allow for a stock cupboard. All remaining vehicles now have
fluorescent lighting. Commonwealth bogies. ETH 3.

1813–1832. Lot No. 30520 Wolverton 1960. 38 t.
1840–1842. Lot No. 30507 Wolverton 1960. 38 t.
1859–1863. Lot No. 30670 Wolverton 1961–62. 38 t.
1882. Lot No. 30702 Wolverton 1962. 38 t.

Notes: 1842 is refurbished and fitted with a microwave oven.

1861 has had its toilets replaced with store cupboards.

1813	x	**M**	E	*E*	OM	1860	x	**M**	WC *WC*	CS
1832	x	**G**	E		OM	1861	x	**M**	WC *WC*	CS
1840	v	**G**	WC	*WC*	CS	1863	x	**CH**	RV *RV*	CP
1842		**CH**	RV	*RV*	CP	1882	x	**M**	WC *WC*	CS
1859	x	**M**	BK	*BK*	BT					

AJ41 (RBR)   RESTAURANT BUFFET

Mark 1. These vehicles were built as unclassified restaurant (RU). They were rebuilt with buffet counters and 23 fixed polypropylene chairs (RBS), then further refurbished by fitting fluorescent lighting and reclassified RBR. ETH 2X.

s Modified for use as servery vehicle with seating removed.

1953. Lot No. 30575 Swindon 1960. B4/B5 bogies. 36.5 t.
1961. Lot No. 30632 Swindon 1961. Commonwealth bogies. 39 t.

1953	s	**VN**	VS	*VS*	CP	1961	x	**G**	WC *WC* CS

AU51   CHARTER TRAIN STAFF COACHES

Mark 1. Converted from BCKs in 1988. Commonwealth bogies. ETH 2.

Lot No. 30732 Derby 1964. 37 t.

2833	(21270)	**BG**	E	*E*	OM
2834	(21267)	**GC**	E	*E*	OM

AT5G   HM THE QUEEN'S SALOON

Mark 3. Converted from a FO built 1972. Consists of a lounge, bedroom and bathroom for HM The Queen, and a combined bedroom and bathroom for the Queen's dresser. One entrance vestibule has double doors. Air conditioned. BT10 bogies. ETH 9X.

Lot No. 30886 Wolverton 1977. 36 t.

2903	(11001)	**RP**	NR	*RP*	ZN

AT5G HRH THE DUKE OF EDINBURGH'S SALOON

Mark 3. Converted from a TSO built 1972. Consists of a combined lounge/dining room, a bedroom and a shower room for the Duke, a kitchen and a valet's bedroom and bathroom. Air conditioned. BT10 bogies. ETH 15X.

Lot No. 30887 Wolverton 1977. 36 t.

2904	(12001)	**RP**	NR	*RP*	ZN

AT5G   ROYAL HOUSEHOLD SLEEPING CAR

Mark 3A. Built to similar specification as SLE 10647–729. 12 sleeping compartments for use of Royal Household with a fixed lower berth and a hinged upper berth. 2T plus shower room. Air conditioned. BT10 bogies. ETH 11X.

Lot No. 31002 Derby/Wolverton 1985. 44 t.

2915   **RP**   NR *RP*   ZN

AT5G HRH THE PRINCE OF WALES'S DINING CAR

Mark 3. Converted from HST TRUK built 1976. Large kitchen retained, but dining area modified for Royal use seating up to 14 at central table(s). Air conditioned. BT10 bogies. ETH 13X.

Lot No. 31059 Wolverton 1988. 43 t.

2916 (40512)   **RP**   NR *RP*   ZN

AT5G ROYAL KITCHEN/HOUSEHOLD DINING CAR

Mark 3. Converted from HST TRUK built 1977. Large kitchen retained and dining area slightly modified with seating for 22 Royal Household members. Air conditioned. BT10 bogies. ETH 13X.

Lot No. 31084 Wolverton 1990. 43 t.

2917 (40514)   **RP**   NR *RP*   ZN

AT5G   ROYAL HOUSEHOLD CARS

Mark 3. Converted from HST TRUKs built 1976/7. Air conditioned. BT10 bogies. ETH 10X.

Lot Nos. 31083 (31085*) Wolverton 1989. 41.05 t.

2918	(40515)		**RP**	NR		ZN
2919	(40518)	*	**RP**	NR		ZN

AT5B   ROYAL HOUSEHOLD COUCHETTES

Mark 2B. Converted from BFK built 1969. Consists of luggage accommodation, guard's compartment, workshop area, 350 kW diesel generator and staff sleeping accommodation. B5 bogies. ETH2X.

Lot No. 31044 Wolverton 1986. 48 t.

2920 (14109, 17109)   **RP** NR *RP* ZN

Mark 2B. Converted from BFK built 1969. Consists of luggage accommodation, kitchen, brake control equipment and staff accommodation. B5 bogies. ETH7X.

Lot No. 31086 Wolverton 1990. 41.5 t.

2921 (14107, 17107)   **RP** NR *RP* ZN

AT5H HRH THE PRINCE OF WALES'S SLEEPING CAR

Mark 3B. BT10 bogies. Air conditioned. ETH 7X.

Lot No. 31035 Derby/Wolverton 1987.

2922		**RP**	NR	*RP*	ZN

AT5H ROYAL SALOON

Mark 3B. BT10 bogies. Air conditioned. ETH 6X.

Lot No. 31036 Derby/Wolverton 1987.

2923		**RP**	NR	*RP*	ZN

AD11 (FO) OPEN FIRST

Mark 1. 42/– 2T. ETH 3. Many now fitted with table lamps.

3066–3069. Lot No. 30169 Doncaster 1955. B4 bogies. 33 t.
3096–3100. Lot No. 30576 BRCW 1959. B4 bogies. 33 t.

3068 was numbered DB 975606 for a time when in departmental service for British Railways.

3066	**RV**	RV	*RV*	CP		3097	**GC**	RV	*RV*	CP
3068	**CI**	RV	*RV*	CP		3098	x **CH**	RV	*RV*	CP
3069	**RV**	RV	*RV*	CP		3100	x **M**	E		OM
3096	x **M**	BK	*BK*	BT						

Later design with fluorescent lighting, aluminium window frames and Commonwealth bogies.

3105–3128. Lot No. 30697 Swindon 1962–63. 36 t.
3130–3150. Lot No. 30717 Swindon 1963. 36 t.

3128/36/41/3/4/6/7/8 were renumbered 1058/60/3/5/6/8/9/70 when reclassified RUO, then 3600/5/8/9/2/6/4/10 when declassified to SO, but have since regained their original numbers. 3136 was numbered DB977970 for a time when in use with Serco Railtest as a Brake Force Runner.

3105	x **M**	WC	*WC*	CS		3123	**GC**	E	*E*	OM
3107	x **CH**	RV	*RV*	CP		3124	**G**	RV	*RV*	CP
3110	x **M**	RV	*RV*	CP		3125	x **RV**	RV	*RV*	CP
3112	x **CH**	RV	*RV*	CP		3127	**G**	E		OM
3113	x **M**	WC	*WC*	CS		3128	x **M**	WC	*WC*	CS
3114	**G**	E		OM		3130	v **M**	WC	*WC*	CS
3115	x **M**	BK	*BK*	BT		3131	x **M**	E	*E*	OM
3117	x **M**	WC	*WC*	CS		3132	x **M**	E	*E*	OM
3119	**GC**	RV	*RV*	CP		3133	x **M**	E		OM
3120	**GC**	E	*E*	OM		3136	**M**	WC	*WC*	CS
3121	**GC**	E	*E*	OM		3140	x **CH**	RV	*RV*	CP
3122	x **CH**	RV	*RV*	CP		3141	**M**	E	*E*	OM

3143	**M**	WC	*WC*	CS		3148	**BG**	RV	*RV*	CP
3144 x	**M**	RV	*RV*	CP		3149	**GC**	RV	*RV*	CP
3146	**M**	E	*E*	OM		3150	**G**	BK		BT
3147	**GC**	E	*E*	OM						

AD1D (FO)   OPEN FIRST

Mark 2D. Air conditioned. Stones equipment. 42/– 2T. B4 bogies. ETH 5.

† Interior modified to Pullman Car standards with new seating, new panelling tungsten lighting and table lights for VSOE "Northern Belle".

Lot No. 30821 Derby 1971–72. 34 t.

| 3174 † | **VN** | VS | *VS* | CP | | 3188 | **PC** | RA | *WT* | OM |
| 3182 † | **VN** | VS | *VS* | CP | | | | | | |

AD1E (FO)   OPEN FIRST

Mark 2E. Air conditioned. Stones equipment. 42/– 2T (41/– 2T 1W w, 36/– 2T p). B4 bogies. ETH 5.

r Refurbished with new seats.
u Fitted with power supply for Mk. 1 RBR.
† Interior modified to Pullman Car standards with new seating, new panelling tungsten lighting and table lights for VSOE "Northern Belle".

3255 was numbered 3525 for a time when fitted with a pantry.

Lot No. 30843 Derby 1972–73. 32.5 t. (35.8 t. †).

3223		**RV**	RV	*RV*	CP		3247 †	**VN**	VS	*VS*	CP
3228 du		**RV**	H	*RV*	CP		3255 dr	**M**	E	*E*	OM
3229 d		**RV**	H	*RV*	CP		3261 dw	**FP**	H	*RV*	CP
3231 p		**PC**	RA	*WT*	OM		3267 †	**VN**	VS	*VS*	CP
3232 dr		**FP**	H		OO		3269 dr	**M**	E	*E*	OM
3240		**RV**	RV	*RV*	CP		3273 †	**VN**	VS	*VS*	CP
3241 dr		**FP**	H	*CD*	GL		3275 †	**VN**	VS	*VS*	CP
3244 d		**RV**	H	*RV*	CP						

AD1F (FO)   OPEN FIRST

Mark 2F. Air conditioned. 3277–3318/58–81 have Stones equipment, others have Temperature Ltd. 42/– 2T. All now refurbished with power-operated vestibule doors, new panels and new seat trim. B4 bogies. d. ETH 5X.

3277–3318. Lot No. 30845 Derby 1973. 33.5 t.
3325–3426. Lot No. 30859 Derby 1973–74. 33.5 t.
3429–3438. Lot No. 30873 Derby 1974–75. 33.5 t.

r Further refurbished with table lamps, modified seats with burgundy seat trim and new m.a. sets.
s Further refurbished with table lamps and modified seats with burgundy seat trim.
u Fitted with power supply for Mk. 1 RBR.

3277		**AR**	H		*RV*	CP				
3278	r	**BP**	FM		*VI*	EM				
3279	u	**M**	E	*E*		OM				
3285	s	**V**	H			LM				
3292		**M**	E	*E*		OM				
3295		**AR**	H		*RV*	CP				
3299	r	**V**	H			KT				
3300	s	**V**	H			AS				
3303		**AR**	H			OM				
3304	r	**V**	H		*RV*	CP				
3309			H			TM				
3312			H		*VI*	CV				
3313	r	**BP**	CD	*CD*		EM				
3314	r	**V**	H		*RV*	CP				
3318		**M**	E	*E*		OM				
3325	r	**V**	H		*RV*	CP				
3326	r	**BP**	CD	*CD*		EM				
3330	r	**RV**	RV	*RV*		CP				
3331		**M**	E	*E*		OM				
3333	r	**V**	H		*RV*	CP				
3334		**AR**	H		*RV*	CP				
3336	u	**AR**	H		*RV*	CP				
3337	r	**V**	H			AS				
3338	u	**M**	E			OM				
3340	r	**V**	H		*RV*	CP				
3344	r	**V**	H		*RV*	CP				
3345	r	**V**	H		*RV*	CP				
3348	r	**RV**	RV	*RV*		CP				
3350	r	**BP**	CD	*CD*		EM				
3351		**AR**	H			TM				
3352	r	**BP**	CD	*CD*		EM				
3353	s	**V**	DM			MQ				
3354	s	**V**	DM			MQ				
3356	r	**RV**	RV	*RV*		CP				

3358		**M**	E	*E*		OM
3359	s	**V**	FM			OY
3360	s		FM			OY
3362	s		FM			OY
3364	r	**RV**	RV	*RV*		CP
3366	s	**V**	H	*VI*		CV
3368		**M**	E	*E*		OM
3374			H			BH
3375		**M**	E			OM
3379	u	**AR**	H		*RV*	CP
3384	r	**RV**	RV	*RV*		CP
3385	r	**BP**	FM		*VI*	EM
3386	r	**V**		RV	*RV*	CP
3387	s	**V**	DM			MQ
3388		**M**	E	*E*		OM
3390	r	**RV**	RV	*RV*		CP
3392	r	**BP**	CD	*CD*		EM
3395	r	**BP**	CD	*CD*		EM
3397	r	**RV**	RV	*RV*		CP
3399	u	**M**	E	*E*		OM
3400		**M**	E	*E*		OM
3402	s	**V**	DM			MQ
3408	s	**V**	FM			OY
3411	s	**V**	DM			MQ
3414		**M**	E	*E*		OM
3416			H			TM
3417		**AR**	H		*RV*	CP
3424		**M**	E	*E*		OM
3425	s	**V**	DM			MQ
3426	r	**RV**	RV	*RV*		CP
3429	r	**V**	H			AS
3431	r	**BP**	CD	*CD*		EM
3433	r	**V**	H			SN
3438	s	**V**	H			CT

AC21 (TSO)   OPEN STANDARD

Mark 1. –/64 2T. ETH 4.

3766. Lot No. 30079 York 1953. Commonwealth bogies (originally built with BR Mark 1 bogies). This coach has narrower seats than later vehicles. 36 t.

3766	x		**M**	WC	*WC*	CS	

AC21 (TSO)   OPEN STANDARD

Mark 1. These vehicles are a development of the above with fluorescent lighting and modified design of seat headrest. Built with BR Mark 1 bogies. –/64 2T. ETH 4.

4831–4836. Lot No. 30506 Wolverton 1959. Commonwealth bogies. 33 t.
4856. Lot No. 30525 Wolverton 1959–60. B4 bogies. 33 t.

4831	x	**M**	BK	*BK*	BT		4836	x	**M**	BK	*BK*	BT
4832	x	**M**	BK	*BK*	BT		4856	x	**M**	BK	*BK*	BT

Lot No. 30646 Wolverton 1961. Built with Commonwealth bogies, but BR Mark 1 bogies substituted by the SR. All now re-rebogied. 34 t B4, 36 t C.

4902	x B4	**CH**	RV	*RV*	CP		4912	x C	**M**	WC	*WC*	CS
4905	x C	**M**	WC	*WC*	CS							

Lot No. 30690 Wolverton 1961–62. Commonwealth bogies and aluminium window frames. 37 t.

4925		**G**	E		OM		4996	x	**M**	E		OM
4927	x	**CH**	RV	*RV*	CP		4998		**BG**	E	*E*	OM
4931	v	**M**	WC	*WC*	CS		4999		**BG**	E		OM
4940	x	**M**	WC	*WC*	CS		5005		**BG**	E		OM
4946	x	**M**	E		OM		5007		**G**	E		OM
4949	x	**M**	E	*E*	OM		5008	x	**M**	E	*E*	OM
4951	x	**M**	WC	*WC*	CS		5009	x	**CH**	RV	*RV*	CP
4954	v	**M**	WC	*WC*	CS		5023		**G**	E	*E*	OM
4956		**BG**	E		OM		5027		**G**	E		OM
4958	v	**M**	WC	*WC*	CS		5028	x	**M**	BK	*BK*	BT
4959		**BG**	E		OM		5032	x	**M**	WC	*WC*	CS
4960	x	**M**	WC	*WC*	CS		5033	x	**M**	WC	*WC*	CS
4973	x	**M**	WC	*WC*	CS		5035	x	**M**	WC	*WC*	CS
4984	x	**M**	WC	*WC*	CS		5037		**G**	E		OM
4986		**G**	E	*E*	OM		5040	x	**CH**	RV	*RV*	CP
4991		**BG**	E		OM		5044	x	**M**	WC	*WC*	CS
4994	x	**M**	WC	*WC*	CS							

AC2Z (TSO)   OPEN STANDARD

Mark 2. Pressure ventilated. –/64 2T. B4 bogies. ETH 4.

Lot No. 30751 Derby 1965–67. 32 t.

5125	v	**G**	WC		BH		5193	v	**LN**	H		TM
5141	v	**G**	WC		RL		5194	v	**RR**	H		TM
5148	v	**RR**	H		TM		5198	v	**CH**	H	*VT*	TM
5157	v	**CH**	H	*VT*	TM		5199	v	**G**	WC		RL
5171	v	**G**	WC	*WC*	CS		5200	v	**G**	WC	*WC*	CS
5177	v	**CH**	H	*VT*	TM		5212	v	**LN**	H		TM
5179	v	**RR**	H		TM		5216	v	**G**	WC	*WC*	CS
5183	v	**RR**	H		TM		5221	v	**RR**	H		TM
5186	v	**RR**	H		TM		5222	v	**G**	WC	*WC*	CS
5191	v	**CH**	H	*VT*	TM							

AD2Z (SO)   OPEN STANDARD

Mark 2. Pressure ventilated. –/48 2T. B4 bogies. ETH 4.

Lot No. 30752 Derby 1966. 32 t.

5229		**PC**	WT	*WT*	OM	5239		**PC**	WT	*WT*	OM
5236	v	**G**	WC	*WC*	CS	5249	v	**G**	WC	*WC*	CS
5237	v	**G**	WC	*WC*	CS						

AC2A (TSO)   OPEN STANDARD

Mark 2A. Pressure ventilated. –/64 2T (–/62 2T w). B4 bogies. ETH 4.

5276–5341. Lot No. 30776 Derby 1967–68. 32 t.
5350–5419. Lot No. 30787 Derby 1968. 32 t.

Facelifted vehicles.

5276	f	**RV**	RV	*RV*	CP	5350		**RV**	RV	*RV*	CP
5278		**PC**	WT	*WT*	OM	5365		**RV**	RV	*RV*	CP
5292	f	**RV**	RV	*RV*	CP	5366	f	**RV**	RV	*RV*	CP
5299		**M**	WC	*WC*	CS	5376		**RV**	RV	*RV*	CP
5309		**CH**	E		OM	5386	w	**M**	E		OM
5322	f	**RV**	RV	*RV*	CP	5412	w	**M**	BK	*BK*	BT
5331		**M**	E		OM	5419	w	**PC**	WT	*WT*	OM
5341	f	**RV**	RV	*RV*	CP						

AC2B (TSO)   OPEN STANDARD

Mark 2B. Pressure ventilated. –/62 2T. B4 bogies. ETH 4.

Note: 5482 was numbered DB977936 for a time when in departmental service or British Railways.

Lot No. 30791 Derby 1969. 32 t.

5453	d	**M**	WC	*WC*	CS	5482		**M**	RP	*E*	OM
5463	d	**M**	WC	*WC*	CS	5487	d	**M**	WC	*WC*	CS
5478	d	**M**	WC	*WC*	CS	5491	d	**M**	WC	*WC*	CS

AC2C (TSO)   OPEN STANDARD

Mark 2C. Pressure ventilated. –/62 2T. B4 bogies. ETH 4.

Lot No. 30795 Derby 1969–70. 32 t.

5569	d	**M**	WC	*WC*	CS	5600		**M**	WC		CS

AC2D (TSO)   OPEN STANDARD

Mark 2D. Air conditioned. Stones equipment. –/62 2T. B4 bogies. ETH 5.

Refurbished with new seats and end luggage stacks. –/58 2T.

Lot No. 30822 Derby 1971. 33 t.

5631	dr	**M**	E	*E*	OM	5704		**M**	WC		CS
5632	dr	**M**	E	*E*	OM	5710	dr	**FP**	H	*CD*	GL
5657	dr	**M**	E	*E*	OM	5714		**M**	WC		CS
5669	dr	**FP**	H	*CD*	GL	5727		**M**	WC		CS
5679	dr	**FP**	H	*CD*	GL	5737	dr	**FP**	H		OO
5700	dr	**FP**	H	*CD*	GL	5740	dr	**FP**	H		OO

AC2E (TSO)   OPEN STANDARD

Mark 2E. Air conditioned. Stones equipment. –/64 2T (w –/62 2T 1W). B4 bogies
d (except 5756). ETH 5.

5745–5801. Lot No. 30837 Derby 1972. 33.5 t.
5810–5906. Lot No. 30844 Derby 1972–73. 33.5 t.

r Refurbished with new interior panelling.
s Refurbished with new interior panelling, modified design of seat headrest
and centre luggage stack. –/60 2T (w –/58 2T 1W).
t Refurbished with new interior panelling and new seats.

No.	flags				depot
5745	s	V	H		KT
5746	r	V	H		KT
5748	r pt		H	RV	CP
5750	s	V	H		KT
5752	wrpt		H	RV	CP
5754	ws	V	H		KT
5756		M	WC		CS
5769	r		H	RV	CP
5773	s pt	V	H	RV	CP
5776	r		H	RV	CP
5779	r		H		OY
5784	r	V	H		KT
5787	s	V	H		KT
5788	r		H	VI	CV
5789	r pt		H		OY
5791	wr		H	RV	CP
5792	r		H	RV	CP
5793	wspt	V	H		KT
5794	wr		H	RV	CP
5796	wr		H	RV	CP
5797	r★		H	VI	CV
5801	r	V	H		KT
5810	s	V	H		KT
5812	wr		H		OY
5814	r		H		CP
5815	ws	V	H		KT
5816	r pt		H		CD
5821	r pt	V	H		KT
5824	rw		H		LM
5827	r		H		LM
5828	ws	V	H		KT
5843	rw		H	RV	CP
5845	s	V	H		KT
5847	rw	V	H		KT
5852		AR	H		CT
5853	t	AV	AW	AW	CF
5859	s	V	H		KT
5866	r pt★		H	VI	CV
5868	s pt	V	H		KT
5869	t	AV	AW	AW	CF
5874	t	M	WC	WC	CS
5876	s pt	V	H		KT
5881	ws	V	H		KT
5886	s	V	H		KT
5887	wr	AR	H		KT
5888	wr		H		OY
5889	s	V	H		KT
5893	s	V	H		KT
5897	r		H		OY
5899	s	V	H		KT
5900	wspt	V	H		KT
5901	s	V	H		KT
5902	s	V	H		KT
5903	s	V	H		KT
5905	s	V	H	RV	CP
5906	wspt★		H	VI	CV

AC2F (TSO)   OPEN STANDARD

Mark 2F. Air conditioned. Temperature Ltd. equipment. Inter-City 70 seats. A
were refurbished in the 1980s with power-operated vestibule doors, new panel
and new seat trim. –/64 2T. (w –/62 2T 1W) B4 bogies. d. ETH 5X.

5908–5958. Lot No. 30846 Derby 1973. 33 t.
5959–6170. Lot No. 30860 Derby 1973–74. 33 t.
6171–6184. Lot No. 30874 Derby 1974–75. 33 t.

* Early Mark 2 style seats.

These vehicles have undergone a second refurbishment with carpets and new seat trim.
‡ Standard refurbished vehicles with new m.a. sets.

Former Cross-Country vehicles:

s Also fitted with centre luggage stack. –/60 2T.
t Also fitted with centre luggage stack and wheelchair space. –/58 2T 1W.

Former West Coast vehicles:

u As "r" but with two wheelchair spaces. –/60 2T 2W.
* Standard refurbished vehicles with new seat trim.

No.							No.					
5908	r	**V**	H		KT		5951	r	**V**	H		KT
5910	u	**V**	H	*RV*	CP		5952	r	**V**	RV	*RV*	CP
5911	s	**V**	RV	*RV*	CP		5954		**M**	E	*E*	OM
5912	s	**V**	H		OY		5955	r	**V**	RV	*RV*	CP
5913	s	**AV**	AW	*AW*	CF		5957	r	**V**	H		KT
5914	u	**V**	H		KT		5958	s★		H	*VI*	CV
5915	r	**V**	H		SN		5959	n	**M**	E	*E*	OM
5916	t		WC		CS		5960	s	**V**	H	*VI*	CV
5917	s	**V**	WC		CS		5961	s pt	**V**	RV	*RV*	CP
5918	t	**V**	H		KT		5962	s pt	**V**	H		KT
5919	s pt	**V**	H	*VI*	CV		5963	r	**V**	H	*RV*	CP
5920	†	**V**	DM		MQ		5964		**AR**	H	*RV*	CP
5921		**AR**	H	*RV*	CP		5965	t	**AV**	AW	*AW*	CF
5922		**M**	E	*E*	OM		5966		**AR**	H		KT
5924		**M**	E	*E*	OM		5967	t	**V**	H		KT
5925	s pt★		H		MQ		5968		**AR**	H		KT
5926			H		KT		5969	u	**V**	H	*RV*	CP
5928		**AR**	H		TM		5971	s	**AV**	AW	*AW*	CF
5929		**AR**	H	*RV*	CP		5975	s	**V**	H		KT
5930	t	**V**	H		KT		5976	t	**AV**	AW	*AW*	CF
5931	†w	**V**	RV	*RV*	CP		5977	r	**V**	H		KT
5932	r	**V**	H	*RV*	CP		5978	r	**V**	H		KT
5933	r	**V**	H		KT		5980	r	**V**	H		KT
5934	r	**V**	RV	*RV*	CP		5981	s★		H		MQ
5935		**AR**	H		KT		5983	s	**V**	H		OY
5936		**AR**	H		KT		5984	r	**V**	H	*RV*	CP
5937	r	**V**	H	*RV*	CP		5985		**AR**	H	*RV*	CP
5939	r	**V**	H		SN		5986	r	**V**	H	*RV*	CP
5940	u	**V**	H		KT		5987	r	**V**	H	*RV*	CP
5941	r	**V**	H	*RV*	CP		5988	r	**V**	H		KT
5943	rw	**V**	H		KT		5989	t	**V**	H		OY
5944		**AR**	H		KT		5991	s	**V**	H		OY
5945	r	**V**	H	*RV*	CP		5993	*	**AR**	H		KT
5946	r	**V**	H	*RV*	CP		5994		**V**	H		KT
5947	s pt	**V**	H		KT		5995	s	**V**	H	*VI*	CV
5948	u	**V**	H		OY		5996	s pt	**V**	H		KT
5949	u	**V**	H		KT		5997	r	**V**	H	*RV*	CP
5950		**AR**	H	*RV*	CP		5998		**AR**	H	*RV*	CP

No.						No.					
5999	s	**V**	H		KT	6103		**AR**	WC *WC*		CS
6000	t	**V**	WC *WC*		CS	6104	r	**V**	H	*RV*	CP
6001	u	**V**	H		OY	6107	r	**V**	H	*RV*	CP
6002	†	**V**	DM		MQ	6110		**M**	E	*E*	OM
6005	r	**V**	H	*RV*	KT	6111	†	**V**	RV *RV*		CP
6006		**AR**	H	*RV*	CP	6112	s pt	**V**	H		KT
6008	s	**AV**	AW *AW*		CF	6113	†	**V**	RV *RV*		CP
6009	r	**V**	H		KT	6115	s		WC		CS
6010	s	**V**	H		KT	6117	t★	**WX**	H		WY
6011	s	**V**	H		KT	6119	s	**AV**	AW *AW*		CF
6012	r	**V**	H		KT	6120	s	**V**	H		KT
6013	s	**AV**	AW *AW*		CF	6121	†	**V**	H		OY
6014	s pt		WC		CS	6122	s★	**WX**	H		WY
6015	t	**V**	H		KT	6123		**AR**	H		KT
6016	r	**V**	H		KT	6124	s pt★	**AV**	AW		TO
6018	t	**V**	H		KT	6134	†	**V**	H		OY
6021	r	**V**	H		KT	6135	s		WC		CS
6022	s	**V**	WC *WC*		CS	6136	r	**V**	H		KT
6024	s	**V**	RV *RV*		CP	6137	s pt	**AV**	AW *AW*		CF
6025	t	**V**	H		KT	6138	†	**V**	RV *RV*		CP
6026	s	**V**	H		KT	6139	n*	**M**	E	*E*	OM
6027	u	**V**	RV *RV*		CP	6141	u	**V**	RV *RV*		CP
6028		**AR**	H		KT	6142	†*	**V**	RV *RV*		CP
6029	r	**V**	H		KT	6144	†*	**V**	H		CT
6031	r	**V**	H		KT	6145	s pt	**V**	H		KT
6034		**AR**	H		KT	6146	*	**AR**	H		LM
6035	t★	**AV**	AW *AW*		CF	6148	s		WC		CS
6036	*	**M**	E	*E*	OM	6149	u	**V**	H		SN
6037		**AR**	H		KT	6150	s		H		KT
6038	s	**V**	RV *RV*		CP	6151	†*	**V**	H		OY
6041	s	**V**	WC *WC*		CS	6152	*	**M**	E	*E*	OM
6042		**AR**	H	*RV*	CP	6153	†	**V**	H		KT
6043	†	**V**	RV *RV*		CP	6154	r pt		H		KT
6045	†w	**V**	H		OY	6157	s	**V**	H	*RV*	CP
6046	s	**V**	H	*VI*	CV	6158	r	**V**	H	*RV*	CP
6047	†n*		H		CT	6159	s pt	**V**	H		KT
6049	r	**V**	H		OY	6160	*	**AR**	H		LM
6050	s		H		KT	6161	†*	**V**	H		CT
6051	r	**V**	RV *RV*		CP	6162	s pt	**AV**	AW *AW*		CF
6052	tw		H		KT	6163	r	**V**	H	*RV*	CP
6053	*	**AR**	H		KT	6164	†	**V**	H		OY
6054	r	**V**	H	*RV*	CP	6165	r	**V**	H		KT
6056	t	**V**	RV *RV*		CP	6166			H		KT
6059	s	**V**	H	*VI*	CV	6167		**AR**	H		LM
6061	s pt	**V**	H		KT	6168	s★		H		LM
6064	s	**AV**	AW *AW*		CF	6170	s★	**AV**	AW *AW*		CF
6065	r	**V**	H		KT	6171	†	**V**	RV *RV*		CP
6066	s★	**AV**	AW *AW*		CF	6172	s	**V**	H		KT
6067	s pt	**V**	RV *RV*		CP	6173	s★	**WX**	H		WY
6073	s	**V**	H		KT	6174		**AR**	H		KT
6101	r	**V**	H	*RV*	CP	6175	r	**V**	H		KT

6176	t	**V**	RV	*RV*	CP		6181	†wn	**V**	DM		MQ
6177	s	**V**	RV	*RV*	CP		6182	s	**V**	H		KT
6179	r	**V**	H		KT		6183	s	**AV**	AW	*AW*	CF
6180	†w	**V**	RV	*RV*	CP		6184	s	**V**	H		KT

AX51   BRAKE GENERATOR VAN

Mark 1. Renumbered 1989 from BR departmental series. Converted from NDA in 1973 to three-phase supply brake generator van for use with HST trailers. Modified 1999 for use with loco-hauled stock. B5 bogies.

Lot No. 30400 Pressed Steel 1958.

6310	(81448, 975325)	**CH**	RV	*RV*	CP

AX51   GENERATOR VAN

Mark 1. Converted from NDA in 1992 to generator vans for use on Anglo-Scottish sleeping car services. Now normally used on trains hauled by steam locomotives. B4 bogies. ETH75.

6311. Lot No. 30162 Pressed Steel 1958. 37.25 t.
6312. Lot No. 30224 Cravens 1956. 37.25 t.
6313. Lot No. 30484 Pressed Steel 1958. 37.25 t.

6311	(80903, 92911)	**B**	E	*E*	OM
6312	(81023, 92925)	**PC**	WC	*WC*	CS
6313	(81553, 92167)	**PC**	P	*VS*	SL

NW51   DESIRO EMU BARRIER VEHICLE

Mark 1. Converted from GUVs with bodies removed and B4 bogies for use as Eurostar barrier vehicles but modified in 2003 by LNWR Co., Crewe for current use.

6321. Lot No. 30343 York 1957. 40 t.
6322/23. Lot No. 30616 Pressed Steel 1959–60. 40 t.
6324. Lot No. 30403 Glasgow 1958–60. 40 t.
6325. Lot No. 30417 Pressed Steel 1958–59. 40 t.

6321	(86515, 96385)	**B**	SM	*FL*	ZJ
6322	(86859, 96386)	**B**	SM	*FL*	ZJ
6323	(86973, 96387)	**B**	SM	*FL*	ZJ
6324	(86562, 96388)	**B**	SM	*FL*	ZJ
6325	(86135, 96389)	**B**	SM	*FL*	ZJ

GS5 (HSBV)   HST BARRIER VEHICLE

Renumbered from BR departmental series, or converted from various types. B4 bogies (Commonwealth bogies *).

6330. Mark 2A. Lot No. 30786 Derby 1968. 32 t.
6336/38/44. Mark 1. Lot No. 30715 Gloucester 1962. 31 t.
6340. Mark 1. Lot No. 30669 Swindon 1962. 36 t.

6346. Mark 2A. Lot No. 30777 Derby 1967. 31.5 t.
6348. Mark 1. Lot No. 30163 Pressed Steel 1957. 31.5 t.

Non-standard livery: 6340, 6344, 6346 All over dark blue.

6330	(14084, 975629)		**G**	A	*GW*	LA
6336	(81591, 92185)		**G**	A	*GW*	LA
6338	(81581, 92180)		**G**	A	*GW*	LA
6340	(21251, 975678)	*	**O**	A	*GN*	EC
6344	(81263, 92080)		**O**	A	*GN*	EC
6346	(9422)		**O**	A	*GN*	EC
6348	(81233, 92963)		**G**	A	*GW*	LA

AV5A/AV5C (MFBV) MARK 4 BARRIER VEHICLE

Mark 2A/2C. Converted from FK* or BSO. B4 bogies.

6352/3. Mark 2A. Lot No. 30774 Derby 1968. 33 t.
6354/5. Mark 2C. Lot No. 30820 Derby 1970. 32 t.
6358/9. Mark 2A. Lot No. 30788 Derby 1968. 31.5 t.

6352	(13465, 19465)	*	**GN**	H	*GN*	BN
6353	(13478, 19478)	*	**GN**	H	*GN*	BN
6354	(9459)		**GN**	H	*GN*	BN
6355	(9477)		**GN**	H	*GN*	BN
6358	(9432)		**GN**	H	*GN*	BN
6359	(9429)		**GN**	H	*GN*	BN

AW51   EMU TRANSLATOR VEHICLE

Mark 1. Converted 1992 from BG. BR Mark 1 bogies.

6364. Mark 1. Lot No. 30039 Derby 1954. 32 t.
6365. Mark 1. Lot No. 30323 Pressed Steel 1957. 32 t.

6364	(80565)	**RR**	MA	*CT*	SI
6365	(81296, 84296)	**RR**	MA	*CT*	SI

AW51   EMU TRANSLATOR VEHICLE

Mark 1. Converted 1980 from RUO. Commonwealth bogies.

Lot No. 30647 Wolverton 1959–61. 36 t.

6376	(1021, 975973)	**P**	P	*FL*	ZJ
6377	(1042, 975975)	**P**	P	*FL*	ZJ
6378	(1054, 975971)	**P**	P		LM
6379	(1059, 975972)	**P**	P		LM

GS51 (HSBV)   HST BARRIER VEHICLE

Mark 1. Converted from BG in 1994–5. B4 bogies.

6392. Lot No. 30715 Gloucester 1962. 29.5 t.
6393/96/97. Lot No. 30716 Gloucester 1962. 29.5 t.

6394. Lot No. 30162 Pressed Steel 1956–57. 30.5 t.
6395. Lot No. 30484 Pressed Steel 1958. 30.5 t.
6398/99. Lot No. 30400 Pressed Steel 1957–58. 30.5 t.

6392	(81588, 92183)	**P**	P	*MM*	NL
6393	(81609, 92196)	**P**	P	*GN*	EC
6394	(80878, 92906)	**P**	P	*GN*	EC
6395	(81506, 92148)	**P**	MA	*MM*	NL
6396	(81607, 92195)	**P**	MA	*MM*	NL
6397	(81600, 92190)	**P**	P	*MM*	NL
6398	(81471, 92126)	**MA**	MA	*MM*	NL
6399	(81367, 92994)	**MA**	MA	*MM*	NL

AG2C (TSOT)   OPEN STANDARD (TROLLEY)

Mark 2C. Converted from TSO by removal of one seating bay and replacing this by a counter with a space for a trolley. Adjacent toilet removed and converted to steward's washing area/store. Pressure ventilated. –/55 1T. B4 bogies. ETH 4.

Lot No. 30795 Derby 1969–70. 32.5 t.

6528	(5592)	**M**	WC	*WC*	CS

AN1F (RLO)   SLEEPER RECEPTION CAR

Mark 2F. Converted from FO, these vehicles consist of pantry, microwave cooking facilities, seating area for passengers (with "moveable" seats), telephone booth and staff toilet. 6703–8 also have a bar. Converted at RTC, Derby (6700), Ilford (6701–5) and Derby (6706–8). Air conditioned. 6700/1/3/5–8 have Stones equipment and 6702/4 have Temperature Ltd. equipment. 26/– 1T (r 30/– 1T (6700) or 27/– 1T (6704)). B4 bogies. d. ETH 5X.

6700–2/4/8. Lot No. 30859 Derby 1973–74. 33.5 t.
6703/5–7. Lot No. 30845 Derby 1973. 33.5 t.

r refurbished with new "sofa" seating as well as the "moveable" seats.

6700	(3347)	r	**FB**	H	*SR*	IS
6701	(3346)		**FS**	H	*SR*	IS
6702	(3421)		**CS**	H	*SR*	IS
6703	(3308)		**FB**	H	*SR*	IS
6704	(3341)	r	**FS**	H	*SR*	IS
6705	(3310, 6430)		**FS**	H	*SR*	IS
6706	(3283, 6421)		**FB**	H	*SR*	IS
6707	(3276, 6418)		**FS**	H	*SR*	IS
6708	(3370)		**CS**	H	*SR*	IS

AN1D (RMBF)   MINIATURE BUFFET CAR

Mark 2D. Converted from TSOT by the removal of another seating bay and fitting a proper buffet counter with boiler and microwave oven. Now converted to first class with new seating and end luggage stacks. Air conditioned. Stones equipment. 30/– 1T. B4 bogies. d. ETH 5.

Lot No. 30822 Derby 1971. 33 t.

6720	(5622, 6652)	**M**	E	E	OM
6721	(5627, 6660)	**FP**	H		OO
6722	(5736, 6661)	**FP**	H	CD	GL
6723	(5641, 6662)	**FP**	H		OO
6724	(5721, 6665)	**FP**	H		OO

AC2F (TSO)   OPEN STANDARD

Mark 2F. Renumbered from FO and declassified in 1985–6. Converted 1990 to TSO with mainly unidirectional seating and power-operated sliding doors. Air conditioned. 6800–11 were converted by BREL Derby and have Temperature Ltd. air conditioning. 6817–29 were converted by RFS Industries Doncaster and have Stones air conditioning. –/74 2T. B4 bogies. d. ETH 5X.

6800–06. 6811. 6828. Lot No. 30859 Derby 1973–74. 33 t.
6808. Lot No. 30873 Derby 1974–75. 33.5 t.
6817–24. 6829. Lot No. 30845 Derby 1973. 33 t.

6800	(3323, 6435)	**AR**	H	CT
6804	(3396, 6449)		H	CT
6805	(3324, 6436)	**AR**	H	KT
6806	(3342, 6440)	**AR**	H	LM
6808	(3430, 6454)	**AR**	H	KT
6811	(3327, 6437)	**AR**	H	KT
6817	(3311, 6431)	**AR**	H	LM
6820	(3320, 6434)	**AR**	H	LM
6821	(3281, 6458)	**AR**	H	KT
6823	(3289, 6424)	**AR**	H	LM
6824	(3307, 6429)	**AR**	H	KT
6828	(3380, 6464)	**AR**	H	KT
6829	(3288, 6423)	**AR**	H	KT

AH2Z (BSOT)
OPEN BRAKE STANDARD (MICRO-BUFFET)

Mark 2. Converted from BSO by removal of one seating bay and replacing this by a counter with a space for a trolley. Adjacent toilet removed and converted to a steward's washing area/store. –/23 0T. B4 bogies. ETH 4.

Lot No. 30757 Derby 1966. 31 t.

| 9101 | (9398) | v | **CH** | H | VT | TM |
| 9104 | (9401) | v | **G** | WC | | ZA |

AE2Z (BSO)   OPEN BRAKE STANDARD

Mark 2. These vehicles use the same body shell as the Mark 2 BFK and have first class seat spacing and wider tables. Pressure ventilated. –/31 1T. B4 bogies. ETH 4.

Lot No. 30757 Derby 1966. 31.5 t.

| 9391 | | **PC** | WT | *WT* | OM | | 9392 | v | **G** | WC | *WC* | CS |

AE2A (BSO)   OPEN BRAKE STANDARD

Mark 2A. These vehicles use the same body shell as the Mark 2A BFK and have first class seat spacing and wider tables. Pressure ventilated. –/31 1T. B4 bogies. ETH 4. Modified for use as Escort Coaches.

9419. Lot No. 30777 Derby 1970. 31.5 t.
9428. Lot No. 30820 Derby 1970. 31.5 t.

| 9419 | | **DR** | DR | *DR* | KM | | 9428 | | **DR** | DR | *DR* | KM |

AE2C (BSO)   OPEN BRAKE STANDARD

Mark 2C. Pressure ventilated. –/31 1T. B4 bogies. ETH 4.

Lot No. 30798 Derby 1970. 32 t.

| 9440 | d | **M** | WC | *WC* | CS | | 9448 | d | **M** | WC | *WC* | CS |

AE2D (BSO)   OPEN BRAKE STANDARD

Mark 2D. Air conditioned (Stones). –/31 1T. B4 bogies. d. pg. ETH 5.

r Refurbished with new interior panelling.
s Refurbished with new seating –/22 1TD.
w Facelifted –/28 1W 1T.

Lot No. 30824 Derby 1971. 33 t.

9479	r		H		OY		9490	s	**FP**	H	*CD*	GL
9480	w	**FP**	H		KT		9492	w	**FP**	DM		MQ
9481	s	**FP**	H		OO		9493	s	**FP**	H	*CD*	GL
9488	s	**FP**	H	*CD*	GL		9494	s	**M**	E	*E*	OM
9489	r	**V**	H		KT							

AE2E (BSO)   OPEN BRAKE STANDARD

Mark 2E. Air conditioned (Stones). –/32 1T. B4 bogies. d. pg. ETH 5.

Lot No. 30838 Derby 1972. 33 t.

r Refurbished with new interior panelling.
s Refurbished with modified design of seat headrest and new interior panelling.
w Facelifted –/28 1W 1T.

9496	r		H		LM		9504	s	**V**	H	*RV*	CP
9497	r★		H	*VI*	CV		9505	s★		H		MQ
9498	r	**V**	H		KT		9506	s★	**WX**	H		WY
9500	r		H	*VI*	CV		9507	s	**V**	H	*RV*	CP
9501	w	**FP**	DM		MQ		9508	s	**V**	VI		LM
9502	s	**V**	H		KT		9509	s	**AV**	AW	*AW*	CF
9503	s	**AV**	AW	*AW*	CF							

AE2F (BSO)   OPEN BRAKE STANDARD

Mark 2F. Air conditioned (Temperature Ltd.). All now refurbished with power-operated vestibule doors, new panels and seat trim. All now further refurbished with carpets and new m.a. sets. –/32 1T. B4 bogies. d. pg. ETH5X.

Lot No. 30861 Derby 1974. 34 t.

9513		**BP**	FM	*VI*	EM	9526	n★		H	*RV*	CP
9516	n	**V**	H	*VI*	CV	9527	n	**V**	RV	*RV*	CP
9520	n	**V**	RV	*RV*	CP	9529	n	**V**	E		OM
9521	★	**AV**	AW	*AW*	CF	9531		**M**	E	*E*	OM
9522		**V**	H	*VI*	CV	9537	n	**V**	H	*RV*	CP
9523		**V**	H		KT	9538		**V**	H		KT
9524	n★	**AV**	AW		TO	9539		**AV**	AW	*AW*	CF
9525		**WX**	H		WY						

AF2F (DBSO) DRIVING OPEN BRAKE STANDARD

Mark 2F. Air conditioned (Temperature Ltd.). Push & pull (t.d.m. system). Converted from BSO, these vehicles originally had half cabs at the brake end. They have since been refurbished and have had their cabs widened and the cab-end gangways removed. –/30 1W 1T. B4 bogies. d. pg. Cowcatchers. ETH 5X.

9701–9710. Lot No. 30861 Derby 1974. Converted Glasgow 1979. Disc brakes. 34 t.
9711–9713. Lot No. 30861 Derby 1974. Converted Glasgow 1985. 34 t.
9714. Lot No. 30861 Derby 1974. Converted Glasgow 1986. Disc brakes. 34 t.

9701	(9528)	**AR**	H	KT	9709	(9515)	**AR**	H	LM
9702	(9510)	**AR**	NR	KT	9710	(9518)	**1**	H	KT
9703	(9517)	**AR**	NR	KT	9711	(9532)	**AR**	H	KT
9704	(9512)	**AR**	H	LM	9712	(9534)	**AR**	H	KT
9705	(9519)	**AR**	H	KT	9713	(9535)	**AR**	H *RV*	CP
9707	(9511)	**AR**	H	KT	9714	(9536)	**AR**	NR	KT
9708	(9530)	**AR**	NR	KT					

AE4E (BUO)   UNCLASSIFIED OPEN BRAKE

Mark 2E. Converted from TSO with new seating for use on Anglo-Scottish overnight services by Railcare, Wolverton. Air conditioned. Stones equipment. B4 bogies. d. –/31 2T. B4 bogies. ETH 4X.

9801–9803. Lot No. 30837 Derby 1972. 33.5 t.
9804–9810. Lot No. 30844 Derby 1972–73. 33.5 t.

9800	(5751)	**CS**	H *SR*	IS	9806	(5840)	**CS**	H *SR*	IS
9801	(5760)	**CS**	H *SR*	IS	9807	(5851)	**FB**	H *SR*	IS
9802	(5772)	**FS**	H *SR*	IS	9808	(5871)	**FB**	H *SR*	IS
9803	(5799)	**CS**	H *SR*	IS	9809	(5890)	**FS**	H *SR*	IS
9804	(5826)	**FS**	H *SR*	IS	9810	(5892)	**CS**	H *SR*	IS
9805	(5833)	**FS**	H *SR*	IS					

AJ1G (RFM)
RESTAURANT BUFFET FIRST (MODULAR)

Mark 3A. Air conditioned. Converted from HST TRFKs, RFBs and FOs.
Refurbished with table lamps and burgundy seat trim (except *). 18/– plus two
seats for staff use (*24/–). BT10 bogies. d. ETH 14X.

10200–10211. Lot No. 30884 Derby 1977. 39.8 t.
10212–10229. Lot No. 30878 Derby 1975–76. 39.8 t.
10231–10260. Lot No. 30890 Derby 1979. 39.8 t.

Non-standard livery: 10211 EWS dark maroon.

10200	(40519)	* 1	P	*1*	NC	10231	(10016)	**V**	P	LM
10202	(40504)	**V**	P		LM	10232	(10027)	**FP**	P	*GW* OO
10203	(40506)	* 1	P	*1*	NC	10233	(10013)	**V**	P	LM
10204	(40502)	**V**	P		WI	10235	(10015)	**CD**	CD*CD*	GL
10205	(40503)	**V**	P		LM	10236	(10018)	**V**	P	WI
10206	(40507)	**V**	P		NC	10237	(10022)	**V**	DR	KM
10208	(40517)	**V**	P		WI	10240	(10003)	**V**	P	LM
10211	(40510)	**0**	E	*E*	TO	10241	(10009)	* 1	P	*1*	NC
10212	(11049)	**V**	P		WB	10242	(10002)	**V**	P	WI
10213	(11050)	**V**	P		LM	10245	(10019)	**V**	P	WI
10214	(11034)	* 1	P	*1*	NC	10246	(10014)	**V**	P	LM
10215	(11032)	**V**	P		WI	10247	(10011)	* 1	P	*1*	NC
10216	(11041)	* 1	P	*1*	NC	10249	(10012)	**V**	P	WI
10217	(11051)	**V**	P		WB	10250	(10020)	**V**	P	LM
10218	(11053)	**V**	P		LM	10253	(10026)	**V**	P	LM
10219	(11047)	**FP**	P	*GW* OO	10255	(10010)	**V**	P	WI
10223	(11043)	* 1	P	*1*	NC	10256	(10028)	**V**	P	GW
10225	(11014)	**FP**	P	*GW* OO	10257	(10007)	**V**	P	LM
10226	(11015)	**V**	P		WI	10259	(10025)	**V**	P	LM
10228	(11035)	* 1	P	*1*	NC	10260	(10001)	**V**	P	GW
10229	(11059)	* 1	P	*1*	NC					

AG2J (RSB)   KITCHEN BUFFET STANDARD

Mark 4. Air conditioned. BT41 bogies. ETH 6X. Rebuilt from first to standard class
with bar adjacent to seating area instead of adjacent to end of coach. –/30 1T.

Lot No. 31045 Metro-Cammell 1989–1992. 43.2 t.

10300	**GN**	H *GN*	BN	10310	**GN**	H *GN*	BN
10301	**GN**	H *GN*	BN	10311	**GN**	H *GN*	BN
10302	**GN**	H *GN*	BN	10312	**GN**	H *GN*	BN
10303	**GN**	H *GN*	BN	10313	**GN**	H *GN*	BN
10304	**GN**	H *GN*	BN	10315	**GN**	H *GN*	BN
10305	**GN**	H *GN*	BN	10317	**GN**	H *GN*	BN
10306	**GN**	H *GN*	BN	10318	**GN**	H *GN*	BN
10307	**GN**	H *GN*	BN	10319	**GN**	H *GN*	BN
10308	**GN**	H *GN*	BN	10320	**GN**	H *GN*	BN
10309	**GN**	H *GN*	BN	10321	**GN**	H *GN*	BN

10323	**GN**	H	*GN*	BN	10329	**GN**	H	*GN*	BN
10324	**GN**	H	*GN*	BN	10330	**GN**	H	*GN*	BN
10325	**GN**	H	*GN*	BN	10331	**GN**	H	*GN*	BN
10326	**GN**	H	*GN*	BN	10332	**GN**	H	*GN*	BN
10328	**GN**	H	*GN*	BN	10333	**GN**	H	*GN*	BN

AN2G (RMB)
OPEN STANDARD WITH MINIATURE BUFFET

Mark 3A. Air conditioned. Converted from Mark 3 TSOs at Derby 2006. –/52 1T (including 6 Compin Pegasus seats for "priority" use).

Lot No. 30877 Derby 1975–77. 37.8 t.

10401	(12168)	**1**	P	*1*	NC	10404	(12068)	**1**	P *1* NC
10402	(12010)	**1**	P	*1*	NC	10405	(12157)	**1**	P *1* NC
10403	(12135)	**1**	P	*1*	NC	10406	(12020)	**1**	P *1* NC

AU4G (SLEP)   SLEEPING CAR WITH PANTRY

Mark 3A. Air conditioned. Retention toilets. 12 compartments with a fixed lower berth and a hinged upper berth, plus an attendants compartment. 2T BT10 bogies. ETH 7X.

Non-standard livery: 10546 EWS dark maroon.

Lot No. 30960 Derby 1981–83. 41 t.

10501	d	**CS**	P	*SR*	IS	10551	d	**CS**	P	*SR*	IS
10502	d	**CS**	P	*SR*	IS	10553	d	**FS**	P	*SR*	IS
10504	d	**FS**	P	*SR*	IS	10561	d	**FS**	P	*SR*	IS
10506	d	**CS**	P	*SR*	IS	10562	d	**FB**	P	*SR*	IS
10507	d	**FS**	P	*SR*	IS	10563	d	**FP**	P		LM
10508	d	**FS**	P	*SR*	IS	10565	d	**FS**	P	*SR*	IS
10513	d	**FS**	P	*SR*	IS	10569	d	**PC**	VS		CP
10516	d	**FB**	P	*SR*	IS	10580	d	**FS**	P	*SR*	IS
10519	d	**CS**	P	*SR*	IS	10584	d	**FP**	P	*GW*	OO
10520	d	**FS**	P	*SR*	IS	10588	d	**FP**	P		LM
10522	d	**FS**	P	*SR*	IS	10589	d	**FP**	P	*GW*	OO
10523	d	**FS**	P	*SR*	IS	10590	d	**FP**	P	*GW*	OO
10526	d	**FS**	P	*SR*	IS	10594	d	**FP**	P	*GW*	OO
10527	d	**FS**	P	*SR*	IS	10596	d		P		KT
10529	d	**FS**	P	*SR*	IS	10597	d	**FS**	P	*SR*	IS
10531	d	**FS**	P	*SR*	IS	10598	d	**FS**	P	*SR*	IS
10532	d	**FP**	P	*GW*	OO	10600	d	**FS**	P	*SR*	IS
10534	d	**FP**	P	*GW*	OO	10601	d	**FP**	P	*GW*	OO
10542	d	**FS**	P	*SR*	IS	10605	d	**FS**	P	*SR*	IS
10543	d	**FS**	P	*SR*	IS	10607	d	**FS**	P	*SR*	IS
10544	d	**CS**	P	*SR*	IS	10610	d	**CS**	P	*SR*	IS
10546	d	**0**	E	*E*	TO	10612	d	**FP**	P	*GW*	OO
10548	d	**FS**	P	*SR*	IS	10613	d	**FS**	P	*SR*	IS
10614	d	**CS**	P	*SR*	IS	10617	d	**CS**	P	*SR*	IS
10616	d	**FP**	P	*GW*	OO						

AS4G/AQ4G* (SLE/SLED*)   SLEEPING CAR

Mark 3A. Air conditioned. Retention toilets. 13 compartments with a fixed lower berth and a hinged upper berth (* 11 compartments with a fixed lower berth and a hinged upper berth + one compartment for a disabled person). 2T. BT10 bogies. ETH 6X.

Note: 10734 was originally 2914 and used as a Royal Train staff sleeping car. It has 12 berths and a shower room and is ETH11X.

0647–10729. Lot No. 30961 Derby 1980–84. 43.5 t.
10734. Lot No. 31002 Derby/Wolverton 1985. 42.5 t.

0647	d	P		KT		10701	d	P		KT
0648	d***CS**	P	*SR*	IS		10703	d **CS**	P	*SR*	IS
0650	d***CS**	P	*SR*	IS		10706	d***CS**	P	*SR*	IS
0666	d***CS**	P	*SR*	IS		10710	d	CD		KT
0675	d **CS**	P	*SR*	IS		10714	d***FS**	P	*SR*	IS
0680	d***FS**	P	*SR*	IS		10718	d***CS**	P	*SR*	IS
0683	d **CS**	P	*SR*	IS		10719	d***CS**	P	*SR*	IS
0688	d **FS**	P	*SR*	IS		10722	d***FS**	P	*SR*	IS
0689	d***FG**	P	*SR*	IS		10723	d***FS**	P	*SR*	IS
0690	d **CS**	P	*SR*	IS		10729	**VN**	VS	*VS*	CP
0693	d **FS**	P	*SR*	IS		10734	**VN**	VS	*VS*	CP
0699	d***FS**	P	*SR*	IS						

AD1G (FO)   OPEN FIRST

Mark 3A. Air conditioned. All now refurbished with table lamps and new seat cushions and trim. 48/– 2T (* 48/– 1T 1TD). BT10 bogies. d. ETH 6X.

1005–7 were open composites 11905–7 for a time.

Non-standard livery: 11039 EWS dark maroon.

Lot No. 30878 Derby 1975–76. 34.3 t.

1005	**V**	P		LM		11028	**V**	DR		KM
1006	**V**	P		LM		11029	**V**	P		GL
1007	**V**	P		LM		11030	**V**	DR		KM
1011	* **V**	P		WI		11031	**V**	P		WI
1013	**V**	P	*CD*	GL		11033	**V**	CD		GL
1016	**V**	P		LM		11036	**V**	P		LM
1017	**V**	P		LM		11038	**1**	P		LM
1018	**V**	P		WI		11039	**0**	E	*E*	TO
1019	**V**	DR		KM		11040	**V**	P		WI
1020	**V**	P		WI		11042	**V**	P		WI
1021	**V**	P		NC		11044	**V**	DR		KM
1023	**1**	P		LM		11045	**V**	P		LM
1026	**V**	P		WI		11046	**V**	DR		KM
1027	**V**	P		WB		11048	**V**	P		WB

11052	**V**	P	WI	11058	**V**	P	LM
11054	**V**	DR	KM	11060	**V**	P	WI
11055	**V**	P	LM				

AD1H (FO)   OPEN FIRST

Mark 3B. Air conditioned. Inter-City 80 seats. All now refurbished with table lamps and new seat cushions and trim. 48/– 2T. BT10 bogies. d. ETH 6X.

† "One" vehicles fitted with disabled toilet and reduced seating including three Compin "Pegasus" seats of the same type as used in standard class (but regarded as first class!). 34/3 1T 1TD 2W.

Lot No. 30982 Derby 1985. 36.5 t.

11064		**V**	P		WB	11083		**V**	P		LM
11065		**V**	P		LM	11084		**V**	P		LM
11066		**1**	P	*1*	NC	11085	†	**1**	P	*1*	NC
11067		**1**	P	*1*	NC	11086		**V**	P		LM
11068		**1**	P	*1*	NC	11087	†	**1**	P	*1*	NC
11069		**1**	P	*1*	NC	11088	†	**1**	P	*1*	NC
11070		**1**	P	*1*	NC	11089		**V**	P		LM
11071		**V**	P		LM	11090	†	**1**	P	*1*	NC
11072		**1**	P	*1*	NC	11091		**1**	P	*1*	NC
11073		**1**	P	*1*	NC	11092	†	**1**	P	*1*	NC
11074		**V**	P		NC	11093	†	**1**	P	*1*	NC
11075		**1**	P	*1*	NC	11094	†	**1**	P	*1*	NC
11076		**1**	P	*1*	NC	11095	†	**1**	P	*1*	NC
11077		**1**	P	*1*	NC	11096	†	**1**	P	*1*	NC
11078	†	**1**	P	*1*	NC	11097		**V**	P		LM
11079		**V**	P		WB	11098	†	**1**	P	*1*	NC
11080		**1**	P	*1*	NC	11099	†	**1**	P	*1*	NC
11081		**1**	P	*1*	NC	11100	†	**1**	P	*1*	NC
11082		**1**	P	*1*	NC	11101	†	**1**	P	*1*	NC

AD1J (FO)   OPEN FIRST

Mark 4. Air conditioned. Rebuilt with new interior by Bombardier Wakefield 2003–05 (some converted from standard class vehicles) 46/– 1T. BT41 bogies. ETH 6X.

11201–11273. Lot No. 31046 Metro-Cammell 1989–92. 41.3 t .
11277–11299. Lot No. 31049 Metro-Cammell 1989–92. 41.3 t .

11201		**GN** H *GN* BN	11280	(12523)	**GN** H *GN* BN
11219		**GN** H *GN* BN	11281	(12418)	**GN** H *GN* BN
11229		**GN** H *GN* BN	11282	(12524)	**GN** H *GN* BN
11237		**GN** H *GN* BN	11283	(12435)	**GN** H *GN* BN
11241		**GN** H *GN* BN	11284	(12487)	**GN** H *GN* BN
11244		**GN** H *GN* BN	11285	(12537)	**GN** H *GN* BN
11273		**GN** H *GN* BN	11286	(12482)	**GN** H *GN* BN
11277	(12408)	**GN** H *GN* BN	11287	(12527)	**GN** H *GN* BN
11278	(12479)	**GN** H *GN* BN	11288	(12517)	**GN** H *GN* BN
11279	(12521)	**GN** H *GN* BN	11289	(12528)	**GN** H *GN* BN

11290 (12530)	**GN** H *GN* BN	11294 (12529)	**GN** H *GN* BN
11291 (12535)	**GN** H *GN* BN	11295 (12475)	**GN** H *GN* BN
11292 (12451)	**GN** H *GN* BN	11298 (12416)	**GN** H *GN* BN
11293 (12536)	**GN** H *GN* BN	11299 (12532)	**GN** H *GN* BN

AD1J (FOD)   OPEN FIRST (DISABLED)

Mark 4. Air conditioned. Rebuilt from FO by Bombardier Wakefield 2003–05.
42/– 1W 1TD. BT41 bogies. ETH 6X.

Lot No. 31046 Metro-Cammell 1989–92. 40.7 t.

11301 (11215)	**GN** H *GN* BN	11316 (11227)	**GN** H *GN* BN
11302 (11203)	**GN** H *GN* BN	11317 (11223)	**GN** H *GN* BN
11303 (11211)	**GN** H *GN* BN	11318 (11251)	**GN** H *GN* BN
11304 (11257)	**GN** H *GN* BN	11319 (11247)	**GN** H *GN* BN
11305 (11261)	**GN** H *GN* BN	11320 (11255)	**GN** H *GN* BN
11306 (11276)	**GN** H *GN* BN	11321 (11245)	**GN** H *GN* BN
11307 (11217)	**GN** H *GN* BN	11322 (11228)	**GN** H *GN* BN
11308 (11263)	**GN** H *GN* BN	11323 (11235)	**GN** H *GN* BN
11309 (11259)	**GN** H *GN* BN	11324 (11253)	**GN** H *GN* BN
11310 (11272)	**GN** H *GN* BN	11325 (11231)	**GN** H *GN* BN
11311 (11221)	**GN** H *GN* BN	11326 (11206)	**GN** H *GN* BN
11312 (11225)	**GN** H *GN* BN	11327 (11236)	**GN** H *GN* BN
11313 (11210)	**GN** H *GN* BN	11328 (11274)	**GN** H *GN* BN
11314 (11207)	**GN** H *GN* BN	11329 (11243)	**GN** H *GN* BN
11315 (11238)	**GN** H *GN* BN	11330 (11249)	**GN** H *GN* BN

AD1J (FO)   OPEN FIRST

Mark 4. Air conditioned. Rebuilt from FO by Bombardier Wakefield 2003–05.
Separate area for 7 smokers, although smoking is no longer allowed. 46/– 1W
1TD. BT41 bogies. ETH 6X.

Lot No. 31046 Metro-Cammell 1989–92. 42.1 t.

11401 (11214)	**GN** H *GN* BN	11416 (11254)	**GN** H *GN* BN
11402 (11216)	**GN** H *GN* BN	11417 (11226)	**GN** H *GN* BN
11403 (11258)	**GN** H *GN* BN	11418 (11222)	**GN** H *GN* BN
11404 (11202)	**GN** H *GN* BN	11419 (11250)	**GN** H *GN* BN
11405 (11204)	**GN** H *GN* BN	11420 (11242)	**GN** H *GN* BN
11406 (11205)	**GN** H *GN* BN	11421 (11220)	**GN** H *GN* BN
11407 (11256)	**GN** H *GN* BN	11422 (11232)	**GN** H *GN* BN
11408 (11218)	**GN** H *GN* BN	11423 (11230)	**GN** H *GN* BN
11409 (11262)	**GN** H *GN* BN	11424 (11239)	**GN** H *GN* BN
11410 (11260)	**GN** H *GN* BN	11425 (11234)	**GN** H *GN* BN
11411 (11240)	**GN** H *GN* BN	11426 (11252)	**GN** H *GN* BN
11412 (11209)	**GN** H *GN* BN	11427 (11200)	**GN** H *GN* BN
11413 (11212)	**GN** H *GN* BN	11428 (11233)	**GN** H *GN* BN
11414 (11246)	**GN** H *GN* BN	11429 (11275)	**GN** H *GN* BN
11415 (11208)	**GN** H *GN* BN	11430 (11248)	**GN** H *GN* BN

AD1J (FO)   OPEN FIRST

Mark 4. Air conditioned. Converted from TFRB with new interior by Bombardie Wakefield 2005. 46/– 1T. BT41 bogies. ETH 6X.

Lot No. 31046 Metro-Cammell 1989–92. 41.3 t.

| 11998 | (10314) | **GN** H *GN* BN | | 11999 | (10316) | **GN** H *GN* BN |

AC2G (TSO)   OPEN STANDARD

Mark 3A. Air conditioned. All refurbished with modified seat backs and new layout and further refurbished with new seat trim. –/76 2T (s – 70 2T 2W, z –/70 1TD 1T 2W). BT10 bogies. d. ETH 6X.

h Coaches modified for "One" with 8 Compin Pegasus seats at saloon ends fo "priority" use and a high density layout with more unidirectional seating. –/80 2T

Note: 12169–72 were converted from open composites 11908–10/22, formerly FOs 11008–10/22.

12004–12167. Lot No. 30877 Derby 1975–77. 34.3 t.
12169–12172. Lot No. 30878 Derby 1975–76. 34.3 t.

No.				Depot		No.				Depot
12004		**V**	P	WI		12038		**V**	P	LM
12005	h	**1**	P	*1*	NC		12040	h	**1**	P	*1*	NC
12007		**V**	P	WI		12041	h	**1**	P	*1*	NC
12008		**V**	P	WI		12042	h	**1**	P	*1*	NC
12009	h	**1**	P	*1*	NC		12043		**V**	P	LM
12011		**V**	P	WB		12044		**V**	P	LM
12012	h	**1**	P	*1*	NC		12045		**V**	P	WI
12013	h	**1**	P	*1*	NC		12046	h	**1**	P	*1*	NC
12014		**V**	P	LM		12047	z	**V**	P	WI
12015	h	**1**	P	*1*	NC		12048		**V**	P	LM
12016		**1**	P	*1*	NC		12049		**1**	P	*1*	NC
12017		**V**	P	WI		12050	s	**V**	P	WI
12019	h	**1**	P	*1*	NC		12051	h	**1**	P	*1*	NC
12021		**1**	P	*1*	NC		12052		**V**	P	LM
12022		**V**	P	WI		12053		**V**	P	LM
12024	h	**1**	P	*1*	NC		12054	s	**V**	P	WB
12025		**V**	P	WI		12055		**V**	P	WI
12026	h	**1**	P	*1*	NC		12056	h	**1**	P	*1*	NC
12027	h	**1**	P	*1*	NC		12057	h	**1**	P	*1*	NC
12028		**V**	P	WI		12058		**V**	P	LM
12029		**V**	P	WI		12059	s	**V**	P	WI
12030	h	**1**	P	*1*	NC		12060	h	**1**	P	*1*	NC
12031		**1**	P	*1*	NC		12061	h	**1**	P	*1*	NC
12032	h	**1**	P	*1*	NC		12062	h	**1**	P	*1*	NC
12033	z	**V**	P	LM		12063		**V**	P	LM
12034		**1**	P	*1*	NC		12064		**1**	P	*1*	NC
12035	h	**1**	P	*1*	NC		12065		**V**	P	LM
12036	s	**V**	P	WI		12066	h	**1**	P	*1*	NC
12037	h	**1**	P	*1*	NC		12067		**1**	P	*1*	NC

No.					
2069		**V**	P		WI
2071		**V**	P		WI
2072		**V**	P		WI
2073	h	**1**	P	*1*	NC
2075		**V**	P		WI
2076		**V**	P		WI
2077		**V**	P		LM
2078		**V**	P		WB
2079		1	P	*1*	NC
2080		**V**	P		WI
2081	h	1	P	*1*	NC
2082	h	1	P	*1*	NC
2083		**V**	P		WI
2084	h	1	P	*1*	NC
2085	s	**V**	P		WI
2086	s	**V**	P		WI
2087	s	**V**	P		WI
2088	z	1	P		LM
2089		1	P	*1*	NC
2090	h	1	P	*1*	NC
2091	h	1	P	*1*	NC
2092		**V**	P		LM
2093	h	1	P	*1*	NC
2094		**V**	P		LM
2095		**V**	P		WI
2097	h	1	P	*1*	NC
2098		1	P	*1*	NC
2099	h	1	P	*1*	NC
2100	z	**FP**	P	*GW*	OO
2101	s	**V**	P		LM
2102		**V**	P		WI
2103		1	P	*1*	NC
2104		**V**	P		LM
2105	h	1	P	*1*	NC
2106		**V**	P		WI
2107	h	1	P	*1*	NC
2108		1	P	*1*	NC
2109	h	1	P	*1*	NC
2110	h	1	P	*1*	NC
2111	h	1	P	*1*	NC
2112	z	**V**	P		LM
2113		**V**	P		WI
2114	h	1	P	*1*	NC
2115	h	1	P	*1*	NC
2116	h	1	P	*1*	NC
2117		**V**	P		LM
2118		1	P	*1*	NC
2119		**V**	P		LM

No.					
12120	h	1	P	*1*	NC
12121		**V**	P		LM
12122	z	**V**	P		WB
12123		**V**	P		LM
12124		**V**	P		WI
12125	h	1	P	*1*	NC
12126	h	1	P	*1*	NC
12127		**V**	P		LM
12128	s	**V**	P		LM
12129	h	1	P	*1*	NC
12130	h	1	P	*1*	NC
12131		**V**	P		LM
12132		1	P	*1*	NC
12133		**V**	P		WB
12134		**V**	P		WI
12136		**V**	P		LM
12137	h	1	P	*1*	NC
12138		**V**	P		WB
12139		**V**	P		LM
12141		1	P	*1*	NC
12142	z	**V**	P		LM
12143		1	P	*1*	NC
12144	s	**V**	P		WI
12145		**V**	P		LM
12146		1	P	*1*	NC
12147		1	P	*1*	NC
12148		1	P	*1*	NC
12149		**V**	P		LM
12150	h	1	P	*1*	NC
12151		1	P	*1*	NC
12152		**V**	P		LM
12153		1	P	*1*	NC
12154	h	1	P	*1*	NC
12155	s	**V**	P		LM
12156		**V**	P		WI
12158		**V**	P		LM
12159		1	P	*1*	NC
12160	s	**V**	P		WI
12161	z	**FP**	P	*GW*	OO
12163		**V**	P		WI
12164		1	P	*1*	NC
12165		**V**	P		LM
12166		1	P	*1*	NC
12167	h	1	P	*1*	NC
12169	s	**V**	P		WI
12170		1	P	*1*	NC
12171		1	P	*1*	NC
12172	s	**V**	P		LM

AI2J (TSOE)   OPEN STANDARD (END)

Mark 4. Air conditioned. Rebuilt with new interior by Bombardier Wakefield 2003–05. Separate area for 26 smokers, although smoking is no longer allowed. –/76 1T. BT41 bogies. ETH 6X.

Note: 12232 was converted from the original 12405.

12200–12231. Lot No. 31047 Metro-Cammell 1989–91. 39.5 t.
12232. Lot No. 31049 Metro-Cammell 1989–92. 39.5 t.

12200	**GN**	H *GN*	BN		12217	**GN**	H *GN*	BN
12201	**GN**	H *GN*	BN		12218	**GN**	H *GN*	BN
12202	**GN**	H *GN*	BN		12219	**GN**	H *GN*	BN
12203	**GN**	H *GN*	BN		12220	**GN**	H *GN*	BN
12204	**GN**	H *GN*	BN		12222	**GN**	H *GN*	BN
12205	**GN**	H *GN*	BN		12223	**GN**	H *GN*	BN
12207	**GN**	H *GN*	BN		12224	**GN**	H *GN*	BN
12208	**GN**	H *GN*	BN		12225	**GN**	H *GN*	BN
12209	**GN**	H *GN*	BN		12226	**GN**	H *GN*	BN
12210	**GN**	H *GN*	BN		12227	**GN**	H *GN*	BN
12211	**GN**	H *GN*	BN		12228	**GN**	H *GN*	BN
12212	**GN**	H *GN*	BN		12229	**GN**	H *GN*	BN
12213	**GN**	H *GN*	BN		12230	**GN**	H *GN*	BN
12214	**GN**	H *GN*	BN		12231	**GN**	H *GN*	BN
12215	**GN**	H *GN*	BN		12232	**GN**	H *GN*	BN
12216	**GN**	H *GN*	BN					

AL2J (TSOD)
OPEN STANDARD (DISABLED ACCESS)

Mark 4. Air conditioned. Rebuilt with new interior by Bombardier Wakefield 2003–05. –/68 2W 1TD. BT41 bogies. ETH 6X.

Note: 12331 has been converted from TSO 12531.

12300–12330. Lot No. 31048 Metro-Cammell 1989–91. 39.4 t.
12331. Lot No. 31049 Metro-Cammell 1989–92. 39.4 t.

12300	**GN**	H *GN*	BN		12313	**GN**	H *GN*	BN
12301	**GN**	H *GN*	BN		12315	**GN**	H *GN*	BN
12302	**GN**	H *GN*	BN		12316	**GN**	H *GN*	BN
12303	**GN**	H *GN*	BN		12317	**GN**	H *GN*	BN
12304	**GN**	H *GN*	BN		12318	**GN**	H *GN*	BN
12305	**GN**	H *GN*	BN		12319	**GN**	H *GN*	BN
12307	**GN**	H *GN*	BN		12320	**GN**	H *GN*	BN
12308	**GN**	H *GN*	BN		12321	**GN**	H *GN*	BN
12309	**GN**	H *GN*	BN		12322	**GN**	H *GN*	BN
12310	**GN**	H *GN*	BN		12323	**GN**	H *GN*	BN
12311	**GN**	H *GN*	BN		12324	**GN**	H *GN*	BN
12312	**GN**	H *GN*	BN		12325	**GN**	H *GN*	BN

2326	**GN**	H *GN*	BN		12329	**GN**	H *GN*	BN
2327	**GN**	H *GN*	BN		12330	**GN**	H *GN*	BN
2328	**GN**	H *GN*	BN		12331	**GN**	H *GN*	BN

AC2J (TSO)   OPEN STANDARD

Mark 4. Air conditioned. Rebuilt with new interior by Bombardier Wakefield 2003–05. –/76 1T. BT41 bogies. ETH 6X.

Lot No. 31049 Metro-Cammell 1989–92. 40.8 t.

Note: 12405 is the second coach to carry that number. It was built from the bodyshell originally intended for 12221. The original 12405 is now 12232.

2400	**GN**	H *GN*	BN		12444	**GN**	H *GN*	BN
2401	**GN**	H *GN*	BN		12445	**GN**	H *GN*	BN
2402	**GN**	H *GN*	BN		12446	**GN**	H *GN*	BN
2403	**GN**	H *GN*	BN		12447	**GN**	H *GN*	BN
2404	**GN**	H *GN*	BN		12448	**GN**	H *GN*	BN
2405	**GN**	H *GN*	BN		12449	**GN**	H *GN*	BN
2406	**GN**	H *GN*	BN		12450	**GN**	H *GN*	BN
2407	**GN**	H *GN*	BN		12452	**GN**	H *GN*	BN
2409	**GN**	H *GN*	BN		12453	**GN**	H *GN*	BN
2410	**GN**	H *GN*	BN		12454	**GN**	H *GN*	BN
2411	**GN**	H *GN*	BN		12455	**GN**	H *GN*	BN
2414	**GN**	H *GN*	BN		12456	**GN**	H *GN*	BN
2415	**GN**	H *GN*	BN		12457	**GN**	H *GN*	BN
2417	**GN**	H *GN*	BN		12458	**GN**	H *GN*	BN
2419	**GN**	H *GN*	BN		12459	**GN**	H *GN*	BN
2420	**GN**	H *GN*	BN		12460	**GN**	H *GN*	BN
2421	**GN**	H *GN*	BN		12461	**GN**	H *GN*	BN
2422	**GN**	H *GN*	BN		12462	**GN**	H *GN*	BN
2423	**GN**	H *GN*	BN		12463	**GN**	H *GN*	BN
2424	**GN**	H *GN*	BN		12464	**GN**	H *GN*	BN
2425	**GN**	H *GN*	BN		12465	**GN**	H *GN*	BN
2426	**GN**	H *GN*	BN		12466	**GN**	H *GN*	BN
2427	**GN**	H *GN*	BN		12467	**GN**	H *GN*	BN
2428	**GN**	H *GN*	BN		12468	**GN**	H *GN*	BN
2429	**GN**	H *GN*	BN		12469	**GN**	H *GN*	BN
2430	**GN**	H *GN*	BN		12470	**GN**	H *GN*	BN
2431	**GN**	H *GN*	BN		12471	**GN**	H *GN*	BN
2432	**GN**	H *GN*	BN		12472	**GN**	H *GN*	BN
2433	**GN**	H *GN*	BN		12473	**GN**	H *GN*	BN
2434	**GN**	H *GN*	BN		12474	**GN**	H *GN*	BN
2436	**GN**	H *GN*	BN		12476	**GN**	H *GN*	BN
2437	**GN**	H *GN*	BN		12477	**GN**	H *GN*	BN
2438	**GN**	H *GN*	BN		12478	**GN**	H *GN*	BN
2439	**GN**	H *GN*	BN		12480	**GN**	H *GN*	BN
2440	**GN**	H *GN*	BN		12481	**GN**	H *GN*	BN
2441	**GN**	H *GN*	BN		12483	**GN**	H *GN*	BN
2442	**GN**	H *GN*	BN		12484	**GN**	H *GN*	BN
2443	**GN**	H *GN*	BN		12485	**GN**	H *GN*	BN

12486	**GN**	H *GN*	BN		12519	**GN**	H *GN*	BN
12488	**GN**	H *GN*	BN		12520	**GN**	H *GN*	BN
12489	**GN**	H *GN*	BN		12522	**GN**	H *GN*	BN
12513	**GN**	H *GN*	BN		12526	**GN**	H *GN*	BN
12514	**GN**	H *GN*	BN		12533	**GN**	H *GN*	BN
12515	**GN**	H *GN*	BN		12534	**GN**	H *GN*	BN
12518	**GN**	H *GN*	BN		12538	**GN**	H *GN*	BN

AA11 (FK)   CORRIDOR FIRS

Mark 1. 42/– 2T. ETH 3.

13229–13230. Lot No. 30381 Swindon 1959. B4 bogies. 33 t.
13321. Lot No. 30667 Swindon 1962. Commonwealth bogies. 36 t.

13229	xk	**M**	BK *BK*	BT		13321	x	**M**	WC	CS
13230	xk	**M**	BK *BK*	BT						

AA1A (FK)   CORRIDOR FIRS

Mark 2A. Pressure ventilated. 42/– 2T. B4 bogies. ETH 4.

13440. Lot No. 30774 Derby 1968. 33 t.

13440	v	**G**	WC *WC*	CS	

AD1B (FO)   OPEN FIRS

Mark 2B. Pressure ventilated. 42/– 2T. B4 bogies. ETH 4.

Lot No. 30789 Derby 1968. 33 t.

This vehicle was built as a FK, sold to Northern Ireland Railways 1980 an
regauged to 5'3". NIR converted it to a 56-seater TSO. Since withdraw
repatriated to Britain and converted back to standard gauge 2002/03. Und
conversion to FO.

13508	(13508, NIR924)	**PC**	RA	CS

AB11 (BFK)   CORRIDOR BRAKE FIRS

Mark 1. 24/– 1T. Commonwealth bogies. ETH 2.

14007. Lot No. 30382 Swindon 1959. 35 t.
17013–17019. Lot No. 30668 Swindon 1961. 36 t.
17023. Lot No. 30718 Swindon 1963. Metal window frames. 36 t.

Originally numbered in 14xxx series and then renumbered in 17xxx series.

14007	x	**M**	B1	*LS*	BH		17018	v	**CH**	VT	*VT*	TM
17013		**PC**	JH	*LS*	SO		17019	x	**M**	92	*LS*	TM
17015	x	**G**	RV	*RV*	CP		17023	x	**G**	E		SL

AB1Z (BFK)   CORRIDOR BRAKE FIRST

Mark 2. Pressure ventilated. 24/– 1T. B4 bogies. ETH 4.

Lot No. 30756 Derby 1966. 31.5 t.

Originally numbered 14041.

| 17041 | **M** | DG | *LS* | BQ | |

AB1A (BFK)   CORRIDOR BRAKE FIRST

Mark 2A. Pressure ventilated. 24/– 1T. B4 bogies. ETH 4.

17056–17077. Lot No. 30775 Derby 1967–8. 32 t.
17086–17102. Lot No. 30786 Derby 1968. 32 t.

Originally numbered 14056–102. 17089 and 17090 were numbered 35502 and 35503 for a time when declassified.

17056	**M**	E		OM		17090	v **CH**	H		TM
17077	**RV**	RV	*RV*	CP		17096	**G**	MN	*LS*	SL
17086	**RV**	RV		CD		17102	**M**	WC	*WC*	CS
17089	v **G**	WC		RL						

AX5B   COUCHETTE/GENERATOR COACH

Mark 2B. Formerly part of Royal Train. Converted from a BFK built 1969. Consists of luggage accommodation, guard's compartment, 350 kW diesel generator and staff sleeping accommodation. Pressure ventilated. B5 bogies. ETH 5X.

Non-standard livery: 17105 Oxford blue.

Lot No. 30888 Wolverton 1977. 46 t.

| 17105 | (14105, 2905) | **0** | RV | *RV* | CP |

AB1D (BFK)   CORRIDOR BRAKE FIRST

Mark 2D. Air conditioned (Stones equipment). 24/– 1T. B4 Bogies. ETH 5.

Lot No. 30823 Derby 1971–72. 33.5 t.

Originally numbered 14144–70.

17144		FM		CV		17167	**VN**	VS	*VS*	CP
17153	**WR**	E		CS		17168	d **M**	WC	*WC*	CS
17159	**CH**	RV		SL		17169		E		CS
17161		E		OM		17170		FM		CV
17163		VS		CO						

AE1H (BFO)   OPEN BRAKE FIRST

Mark 3B. Air conditioned. Fitted with hydraulic handbrake. Refurbished with
table lamps and burgundy seat trim. 36/– 1T (w 35/– 1T) BT10 bogies. pg. d.
ETH 5X.

Lot No. 30990 Derby 1986. 35.81 t.

17173		**FP**	P	*GW*	OO		17175	w	**FP**	P	*GW*	OO
17174		**FP**	P	*GW*	OO							

AA21 (SK)   CORRIDOR STANDARD

Mark 1. Each vehicle has eight compartments. All remaining vehicles have metal
window frames and melamine interior panelling. Commonwealth bogies. –/48
2T. ETH 4.

Lot No. 30685 Derby 1961–62. 36 t.

t Rebuilt internally as TSO using components from 4936. –/64 2T.

Originally numbered 25756–25893.

18756	x	**M**	WC	*WC*	CS		18808	x	**M**	WC	*WC*	CS
18767	x	**M**	WC	*WC*	CS		18862	x	**M**	WC	*WC*	CS
18806	xt	**M**	WC	*WC*	CS		18893	x	**CH**	WC		CS

AB31 (BCK)   CORRIDOR BRAKE COMPOSITE

Mark 1. There are two variants depending upon whether the standard class
compartments have armrests. Each vehicle has two first class and three standard
class compartments. 12/18 2T (12/24 2T *). ETH 2.

21232. Lot No. 30574 GRCW 1960. B4 bogies. 34 t.
21241–21246. Lot No. 30669 Swindon 1961–62. Commonwealth bogies. 36 t.
21256. Lot No. 30731 Derby 1963. Commonwealth bogies. 37 t.
21266–21272. Lot No. 30732 Derby 1964. Commonwealth bogies. 37 t.

21232	x	**CI**	62	*LS*	SK		21266	x*	**M**	WC	*WC*	CS
21241	x	**M**	BK	*BK*	BT		21268	*		BS		SO
21245	x	**M**	E		OM		21269	*	**GC**	E	*E*	OM
21246		**BG**	E	*E*	OM		21272	x*	**CH**	RV	*RV*	CP
21256	x	**M**	WC	*WC*	CS							

AB21 (BSK)   CORRIDOR BRAKE STANDARD

Mark 1. There are two variants depending upon whether the compartments have armrests. Each vehicle has four compartments. Lots 30699 and 30721 have metal window frames and melamine interior panelling. –/24 1T. ETH2.

g Fitted with an e.t.s. generator. Weight unknown.

35185. Lot No. 30427 Wolverton 1959. B4 bogies. 33 t.
35317–35333. Lot No. 30699 Wolverton 1962–63. Commonwealth bogies. 37 t.
35449. Lot No. 30728 Wolverton 1963. Commonwealth bogies. 37 t.
35452–35486. Lot No. 30721 Wolverton 1963. Commonwealth bogies. 37 t.

35185	x	**M**	BK *BK*	BT	35463	v	**M**	WC *LS*	CS
35317	x	**G**	IR *LS*	BQ	35465	x	**CI**	LW *LS*	CP
35329	v	**G**	MH *LS*	RL	35468	v	**M**	NM *LS*	YK
35333	x	**CH**	24 *LS*	DI	35469	xg	**M**	E *E*	OM
35449	x	**M**	BE *LS*	RL	35470	v	**CH**	VT *LS*	TM
35452	x	**RR**	LW	CP	35476	x	**M**	62 *LS*	SK
35453	x	**CH**	GW *LS*	DI	35479	v	**M**	SV *LS*	KR
35459	x	**M**	WC *WC*	CS	35486	x	**M**	SV *LS*	KR
35461	x	**CH**	RV *LS*	OM					

AB1C (BFK)   CORRIDOR BRAKE FIRST

Mark 2C. Pressure ventilated. Renumbered when declassified. –/24 1T. B4 bogies. ETH 4.

Lot No. 30796 Derby 1969–70. 32.5 t.

35508	(14128, 17128)	**M**	IR	*LS*	BQ

AB5C   BRAKE/POWER KITCHEN

Mark 2C. Pressure ventilated. Converted from BFK (declassified to BSK) built 1970. Converted at West Coast Railway Company 2000–01. Consists of 60 kVA generator, guard's compartment and electric kitchen. B5 bogies. ETH 4.

Non-standard livery: British Racing Green with gold lining.

Lot No. 30796 Derby 1969–70. 32.5 t.

35511	(14130, 17130)	**0**	RA		CP

AB1A (BFK)   CORRIDOR BRAKE FIRST

Mark 2A. Pressure ventilated. Renumbered when declassified. –/24 1T. B4 bogies. Cage removed from brake compartment. ETH 4.

Lot No. 30786 Derby 1968. 32 t.

35517	(14088, 17088)	**M**	IR	*LS*	BQ
35518	(14097, 17097)	**PC**	IR	*LS*	OM

NAMED COACHES

The following miscellaneous coaches carry names:

1200	AMBER	3330	BRUNEL
1659	CAMELOT	3348	GAINSBOROUGH
1800	TINTAGEL	3356	TENNYSON
3105	JULIA	3364	SHAKESPEARE
3113	JESSICA	3384	DICKENS
3117	CHRISTINA	3390	CONSTABLE
3128	VICTORIA	3397	WORDSWORTH
3130	PAMELA	3426	ELGAR
3136	DIANA	5193	CLAN MACLEOD
3143	PATRICIA	5212	CAPERKAILZIE
3174	GLAMIS	5229	THE GREEN KNIGHT
3182	WARWICK	5239	THE RED KNIGHT
3188	SOVEREIGN	5278	MELISANDE
3223	DIAMOND	5365	Deborah
3228	AMETHYST	5376	Michaela
3229	JADE	5419	SIR LAUNCELOT
3231	Apollo	9391	PENDRAGON
3240	SAPPHIRE	10569	LEVIATHAN
3244	EMERALD	10729	CREWE
3247	CHATSWORTH	10734	BALMORAL
3267	BELVOIR	17013	ALBANNACH SGIATHACH
3273	ALNWICK	17086	Georgina
3275	HARLECH	35518	MERLIN

2.2. HIGH SPEED TRAIN TRAILER CARS

HSTs consist of a number of trailer cars (usually seven to nine) with a power car at each end. All trailer cars are classified Mark 3 and have BT10 bogies with disc brakes and central door locking. Heating is by a 415 V three-phase supply and vehicles have air conditioning. Maximum speed is 125 m.p.h.

All vehicles underwent a mid-life refurbishment in the 1980s, and a further refurbishment programme was completed in November 2000, with each train operating company having a different scheme as follows:

First Great Western. Green seat covers and extra partitions between seat bays.

Great North Eastern Railway. New ceiling lighting panels and brown seat covers. First class vehicles have table lamps and imitation walnut plastic end panels.

Virgin Cross-Country. Green seat covers. Standard class vehicles had four seats in the centre of each carriage replaced with a luggage stack. All have now passed to other operators or are in store.

Midland Mainline. Grey seat covers, redesigned seat squabs, side carpeting and two seats in the centre of each standard class carriage and one in first class carriages replaced with a luggage stack.

Since then the remaining three operators of HSTs have embarked on separate, and very different, refurbishment projects:

Midland Mainline were first to refurbish their vehicles a second time during 2003/04. This involved fitting new fluorescent and halogen ceiling lighting, although the original seats were retained in first and standard class, but with blue upholstery.

First Great Western started a major rebuild of their HST sets in late 2006, although the first set was not due to enter traffic until February 2007. By the end of 2007 the company plans to have 53 sets in traffic with new interiors featuring new lighting and seating throughout. First class seats, with leather upholstery, are made by Primarius UK and standard class seats are made by Grammer. Some sets are being reduced to 7-cars with "high density" seating layouts in standard class, with almost all seats arranged in a unidirectional layout. The refurbishment work is being carried out at Derby and Ilford Works by Bombardier.

GNER modernised their buffet cars with new corner bars in 2004 and at the same time each HST set was made up to 9-cars with an extra standard class vehicle added with a disabled persons toilet.

At the end of 2006 GNER embarked on a major rebuild of its HST sets, with the work being carried out at Wabtec, Doncaster. All vehicles will have similar interiors to the Mark 4 "Mallard" fleet, with new seats throughout. 13 sets are to be refurbished and the work is due for completion by March 2009.

Ten sets ex-Virgin Cross-Country, and some spare vehicles, were temporarily allocated to Midland Mainline for the interim service to Manchester during 2003/04 and had a facelift. Buffet cars were converted from TRSB to TRFB and renumbered in the 408xx series. These sets are now in use with First Great Western, GNER or are undergoing refurbishment for FGW.

TOPS Type Codes

TOPS type codes for HST trailer cars are made up as follows:

(1) Two letters denoting the layout of the vehicle as follows:

GH Open	GL Kitchen
GJ Open with Guard's compartment	GN Buffet

(2) A digit for the class of passenger accommodation

1 First	2 Standard (formerly second).

(3) A suffix relating to the build of coach.

G   Mark 3

Operator Codes

The normal operator codes are given in brackets after the TOPS codes. These
are as follows:

TF	Trailer First	TGS	Trailer Guard's Standard
TRB	Trailer Buffet First	TRSB	Trailer Buffet Standard
TRFB	Trailer Buffet First	TS	Trailer Standard

General Note: + Assigned for lease to First Great Western after refurbishment.

GN1G (TRFB)   TRAILER BUFFET FIRST

Converted from TRSB by fitting first class seats. Renumbered from 404xx series
by subtracting 200. 23/–.

40204–40228. Lot No. 30883 Derby 1976–77. 36.12 t.
40231. Lot No. 30899 Derby 1978–79. 36.12 t.

* Refurbished First Great Western vehicles. New Primarius leather seats.

40204		**FG**	A	*GW*	LA	40210		**FG**	A	*GW*	LA
40205		**FG**	A	*GW*	LA	40221		**FG**	A	*GW*	LA
40207		**FG**	A	*GW*	LA	40228		**FG**	A	*GW*	LA
40208		**FG**	A	*GW*	LA	40231	*	**FD**	A	*GW*	LA
40209		**FG**	A	*GW*	LA						

GK2G (TRSB)   TRAILER BUFFET STANDARD

Renumbered from 400xx series by adding 400. –/33 1W.

40402–40426. Lot No. 30883 Derby 1976–77. 36.12 t.
40433/40434. Lot No. 30899 Derby 1978–79. 36.12 t.

Note: 40433/40434 were numbered 40233/40234 for a time when fitted with 23
first class seats.

40402	**V**	P	LM	40424	**V**	P	LM
40403	**V**	P	LM	40425	**V**	P	LM
40416	**V**	P	LM	40426	**V**	P	LM
40417	**V**	P	LM	40433	**V**	P	LM
40419	**V**	P	LM	40434	**V**	P	LM

GK1G (TRFB)   **TRAILER BUFFET FIRST**

These vehicles have larger kitchens than the 402xx and 404xx series vehicles,
and are used in trains where full meal service is required. They were renumbered
from the 403xx series (in which the seats were unclassified) by adding 400 to
the previous number. 17/–.

40700–40721. Lot No. 30921 Derby 1978–79. 38.16 t.
40722–40735. Lot No. 30940 Derby 1979–80. 38.16 t.
40736–40753. Lot No. 30948 Derby 1980–81. 38.16 t.
40754–40757. Lot No. 30966 Derby 1982. 38.16 t.

r Modified with new corner bar.
† Fitted with transceiver "dome" for wi-fi.

40700	**MN**	P	*MM*	NL	40730	**MN**	P	*MM*	NL
40701	**MN**	P	*MM*	NL	40731	**FG**	A	*GW*	LA
40702	**MN**	P	*MM*	NL	40732	**MN**	A	*MM*	NL
40703	**FG**	A	*GW*	LA	40733	**FG**	A	*GW*	LA
40704 r†	**GN**	A	*GN*	EC	40734	**FG**	A	*GW*	LA
40705 r†	**GN**	A	*GN*	EC	40735 r†	**GN**	A	*GN*	EC
40706 r†	**GN**	A	*GN*	EC	40736	**FG**	A	*GW*	LA
40707	**FG**	A	*GW*	LA	40737 r†	**GN**	A	*GN*	EC
40708	**MN**	P	*MM*	NL	40738	**FG**	A	*GW*	LA
40709	**FG**	A	*GW*	LA	40739	**FG**	A	*GW*	LA
40710	**FG**	A	*GW*	LA	40740 r†	**GN**	A	*GN*	EC
40711 r†	**GN**	A	*GN*	EC	40741	**MN**	P	*MM*	NL
40712	**FG**	A	*GW*	LA	40742 r†	**GN**	A	*GN*	EC
40713	**FG**	A	*GW*	LA	40743	**FG**	A	*GW*	LA
40714	**FG**	A	*GW*	LA	40744	**FG**	A	*GW*	LA
40715	**FG**	A	*GW*	LA	40745	**FG**	A	*GW*	LA
40716	**FG**	A	*GW*	LA	40746	**MN**	P	*MM*	NL
40717	**FG**	A	*GW*	LA	40747	**FG**	A	*GW*	LA
40718	**FG**	A	*GW*	LA	40748 r†	**GN**	A	*GN*	EC
40720 r†	**GN**	A	*GN*	EC	40749	**MN**	P	*MM*	NL
40721	**FG**	A	*GW*	LA	40750 r†	**GN**	A	*GN*	EC
40722	**FG**	A	*GW*	LA	40751	**MN**	P	*MM*	NL
40723	**MN**	A	*MM*	NL	40752	**FT**	A	*GW*	LA
40724	**FG**	A	*GW*	LA	40753	**MN**	P	*MM*	NL
40725	**FG**	A	*GW*	LA	40754	**MN**	P	*MM*	NL
40726	**FG**	A	*GW*	LA	40755	**FG**	A	*GW*	LA
40727	**FG**	A	*GW*	LA	40756	**MN**	P	*MM*	NL
40728	**MN**	P	*MM*	NL	40757	**FG**	A	*GW*	LA
40729	**MN**	P	*MM*	NL					

GL1G (TRFB)   **TRAILER BUFFET FIRST**

These vehicles have been converted from TRSBs in the 404xx series to be similar
to the 407xx series vehicles. 17/–.

40801–40803/40805/40808/40809/40811. Lot No. 30883 Derby 1976–77. 38.16 t.
40804/40806/40807/40810. Lot No. 30899 Derby 1978–79. 38.16 t.

Note: 40802/40804/40811 were numbered 40212/40232/40211 for a time when fitted with 23 first class seats.

40801	(40027, 40427)	**FG**	P	*GW*	LA
40802	(40012, 40412)	**FG**	P	*GW*	LA
40803	(40018, 40418)	**FG**	P	*GW*	LA
40804	(40032, 40432)	**MN**	P		LM
40805	(40020, 40420)	**GN**	P	*GN*	EC
40806	(40029, 40429)	**FG**	P	*GW*	LA
40807	(40035, 40435)	**FG**	P	*GW*	LA
40808	(40015, 40415)	**FG**	P	*GW*	LA
40809	(40014, 40414)	**FG**	P	*GW*	LA
40810	(40030, 40430)	**FG**	P	*GW*	LA
40811	(40011, 40411)	**GN**	P	*GN*	EC

GN1G (TRB)   TRAILER BUFFET FIRST

Vehicles owned by First Group. Converted or undergoing conversion from TRSB by First Great Western. 23/–.
40900/40902/40904. Lot No. 30883 Derby 1976–77. 36.12 t.
40901/40903. Lot No. 30899 Derby 1978–79. 36.12 t.

40900	(40022, 40422)	**FG**	FG	*GW*	LA
40901	(40036, 40436)	**V**	FG		ZI
40902	(40023, 40423)	**FT**	FG		ZI
40903	(40037, 40437)	**V**	FG		ZI
40904	(40001, 40401)	**V**	FG		ZI

GH1G (TF)   TRAILER FIRST

41003–41056. Lot No. 30881 Derby 1976–77. 33.66 t.
41057–41120. Lot No. 30896 Derby 1977–78. 33.66 t.
41121–41148. Lot No. 30938 Derby 1979–80. 33.66 t.
41149–41166. Lot No. 30947 Derby 1980. 33.66 t.
41167–41169. Lot No. 30963 Derby 1982. 33.66 t.
41170. Lot No. 30967 Derby 1982. Former prototype vehicle. 33.66 t.
41179–41180. Lot No. 30884 Derby 1977. 33.66 t.
41181–41184/41189. Lot No. 30939 Derby 1979–80. 33.66 t.
41185–41188. Lot No. 30969 Derby 1982. 33.66 t.

As built 48/– 2T.
* Refurbished First Great Western vehicles. New Primarius leather seats.
s Fitted with centre luggage stack, disabled toilet and wheelchair space.   46/– 1T 1TD 1W.
: Fitted with disabled toilet and wheelchair space. 47/– 1T 1TD 1W.
w Wheelchair space 47/– 2T 1W.

41003	**FT**	A	*GW*	LA		41008	**FG**	A	*GW*	LA
41004	**FG**	A	*GW*	LA		41009	**FG**	A	*GW*	LA
41005	**FG**	A	*GW*	LA		41010	**FG**	A	*GW*	LA
41006	**FG**	A	*GW*	LA		41011	**FG**	A	*GW*	LA
41007	**FG**	A	*GW*	LA		41012	**FG**	A	*GW*	LA

41015		**FG**	A	*GW*	LA	41077		**MN**	P	*MM*	NL
41016		**FG**	A	*GW*	LA	41078		**MN**	P	*MM*	NL
41017		**FG**	A	*GW*	LA	41079		**MN**	P	*MM*	NL
41018		**FG**	A	*GW*	LA	41080	s	**MN**	P	*MM*	NL
41019		**FG**	A	*GW*	LA	41081	w	**MN**	P		ZD+
41020		**FG**	A	*GW*	LA	41083		**MN**	P	*MM*	NL
41021		**FG**	A	*GW*	LA	41084	s	**MN**	P	*MM*	NL
41022		**FG**	A	*GW*	LA	41085		**FD**	FG	*GW*	LA
41023		**FG**	A	*GW*	LA	41086	w	**V**	FG		ZD+
41024		**FG**	A	*GW*	LA	41087		**GN**	A	*GN*	EC
41025	t	**MN**	A	*MM*	NL	41088	w	**GN**	A	*GN*	EC
41026		**MN**	A	*MM*	NL	41089		**FG**	A	*GW*	LA
41027		**FG**	A	*GW*	LA	41090	w	**GN**	A	*GN*	EC
41028		**FG**	A	*GW*	LA	41091		**GN**	A	*GN*	EC
41029		**FG**	A	*GW*	LA	41092	w	**GN**	A	*GN*	EC
41030		**FG**	A	*GW*	LA	41093		**FG**	A	*GW*	LA
41031		**FG**	A	*GW*	LA	41094		**FG**	A	*GW*	LA
41032		**FG**	A	*GW*	LA	41095	w	**GN**	P	*GN*	EC
41033		**FG**	A	*GW*	LA	41096	w	**MN**	P		ZD+
41034		**FG**	A	*GW*	LA	41097		**GN**	A	*GN*	EC
41035		**MN**	A	*MM*	NL	41098	w	**GN**	A	*GN*	EC
41036	t	**MN**	A	*MM*	NL	41099		**GN**	A	*GN*	EC
41037		**FG**	A	*GW*	LA	41100	w	**GN**	A	*GN*	EC
41038		**FG**	A	*GW*	LA	41101		**FG**	A	*GW*	LA
41039		**GN**	A	*GN*	EC	41102		**FG**	A	*GW*	LA
41040	w	**GN**	A	*GN*	EC	41103		**FG**	A	*GW*	LA
41041	s	**MN**	P	*MM*	NL	41104		**FG**	A	*GW*	LA
41044	w	**GN**	A	*GN*	EC	41105		**FG**	A	*GW*	LA
41045	w	**V**	FG		ZD+	41106		**FG**	A	*GW*	LA
41046	s	**MN**	P	*MM*	NL	41107	w	**FG**	P	*GW*	LA
41051		**FG**	A	*GW*	LA	41108	w	**MN**	P		ZD+
41052		**FG**	A	*GW*	LA	41109	w	**FG**	P	*GW*	ZA
41055		**FG**	A	*GW*	LA	41110		**FG**	A	*GW*	LA
41056		**FG**	A	*GW*	LA	41111		**MN**	P	*MM*	NL
41057		**MN**	P	*MM*	NL	41112		**MN**	P	*MM*	NL
41058	s	**MN**	P	*MM*	NL	41113	s	**MN**	P	*MM*	NL
41059	w	**V**	FG		ZD+	41114	w	**FG**	FG	*GW*	LA
41061		**MN**	P	*MM*	NL	41115	w	**GN**	P	*GN*	EC
41062	w	**MN**	P	*MM*	NL	41116		**FG**	A	*GW*	LA
41063		**MN**	P	*MM*	NL	41117		**MN**	P	*MM*	NL
41064	s	**MN**	P	*MM*	NL	41118	w	**GN**	A	*GN*	EC
41065		**FG**	A	*GW*	LA	41119	w	**MN**	P		ZD+
41066		**GN**	A	*GN*	EC	41120		**GN**	A	*GN*	EC
41067	s	**MN**	P	*MM*	NL	41121		**FG**	A	*GW*	LA
41068	s	**MN**	P	*MM*	NL	41122		**FG**	A	*GW*	LA
41069	s	**MN**	P	*MM*	NL	41123		**FG**	A	*GW*	LA
41070	s	**MN**	P	*MM*	NL	41124		**FG**	A	*GW*	LA
41071		**MN**	P	*MM*	NL	41125		**FG**	A	*GW*	LA
41072	s	**MN**	P	*MM*	NL	41126		**FG**	A	*GW*	LA
41075		**MN**	P	*MM*	NL	41127		**FG**	A	*GW*	LA
41076	s	**MN**	P	*MM*	NL	41128		**FG**	A	*GW*	LA

41129	FG	A	GW	LA		41150 w	GN	A	GN	EC
41130	FG	A	GW	LA		41151	GN	A	GN	EC
41131	FG	A	GW	LA		41152	GN	A	GN	EC
41132	FG	A	GW	LA		41153	MN	P	MM	NL
41133	FG	A	GW	LA		41154 s	MN	P	MM	NL
41134	FG	A	GW	LA		41155	MN	P	MM	NL
41135	FG	A	GW	LA		41156	MN	P	MM	NL
41136	FG	A	GW	LA		41157	FG	A	GW	LA
41137	FG	A	GW	LA		41158	FG	A	GW	LA
41138	FG	A	GW	LA		41159 w	GN	P	GN	EC
41139	FG	A	GW	LA		41160 w	V	FG		ZD+
41140	FG	A	GW	LA		41161 w	MN	P		ZD+
41141	FG	A	GW	LA		41162 w	FG	FG GW		LA
41142	FG	A	GW	LA		41163 w	V	FG		ZD+
41143	FG	A	GW	LA		41164 w	GN	A	GN	EC
41144	FG	A	GW	LA		41165 w	GN	P	GN	EC
41145	FG	A	GW	LA		41166 w	V	FG		ZD+
41146	FG	A	GW	LA		41167 *w	FD	FG GW		LA
41147 w	FG	P	GW	LA		41168 w	FG	P	GW	LA
41148 w	V	P		ZD+		41169 w	V	P		ZD+
41149 w	FG	P	GW	LA						

41170 (41001)	GN	A	GN	EC		41184 (42270)	MN	P		ZD+
41179 (40505)	FG	A	GW	LA		41185 (42313)	GN	P	GN	EC
41180 (40511)	FG	A	GW	LA		41186 (42312)	FG	P	GW	LA
41181 (42282)	FG	P	GW	LA		41187 (42311)	MN	P		ZD+
41182 (42278)	FG	P	GW	LA		41188 (42310)	FG	P	GW	LA
41183 (42274)	FG	P	GW	LA		41189 (42298)	MN	P		LA+

GH2G (TS)   TRAILER STANDARD

42003–42090/42362. Lot No. 30882 Derby 1976–77. 33.60 t.
42091–42250. Lot No. 30897 Derby 1977–79. 33.60 t.
42251–42305. Lot No. 30939 Derby 1979–80. 33.60 t.
42306–42322. Lot No. 30969 Derby 1982. 33.60 t.
42323–42341. Lot No. 30983 Derby 1984–85. 33.60 t.
42342/42360. Lot No. 30949 Derby 1982. 33.47 t. Converted from TGS.
42343/42345. Lot No. 30970 Derby 1982. 33.47 t. Converted from TGS.
42344/42361. Lot No. 30964 Derby 1982. 33.47 t. Converted from TGS.
42346/42347/42350/42351. Lot No. 30881 Derby 1976–77. 33.66 t. Converted from TF.
42348/42349/42363. Lot No. 30896 Derby 1977–78. 33.66 t. Converted from TF.
42352/42354. Lot No. 30897 Derby 1977. Were TF from 1983 to 1992. 33.66 t.
42353/42355–42357. Lot No. 30967 Derby 1982. Ex-prototype vehicles. 33.66 t.

Standard seating –/76 2T.
* Refurbished First Great Western vehicles. New Grammer seating.
d disabled persons toilet and 5 tip-up seats. –/65 1T 1TD.
k "High density" FGW vehicle with disabled persons toilet and 5 tip-up seats. –/72 1T 1TD 2W.
h "High density" FGW vehicles. –/84 2T.
s Centre luggage stack –/72 2T.

u Centre luggage stack –/74 2T.
w Centre luggage stack and wheelchair space –72 2T 1W.
z Seats removed for wheelchair spaces –/70 2T 2W.
† Disabled persons toilet. –/62 1T 1TD 1W.
e Rebuilt VOLO TV "entertainment" coach with new seats and on-train
   entertainment systems. 36 seats had monitors fixed to the seatbacks but
   these have now been removed.

42158 was numbered 41177 for a time when fitted with first class seats.

Non-standard livery: 42076 – VOLO TV (all over silver with various images).

42003		**FG**	A	*GW*	LA	42048		**FG**	A	*GW*	LA

42003		**FG**	A	*GW*	LA	42048		**FG**	A	*GW*	LA
42004	d	**FG**	A	*GW*	LA	42049		**FG**	A	*GW*	LA
42005		**FG**	A	*GW*	LA	42050		**FG**	A	*GW*	LA
42006		**FG**	A	*GW*	LA	42051	u	**MN**	A	*MM*	NL
42007	d	**FG**	A	*GW*	LA	42052	u	**MN**	A	*MM*	NL
42008	d	**FG**	A	*GW*	LA	42053	u	**MN**	A	*MM*	NL
42009		**FG**	A	*GW*	LA	42054		**FG**	A	*GW*	LA
42010	d	**FG**	A	*GW*	LA	42055		**FG**	A	*GW*	LA
42012	d	**FG**	A	*GW*	LA	42056		**FG**	A	*GW*	LA
42013		**FG**	A	*GW*	LA	42057		**GN**	A	*GN*	EC
42014		**FG**	A	*GW*	LA	42058		**GN**	A	*GN*	EC
42015	d	**FG**	A	*GW*	LA	42059		**GN**	A	*GN*	EC
42016		**FG**	A	*GW*	LA	42060		**FG**	A	*GW*	LA
42019		**FG**	A	*GW*	LA	42061		**FG**	A	*GW*	LA
42021	d	**FG**	A	*GW*	LA	42062	d	**FG**	A	*GW*	LA
42023		**FG**	A	*GW*	LA	42063		**GN**	A	*GN*	EC
42024	d	**FG**	A	*GW*	LA	42064		**GN**	A	*GN*	EC
42025		**FG**	A	*GW*	LA	42065		**GN**	A	*GN*	EC
42026		**FG**	A	*GW*	LA	42066	d	**FG**	A	*GW*	LA
42027		**FG**	A	*GW*	LA	42067		**FG**	A	*GW*	LA
42028		**FG**	A	*GW*	LA	42068		**FG**	A	*GW*	LA
42029		**FG**	A	*GW*	LA	42069	d	**FG**	A	*GW*	LA
42030	d	**FG**	A	*GW*	LA	42070		**FG**	A	*GW*	LA
42031		**FG**	A	*GW*	LA	42071		**FG**	A	*GW*	LA
42032		**FG**	A	*GW*	LA	42072		**FG**	A	*GW*	LA
42033		**FG**	A	*GW*	LA	42073		**FG**	A	*GW*	LA
42034		**FG**	A	*GW*	LA	42074		**FG**	A	*GW*	LA
42035		**FG**	A	*GW*	LA	42075		**FG**	A	*GW*	LA
42036	u	**MN**	A	*MM*	NL	42076	e	**0**	A	*GW*	LA
42037	u	**MN**	A	*MM*	NL	42077		**FG**	A	*GW*	LA
42038	u	**MN**	A	*MM*	NL	42078		**FG**	A	*GW*	LA
42039		**FG**	A	*GW*	LA	42079		**FG**	A	*GW*	LA
42040		**FG**	A	*GW*	LA	42080		**FG**	A	*GW*	LA
42041		**FG**	A	*GW*	LA	42081	d	**FG**	A	*GW*	LA
42042		**FG**	A	*GW*	LA	42083		**FG**	A	*GW*	LA
42043		**FG**	A	*GW*	LA	42084	s	**MN**	P		LA+
42044		**FG**	A	*GW*	LA	42085	s	**MN**	P		LA+
42045		**FG**	A	*GW*	LA	42086	s	**MN**	P		LA+
42046		**FG**	A	*GW*	LA	42087	s	**MN**	P		LA+
42047		**FG**	A	*GW*	LA	42088	s	**V**	P		LM

42089	**FG**	A	*GW*	LA
42090 s	**V**	P		ZD+
42091 †	**GN**	A	*GN*	EC
42092	**V**	FG		LA+
42093 s	**V**	FG		ZD+
42094 s	**V**	FG		ZD+
42095	**FG**	FG	*GW*	LA
42096	**FG**	A	*GW*	LA
42097 w	**MN**	A	*MM*	NL
42098	**FG**	A	*GW*	LA
42099	**FG**	A	*GW*	LA
42100 u	**MN**	P	*MM*	NL
42101 w	**MN**	P	*MM*	NL
42102 u	**MN**	P	*MM*	NL
42103 z	**GN**	FG		ZI+
42104	**GN**	A	*GN*	EC
42105 s	**V**	FG		ZI+
42106	**GN**	A	*GN*	EC
42107	**FG**	A	*GW*	LA
42108 s	**V**	FG		ZD+
42109	**GN**	P	*GN*	EC
42110	**GN**	P	*GN*	EC
42111 u	**MN**	P	*MM*	NL
42112 u	**MN**	P	*MM*	NL
42113 u	**MN**	P	*MM*	NL
42115 s	**MN**	P		LA+
42116 †	**GN**	A	*GN*	EC
42117	**GN**	P	*GN*	EC
42118	**FG**	A	*GW*	LA
42119 u	**MN**	P	*MM*	NL
42120 u	**MN**	P	*MM*	NL
42121 u	**MN**	P	*MM*	NL
42122	**GN**	A	*GN*	EC
42123 u	**MN**	P	*MM*	NL
42124 u	**MN**	P	*MM*	NL
42125 u	**MN**	P	*MM*	NL
42126	**FG**	A	*GW*	LA
42127 †	**GN**	A	*GN*	EC
42128 †	**GN**	A	*GN*	EC
42129	**FG**	A	*GW*	LA
42130 s	**V**	P		LM
42131 u	**MN**	P	*MM*	NL
42132 u	**MN**	P	*MM*	NL
42133 u	**MN**	P	*MM*	NL
42134	**GN**	A	*GN*	EC
42135 u	**MN**	P	*MM*	NL
42136 u	**MN**	P	*MM*	NL
42137 u	**MN**	P	*MM*	NL
42138 d	**FG**	A	*GW*	LA
42139 u	**MN**	P	*MM*	NL
42140 u	**MN**	P	*MM*	NL
42141 u	**MN**	P	*MM*	NL
42143	**FG**	A	*GW*	LA
42144	**FG**	A	*GW*	LA
42145	**FG**	A	*GW*	LA
42146	**GN**	A	*GN*	EC
42147 u	**MN**	P	*MM*	NL
42148 u	**MN**	P	*MM*	NL
42149 u	**MN**	P	*MM*	NL
42150	**GN**	A	*GN*	EC
42151 w	**MN**	P	*MM*	NL
42152 u	**MN**	P	*MM*	NL
42153 u	**MN**	P	*MM*	NL
42154	**GN**	A	*GN*	EC
42155 w	**MN**	P	*MM*	NL
42156 u	**MN**	P	*MM*	NL
42157 u	**MN**	P	*MM*	NL
42158	**GN**	A	*GN*	EC
42159	**GN**	P	*GN*	EC
42160	**GN**	P	*GN*	EC
42161 †	**GN**	A	*GN*	EC
42162	**FG**	P	*GW*	LA
42163 w	**MN**	P	*MM*	NL
42164 u	**MN**	P	*MM*	NL
42165 u	**MN**	P	*MM*	NL
42166	**FG**	P	*GW*	LA
42167 *h	**FD**	FG	*GW*	LA
42168 *h	**FD**	FG	*GW*	LA
42169 *h	**FD**	FG	*GW*	LA
42170	**FG**	P	*GW*	LA
42171	**GN**	A	*GN*	EC
42172	**GN**	A	*GN*	EC
42173	**FG**	P	*GW*	LA
42174	**FG**	P	*GW*	LA
42175 s	**V**	FG		ZD+
42176 s	**V**	FG		ZD+
42177 s	**V**	FG		ZD+
42178 s	**MN**	P		ZD+
42179	**GN**	A	*GN*	EC
42180	**GN**	A	*GN*	EC
42181	**GN**	A	*GN*	EC
42182	**GN**	A	*GN*	EC
42183 d	**FG**	A	*GW*	LA
42184	**FG**	A	*GW*	LA
42185	**FG**	A	*GW*	LA
42186	**GN**	A	*GN*	EC
42187 s	**MN**	P		LA+
42188 †	**GN**	A	*GN*	EC
42189 †	**GN**	A	*GN*	EC
42190	**GN**	A	*GN*	EC
42191	**GN**	A	*GN*	EC
42192	**GN**	A	*GN*	EC

42193		**GN**	A	*GN*	EC		42244		**GN**	A	*GN*	EC
42194	w	**MN**	P	*MM*	NL		42245		**FG**	A	*GW*	LA
42195		**FG**	P	*GW*	LA		42246	s	**MN**	P		ZD+
42196		**FG**	A	*GW*	LA		42247	s	**MN**	P		ZD+
42197		**FG**	A	*GW*	LA		42248	s	**MN**	P		ZD+
42198		**GN**	A	*GN*	EC		42249	s	**MN**	P		ZD+
42199		**GN**	A	*GN*	EC		42250		**FG**	A	*GW*	LA
42200	d	**FG**	A	*GW*	LA		42251	d	**FG**	A	*GW*	LA
42201	d	**FG**	A	*GW*	LA		42252		**FG**	A	*GW*	LA
42202	d	**FG**	A	*GW*	LA		42253		**FG**	A	*GW*	LA
42203		**FG**	A	*GW*	LA		42254		**FG**	P	*GW*	LA
42204		**FG**	A	*GW*	LA		42255	d	**FG**	A	*GW*	LA
42205	u	**MN**	P	*MM*	NL		42256		**FG**	A	*GW*	LA
42206	d	**FG**	A	*GW*	LA		42257		**FG**	A	*GW*	LA
42207	d	**FG**	A	*GW*	LA		42258		**FG**	P	*GW*	LA
42208		**FG**	A	*GW*	LA		42259	*k	**FD**	A	*GW*	LA
42209		**FG**	A	*GW*	LA		42260		**FG**	A	*GW*	LA
42210	u	**MN**	P	*MM*	NL		42261		**FG**	A	*GW*	LA
42211	d	**FG**	A	*GW*	LA		42262		**FG**	P	*GW*	LA
42212		**FG**	A	*GW*	LA		42263		**FG**	A	*GW*	LA
42213		**FG**	A	*GW*	LA		42264	d	**FG**	A	*GW*	LA
42214		**FG**	A	*GW*	LA		42265		**FG**	P	*GW*	LA
42215		**GN**	A	*GN*	EC		42266		**FG**	A	*GW*	LA
42216		**FG**	A	*GW*	LA		42267	d	**FG**	A	*GW*	LA
42217		**FG**	P	*GW*	LA		42268	d	**FG**	A	*GW*	LA
42218		**FG**	P	*GW*	LA		42269	d	**FG**	A	*GW*	LA
42219		**GN**	A	*GN*	EC		42271	d	**FG**	A	*GW*	LA
42220	w	**MN**	P	*MM*	NL		42272		**FG**	A	*GW*	LA
42221		**FG**	A	*GW*	LA		42273		**FG**	A	*GW*	LA
42222		**FG**	P	*GW*	LA		42275	d	**FG**	A	*GW*	LA
42223		**FG**	P	*GW*	LA		42276		**FG**	A	*GW*	LA
42224		**FG**	P	*GW*	LA		42277		**FG**	A	*GW*	LA
42225	u	**MN**	P	*MM*	NL		42279	d	**FG**	A	*GW*	LA
42226		**GN**	A	*GN*	EC		42280		**FG**	A	*GW*	LA
42227	u	**MN**	P	*MM*	NL		42281		**FG**	A	*GW*	LA
42228	u	**MN**	P	*MM*	NL		42283		**FG**	A	*GW*	LA
42229	u	**MN**	P	*MM*	NL		42284		**FG**	A	*GW*	LA
42230	u	**MN**	P	*MM*	NL		42285		**FG**	A	*GW*	LA
42231		**FG**	FG	*GW*	LA		42286	s	**V**	P		LM
42232		**FG**	FG	*GW*	LA		42287	d	**FG**	A	*GW*	LA
42233		**FG**	FG	*GW*	LA		42288		**FG**	A	*GW*	LA
42234	s	**V**	P		LM		42289		**FG**	A	*GW*	LA
42235		**GN**	A	*GN*	EC		42290	s	**V**	P		LM
42236		**FG**	A	*GW*	LA		42291	d	**FG**	A	*GW*	LA
42237	s	**GN**	P	*GN*	EC		42292	d	**FG**	A	*GW*	LA
42238	†	**GN**	A	*GN*	EC		42293		**FG**	A	*GW*	LA
42239	†	**GN**	A	*GN*	EC		42294	s	**V**	P		LM
42240		**GN**	A	*GN*	EC		42295	d	**FG**	A	*GW*	LA
42241		**GN**	A	*GN*	EC		42296		**FG**	A	*GW*	LA
42242		**GN**	A	*GN*	EC		42297		**FG**	A	*GW*	LA
42243		**GN**	A	*GN*	EC		42299	d	**FG**	A	*GW*	LA

42300		**FG**	A	*GW*	LA	42323		**GN**	A	*GN*	EC
42301		**FG**	A	*GW*	LA	42324	w	**MN**	P	*MM*	NL
42302	s	**V**	FG		ZI+	42325		**FG**	A	*GW*	LA
42303	s	**V**	FG		ZD+	42326	s	**GN**	P	*GN*	EC
42304	s	**V**	FG		ZD+	42327	w	**MN**	P	*MM*	NL
42305	s	**V**	FG		ZD+	42328	w	**MN**	P	*MM*	NL
42306	s	**GN**	P	*GN*	EC	42329	w	**MN**	P	*MM*	NL
42307	s	**GN**	P	*GN*	EC	42330	s	**GN**	P	*GN*	EC
42308	s	**MN**	P		ZD+	42331	w	**MN**	P	*MM*	NL
42309	s	**MN**	P		ZD+	42332		**FG**	A	*GW*	LA
42314		**FG**	P	*GW*	LA	42333		**FG**	A	*GW*	LA
42315		**FG**	P	*GW*	LA	42334		**FG**	A	*GW*	LA
42316		**FG**	P	*GW*	LA	42335	u	**MN**	P	*MM*	NL
42317		**FG**	P	*GW*	LA	42336	s	**MN**	P		ZD+
42318	s	**V**	P		ZD+	42337	w	**MN**	P	*MM*	NL
42319	s	**V**	P		ZD+	42338	s	**MN**	P		ZD+
42320	s	**V**	P		ZD+	42339	w	**MN**	P	*MM*	NL
42321	s	**V**	P		ZD+	42340		**GN**	A	*GN*	EC
42322	s	**V**	P		LM	42341	u	**MN**	P	*MM*	NL

42342	(44082)	u	**MN**	A	*MM*	NL
42343	(44095)		**FG**	A	*GW*	LA
42344	(44092)	d	**FG**	A	*GW*	LA
42345	(44096)	d	**FG**	A	*GW*	LA
42346	(41053)		**FG**	A	*GW*	LA
42347	(41054)	d	**FG**	A	*GW*	LA
42348	(41073)	d	**FG**	A	*GW*	LA
42349	(41074)		**FG**	A	*GW*	LA
42350	(41047)		**FG**	A	*GW*	LA
42351	(41048)		**FG**	A	*GW*	LA
42352	(42142, 41176)	u	**MN**	P	*MM*	NL
42353	(42001, 41171)		**FT**	FG		ZD+
42354	(42114, 41175)		**GN**	A	*GN*	EC
42355	(42000, 41172)		**GN**	A	*GN*	EC
42356	(42002, 41173)		**FG**	A	*GW*	LA
42357	(41002, 41174)		**GN**	A	*GN*	EC
42360	(44084, 45084)		**FG**	A	*GW*	LA
42361	(44099, 42000)		**FG**	A	*GW*	LA
42362	(42011, 41178)		**FG**	A	*GW*	LA
42363	(41082)	†	**GN**	A	*GN*	EC

GJ2G (TGS)   TRAILER GUARD'S STANDARD

44000. Lot No. 30953 Derby 1980. 33.47 t.
44001–44090. Lot No. 30949 Derby 1980–82. 33.47 t.
44091–44094. Lot No. 30964 Derby 1982. 33.47 t.
44097–44101. Lot No. 30970 Derby 1982. 33.47 t.

As built –/65 1T (w –/63 1T 1W).
* Refurbished First Great Western vehicles. New Grammer seating.
h "High density" FGW vehicles with toilet removed for trolley store. –/71.
s Fitted with centre luggage stack –/63 1T.
t Fitted with centre luggage stack –/61 1T.

44000 w	**FG**	P	*GW*	LA		44047 s	**MN**	P	*MM*	NL
44001 w	**FG**	A	*GW*	LA		44048 s	**MN**	P	*MM*	NL
44002 w	**FG**	A	*GW*	LA		44049 w	**FT**	A	*GW*	LA
44003 w	**FG**	A	*GW*	LA		44050 s	**MN**	P	*MM*	NL
44004 w	**FG**	A	*GW*	LA		44051 s	**MN**	P	*MM*	NL
44005 w	**FG**	A	*GW*	LA		44052 s	**MN**	P	*MM*	NL
44007 w	**FG**	A	*GW*	LA		44054 s	**MN**	P	*MM*	NL
44008 w	**FG**	A	*GW*	LA		44055 w	**GN**	FG		ZD+
44009 w	**FG**	A	*GW*	LA		44056 w	**GN**	A	*GN*	EC
44010 w	**FG**	A	*GW*	LA		44057 w	**GN**	P	*GN*	EC
44011 w	**FG**	A	*GW*	LA		44058 w	**GN**	A	*GN*	EC
44012 s	**MN**	A	*MM*	NL		44059 w	**FG**	A	*GW*	LA
44013 w	**FG**	A	*GW*	LA		44060 t	**MN**	P		ZD+
44014 w	**FG**	A	*GW*	LA		44061 w	**GN**	A	*GN*	EC
44015 w	**FG**	A	*GW*	LA		44063 w	**GN**	A	*GN*	EC
44016 w	**FG**	A	*GW*	LA		44064 w	**FG**	A	*GW*	LA
44017 s	**MN**	A	*MM*	NL		44065 t	**V**	P		LM
44018 w	**FG**	A	*GW*	LA		44066 w	**FG**	A	*GW*	LA
44019 w	**GN**	A	*GN*	EC		44067 w	**FG**	A	*GW*	LA
44020 w	**FG**	A	*GW*	LA		44068 *h	**FD**	FG	*GW*	LA
44021 t	**V**	P		LM		44069 t	**MN**	P		LA+
44022 w	**FG**	A	*GW*	LA		44070 s	**MN**	P	*MM*	NL
44023 w	**FG**	A	*GW*	LA		44071 s	**MN**	P	*MM*	NL
44024 w	**FG**	A	*GW*	LA		44072 t	**V**	P		LM
44025 w	**FG**	A	*GW*	LA		44073 s	**MN**	P	*MM*	NL
44026 w	**FG**	A	*GW*	LA		44074 s	**FG**	FG	*GW*	LA
44027 s	**MN**	P	*MM*	NL		44075 t	**GN**	P	*GN*	EC
44028 w	**FG**	A	*GW*	LA		44076 t	**V**	FG		ZD+
44029 w	**FG**	A	*GW*	LA		44077 w	**GN**	A	*GN*	EC
44030 w	**FG**	A	*GW*	LA		44078 t	**MN**	P		ZD+
44031 w	**GN**	A	*GN*	EC		44079 w	**FG**	P	*GW*	LA
44032 w	**FG**	A	*GW*	LA		44080 w	**GN**	A	*GN*	EC
44033 w	**FG**	A	*GW*	LA		44081 t	**V**	FG		ZD+
44034 w	**FG**	A	*GW*	LA		44083 s	**MN**	P	*MM*	NL
44035 w	**FG**	A	*GW*	LA		44085 s	**MN**	P	*MM*	NL
44036 w	**FG**	A	*GW*	LA		44086 w	**FG**	A	*GW*	LA
44037 w	**FG**	A	*GW*	LA		44088 t	**V**	P		LM
44038 w	**FG**	A	*GW*	LA		44089 t	**V**	P		LM
44039 w	**FG**	A	*GW*	LA		44090 w	**FG**	P	*GW*	LA
44040 w	**FG**	A	*GW*	LA		44091 t	**V**	P		ZD+
44041 s	**MN**	P	*MM*	NL		44093 w	**FG**	A	*GW*	LA
44042 t	**MN**	P		ZD+		44094 w	**GN**	A	*GN*	EC
44043 w	**FG**	A	*GW*	LA		44097 w	**FG**	P	*GW*	LA
44044 w	**MN**	P	*MM*	NL		44098 w	**GN**	A	*GN*	EC
44045 w	**GN**	A	*GN*	EC		44100 t	**V**	FG		LA+
44046 s	**MN**	P	*MM*	NL		44101 w	**FG**	P	*GW*	LA

▲ **Passenger Carrying Coaching Stock.** Riviera Trains Oxford Blue-liveried Mark 1 Restaurant Buffet 1683 is seen at Pantyffynnon on 15/07/06. **Bob Sweet**

▼ Newly repainted into BR Southern Region Green, Mark 1 Restaurant Buffet 1961 is seen at Derby on 30/08/06. **Ryan Tranmer**

▲ BR Western Region Chocolate & Cream-liveried Mark 1 FO 3140 passes
Llandeilo on 15/07/06.   **Bob Sweet**

▼ BR Maroon-liveried Mark 1 TSO 4912 (carrying the number 99318) is seen at
Abbotswood Junction on 12/05/06.   **Bob Sweet**

▲ Riviera Trains-liveried Facelifted Mark 2A TSO 5366 is seen at Bedford on 10/06/06.   **Mark Beal**

▼ Royal Train-liveried Mark 2B Royal Household Couchette 2920 is seen at Hexthorpe, Doncaster on 13/07/06.   **Robert Pritchard**

▲ VSOE Northern Belle-liveried Mark 2D FO 3174 "GLAMIS" is seen near Sheffield on 30/05/06 forming part of the VSOE Northern Belle luxury train.
Robert Pritchard

▼ Blue Pullman-liveried Mark 2F FO 3350 is seen at Milton Keynes Central on 08/04/06. **Mark Beal**

▲ Arriva Trains-liveried Mark 2F TSO 6013 is seen at Fishguard Harbour on
06/09/06.   **Robert Pritchard**

▼ Inter-City-liveried Mark 2F BSO 9526 is seen at Hereford on 19/11/05.
                                                          Stephen Widdowson

▲ "One"-liveried Mark 3A Restaurant Buffet First 10241 is seen at Pudding Mill Lane on 08/09/06.   **Robert Pritchard**

▼ EWS maroon-liveried Mark 3A FO 11039 is seen at Colton Junction South forming part of the EWS Company Train on 30/07/06.   **Bob Sweet**

▲ "One"-liveried Mark 3A TSO 12082 is seen at Manningtree on 02/05/06.
Robert Pritchard

▼ First Great Western replaced the Mark 2 day coaches on their Sleeper service with Mark 3s in 2006. On 03/06/06 Mark 3B BFO 17173 is seen at London Paddington.
Mark Beal

▲ Old First Great Western-liveried Mark 3A Sleeping Car 10532 is seen at Long Rock depot, Penzance on 01/07/06. **Stephen Widdowson**

▼ First Group-liveried Mark 3A Sleeping Car 10680 passes Bridge of Orchy on 10/06/06. **Robert Pritchard**

▲ Midland Mainline-liveried HST Trailer Buffet First 40754 is seen at Chesterfield on 06/07/06. **Robert Pritchard**

▼ New First Group "Dynamic Lights"-liveried HST Trailer First 41003 is seen at Newton Abbot on 03/04/06. **Robert Pritchard**

▲ HST Trailer Guard's Standard 44094 in GNER livery is seen at Falkirk Grahamston on 13/07/06. **Adrian Sumner**

▼ Refurbished GNER-liveried "Mallard" Mark 4 FO 11282 is seen at Doncaster on 30/06/06. **Robert Pritchard**

▲ GWR First Class Saloon 9004 is seen at Ascot on 22/06/06 as part of the Queen of Scots luxury train.   **Mark Beal**

▼ Royal Scotsman Saloon 99967 is seen at Haymarket on 22/07/06.   **Mark Beal**

▲ Pullman First Bar 310 "PEGASUS", also carrying "THE TRIANON BAR" branding, is seen at Eastleigh on 16/07/05.　　　　**Bob Sweet**

▼ **Non-Passenger Carrying Coaching Stock.** Newly converted Nanking Blue-liveried Mark 1 Kitchen Car 80042 is seen passing Reedham, forming part of the Blue Pullman set, on 09/09/06.　　　　**Robert Pritchard**

▲ "One"-liveried Mark 3B DVT 82121 leads the 09.00 London Liverpool Street–Norwich through Pudding Mill Lane on 08/09/06, with 90015 providing power at the rear. **Robert Pritchard**

▼ GNER-liveried Mark 4 DVT 82202 leaves Newark North Gate with the 13.30 Edinburgh–Finsbury Park on 29/04/06. **Paul Shannon**

▲ Porterbrook-liveried Translator/barrier vehicle 6378 is seen at Norton Junction on 19/07/06. **Bob Sweet**

▼ HSBC Rail-liveried EMU Translator Vehicle 975867 is seen at Mossend Yard on 30/05/06. **Ian Lothian**

▲ Network Rail Spray Coach 99019 is seen at Rugby as part of the Network Rail Railhead Treatment Train on 11/08/05. **Bob Sweet**

▼ Structure Gauging Train Driving Trailer Coach 975081 (converted from a BR Mark 1 BSK) is seen at Derby RTC on 24/09/05. **Paul Robertson**

▲ Network Rail New Measurement Train Conference Coach 975814 is seen at Doncaster on 21/01/06. **Simon Wright**

▼ Serco Railtest-liveried Track Recording Coach 999508 is seen at Derby RTC on 16/07/06. **Paul Robertson**

2.3. SALOONS

Several specialist passenger carrying vehicles, normally referred to as saloons are permitted to run on the National Rail system. Many of these are to pre-nationalisation designs.

WCJS FIRST SALOON

Built 1892 by LNWR, Wolverton. Originally dining saloon mounted on six-wheel bogies. Rebuilt with new underframe with four-wheel bogies in 1927. Rebuilt 1960 as observation saloon with DMU end. Gangwayed at other end. The interior has a saloon, kitchen, guards vestibule and observation lounge. Gresley bogies. 19/– 1T. 28.5 t. 75 m.p.h.

Non-standard livery: London & North Western Railway.

41   (484, 45018)   x   **0**   SH   *SH*   CJ

LNWR DINING SALOON

Built 1890 by LNWR, Wolverton. Mounted on the underframe of LMS GUV 37908 in the 1980s. Contains kitchen and dining area seating 12 at tables for two. Gresley bogies. 10/–. 75 m.p.h. 25.4 t.

Non-standard livery: London & North Western Railway.

159   (5159)   x   **0**   SH   *SH*   CJ

GNR FIRST CLASS SALOON

Built 1912 by GNR, Doncaster. Contains entrance vestibule, lavatory, two separate saloons, library and luggage space. Gresley bogies. 19/– 1T. 75 m.p.h. 29.4 t.

Non-standard livery: Teak.

807   (4807)   x   **0**   SH   *SH*   CJ

LNER GENERAL MANAGERS SALOON

Built 1945 by LNER, York. Gangwayed at one end with a veranda at the other. The interior has a dining saloon seating 12, kitchen, toilet, office and nine seat lounge. 21/– 1T. B4 bogies. 75 m.p.h. ETH3. 35.7 t.

1999   (902260)   **M**   GS   *GS*   CS   DINING CAR No. 2

GENERAL MANAGER'S SALOON

Renumbered 1989 from London Midland Region departmental series. Formerly the LMR General Manager's saloon. Rebuilt from LMS period 1 BFK M 5033 M to dia. 1654 and mounted on the underframe of BR suburban BS M 43232. Screw couplings have been removed. B4 bogies. 100 m.p.h. ETH2X.

LMS Lot No. 326 Derby 1927. 27.5 t.

6320   (5033, DM 395707) x   **M**   62   *62*   SK

GWR FIRST CLASS SALOON

Built 1930 by GWR, Swindon. Contains saloons at either end with body end observation windows, staff compartment, central kitchen and pantry/bar. Numbered DE321011 when in departmental service with British Railways. 20/– 1T. GWR bogies. 75 m.p.h. 34 t.

GWR Lot No. 1431 1930.

9004   **CH**   RA *SH*   CJ

LMS INSPECTION SALOONS

Built as engineers' inspection saloons. Non-gangwayed. Observation windows at each end. The interior layout consists of two saloons interspersed by a central lavatory/kitchen/guards section. BR Mark 1 bogies. 80 m.p.h. 31.5 t.

45020–45026. Lot No. LMS 1356 Wolverton 1944.
45029. Lot No. LMS 1327 Wolverton 1942.
999503. Lot No. BR Wagon Lot. 3093 Wolverton 1957.

45020		**E**	E	*E*	ML
45026	v	**M**	HN		CS
45029	v	**E**	E		ML
999503	v	**M**	E		OM

"QUEEN OF SCOTS" SERVICE CARS

Converted from BR Mark 1 BSKs. Commonwealth bogies. 100 m.p.h. ETH2.

Non-standard livery: London & North Western Railway.

99035. Lot No. 30699 Wolverton 1962–63.
99886. Lot No. 30721 Wolverton 1963.

99035	(35322)	x	**0**	SH	*SH*	CJ	SERVICE CAR No. 2
99886	(35407)	x	**0**	SH	*SH*	CJ	SERVICE CAR No. 1

VSOE SUPPORT CARS

Converted 1983 (§ 199x) from BR Mark 1 BSK (§ Courier vehicle converted from Mark 1 BSK 1986–87). Toilet retained and former compartment area replaced with train manager's office, crew locker room, linen store and dry goods store. The former luggage area has been adapted for use as an engineers' compartment and workshop. Commonwealth bogies. 100 m.p.h. ETH2.

99538. Lot No. 30229 Metro-Cammell 1955–57. 36 t.
99545. Lot No. 30721 Wolverton 1963. 37 t.

99538 (34991)		**PC**	VS	*VS*	SL	BAGGAGE CAR No. 9
99545 (35466, 80207) §	**PC**	VS	*VS*	SL	BAGGAGE CAR No. 11

VSOE BRAKE LUGGAGE VAN

Converted 199x from BR Mark 1 BG. Guard's compartment retained and former baggage area adapted for stowage of passengers' luggage. pg. B4 bogies. 100 m.p.h. ETH1X.

Lot No. 30162 Pressed Steel 1956–57. 30.5 t.

99554 (80867, 92904)	**G**	VS	CP

RAILFILMS KITCHEN/SLEEPING SALOON

Converted from BR Mark 1 SK. Contains three sleeping cabins with showers and toilets and a large kitchen/pantry. Commonwealth bogies. 100 m.p.h. ETH 4.

Lot No. 30726 York 1963.

Non-standard livery: London & North Western Railway.

99884 (26208, 19208)	**0**	RA	CS	State Car No. 84

ROYAL SCOTSMAN SALOONS

Built 1960 by Metro-Cammell as Pullman Parlour First (§ Pullman Kitchen First) for East Coast Main Line services. Rebuilt 1990 as sleeping cars with four twin sleeping rooms (*§ three twin sleeping rooms and two single sleeping rooms at each end). Commonwealth bogies. 38.5 t.

99961 (324 AMBER) *	**M**	GS	*GS*	CS	STATE CAR 1
99962 (329 PEARL)	**M**	GS	*GS*	CS	STATE CAR 2
99963 (331 TOPAZ)	**M**	GS	*GS*	CS	STATE CAR 3
99964 (313 FINCH) §	**M**	GS	*GS*	CS	STATE CAR 4

Built 1960 by Metro-Cammell as Pullman Kitchen First for East Coast Main Line services. Rebuilt 1990 as observation car with open verandah seating 32. Commonwealth bogies. 38.5 t.

99965 (319 SNIPE)   M   GS   *GS*   CS   OBSERVATION CAR

Built 1960 by Metro-Cammell as Pullman Kitchen First for East Coast Main Line services. Rebuilt 1993 as dining car. Commonwealth bogies. 38.5 t.

99967 (317 RAVEN)   M   GS   *GS*   CS   DINING CAR

Mark 3A. Converted from SLEP at Carnforth Railway Restoration and Engineering Services in 1997. BT10 bogies. Attendant's and adjacent two sleeping compartments converted to generator room containing a 160 kW Volvo unit. In 99968 four sleeping compartments remain for staff use with another converted for use as a staff shower and toilet. The remaining five sleeping compartments have been replaced by two passenger cabins. In 99969 seven sleeping compartments remain for staff use. A further sleeping compartment, along with one toilet, have been converted to store rooms. The other two sleeping compartments have been combined to form a crew mess. ETH7X. 41.5 t.

Lot. No. 30960 Derby 1981–3.

99968 (10541)   M   GS   *GS*   CS   STATE CAR 5
99969 (10556)   M   GS   *GS*   CS   SERVICE CAR

RAILFILMS "LMS CLUB CAR"

Converted from BR Mark 1 TSO at Carnforth Railway Restoration and Engineering Services in 1994. Contains kitchen, pantry and two dining saloons. 20/– 1T. Commonwealth bogies. 100 m.p.h. ETH 4.

Lot. No. 30724 York 1963. 37 t.

99993 (5067)   M   RA   *WT*   OM   LMS CLUB CAR

BR INSPECTION SALOON

Mark 1. Short frames. Non-gangwayed. Observation windows at each end. The interior layout consists of two saloons interspersed by a central lavatory/kitchen/guards/luggage section. BR Mark 1 bogies. 90 m.p.h.

Lot No. BR Wagon Lot. 3379 Swindon 1960. 30.5 t.

999509   E   E   *E*   ML

2.4. PULLMAN CAR COMPANY SERIES

Pullman cars have never generally been numbered as such, although many have carried numbers, instead they have carried titles. However, a scheme of schedule numbers exists which generally lists cars in chronological order. In this section those numbers are shown followed by the car's title. Cars described as "kitchen" contain a kitchen in addition to passenger accommodation and have gas cooking unless otherwise stated. Cars described as "parlour" consist entirely of passenger accommodation. Cars described as "brake" contain a compartment for the use of the guard and a luggage compartment in addition to passenger accommodation.

PULLMAN PARLOUR FIRST

Built 1927 by Midland Carriage and Wagon Company. Gresley bogies. 26/– 2T. ETH 2. 41 t.

213 MINERVA   **PC** VS *VS* SL

PULLMAN PARLOUR FIRST

Built 1928 by Metropolitan Carriage and Wagon Company. Gresley bogies. 24/– 2T. ETH 4. 40 t.

| 239 | AGATHA | **PC** | VS | | SL |
| 243 | LUCILLE | **PC** | VS | *VS* | SL |

PULLMAN KITCHEN FIRST

Built 1925 by BRCW. Rebuilt by Midland Carriage & Wagon Company in 1928. Gresley bogies. 20/– 1T. ETH 4. 41 t.

245 IBIS   **PC** VS *VS* SL

PULLMAN PARLOUR FIRST

Built 1928 by Metropolitan Carriage and Wagon Company. Gresley bogies. 24/– 2T. ETH 4.

254 ZENA   **PC** VS *VS* SL

PULLMAN KITCHEN FIRST

Built 1928 by Metropolitan Carriage and Wagon Company. Gresley bogies. 20/– 1T. ETH 4. 42 t.

255 IONE   **PC** VS *VS* SL

PULLMAN KITCHEN COMPOSITE

Built 1932 by Metropolitan Carriage and Wagon Company. Originally included in 6-Pul EMU. Electric cooking. EMU bogies. 12/16 1T.

264	RUTH	**PC**	VS		SL

PULLMAN KITCHEN FIRST

Built 1932 by Metropolitan Carriage and Wagon Company. Originally included in "Brighton Belle" EMUs but now used as hauled stock. Electric cooking. B5 (SR) bogies (§ EMU bogies). 20/– 1T. ETH 2. 44 t.

280	AUDREY		**PC**	VS	*VS*	SL
281	GWEN		**PC**	VS	*VS*	SL
283	MONA	§	**PC**	VS		SL
284	VERA		**PC**	VS	*VS*	SL

PULLMAN PARLOUR THIRD

Built 1932 by Metropolitan Carriage and Wagon Company. Originally included in "Brighton Belle" EMUs. EMU bogies. –/56 2T.

285	CAR No. 85	**PC**	VS	SL
286	CAR No. 86	**PC**	VS	SL

PULLMAN BRAKE THIRD

Built 1932 by Metropolitan Carriage and Wagon Company. Originally driving motor cars in "Brighton Belle" EMUs. Traction and control equipment removed for use as hauled stock. EMU bogies. –/48 1T.

288	CAR No. 88	**PC**	VS	SL
292	CAR No. 92	**PC**	VS	SL
293	CAR No. 93	**PC**	VS	SL

PULLMAN PARLOUR FIRST

Built 1951 by Birmingham Railway Carriage and Wagon Company. Gresley bogies. 32/– 2T. ETH 3. 39 t.

301	PERSEUS	**PC**	VS	*VS*	SL

Built 1952 by Pullman Car Company, Preston Park using underframe and bogies from 176 RAINBOW, the body of which had been destroyed by fire. Gresley bogies. 26/– 2T. ETH 4. 38 t.

302	PHOENIX	**PC**	VS	*VS*	SL

PULLMAN PARLOUR FIRST

Built 1951 by Birmingham Railway Carriage & Wagon Company. Gresley bogies. 32/– 2T. ETH 3. 39 t.

308 CYGNUS   **PC**   VS   *VS*   SL

PULLMAN FIRST BAR

Built 1951 by Birmingham Railway Carriage & Wagon Company. Rebuilt 1999 by Blake Fabrications, Edinburgh with original timber-framed body replaced by a new fabricated steel body. Contains kitchen, bar, dining saloon and coupé. Electric cooking. Gresley bogies. 14/– 1T. ETH 3.

310 PEGASUS   **PC**   RA   *WT*   OM

Also carries "THE TRIANON BAR" branding.

PULLMAN KITCHEN SECOND

Built 1960–1961 by Metro-Cammell for East Coast Main Line services. Commonwealth bogies. –/30 1T. 40 t.

335 CAR No. 335   x **PC**   VT   *VT*   TM

PULLMAN PARLOUR SECOND

Built 1960–1961 by Metro-Cammell for East Coast Main Line services. Commonwealth bogies. –/42 2T. 38.5 t.

348 CAR No. 348   x **M**   WC   *WC*   CS
349 CAR No. 349   x **PC**   VT   *VT*   TM
353 CAR No. 353   x **PC**   VT   *VT*   TM

PULLMAN SECOND BAR

Built 1960–1961 by Metro-Cammell for East Coast Main Line services. Commonwealth bogies. –/24 + 17 bar seats. 38.5 t.

354 THE HADRIAN BAR x **PC**   WC   *WC*   CS

2.5. PASSENGER COACHING STOCK AWAITING DISPOSAL

This list contains the last known locations of coaching stock awaiting disposal. The definition of which vehicles are "awaiting disposal" is somewhat vague, but generally speaking these are vehicles of types not now in normal service or vehicles which have been damaged by fire, vandalism or collision.

1644 CS	5475 CT	10201 ZB
1650 CS	5480 KT	10327 ZC
1652 CS	5505 CS	10515 IS
1655 CS	5647 CD	10540 OM
1663 CS	5780 CT	10547 IS
1670 CS	5781 CT	10554 TO
1674 SL	5800 CT	10555 AS
1688 CS	5831 CT	10663 IS
1981 TH	5836 CT	10682 TO
2127 CS	5973 CT	10709 ZN
3181 CD	6155 CT	10713 OM
3521 BR	6178 HM	11024 ZH
4849 CD	6335 LA	11037 ZD
4854 CD	6339 EC	12023 ZD
4860 CS	6345 EC	12070 ZD
4932 BR	6356 CV	12096 ZN
4997 CS	6357 CV	13306 CS
5226 BH	6360 NL	13320 CS
5267 KT	6361 NL	13323 CS
5354 SN	6523 CS	18837 CS
5389 OM	6813 CT	19013 CS
5410 CT	6816 CT	34525 CS
5420 OM	6825 CT	35513 CD
5443 CT	6900 Cambridge Station Yard	35516 CD
5446 KT	6901 Cambridge Station Yard	41043 ZB
5454 CT	9458 ZB	
5471 CT	9482 NL	

Former Gatwick Express stock awaiting disposal:

Advertising livery: As **GX** but with a deep blue instead of a white lower bodyside, advertising Continental Airlines.

8208	**AL**	GB	PB	72507 (3412)	72643 (6040)		
8312	**GX**	GB	SN	72622 (6004)	72711 (6109)	72623 (6118)	
8315	**GX**	GB	SN	72636 (6071)	72714 (6092)	72645 (5942)	
Spare	**GX**	NR	AS	72608 (6077)			
Spare	**AL**	NR	AS	72641 (6079)			
Spare	**GX**	NR	AS	72702 (6099)			

2.6. 99xxx RANGE NUMBER CONVERSION TABLE

The following table is presented to help readers identify vehicles which may carry numbers in the 99xxx range, the former private owner number series which is no longer in general use.

99xxx	BR No.	99xxx	BR No.	99xxx	BR No.	99xxx	BR No.
99040	21232	99322	5600	99532 Pullman 308		99675	552
99041	35476	99323	5704	99534 Pullman 245		99676	553
99052	Saloon 41	99324	5714	99535 Pullman 213		99677	586
99121	3105	99325	5727	99536 Pullman 254		99678	504
99125	3113	99326	4954	99537 Pullman 280		99679	506
99127	3117	99327	5044	99539 Pullman 255		99680	17102
99128	3130	99328	5033	99541 Pullman 243		99710	18767
99131	1999	99329	4931	99542	889202	99712	18893
99141	17041	99348 Pullman 348		99543 Pullman 284		99716	18808
99241	35449	99349 Pullman 349		99546 Pullman 281		99718	18862
99304	21256	99353 Pullman 353		99547 Pullman 292		99721	18756
99311	1882	99354 Pullman 354		99548 Pullman 293		99722	18806
99312	35463	99361 Pullman 361		99670	546	99723	35459
99316	13321	99371	3128	99671	548	99792	17019
99317	3766	99405	35486	99672	549	99880	159
99318	4912	99530 Pullman 301		99673	550	99881	807
99319	17168	99531 Pullman 302		99674	551	99953	35468
99321	5299						

2.7. PRESERVED LOCOMOTIVE SUPPORT COACHES TABLE

The following table lists support coaches and the BR numbers of the locomotives which they normally support at present. These coaches can spend considerable periods of time off the National Rail system when the locomotives they support are not being used on that system.

14007	61264	35329	RL locos	35465	46201	35508	BQ locos
17013	60019	35333	6024	35468	NM locos	35517	BQ locos
17019	30777	35449	45231	35470	TM locos	35518	34067
17041	71000	35453	5051	35476	46233	80204	WC locos
17096	35028	35461	5029	35479	SV locos	80217	WC locos
21232	46233	35463	WC locos	35486	SV locos	80220	62005
35317	30850						

2.8. MARK 4 FIXED FORMATION SETS

The GNER Mark 4 sets generally run in fixed formations since their "Mallard" refurbishment at Bombardier, Wakefield (2003–05). These rakes are listed below. Class 91 locomotives are positioned next to Coach B.

Set	B	C	D	E	G	H	K	L	M	DVT
BN01	12207	12417	12415	12414	12307	10307	11298	11301	11401	82207
BN02	12232	12402	12450	12448	12302	10302	11299	11302	11402	82202
BN03	12201	12401	12459	12478	12301	10320	11277	11303	11403	82219
BN04	12202	12480	12421	12518	12327	10303	11278	11304	11404	82209
BN05	12209	12486	12520	12522	12300	10326	11219	11305	11405	82210
BN06	12208	12406	12420	12422	12313	10309	11279	11306	11406	82208
BN07	12231	12411	12405	12489	12329	10323	11280	11307	11407	82204
BN08	12205	12481	12485	12407	12328	10300	11229	11308	11408	82211
BN09	12230	12513	12483	12514	12308	10331	11281	11309	11409	82215
BN10	12214	12419	12488	12443	12305	10304	11282	11310	11410	82205
BN11	12203	12437	12436	12484	12315	10308	11283	11311	11411	82218
BN12	12212	12431	12404	12426	12330	10333	11284	11312	11412	82212
BN13	12228	12469	12430	12424	12311	10313	11285	11313	11413	82213
BN14	12229	12410	12526	12423	12312	10332	11201	11314	11414	82206
BN15	12226	12442	12409	12515	12309	10306	11286	11315	11415	82214
BN16	12213	12428	12445	12433	12304	10315	11287	11316	11416	82225
BN17	12223	12444	12427	12432	12303	10324	11288	11317	11417	82222
BN18	12215	12453	12468	12467	12324	10305	11289	11318	11418	82220
BN19	12211	12434	12400	12470	12310	10318	11290	11319	11419	82201
BN20	12224	12477	12439	12440	12326	10321	11241	11320	11420	82200
BN21	12222	12461	12441	12476	12323	10330	11244	11321	11421	82227
BN22	12210	12452	12460	12473	12316	10301	11291	11322	11422	82230
BN23	12225	12454	12456	12455	12318	10325	11292	11323	11423	82226
BN24	12219	12447	12425	12403	12319	10328	11293	11324	11424	82229
BN25	12217	12446	12519	12464	12322	10312	11294	11325	11425	82216
BN26	12220	12474	12465	12429	12325	10311	11295	11326	11426	82223
BN27	12216	12449	12466	12538	12317	10319	11237	11327	11427	82228
BN28	12218	12458	12463	12533	12320	10310	11273	11328	11428	82217
BN29	12204	12462	12457	12438	12321	10317	11998	11329	11429	82231
BN30	12227	12471	12534	12472	12331	10329	11999	11330	11430	82203
Spare	12200									82224

3. DIESEL MULTIPLE UNITS

INTRODUCTION

DMU CLASSES

DMU Classes are listed in class number order. Principal details and dimensions are quoted for each class in metric and/or imperial units as considered appropriate bearing in mind common usage in the UK.

All dimensions and weights are quoted for vehicles in an "as new" condition with all necessary supplies (e.g. oil, water, sand) on board. Dimensions are quoted in the order Length – Width. All lengths quoted are over buffers or couplers as appropriate. Where two lengths are quoted, the first refers to outer vehicles in a set and the second to inner vehicles. All width dimensions quoted are maxima.

NUMERICAL LISTINGS

DMUs are listed in numerical order of set – using current numbers as allocated by the RSL. Individual "loose" vehicles are listed in numerical order after vehicles formed into fixed formations. Where numbers carried are different from those officially allocated these are noted in class headings where appropriate. Where sets or vehicles have been renumbered in recent years, former numbering detail is shown in parentheses. Each entry is laid out as in the following example:

Set No.	Detail	Livery	Owner	Operator	Depot	Formation		Name
142 073	v	**AV**	A	*AW*	CF	55723	55769	Myfanwy

Detail Differences. Detail differences which currently affect the areas and types of train which vehicles may work are shown, plus differences in interior layout. Where such differences occur within a class, these are shown either in the heading information or alongside the individual set or vehicle number. The following standard abbreviation is used:

r   Radio Electronic Token Block (RETB) equipment fitted.

In all cases use of the above abbreviation indicates the equipment indicated is normally operable. Meaning of non-standard abbreviations is detailed in individual class headings.

Set Formations. Regular set formations are shown where these are normally maintained. Readers should note set formations might be temporarily varied from time to time to suit maintenance and/or operational requirements. Vehicles shown as "spare" are not formed in any regular set formation.

Codes. Codes are used to denote the livery, owner, operator and depot of each unit. Details of these will be found in section 7 of this book. Where a unit or spare car is off-lease, the operator column will be left blank.

Names. Only names carried with official sanction are listed. As far as possible names are shown in UPPER/lower case characters as actually shown on the name carried on the vehicle(s). Unless otherwise shown, complete units are regarded as named rather than just the individual car(s) which carry the name.

GENERAL INFORMATION

CLASSIFICATION AND NUMBERING

First generation ("Heritage") DMUs are classified in the series 100–139.
Second generation DMUs are classified in the series 140–199.
Diesel-electric multiple units are classified in the series 200–249.
Service units are classified in the series 930–999.
First and second generation individual cars are numbered in the series 50000–59999 and 79000–79999.

DEMU individual cars are numbered in the series 60000–60999, except for a few former EMU vehicles which retain their EMU numbers.

Service stock individual cars are numbered in the series 975000–975999 and 977000–977999, although this series is not exclusively used for DMU vehicles.

OPERATING CODES

These codes are used by train operating company staff to describe the various different types of vehicles and normally appear on data panels on the inner (i.e. non driving) ends of vehicles.

The first part of the code describes whether or not the car has a motor or a driving cab as follows:

DM Driving motor.
M   Motor
DT Driving trailer
T   Trailer

The next letter is a "B" for cars with a brake compartment.

This is followed by the saloon details:

F   First
S   Standard
C   Composite

so denotes a semi-open vehicle (part compartments, part open). All other vehicles are assumed to consist solely of open saloons.

L denotes a vehicle with a lavatory compartment.

Finally vehicles with a buffet are suffixed RB or RMB for a miniature buffet.

Where two vehicles of the same type are formed within the same unit, the above codes may be suffixed by (A) and (B) to differentiate between the vehicles.

A composite is a vehicle containing both first and standard class accommodation, whilst a brake vehicle is a vehicle containing separate specific accommodation for the conductor.

Special Note: Where vehicles have been declassified, the correct operating code which describes the actual vehicle layout is quoted in this publication.

BUILD DETAILS

Lot Numbers
Vehicles ordered under the auspices of BR were allocated a lot (batch) number when ordered and these are quoted in class headings and sub-headings.

Builders
These are shown in class headings. Abbreviations used are found in section 8.7.

Information on sub-contracting works which built parts of vehicles e.g. the underframes etc. is not shown.

ACCOMMODATION

The information given in class headings and sub-headings is in the form F/S nT (or TD) nW. For example 12/54 1T 1W denotes 12 first class and 54 standard class seats, one toilet and one space for a wheelchair. A number in brackets denotes tip-up seats (in addition to the fixed seats). Tip-up seats in vestibules do not count. The seating layout of open saloons is shown as 2+1, 2+2 or 3+2 as the case may be. Where units have first class accommodation as well as standard and the layout is different for each class then these are shown separately prefixed by "1:" and "2:". TD denotes a toilet suitable for use by a disabled person.

3.1. DIESEL MECHANICAL & DIESEL HYDRAULIC UNITS

3.1.1. FIRST GENERATION UNITS

CLASS 121   PRESSED STEEL SUBURBAN

First generation units used by Chiltern Railways on selected Aylesbury–Princes Risborough services (121 020) and by Arriva Trains Wales on Cardiff Queen Street–Cardiff Bay shuttles (121 032).
Construction: Steel.
Engines: Two Leyland 1595 of 112 kW (150 h.p.) at 1800 r.p.m.
Transmission: Mechanical. Cardan shaft and freewheel to a four-speed epicyclic gearbox and final drive.
Bogies: DD10.
Brakes: Vacuum.
Couplers: Screw.
Dimensions: 20.45 x 2.82 m.
Gangways: Non gangwayed single cars with cabs at each end.
Wheel arrangement: 1-A + A-1.
Doors: Manually-operated slam.
Maximum Speed: 70 m.p.h.
Seating Layout: 3+2 facing.
Multiple Working: "Blue Square" coupling code. First Generation vehicles cannot be coupled to Second Generation units.

55020/55032. DMBS. Lot No. 30518 1960/1961. –/65. 38.0 t.

Non-standard livery: 121 032 All over Chiltern blue with a silver stripe.

Notes: Fitted with central door locking.

121 020 formerly in departmental use as unit 960 002 (977722).

121 032 formerly in departmental use as 977842, and more recently in preservation at The Railway Age, Crewe.

121 020	**0**	CR	*CR*	AL	55020
121 032	**AV**	AW	*AW*	CF	55032

3.1.2. SECOND GENERATION UNITS

All units in this section have air brakes and are equipped with public address, with transmission equipment on driving vehicles and flexible diaphragm gangways. Except where otherwise stated, transmission is Voith 211r hydraulic with a cardan shaft to a Gmeinder GM190 final drive.

CLASS 142   PACER   BREL DERBY/LEYLAND

DMS–DMSL.

Construction: Steel underframe, aluminium alloy body and roof. Built from Leyland National bus parts on four-wheeled underframes.
Engines: One Cummins LTA10-R of 172 kW (230 h.p.) at 2100 r.p.m.
Couplers: BSI at outer ends, bar within unit.
Dimensions: 15.45 x 2.80 m.
Gangways: Within unit only.   **Wheel Arrangement:** 1-A + A-1.
Doors: Twin-leaf inward pivoting.   **Maximum Speed:** 75 m.p.h.
Seating Layout: 3+2 mainly unidirectional bus/bench style unless stated.
Multiple Working: Within class and with Classes 143, 144, 150, 153, 155, 156, 158 and 159.

55542–55591. DMS. Lot No. 31003 1985–1986. –/62 (s –/56, t –/53 or 55 1W, u –/52 or 54 1W, v –/46(6) 2W). 24.5 t.
55592–55641. DMSL. Lot No. 31004 1985–1986. –/59 1T (s –/50 1T, u –/60 1T, v –/44(6) 1T 2W). 25.0 t.
55701–55746. DMS. Lot No. 31013 1986–1987. –/62 (s –/56, t –/53 or 55 1W, u –/52 or 54 1W, v –/46(6) 2W). 24.5 t.
55747–55792. DMSL. Lot No. 31014 1986–1987. –/59 1T (s –/50 1T, u –/60 1T, v–/44(6) 1T 2W). 25.0 t.

Notes: s Fitted with 2+2 individual high-back seating.

t Northern (ex-First North Western) facelifted units – DMS fitted with a luggage/ bicycle rack and wheelchair space.

u Merseytravel units – Fitted with 3+2 individual low-back seating.

v Refurbished Arriva Trains Wales units. Fitted with 2+2 individual Chapman seating.

142 001	t	**NW**	A	*NO*	NH	55542	55592
142 002	v	**AV**	A	*AW*	CF	55543	55593
142 003		**NW**	A	*NO*	NH	55544	55594
142 004	t	**NW**	A	*NO*	NH	55545	55595
142 005	t	**NW**	A	*NO*	NH	55546	55596
142 006	v	**AV**	A	*AW*	CF	55547	55597
142 007	t	**NW**	A	*NO*	NH	55548	55598
142 009	t	**NW**	A	*NO*	NH	55550	55600	Newton Heath 125 1876–2001
142 010	v	**AV**	A	*AW*	CF	55551	55601
142 011	t	**NW**	A	*NO*	NH	55552	55602
142 012	t	**NW**	A	*NO*	NH	55553	55603

142 013		**NW**	A	*NO*	NH	55554	55604
142 014	t	**NW**	A	*NO*	NH	55555	55605
142 015	s	**AV**	A	*NO*	HT	55556	55606
142 016	s	**AV**	A	*NO*	HT	55557	55607
142 017	s	**AV**	A	*NO*	HT	55558	55608
142 018	s	**AV**	A	*NO*	HT	55559	55609
142 019	s	**AV**	A	*NO*	HT	55560	55610
142 020	s	**AV**	A	*NO*	HT	55561	55611
142 021	s	**AV**	A	*NO*	HT	55562	55612
142 022	s	**AV**	A	*NO*	HT	55563	55613
142 023	t	**NW**	A	*NO*	NH	55564	55614
142 024	s	**AV**	A	*NO*	HT	55565	55615
142 025	s	**NS**	A	*NO*	HT	55566	55616
142 026	s	**AV**	A	*NO*	HT	55567	55617
142 027	t	**NW**	A	*NO*	NH	55568	55618
142 028	t	**NW**	A	*NO*	NH	55569	55619
142 029		**NW**	A	*NO*	NH	55570	55620
142 030		**NW**	A	*NO*	NH	55571	55621
142 031	t	**NW**	A	*NO*	NH	55572	55622
142 032	t	**NW**	A	*NO*	NH	55573	55623
142 033	t	**NW**	A	*NO*	NH	55574	55624
142 034	t	**NW**	A	*NO*	NH	55575	55625
142 035	t	**NW**	A	*NO*	NH	55576	55626
142 036	t	**NW**	A	*NO*	NH	55577	55627
142 037	t	**NW**	A	*NO*	NH	55578	55628
142 038	t	**NW**	A	*NO*	NH	55579	55629
142 039	t	**NW**	A	*NO*	NH	55580	55630
142 040	t	**NW**	A	*NO*	NH	55581	55631
142 041	u	**MY**	A	*NO*	NH	55582	55632
142 042	u	**MY**	A	*NO*	NH	55583	55633
142 043	u	**MY**	A	*NO*	NH	55584	55634
142 044	u	**MY**	A	*NO*	NH	55585	55635
142 045	u	**MY**	A	*NO*	NH	55586	55636
142 046	u	**MY**	A	*NO*	NH	55587	55637
142 047	u	**MY**	A	*NO*	NH	55588	55638
142 048	u	**MY**	A	*NO*	NH	55589	55639
142 049	u	**MY**	A	*NO*	NH	55590	55640
142 050	s	**NS**	A	*NO*	HT	55591	55641
142 051	u	**MY**	A	*NO*	NH	55701	55747
142 052	u	**MY**	A	*NO*	NH	55702	55748
142 053	u	**MY**	A	*NO*	NH	55703	55749
142 054	u	**MY**	A	*NO*	NH	55704	55750
142 055	u	**MY**	A	*NO*	NH	55705	55751
142 056	u	**MY**	A	*NO*	NH	55706	55752
142 057	u	**MY**	A	*NO*	NH	55707	55753
142 058	u	**MY**	A	*NO*	NH	55708	55754
142 060	t	**NW**	A	*NO*	NH	55710	55756
142 061	t	**NW**	A	*NO*	NH	55711	55757
142 062	t	**NW**	A	*NO*	NH	55712	55758
142 063	t	**NW**	A	*NO*	NH	55713	55759
142 064	t	**NW**	A	*NO*	NH	55714	55760

142 065	s	**NS**	A	*NO*	HT	55715	55761	
142 066	s	**NS**	A	*NO*	HT	55716	55762	
142 067		**NW**	A	*NO*	NH	55717	55763	
142 068	t	**NW**	A	*NO*	NH	55718	55764	
142 069	v	**AV**	A	*AW*	CF	55719	55765	
142 070	t	**NW**	A	*NO*	NH	55720	55766	
142 071	v	**AV**	A	*NO*	HT	55721	55767	
142 072	v	**AV**	A	*AW*	CF	55722	55768	
142 073	v	**AV**	A	*AW*	CF	55723	55769	Myfanwy
142 074	v	**AV**	A	*AW*	CF	55724	55770	
142 075	v	**AV**	A	*AW*	CF	55725	55771	
142 076	v	**AV**	A	*AW*	CF	55726	55772	
142 077	v	**AV**	A	*AW*	CF	55727	55773	
142 078	s	**AV**	A	*NO*	HT	55728	55774	
142 079	s	**AV**	A	*NO*	HT	55729	55775	
142 080	v	**AV**	A	*AW*	CF	55730	55776	
142 081	v	**AV**	A	*AW*	CF	55731	55777	
142 082	v	**AV**	A	*AW*	CF	55732	55778	
142 083	v	**AV**	A	*AW*	CF	55733	55779	
142 084	s	**AV**	A	*NO*	HT	55734	55780	
142 085	v	**AV**	A	*AW*	CF	55735	55781	
142 086	s	**AV**	A	*NO*	HT	55736	55782	
142 087	s	**AV**	A	*NO*	HT	55737	55783	
142 088	s	**AV**	A	*NO*	HT	55738	55784	
142 089	s	**AV**	A	*NO*	HT	55739	55785	
142 090	s	**AV**	A	*NO*	HT	55740	55786	
142 091	s	**AV**	A	*NO*	HT	55741	55787	
142 092	s	**AV**	A	*NO*	HT	55742	55788	
142 093	s	**AV**	A	*NO*	HT	55743	55789	
142 094	s	**AV**	A	*NO*	HT	55744	55790	
142 095	s	**AV**	A	*NO*	HT	55745	55791	
142 096	s	**AV**	A	*NO*	HT	55746	55792	

CLASS 143   PACER   ALEXANDER/BARCLAY

DMS–DMSL. Similar design to Class 142, but bodies built by W. Alexander with Barclay underframes.

Construction: Steel underframe, aluminium alloy body and roof. Alexander bus bodywork on four-wheeled underframes.
Engines: One Cummins LTA10-R of 172 kW (230 h.p.) at 2100 r.p.m.
Couplers: BSI at outer ends, bar within unit.
Dimensions: 15.45 x 2.80 m.
Gangways: Within unit only.   **Wheel Arrangement:** 1-A + A-1.
Doors: Twin-leaf inward pivoting.   **Maximum Speed:** 75 m.p.h.
Seating Layout: 2+2 high-back Chapman seating, mainly unidirectional.
Multiple Working: Within class and with Classes 142, 144, 150, 153, 155, 156, 158 and 159.

DMS. Lot No. 31005 Andrew Barclay 1985–1986. –/48(6) 2W. 24.0 t.
DMSL. Lot No. 31006 Andrew Barclay 1985–1986. –/44(6) 1T 2W. 24.5 t.

143 601	**AV**	BC	*AW*	CF	55642	55667	
143 602	**AV**	P	*AW*	CF	55651	55668	
143 603	**BI**	P	*GW*	PM	55658	55669	
143 604	**AV**	P	*AW*	CF	55645	55670	
143 605	**AV**	P	*AW*	CF	55646	55671	
143 606	**AV**	P	*AW*	CF	55647	55672	
143 607	**AV**	P	*AW*	CF	55648	55673	
143 608	**AV**	P	*AW*	CF	55649	55674	
143 609	**AV**	CC	*AW*	CF	55650	55675	Sir Tom Jones
143 610	**AV**	BC	*AW*	CF	55643	55676	
143 611	**BI**	P	*GW*	PM	55652	55677	
143 612	**BI**	P	*GW*	PM	55653	55678	
143 614	**AV**	BC	*AW*	CF	55655	55680	
143 616	**AV**	P	*AW*	CF	55657	55682	
143 617	**BI**	RI	*GW*	PM	55644	55683	
143 618	**BI**	RI	*GW*	PM	55659	55684	
143 619	**BI**	RI	*GW*	PM	55660	55685	
143 620	**BI**	P	*GW*	PM	55661	55686	
143 621	**BI**	P	*GW*	PM	55662	55687	
143 622	**AV**	P	*AW*	CF	55663	55688	
143 623	**AV**	P	*AW*	CF	55664	55689	
143 624	**AV**	P	*AW*	CF	55665	55690	
143 625	**AV**	P	*AW*	CF	55666	55691	

CLASS 144   PACER   ALEXANDER/BREL DERBY

DMS–DMSL or DMS–MS–DMSL. As Class 143, but underframes built by BREL.

Construction: Steel underframe, aluminium alloy body and roof. Alexander bus bodywork on four-wheeled underframes.
Engines: One Cummins LTA10-R of 172 kW (230 h.p.) at 2100 r.p.m.
Couplers: BSI at outer ends, bar within unit.
Dimensions: 15.45/15.43 x 2.80 m.
Gangways: Within unit only.   **Wheel Arrangement:** 1-A + A-1.
Doors: Twin-leaf inward pivoting.   **Maximum Speed:** 75 m.p.h.
Seating Layout: 2+2 high-back Richmond seating, mainly unidirectional.
Multiple Working: Within class and with Classes 142, 143, 150, 153, 155, 156, 158 and 159.

DMS. Lot No. 31015 BREL Derby 1986–1987. –/45(3) 1W 24.0 t.
MS. Lot No. BREL Derby 31037 1987. –/58. 23.5 t.
DMSL. Lot No. BREL Derby 31016 1986–1987. –/42(3) 1T. 24.5 t.

Note: The centre cars of the 3-car units are owned by West Yorkshire PTE, although managed by Porterbrook Leasing Company.

144 001	**YP**	P	*NO*	NL	55801	55824
144 002	**YP**	P	*NO*	NL	55802	55825
144 003	**YP**	P	*NO*	NL	55803	55826
144 004	**YP**	P	*NO*	NL	55804	55827
144 005	**YP**	P	*NO*	NL	55805	55828
144 006	**YP**	P	*NO*	NL	55806	55829

144 007	**YP**	P	*NO*	NL	55807		55830
144 008	**YP**	P	*NO*	NL	55808		55831
144 009	**YP**	P	*NO*	NL	55809		55832
144 010	**YP**	P	*NO*	NL	55810		55833
144 011	**YP**	P	*NO*	NL	55811		55834
144 012	**YP**	P	*NO*	NL	55812		55835
144 013	**YP**	P	*NO*	NL	55813		55836
144 014	**YP**	P	*NO*	NL	55814	55850	55837
144 015	**YP**	P	*NO*	NL	55815	55851	55838
144 016	**YP**	P	*NO*	NL	55816	55852	55839
144 017	**YP**	P	*NO*	NL	55817	55853	55840
144 018	**YP**	P	*NO*	NL	55818	55854	55841
144 019	**YP**	P	*NO*	NL	55819	55855	55842
144 020	**YP**	P	*NO*	NL	55820	55856	55843
144 021	**YP**	P	*NO*	NL	55821	55857	55844
144 022	**YP**	P	*NO*	NL	55822	55858	55845
144 023	**YP**	P	*NO*	NL	55823	55859	55846

Name (carried on DMSL):

144 001 THE PENISTONE LINE PARTNERSHIP

CLASS 150/0   SPRINTER   BREL YORK

DMSL–MS–DMS. Prototype Sprinter.

Construction: Steel.
Engines: One Cummins NT-855-R4 of 213 kW (285 h.p.) at 2100 r.p.m.
Bogies: BX8P (powered), BX8T (non-powered).
Couplers: BSI at outer end of driving vehicles, bar non-driving ends.
Dimensions: 20.06/20.18 x 2.82 m.
Gangways: Within unit only.   **Wheel Arrangement:** 2-B + 2-B + B-2.
Doors: Twin-leaf sliding.   **Maximum Speed:** 75 m.p.h.
Seating Layout: 3+2 (mainly unidirectional).
Multiple Working: Within class and with Classes 142, 143, 144, 153, 155, 156, 158, 159 and 170.

DMSL. Lot No. 30984 1984. –/72 1T. 35.4 t.
MS. Lot No. 30986 1984. –/92. 34.1 t.
DMS. Lot No. 30985 1984. –/76. 29.5 t.

| 150 001 | **CC** | A | *CT* | TS | 55200 | 55400 | 55300 |
| 150 002 | **CC** | A | *CT* | TS | 55201 | 55401 | 55301 |

CLASS 150/1 SPRINTER BREL YORK

DMSL–DMS or DMSL–DMSL–DMS or DMSL–DMS–DMS.

Construction: Steel.
Engines: One Cummins NT855R5 of 213 kW (285 h.p.) at 2100 r.p.m.
Bogies: BP38 (powered), BT38 (non-powered).
Couplers: BSI.
Dimensions: 19.74 x 2.82 m.
Gangways: Within unit only.
Doors: Twin-leaf sliding.
Wheel Arrangement: 2-B (+ 2–B) + B-2.
Maximum Speed: 75 m.p.h.
Seating Layout: 3+2 facing as built but Centro units were reseated with mainly unidirectional seating.
Multiple Working: Within class and with Classes 142, 143, 144, 153, 155, 156, 158, 159 and 170.

DMSL. Lot No. 31011 1985–1986. –/72 1T (s –/59 1TD (except 52144 which is –/62 1TD), t –/71 1W 1T, u –/71 1T). 38.3 t.
DMS. Lot No. 31012 1985–1986. –/76 (s –/65, u –/70). 38.1 t.

Non-standard livery: 150 134 Plain dark blue.

Notes: The centre cars of 3-car units are Class 150/2 vehicles. For details see Class 150/2.

150 133–150 150 have been refurbished with individual Chapman seating.

150 003	u	**CO**	A	*CT*	TS	52103	57210	57103
150 004	u	**CC**	A	*CT*	TS	52104	52216	57104
150 005	u	**CC**	A	*CT*	TS	52105	57210	57105
150 006	u	**CC**	A	*CT*	TS	52106	57214	57106
150 007	u	**CC**	A	*CT*	TS	52107	52202	57107
150 008	u	**CC**	A	*CT*	TS	52108	57216	57108
150 009	u	**CC**	A	*CT*	TS	52109	57202	57109
150 010	u	**CC**	A	*CT*	TS	52110	57226	57110
150 011	u	**CC**	A	*CT*	TS	52111	52204	57111
150 012	u	**CC**	A	*CT*	TS	52112	57206	57112
150 013	u	**CC**	A	*CT*	TS	52113	52226	57113
150 014	u	**CC**	A	*CT*	TS	52114	57204	57114
150 015	u	**CC**	A	*CT*	TS	52115	52206	57115
150 016	u	**CC**	A	*CT*	TS	52116	57212	57116
150 017	u	**CC**	A	*CT*	TS	52117	57209	57117
150 018	u	**CO**	A	*CT*	TS	52118	52220	57118
150 019	u	**CC**	A	*CT*	TS	52119	57220	57119
150 022	u	**CC**	A	*CT*	TS	52122	57214	57122
150 101	u	**CC**	A	*CT*	TS	52101	57101	
150 102	u	**CC**	A	*CT*	TS	52102	57102	
150 120	t	**SL**	A	*SL*	WN	52120	57120	Gospel Oak–Barking 2000
150 121	u	**SL**	A	*SL*	WN	52121	57121	Willesden Eight
150 123	t	**SL**	A	*SL*	WN	52123	57123	Richard Crane
150 124	u	**CC**	A	*CT*	TS	52124	57124	
150 125	u	**CC**	A	*CT*	TS	52125	57125	
150 126	u	**CO**	A	*CT*	TS	52126	57126	

150 127	t	**SL**	A	*SL*	WN	52127	57127	Bletchley TMD
150 128	t	**SL**	A	*SL*	WN	52128	57128	Community Forest
150 129	t	**SL**	A	*SL*	WN	52129	57129	MARSTON VALE
150 130	t	**SL**	A	*SL*	WN	52130	57130	Bedford–Bletchley 150
150 131	t	**SL**	A	*SL*	WN	52131	57131	LESLIE CRABBE
150 132		**CO**	A	*CT*	TS	52132	57132	
150 133	s	**NW**	A	*SL*	WN	52133	57133	Northern Star
150 134	s	**O**	A	*NO*	NH	52134	57134	
150 135	s	**NW**	A	*NO*	NH	52135	57135	
150 136	s	**NW**	A	*NO*	NH	52136	57136	
150 137	s	**NW**	A	*NO*	NH	52137	57137	
150 138	s	**NW**	A	*NO*	NH	52138	57138	
150 139	s	**NW**	A	*NO*	NH	52139	57139	
150 140	s	**NW**	A	*NO*	NH	52140	57140	
150 141	s	**NW**	A	*NO*	NH	52141	57141	
150 142	s	**NW**	A	*NO*	NH	52142	57142	
150 143	s	**NW**	A	*NO*	NH	52143	57143	
150 144	s	**NW**	A	*NO*	NH	52144	57144	
150 145	s	**NO**	A	*NO*	NH	52145	57145	
150 146	s	**NW**	A	*NO*	NH	52146	57146	
150 147	s	**NW**	A	*NO*	NH	52147	57147	
150 148	s	**NW**	A	*NO*	NH	52148	57148	
150 149	s	**NW**	A	*NO*	NH	52149	57149	
150 150	s	**NW**	A	*NO*	NH	52150	57150	

CLASS 150/2   SPRINTER   BREL YORK

DMSL–DMS.

Construction: Steel.
Engines: One Cummins NT855R5 of 213 kW (285 h.p.) at 2100 r.p.m.
Bogies: BP38 (powered), BT38 (non-powered).
Couplers: BSI.   **Dimensions:** 19.74 x 2.82 m.
Gangways: Throughout.   **Wheel Arrangement:** 2-B + B-2.
Doors: Twin-leaf sliding.   **Maximum Speed:** 75 m.p.h.
Seating Layout: 3+2 mainly unidirectional seating as built, but many units have now been refurbished with 2+2 seating.
Multiple Working: Within class and with Classes 142, 143, 144, 153, 155, 156, 158, 159 and 170.

DMSL. Lot No. 31017 1986–1987. –/73 1T (s –/62 1TD, t –/60(4) 1T, v –/60(8) 1T, w –/60(8) 1T). 37.5 t.
DMS. Lot No. 31018 1986–1987. –/76 (* –/68, s –/70, t –/56(10) 1W, v –/56(15), w –/56(17)). 36.5 t.

Notes: Units in **NW** livery have been refurbished with 3+2 Chapman seating.

Units in **AR** livery (now in use with Central Trains) have 3+2 Chapman seating and Central decals applied on their Anglia livery.

t Refurbished Arriva Trains Wales units with 2+2 Primarius seating.

vw Refurbished Arriva Trains Wales and First Great Western units with 2+2 Chapman seating.

150 201	s	**NW**	A	*NO*	NH	52201	57201
150 203	s	**NW**	A	*NO*	NH	52203	57203
150 205	s	**NW**	A	*NO*	NH	52205	57205
150 207	s	**NW**	A	*NO*	NH	52207	57207
150 208	t	**AV**	P	*AW*	CF	52208	57208
150 211	s	**NW**	A	*NO*	NH	52211	57211
150 213	*	**AR**	P	*CT*	TS	52213	57213
150 215	s	**NW**	A	*NO*	NH	52215	57215
150 217	*	**AR**	P	*CT*	TS	52217	57217
150 218	s	**NW**	A	*NO*	NH	52218	57218
150 219	w	**WZ**	P	*GW*	PM	52219	57219
150 221	w	**WZ**	P	*GW*	PM	52221	57221
150 222	s	**NW**	A	*NO*	NH	52222	57222
150 223	s	**NW**	A	*NO*	NH	52223	57223
150 224	s	**NW**	A	*NO*	NH	52224	57224
150 225	s	**NW**	A	*NO*	NH	52225	57225
150 227	*	**AR**	P	*CT*	TS	52227	57227
150 228		**NO**	P	*NO*	NH	52228	57228
150 229	*	**AR**	P	*CT*	TS	52229	57229
150 230	*	**AR**	P	*AW*	CF	52230	57230	The Tamar Kingfisher
150 231	*	**AR**	P	*CT*	TS	52231	57231
150 232	w	**WZ**	P	*GW*	PM	52232	57232	The Coastal Connection
150 233	w	**WZ**	P	*GW*	PM	52233	57233	The Lady Margaret of Looe Valley
150 234	w	**WZ**	P	*GW*	PM	52234	57234	The National Trust
150 235	*	**AR**	P	*CT*	TS	52235	57235
150 236	w	**WZ**	P	*AW*	CF	52236	57236
150 237	*	**AR**	P	*CT*	TS	52237	57237
150 238	w	**WZ**	P	*GW*	PM	52238	57238	Exeter Explorer
150 239	w	**WZ**	P	*GW*	PM	52239	57239
150 240	w	**WZ**	P	*AW*	CF	52240	57240
150 241	w	**WZ**	P	*AW*	CF	52241	57241	The Tarka Belle
150 242	w	**WZ**	P	*AW*	CF	52242	57242
150 243	w	**WZ**	P	*GW*	PM	52243	57243
150 244	w	**FI**	P	*GW*	PM	52244	57244
150 245	t	**AV**	P	*AW*	CF	52245	57245
150 246	w	**WZ**	P	*GW*	PM	52246	57246
150 247	w	**WZ**	P	*GW*	PM	52247	57247
150 248	w	**WZ**	P	*GW*	PM	52248	57248	The Great Gardens of Cornwall
150 249	w	**FI**	P	*GW*	PM	52249	57249
150 250	t	**AV**	P	*AW*	CF	52250	57250
150 251	w	**WZ**	P	*AW*	CF	52251	57251
150 252	t	**AV**	P	*AW*	CF	52252	57252
150 253	w	**WZ**	P	*AW*	CF	52253	57253	The Exmouth Avocet
150 254	w	**WZ**	P	*AW*	CF	52254	57254
150 255	*	**AR**	P	*CT*	TS	52255	57255
150 256	t	**AV**	P	*AW*	CF	52256	57256
150 257	*	**AR**	P	*CT*	TS	52257	57257
150 258	t	**AV**	P	*AW*	CF	52258	57258
150 259	t	**AV**	P	*AW*	CF	52259	57259

150 260	t	**AV**	P	*AW*	CF	52260	57260	
150 261	w	**WZ**	P	*GW*	PM	52261	57261	The Riviera Flyer
150 262	t	**AV**	P	*AW*	CF	52262	57262	
150 263	w	**WZ**	P	*GW*	PM	52263	57263	The Castles of Cornwall
150 264	t	**AV**	P	*AW*	CF	52264	57264	
150 265	w	**WZ**	P	*GW*	PM	52265	57265	The Falmouth Flyer
150 266	w	**WZ**	P	*GW*	PM	52266	57266	The Whitley Wonder
150 267	v	**AV**	P	*AW*	CF	52267	57267	
150 268		**NO**	P	*NO*	NH	52268	57268	
150 269		**NO**	P	*NO*	NH	52269	57269	
150 270		**NO**	P	*NO*	NH	52270	57270	
150 271		**NO**	P	*NO*	NH	52271	57271	
150 272		**NO**	P	*NO*	NH	52272	57272	
150 273		**NO**	P	*NO*	NH	52273	57273	
150 274		**NO**	P	*NO*	NH	52274	57274	
150 275		**NO**	P	*NO*	NH	52275	57275	
150 276		**NO**	P	*NO*	NH	52276	57276	
150 277		**NO**	P	*NO*	NH	52277	57277	
150 278	v	**AV**	P	*AW*	CF	52278	57278	
150 279	v	**AV**	P	*AW*	CF	52279	57279	
150 280	v	**AV**	P	*AW*	CF	52280	57280	
150 281	v	**AV**	P	*AW*	CF	52281	57281	
150 282	v	**AV**	P	*AW*	CF	52282	57282	
150 283	t	**AV**	P	*AW*	CF	52283	57283	
150 284	t	**AV**	P	*AW*	CF	52284	57284	
150 285	t	**AV**	P	*AW*	CF	52285	57285	

CLASS 153   SUPER SPRINTER   LEYLAND BUS

DMSL. Converted by Hunslet-Barclay, Kilmarnock from Class 155 2-car units.

Construction: Steel underframe, aluminium alloy body and roof. Built from Leyland National bus parts on bogied underframes.
Engine: One Cummins NT855R5 of 213 kW (285 h.p.) at 2100 r.p.m.
Bogies: One P3-10 (powered) and one BT38 (non-powered).
Couplers: BSI.
Dimensions: 23.21 x 2.70 m.
Gangways: Throughout.   **Wheel Arrangement:** 2-B.
Doors: Single-leaf sliding plug.   **Maximum Speed:** 75 m.p.h.
Seating Layout: 2+2 facing/unidirectional.
Multiple Working: Within class and with Classes 142, 143, 144, 150, 155, 156, 158, 159 and 170.

52301–52335. DMSL. Lot No. 31026 1987–1988. Converted under Lot No. 31115 1991–1992. –/72(3) 1T 1W (* –/69 1T 1W, s –/72 1T 1W, t –/72(2) 1T 1W, u –/70(3) 1T 1W). 41.2 t.

57301–57335. DMSL. Lot No. 31027 1987–1988. Converted under Lot No. 31115 1991–1992. –/72(3) 1T 1W (* –/69 1T 1W, u –/70(3) 1T 1W). 41.2 t.

Advertising liveries: 153 329 St. Ives Line promotional livery (light blue with dark blue doors & various images).

153 369 Looe Valley Line promotional livery (light blue with dark blue doors & various images).

Notes: Cars numbered in the 573xx series were renumbered by adding 50 to their original number so that the last two digits correspond with the set number.

Central Trains and Northern (**NW** livery) units are fitted with Chapman seating, as are Arriva Trains Wales units in **NW** livery.

Northern (**AV** livery) units are fitted with Richmond seating.

Most Arriva Trains Wales/First Great Western units have been reseated with seats removed from the company's Class 158 units.

* Chapman seating and bicycle rack.

153 301		**AV**	A	*NO*	NL	52301
153 302		**DC**	A		ZG	52302
153 303		**HW**	A	*AW*	CF	52303
153 304		**AV**	A	*NO*	NL	52304
153 305		**WX**	A	*GW*	PM	52305
153 306	r*	**1**	P	*1*	NC	52306
153 307		**AV**	A	*NO*	NL	52307
153 308		**DC**	A		ZG	52308
153 309	r*	**AR**	P	*1*	NC	52309	GERARD FIENNES
153 310		**NW**	P	*AW*	CF	52310
153 311	*	**PS**	P		CF	52311
153 312	s	**HW**	A	*AW*	CF	52312
153 313		**NW**	P		CF	52313
153 314	r*	**1**	P	*1*	NC	52314
153 315		**AV**	A	*NO*	NL	52315
153 316		**NW**	P	*NO*	NL	52316
153 317		**AV**	A	*NO*	NL	52317
153 318		**WX**	A	*GW*	PM	52318
153 319		**AV**	A	*NO*	NL	52319
153 320		**HW**	P	*AW*	CF	52320
153 321		**HW**	P	*AW*	CF	52321
153 322	r*	**AR**	P	*1*	NC	52322	BENJAMIN BRITTEN
153 323		**AV**	P	*AW*	CF	52323
153 324		**NW**	P	*NO*	NL	52324
153 325		**CT**	P	*CT*	TS	52325
153 326	*	**PS**	P		CF	52326
153 327		**HW**	A	*AW*	CF	52327
153 328		**AV**	A	*NO*	NL	52328
153 329	u	**AL**	P	*GW*	PM	52329	The St. Ives Bay Belle
153 330	s	**NW**	P	*NO*	NL	52330
153 331		**AV**	A	*NO*	NL	52331
153 332		**NW**	P	*NO*	NL	52332
153 333	s	**CT**	P	*CT*	TS	52333
153 334	t	**CT**	P	*CT*	TS	52334
153 335	r*	**AR**	P	*1*	NC	52335	MICHAEL PALIN
153 351		**AV**	A	*NO*	NL	57351
153 352		**AV**	A	*NO*	NL	57352
153 353		**AV**	A	*AW*	CF	57353

153 354	**CT**	P	*CT*	TS	57354	
153 355	**WX**	A		ZG	57355	
153 356	**CT**	P	*CT*	TS	57356	
153 357	**AV**	A	*NO*	NL	57357	
153 358	**NW**	P	*NO*	NL	57358	
153 359	**NW**	P	*NO*	NL	57359	
153 360	**NW**	P	*NO*	NL	57360	
153 361	**NW**	P	*AW*	CF	57361	
153 362	**HW**	A	*AW*	CF	57362	Dylan Thomas 1914–1953
153 363	s	**NW**	P	*NO*	NL	57363	
153 364	**CT**	P	*CT*	TS	57364	
153 365	**CT**	P	*CT*	TS	57365	
153 366	**CT**	P	*CT*	TS	57366	
153 367	**AV**	P	*AW*	CF	57367	
153 368	s	**WX**	A	*GW*	PM	57368	
153 369	u	**AL**	P	*GW*	PM	57369	The Looe Valley Explorer
153 370	**WX**	A	*GW*	PM	57370	
153 371	**CT**	P	*CT*	TS	57371	
153 372	**WX**	A	*GW*	PM	57372	
153 373	**WX**	A	*GW*	PM	57373	
153 374	**DC**	A		ZG	57374	
153 375	**CT**	P	*CT*	TS	57375	
153 376	**CT**	P	*CT*	TS	57376	
153 377	**DC**	A	*GW*	PM	57377	
153 378	**AV**	A	*NO*	NL	57378	
153 379	**CT**	P	*CT*	TS	57379	
153 380	**DC**	A	*GW*	PM	57380	
153 381	**CT**	P	*CT*	TS	57381	
153 382	**DC**	A	*GW*	PM	57382	
153 383	**CT**	P	*CT*	TS	57383	
153 384	**CT**	P	*CT*	TS	57384	
153 385	**CT**	P	*CT*	TS	57385	

CLASS 155   SUPER SPRINTER   LEYLAND BUS

DMSL–DMS.

Construction: Steel underframe, aluminium alloy body and roof. Built from Leyland National bus parts on bogied underframes.
Engines: One Cummins NT855R5 of 213 kW (285 h.p.) at 2100 r.p.m.
Bogies: One P3-10 (powered) and one BT38 (non-powered).
Couplers: BSI.
Dimensions: 23.21 x 2.70 m.
Gangways: Throughout.   **Wheel Arrangement:** 2-B + B-2.
Doors: Single-leaf sliding plug.   **Maximum Speed:** 75 m.p.h.
Seating Layout: 2+2 facing/unidirectional.
Multiple Working: Within class and with Classes 142, 143, 144, 150, 153, 156, 158, 159 and 170.

DMSL. Lot No. 31057 1988. –/80 1TD 1W (* –/76 1TD 1W). 39.0 t.
DMS. Lot No. 31058 1988. –/80. 38.6 t.

Note: These units are owned by West Yorkshire PTE, although managed by Porterbrook Leasing Company.

155 341	*	**NO**	P	*NO*	NL	52341	57341
155 342		**WY**	P	*NO*	NL	52342	57342
155 343		**WY**	P	*NO*	NL	52343	57343
155 344		**WY**	P	*NO*	NL	52344	57344
155 345	*	**NO**	P	*NO*	NL	52345	57345
155 346	*	**NO**	P	*NO*	NL	52346	57346
155 347	*	**NO**	P	*NO*	NL	52347	57347

CLASS 156 SUPER SPRINTER METRO-CAMMELL

DMSL–DMS.

Construction: Steel.
Engines: One Cummins NT855R5 of 213 kW (285 h.p.) at 2100 r.p.m.
Bogies: One P3-10 (powered) and one BT38 (non-powered).
Couplers: BSI.
Dimensions: 23.03 x 2.73 m.
Gangways: Throughout.   **Wheel Arrangement:** 2-B + B-2.
Doors: Single-leaf sliding.   **Maximum Speed:** 75 m.p.h.
Seating Layout: 2+2 facing/unidirectional.
Multiple Working: Within class and with Classes 142, 143, 144, 150, 153, 155, 158, 159 and 170.

DMSL. Lot No. 31028 1988–1989. –/74 (†* –/72, st –/70, u –/68) 1TD 1W. 38.6 t.
DMS. Lot No. 31029 1987–1989. –/76 (q –/78, † –/74, tu –/72) 37.9 t.

Notes: s Fitted with Chapman seating.

q Fitted with Richmond seating.

Non-standard liveries: 156 451 Northern experimental(1). Two-tone lilac with a white swoosh.
156 425, 156 460 and 156 464 Northern experimental(2). White with two-tone lilac swooshs.

Advertising livery: 156 402 Anglia in Bloom. White with various images.

156 401	*	**CT**	P	*CT*	TS	52401	57401
156 402	r*	**AL**	P	*1*	NC	52402	57402
156 403	*	**CT**	P	*CT*	TS	52403	57403
156 404	*	**CT**	P	*CT*	TS	52404	57404
156 405	*	**CT**	P	*CT*	TS	52405	57405
156 406	*	**CT**	P	*CT*	TS	52406	57406
156 407	r*	**CT**	P	*1*	NC	52407	57407
156 408	*	**CT**	P	*CT*	TS	52408	57408
156 409	r*	**1**	P	*1*	NC	52409	57409
156 410	*	**CT**	P	*CT*	TS	52410	57410
156 411	*	**CT**	P	*CT*	TS	52411	57411
156 412	r*	**CT**	P	*1*	NC	52412	57412
156 413	*	**CT**	P	*CT*	TS	52413	57413
156 414	*	**CT**	P	*CT*	TS	52414	57414

156 415	*	CT	P	CT	TS	52415	57415
156 416	r*	1	P	1	NC	52416	57416
156 417	r*	1	P	1	NC	52417	57417
156 418	r*	CT	P	1	NC	52418	57418
156 419	r*	CT	P	1	NC	52419	57419
156 420	s	FS	P	NO	NH	52420	57420
156 421	s	FS	P	NO	NH	52421	57421
156 422	r*	1	P	1	NC	52422	57422
156 423	s	FS	P	NO	NH	52423	57423
156 424	s	FS	P	NO	NH	52424	57424
156 425	s	0	P	NO	NH	52425	57425
156 426	s	FB	P	NO	NH	52426	57426
156 427	s	FB	P	NO	NH	52427	57427
156 428	s	FS	P	NO	NH	52428	57428
156 429	s	FB	P	NO	NH	52429	57429
156 430	t	SC	A	SR	CK	52430	57430
156 431	t	SC	A	SR	CK	52431	57431
156 432	t	SC	A	SR	CK	52432	57432
156 433	t	SC	A	SR	CK	52433	57433
156 434	t	SC	A	SR	CK	52434	57434
156 435	t	SC	A	SR	CK	52435	57435
156 436	†	SC	A	SR	CK	52436	57436
156 437	t	SC	A	SR	CK	52437	57437
156 438	q	NS	A	NO	HT	52438	57438
156 439	t	SC	A	SR	CK	52439	57439
156 440	s	FS	P	NO	NH	52440	57440
156 441	s	FS	P	NO	NH	52441	57441
156 442	t	SC	A	SR	CK	52442	57442
156 443	q	NS	A	NO	HT	52443	57443
156 444	q	NS	A	NO	HT	52444	57444
156 445	u	SC	A	SR	CK	52445	57445
156 446	rt	FS	A	SR	CK	52446	57446
156 447	ru	FS	A	SR	CK	52447	57447
156 448	q	NS	A	NO	HT	52448	57448
156 449	u	FS	A	SR	CK	52449	57449
156 450	ru	FS	A	SR	CK	52450	57450
156 451	q	0	A	NO	HT	52451	57451
156 452	s	FS	P	NO	NH	52452	57452
156 453	ru	FS	A	SR	CK	52453	57453
156 454	q	NS	A	NO	HT	52454	57454
156 455	s	FB	P	NO	NH	52455	57455
156 456	rt	FS	A	SR	CK	52456	57456
156 457	rt	FS	A	SR	CK	52457	57457
156 458	rt	FS	A	SR	CK	52458	57458
156 459	s	FB	P	NO	NH	52459	57459
156 460	s	0	P	NO	NH	52460	57460
156 461	s	NO	P	NO	NH	52461	57461
156 462		FS	A	SR	CK	52462	57462
156 463	q	NS	A	NO	HT	52463	57463
156 464	s	0	P	NO	NH	52464	57464
156 465	ru	FS	A	SR	CK	52465	57465

156 466	s	**FS**	P	*NO*	NH	52466	57466
156 467		**FS**	A	*SR*	CK	52467	57467
156 468	q	**NS**	A	*NO*	NH	52468	57468
156 469	q	**NO**	A	*NO*	HT	52469	57469
156 470	q	**NS**	A	*NO*	NH	52470	57470
156 471	q	**NS**	A	*NO*	NH	52471	57471
156 472	q	**NS**	A	*NO*	NH	52472	57472
156 473	q	**NS**	A	*NO*	NL	52473	57473
156 474	rt	**FS**	A	*SR*	CK	52474	57474
156 475	q	**NS**	A	*NO*	NL	52475	57475
156 476	rt	**FS**	A	*SR*	CK	52476	57476
156 477	t	**FS**	A	*SR*	CK	52477	57477
156 478	rt	**FS**	A	*SR*	CK	52478	57478
156 479	q	**NS**	A	*NO*	NL	52479	57479
156 480	q	**NS**	A	*NO*	NL	52480	57480
156 481	q	**NS**	A	*NO*	NL	52481	57481
156 482	q	**NS**	A	*NO*	NL	52482	57482
156 483	q	**NS**	A	*NO*	NL	52483	57483
156 484	q	**NS**	A	*NO*	NL	52484	57484
156 485	ru	**FS**	A	*SR*	CK	52485	57485
156 486	q	**NS**	A	*NO*	NL	52486	57486
156 487	q	**NS**	A	*NO*	NL	52487	57487
156 488	q	**NS**	A	*NO*	NL	52488	57488
156 489	q	**NS**	A	*NO*	NH	52489	57489
156 490	q	**NS**	A	*NO*	NL	52490	57490
156 491	q	**NS**	A	*NO*	NL	52491	57491
156 492	†	**FS**	A	*SR*	CK	52492	57492
156 493	rt	**FS**	A	*SR*	CK	52493	57493
156 494	§	**SC**	A	*SR*	CK	52494	57494
156 495	u	**SC**	A	*SR*	CK	52495	57495
156 496	ru	**FS**	A	*SR*	CK	52496	57496
156 497	q	**NS**	A	*NO*	NL	52497	57497
156 498	q	**NS**	A	*NO*	NH	52498	57498
156 499	rt	**FS**	A	*SR*	CK	52499	57499
156 500	u	**SC**	A	*SR*	CK	52500	57500
156 501		**SC**	A	*SR*	CK	52501	57501
156 502		**SC**	A	*SR*	CK	52502	57502
156 503		**SC**	A	*SR*	CK	52503	57503
156 504		**SC**	A	*SR*	CK	52504	57504
156 505		**SC**	A	*SR*	CK	52505	57505
156 506		**SC**	A	*SR*	CK	52506	57506
156 507		**SC**	A	*SR*	CK	52507	57507
156 508		**SC**	A	*SR*	CK	52508	57508
156 509		**SC**	A	*SR*	CK	52509	57509
156 510		**SC**	A	*SR*	CK	52510	57510
156 511		**SC**	A	*SR*	CK	52511	57511
156 512		**SC**	A	*SR*	CK	52512	57512
156 513		**SC**	A	*SR*	CK	52513	57513
156 514		**SC**	A	*SR*	CK	52514	57514

Names:

156 416   Saint Edmund
156 420   LA' AL RATTY Ravenglass & Eskdale Railway
156 433   The Kilmarnock Edition
156 466   BUXTON Festival

CLASS 158/0 BREL

DMSL(B)–DMSL(A) or DMCL–DMSL or DMCL–MSL–DMSL.

Construction: Welded aluminium.
Engines: 158 701–158 814: One Cummins NTA855R of 260 kW (350 h.p.) at 1900 r.p.m.
158 815–158 862: One Perkins 2006-TWH of 260 kW (350 h.p.) at 1900 r.p.m.
158 863–158 872: One Cummins NTA855R of 300 kW (400 h.p.) at 2100 r.p.m.
Bogies: One BREL P4 (powered) and one BREL T4 (non-powered) per car.
Couplers: BSI.
Dimensions: 23.21 x 2.70 m.
Gangways: Throughout.
Doors: Twin-leaf swing plug.
Seating Layout: 2+2 facing/unidirectional in all standard and first class except
2+1 in South West Trains first class.
Multiple Working: Within class and with Classes 142, 143, 144, 150, 153, 155,
156, 159 and 170.

Wheel Arrangement: 2-B + B-2.		
Maximum Speed: 90 m.p.h.		

DMSL(B). Lot No. 31051 BREL Derby 1989–1992. –/68 1TD 1W. († –/66 1TD 1W,
t –/64 1TD 1W). 38.5 t.
MSL. Lot No. 31050 BREL Derby 1991. –/70 1T. 38.5 t.
DMSL(A). Lot No. 31052 BREL Derby 1989–1992. –/70 1T († –/68 1T, t –/66 1T).
38.5 t.

The above details refer to the "as built" condition. The following DMSL(B) have
now been converted to DMCL as follows:

52701–52744 (First ScotRail/Trans-Pennine Express). 15/51 1TD 1W (* 15/53
1TD 1W).
52747–52751. (First Great Western). 9/51 1TD 1W.
52760–52779/52781. (Trans-Pennine Express/former TPX 2-car units). 16/48
1TD 1W.
52786/52789 (South West Trains). 13/44 1TD 1W.
52798–52814 (Trans-Pennine Express/former TPX 3-car units). 32/32 1TD 1W.

Notes: First ScotRail units 158 701–736/738–741 are fitted with Richmond seating.

s – Trans-Pennine and Central Trains units have been refurbished with new shape
seat cushions. Trans-Pennine units are also fitted with table lamps in first class.

t – Arriva Trains Wales and Trans-Pennine Express/Northern units with some
seats removed for additional luggage space.

u – Refurbished South West Trains units with Class 159-style interiors, including
first class seating.

† – First Great Western and Arriva Trains Wales units fitted with Chapman seating.

All First ScotRail 158s are "fitted" for RETB. When a unit arrives at Inverness the cab display unit is clipped on and plugged in. Similarly Arriva Trains Wales units have RETB plugged in at Shrewsbury for working the Cambrian Lines.

Non-standard livery: 158 750 As **RE** but with a Trans-Pennine Express blue band along the lower bodyside.

158 701	*	**FS**	P	*SR*	IS	52701 57701
158 702	*	**FS**	P	*SR*	IS	52702 57702
158 703	*	**FS**	P	*SR*	IS	52703 57703
158 704	*	**FS**	P	*SR*	IS	52704 57704
158 705	*	**FS**	P	*SR*	IS	52705 57705
158 706	*	**FS**	P	*SR*	IS	52706 57706
158 707	*	**FS**	P	*SR*	IS	52707 57707
158 708	*	**FS**	P	*SR*	IS	52708 57708
158 709	*	**SR**	P	*SR*	IS	52709 57709
158 710	*	**FS**	P	*SR*	IS	52710 57710
158 711	*	**FS**	P	*SR*	IS	52711 57711
158 712	*	**FS**	P	*SR*	IS	52712 57712
158 713	*	**SR**	P	*SR*	IS	52713 57713
158 714	*	**SR**	P	*SR*	IS	52714 57714
158 715	*	**FS**	P	*SR*	IS	52715 57715
158 716	*	**FS**	P	*SR*	IS	52716 57716
158 717	*	**SR**	P	*SR*	IS	52717 57717
158 718	*	**FS**	P	*SR*	IS	52718 57718
158 719	*	**SR**	P	*SR*	IS	52719 57719
158 720	*	**FS**	P	*SR*	IS	52720 57720
158 721	*	**SR**	P	*SR*	IS	52721 57721
158 722	*	**FS**	P	*SR*	IS	52722 57722
158 723	*	**FS**	P	*SR*	IS	52723 57723
158 724	*	**SR**	P	*SR*	IS	52724 57724
158 725	*	**FS**	P	*SR*	IS	52725 57725
158 726	*	**FS**	P	*SR*	HA	52726 57726
158 727	*	**FS**	P	*SR*	HA	52727 57727
158 728	*	**FS**	P	*SR*	HA	52728 57728
158 729	*	**FS**	P	*SR*	HA	52729 57729
158 730	*	**FS**	P	*SR*	HA	52730 57730
158 731	*	**FS**	P	*SR*	HA	52731 57731
158 732	*	**FS**	P	*SR*	HA	52732 57732
158 733	*	**FS**	P	*SR*	HA	52733 57733
158 734	*	**FS**	P	*SR*	HA	52734 57734
158 735	*	**FS**	P	*SR*	HA	52735 57735
158 736	*	**FS**	P	*SR*	HA	52736 57736
158 737		**TP**	P	*TP*	NL	52737 57737
158 738	*	**FS**	P	*SR*	HA	52738 57738
158 739	*	**FS**	P	*SR*	HA	52739 57739
158 740	*	**FS**	P	*SR*	HA	52740 57740
158 741	*	**FS**	P	*SR*	HA	52741 57741
158 742		**TP**	P	*SW*	SA	52742 57742
158 743		**TP**	P	*SW*	SA	52743 57743
158 744		**TP**	P	*SW*	SA	52744 57744
158 745	†	**WT**	P	*GW*	PM	52745 57745

158 746	†	**WT**	P	*GW*	PM	52746	57746	
158 747		**WE**	P	*GW*	PM	52747	57747	
158 748		**WT**	P	*GW*	PM	52748	57748	
158 749		**WT**	P	*GW*	PM	52749	57749	
158 750		**0**	P	*GW*	PM	52750	57750	
158 751		**WT**	P	*GW*	PM	52751	57751	
158 752		**NW**	P	*NO*	NL	52752	57752	
158 753		**NW**	P	*NO*	NL	52753	57753	
158 754		**NW**	P	*NO*	NL	52754	57754	
158 755		**NW**	P	*NO*	NL	52755	57755	
158 756		**NW**	P	*NO*	NL	52756	57756	
158 757		**NW**	P	*NO*	NL	52757	57757	
158 758		**NW**	P	*NO*	NL	52758	57758	
158 759		**NW**	P	*NO*	NL	52759	57759	
158 760	s	**TP**	P	*GW*	PM	52760	57760	
158 761	s	**TP**	P	*GW*	PM	52761	57761	
158 762	s	**TP**	P	*GW*	PM	52762	57762	
158 763	s	**TP**	P	*GW*	PM	52763	57763	
158 764	s	**TP**	P	*GW*	PM	52764	57764	
158 765	s	**TP**	P	*GW*	PM	52765	57765	
158 766	s	**TP**	P	*GW*	PM	52766	57766	
158 767	s	**TP**	P	*GW*	PM	52767	57767	
158 768	s	**TP**	P	*GW*	PM	52768	57768	
158 769	s	**TP**	P	*GW*	PM	52769	57769	
158 770	s	**TP**	P	*TP*	NL	52770		57770
158 771	s	**TP**	P	*GW*	PM	52771		57771
158 772	s	**TP**	P	*TP*	NL	52772		57772
158 773	s	**TP**	P	*TP*	NL	52773		57773
158 774	s	**TP**	P	*TP*	NL	52774		57774
158 775	s	**TP**	P	*TP*	NL	52775		57775
158 776	s	**TP**	P	*GW*	PM	52776		57776
158 777	s	**TP**	P	*TP*	NL	52777		57777
158 778	s	**TP**	P	*GW*	PM	52778		57778
158 779	s	**TP**	P	*TP*	NL	52779		57779
158 780	s	**CT**	A	*CT*	TS	52780		57780
158 781	s	**TP**	P	*TP*	NL	52781		57781
158 782	s	**WT**	A		ZC	52782		57782
158 783	s	**CT**	A	*CT*	TS	52783		57783
158 784	st	**CT**	A	*GW*	PM	52784		57784
158 785	s	**CT**	A	*CT*	TS	52785		57785
158 786	u	**SW**	A	*SW*	SA	52786		57786
158 787	s	**NO**	A	*NO*	NL	52787		57787
158 788	s	**CT**	A	*CT*	TS	52788		57788
158 789	u	**SW**	A	*SW*	SA	52789		57789
158 790	st	**CT**	A	*GW*	PM	52790		57790
158 791	st	**CT**	A	*TP*	NL	52791		57791
158 792	s	**CT**	A	*NO*	NL	52792		57792
158 793	s	**CT**	A	*NO*	NL	52793		57793
158 794	s	**CT**	A	*NO*	NL	52794		57794
158 795	s	**CT**	A	*NO*	NL	52795		57795
158 796	s	**CT**	A	*NO*	NL	52796		57796

▲ Merseytravel-liveried 142 043 is seen at Pemberton with the 10.55 Kirkby–Rochdale on 10/05/06. **Paul Senior**

▼ Arriva Trains-liveried 143 623 leaves Cardiff Central with the 10.04 Radyr–Coryton on 06/09/06. **Robert Pritchard**

New West Yorkshire PTE-liveried 144 008 approaches Hatfield & Stainforth with the 08.25 Sheffield–Scunthorpe stopping service on 01/10/05.

Andrew Wills

Silverlink operate eight 150s and they are used on the Bedford–Bletchley and Gospel Oak–Barking lines. Here 150 123 arrives at Lidlington with the 08.39 Bletchley–Bedford on 11/04/05. **Kim Fullbrook**

▲ 153 314, in "One" livery, is seen after arrival at Lowestoft on 10/09/06 with the 12.57 from Norwich (coupled to 156 416). 156 417 is in the adjacent platform.
Alan Yearsley

▼ Newly repainted into Northern livery, 155 346 leaves Bradford Interchange with the 16.24 Manchester Victoria–Leeds on 28/08/06.
Gavin Morrison

Carrying the second experimental Northern livery 156 460 and 156 455 (in all over dark blue livery) have just emerged from Blea Moor Tunnel with the 14.26 Carlisle–Leeds on 04/03/06. **Robert Pritchard**

▲ First Group-liveried 158 727 is seen leaving Bathgate with the 11.23 to Newcraighall on 17/03/06. **Ian Lothian**

▼ South West Trains-liveried 159 008 and 159 012 are seen at Worting Junction with the 06.41 Exeter St. Davids–London Waterloo on 04/05/06. **Chris Wilson**

▲ Chiltern Railways-liveried 165 002 leads 168 218 at Hatton with the 16.35 London Marylebone–Stratford-upon-Avon on 27/06/05. **Scott Borthwick**

▼ Newly vinyled in the First Group "Dynamic Lights" livery 166 220 is seen at Reading depot on 30/09/06. This was the first Class 166 to receive this livery. **Darren Ford**

One of the original Class 168s, 168 005, passes Bishops Itchington, south of Leamington Spa with the 08.10 Kidderminster–London Marylebone on 23/06/06.
Scott Borthwick

Central Trains-liveried 170 502 has just emerged from Milford Tunnel with the 06.57 Derby–Matlock on 24/07/06.

Paul Robertson

▲ Looking superb in Strathclyde PTE livery, 170 477 pauses at North Queensferry with the 14.47 "Fife Circle" service to Edinburgh Waverley on 27/06/05.

Adrian Sumner

▼ Southern-liveried 171 727 and 171 721 leave a very foggy Norwood Junction with the 09.07 London Bridge–Uckfield on 19/11/05. **Alex Dasi-Sutton**

▲ Arriva Trains Wales-liveried 175 008 and First Group-liveried 175 116, are seen at Leyland with the 15.42 Blackpool North–Manchester Airport on 27/04/06.
Rodney Lissenden

▼ 180 113 and 180 109 pass Denchworth with the 09.30 Plymouth–London Paddington (via Bristol) on 17/11/05.
Brian Denton

The Siemens-built Class 185s entered service with Trans-Pennine Express in 2006. One of the first routes that saw the new units was the South Trans-Pennine. On 14/07/06 185 109, in the new First Group "Dynamic Lights" livery, passes Kilnhurst, just south of Swinton, with the 06.56 Manchester Airport–Cleethorpes.   **Andrew Wills**

With a dusting of snow on the ground 220 019 "Mersey Voyager" leads 221 104 "Sir John Franklin" through Ribblehead station on the scenic Settle & Carlisle line with the diverted 10.10 Glasgow–Plymouth on 04/03/06. **Robert Pritchard**

221 108 "Sir Ernest Shackleton" passes Craigo, just north of Montrose, with the 12.03 Birmingham New Street–Aberdeen on 01/06/06.

Andrew Wills

▲ Midland Mainline-liveried 9-car "Meridian" 222 007 passes Harrowden Junction with the 16.30 Nottingham–St. Pancras on 30/08/05.			**Gavin Morrison**

▼ South West Trains Route Learning Unit 960 012 "John Cameron", converted from a Class 121, passes Old Basing on 06/04/06 with the 12.05 Waterloo–Salisbury crew training run.			**Chris Wilson**

▲ The Network Rail Track Assessment Unit No. 950 001 is based on the Class 150/1 design. On 26/07/06 it pauses at Achnasheen with the 2Z08 Strathcarron–Inverness test train. **Jason Rogers**

▼ Eurailscout GB Track Assessment/Recording Unit 999700/701 crosses Manningtree Viaduct with an unidentified southbound service on 06/06/06. **David Moulden**

158 797	st	**CT**	A	*NO*	NL	52797		57797
158 798	s	**TP**	P	*GW*	PM	52798	58715	57798
158 799	s	**TP**	P	*TP*	HT	52799	58716	57799
158 802	s	**TP**	P		ZB	52802		57802
158 806	s	**TP**	P	*TP*	HT	52806	58706	57806
158 808	s	**TP**	P	*SW*	SA	52808		57808
158 810	s	**TP**	P	*TP*	HT	52810	58710	57810
158 812	s	**TP**	P	*TP*	HT	52812	58712	57812
158 813	s	**TP**	P	*TP*	HT	52813	58713	57813
158 814	s	**TP**	P	*SW*	SA	52814		57814
158 815	†	**WT**	A	*GW*	PM	52815	57815	
158 816	†	**WT**	A	*GW*	PM	52816	57816	
158 817	†	**WT**	A	*GW*	PM	52817	57817	
158 818	†	**AV**	A	*AW*	CF	52818	57818	
158 819	†	**WB**	A	*AW*	CF	52819	57819	
158 820	†	**AV**	A	*AW*	CF	52820	57820	
158 821	†	**WB**	A	*AW*	CF	52821	57821	
158 822	†	**WB**	A	*AW*	CF	52822	57822	
158 823	†	**AV**	A	*AW*	CF	52823	57823	
158 824	†	**WB**	A	*AW*	CF	52824	57824	
158 825	†	**WB**	A	*AW*	CF	52825	57825	
158 826	†	**WB**	A	*AW*	CF	52826	57826	
158 827	†	**WB**	A	*AW*	CF	52827	57827	
158 828	†	**AV**	A	*AW*	CF	52828	57828	
158 829	†	**AV**	A	*AW*	CF	52829	57829	
158 830	†	**WB**	A	*AW*	CF	52830	57830	
158 831	†	**WB**	A	*AW*	CF	52831	57831	
158 832	†	**WB**	A	*AW*	CF	52832	57832	
158 833	†	**WB**	A	*AW*	CF	52833	57833	
158 834	†	**WB**	A	*AW*	CF	52834	57834	
158 835	†	**WB**	A	*AW*	CF	52835	57835	
158 836	†	**WB**	A	*AW*	CF	52836	57836	
158 837	†	**AV**	A	*AW*	CF	52837	57837	
158 838	†	**WB**	A	*AW*	CF	52838	57838	
158 839	†	**WB**	A	*AW*	CF	52839	57839	
158 840	†	**AV**	A	*AW*	CF	52840	57840	
158 841	†	**WB**	A	*AW*	CF	52841	57841	
158 842	†	**WB**	A		ZG	52842	57842	
158 843	†	**WB**	A		ZG	52843	57843	
158 844	t	**CT**	A		ZG	52844	57844	
158 845	t	**CT**	A		ZG	52845	57845	
158 846	t	**CT**	A	*CT*	TS	52846	57846	
158 847	t	**CT**	A	*CT*	TS	52847	57847	
158 848	t	**CT**	A		ZG	52848	57848	
158 849	t	**CT**	A		ZG	52849	57849	
158 850	t	**CT**	A		ZG	52850	57850	
158 851	t	**CT**	A		ZG	52851	57851	
158 852	t	**CT**	A	*CT*	TS	52852	57852	
158 853	t	**CT**	A		ZG	52853	57853	
158 854	t	**CT**	A	*CT*	TS	52854	57854	
158 855	s	**WE**	A	*GW*	PM	52855	57855	

158 856	s	**CT**	A	*CT*	TS	52856	57856
158 857	s	**CT**	A	*CT*	TS	52857	57857
158 858	s	**CT**	A	*CT*	TS	52858	57858
158 859	s	**WT**	A		ZC	52859	57859
158 860	s	**WE**	A		ZG	52860	57860
158 861	s	**WT**	A		ZC	52861	57861
158 862	s	**CT**	A	*CT*	TS	52862	57862
158 863	†	**WT**	A	*SR*	HA	52863	57863
158 864	†	**WT**	A	*GW*	PM	52864	57864
158 865	†	**WT**	A	*GW*	PM	52865	57865
158 866	†	**WT**	A	*GW*	PM	52866	57866
158 867	†	**WT**	A	*GW*	PM	52867	57867
158 868	†	**WT**	A	*GW*	PM	52868	57868
158 869	†	**WT**	A	*GW*	PM	52869	57869
158 870	†	**WT**	A	*GW*	PM	52870	57870
158 871	†	**WT**	A	*GW*	PM	52871	57871
158 872	†	**WT**	A	*GW*	PM	52872	57872
Spare	s	**TP**	P		ZB		58702	(to go into 158 772)
Spare	s	**TP**	P		ZB		58708	(to go into 158 770)
Spare	s	**TP**	P		ZB		58714	(to go into 158 774)

Names:

158 702	BBC Scotland – 75 years
158 707	Far North Line 125th ANNIVERSARY
158 715	Haymarket
158 720	Inverness & Nairn Railway – 150 years
158 747	Richard Trevithick
158 855	Exmoor Explorer
158 860	Isambard Kingdom Brunel
158 861	Spirit of the South West

CLASS 158/9   BREL

DMSL–DMS. Units leased by West Yorkshire PTE. Details as for Class 158/0 except for seating layout and toilets.

DMSL. Lot No. 31051 BREL Derby 1990–1992. –/70 1TD 1W. 38.5 t.
DMS. Lot No. 31052 BREL Derby 1990–1992. –/72 and parcels area. 38.5 t.

Note: These units are leased by West Yorkshire PTE and are now managed by HSBC Rail (UK) on behalf of Midland Montague who own the units.

158 901	**YP**	H	*NO*	NL	52901	57901
158 902	**YP**	H	*NO*	NL	52902	57902
158 903	**YP**	H	*NO*	NL	52903	57903
158 904	**YP**	H	*NO*	NL	52904	57904
158 905	**YP**	H	*NO*	NL	52905	57905
158 906	**YP**	H	*NO*	NL	52906	57906
158 907	**YP**	H	*NO*	NL	52907	57907
158 908	**YP**	H	*NO*	NL	52908	57908
158 909	**YP**	H	*NO*	NL	52909	57909
158 910	**YP**	H	*NO*	NL	52910	57910

CLASS 159/0   BREL

DMCL–MSL–DMSL. Built as Class 158. Converted before entering passenger service to Class 159 by Rosyth Dockyard.

Construction: Welded aluminium.
Engines: One Cummins NTA855R of 300 kW (400 h.p.) at 2100 r.p.m.
Bogies: One BREL P4 (powered) and one BREL T4 (non-powered) per car.
Couplers: BSI.   **Dimensions:** 22.16 x 2.70 m.
Gangways: Throughout.   **Wheel Arrangement:** 2-B + B-2 + B-2.
Doors: Twin-leaf swing plug.   **Maximum Speed:** 90 m.p.h.
Seating Layout: 1: 2+1 facing, 2: 2+2 facing/unidirectional.
Multiple Working: Within class and with Classes 142, 143, 144, 150, 153, 155, 156, 158 and 170.

DMCL. Lot No. 31051 BREL Derby 1992–1993. 24/28 1TD 1W. 38.5 t.
MSL. Lot No. 31050 BREL Derby 1992–1993. –/70(6) 1T. 38.5 t.
DMSL. Lot No. 31052 BREL Derby 1992–1993. –/72 1T. 38.5 t.

159 001	**SW**	P	*SW*	SA	52873	58718	57873	CITY OF EXETER
159 002	**SW**	P	*SW*	SA	52874	58719	57874	CITY OF SALISBURY
159 003	**SW**	P	*SW*	SA	52875	58720	57875	TEMPLECOMBE
159 004	**SW**	P	*SW*	SA	52876	58721	57876	BASINGSTOKE AND DEANE
159 005	**SW**	P	*SW*	SA	52877	58722	57877	
159 006	**SW**	P	*SW*	SA	52878	58723	57878	
159 007	**SW**	P	*SW*	SA	52879	58724	57879	
159 008	**SW**	P	*SW*	SA	52880	58725	57880	
159 009	**SW**	P	*SW*	SA	52881	58726	57881	
159 010	**SW**	P	*SW*	SA	52882	58727	57882	
159 011	**SW**	P	*SW*	SA	52883	58728	57883	
159 012	**SW**	P	*SW*	SA	52884	58729	57884	
159 013	**SW**	P	*SW*	SA	52885	58730	57885	
159 014	**SW**	P	*SW*	SA	52886	58731	57886	
159 015	**SW**	P	*SW*	SA	52887	58732	57887	
159 016	**SW**	P	*SW*	SA	52888	58733	57888	
159 017	**SW**	P	*SW*	SA	52889	58734	57889	
159 018	**SW**	P	*SW*	SA	52890	58735	57890	
159 019	**SW**	P	*SW*	SA	52891	58736	57891	
159 020	**SW**	P	*SW*	SA	52892	58737	57892	
159 021	**SW**	P	*SW*	SA	52893	58738	57893	
159 022	**SW**	P	*SW*	SA	52894	58739	57894	

CLASS 159/1   BREL

DMCL–MSL–DMSL. Units converted or undergoing conversion from Class 158s at Wabtec, Doncaster for use with South West Trains.

Details as Class 158/0 except:
Seating Layout: 1: 2+1 facing, 2: 2+2 facing/unidirectional.

DMCL. Lot No. 31051 BREL Derby 1989–1992. 24/28 1TD 1W. 38.5 t.
MSL. Lot No. 31050 BREL Derby 1989–1992. –/70 1T. 38.5 t.
DMSL. Lot No. 31052 BREL Derby 1989–1992. –/72 1T.38.5 t.

159 101	(158 800)	**SW**	P	*SW*	SA	52800	58717	57800
159 102	(158 803)	**SW**	P	*SW*	SA	52803	58703	57803
159 103	(158 804)	**SW**	P	*SW*	SA	52804	58704	57804
159 104	(158 805)	**SW**	P	*SW*	SA	52805	58705	57805
159 105	(158 807)	**SW**	P		ZB	52807	58707	57811
159 106	(158 809)	**SW**	P		ZB	52809	58709	57809
159 107	(158 811)	**SW**	P		ZB	52811	58711	57807
159 108	(158 801)	**SW**	P		ZB	52801	58701	57801

CLASS 165/0   NETWORK TURBO   BREL

DMSL–DMS and DMSL–MS–DMS. Chiltern Railways units. Refurbished 2003–2005 with first class seats removed and air conditioning fitted.

Construction: Welded aluminium.
Engines: One Perkins 2006-TWH of 260 kW (350 h.p.) at 1900 r.p.m.
Bogies: BREL P3-17 (powered), BREL T3-17 (non-powered).
Couplers: BSI at outer ends, bar within 3-car units.
Dimensions: 23.50/23.25 x 2.81 m.
Gangways: Within unit only.   **Wheel Arrangement:** 2-B (+ B-2) + B-2.
Doors: Twin-leaf swing plug.   **Maximum Speed:** 75 m.p.h.
Seating Layout: 2+2/3+2 facing/unidirectional.
Multiple Working: Within class and with Classes 166 and 168.

Fitted with tripcocks for working over London Underground tracks between Harrow-on-the-Hill and Amersham.

58801–58822/58873–58878. DMSL. Lot No. 31087 BREL York 1990. –/89 1T. 40.1 t.
58823–58833. DMSL. Lot No. 31089 BREL York 1991–1992. –/89 1T. 40.1 t.
MS. Lot No. 31090 BREL York 1991–1992. –/106. 37.0 t.
DMS. Lot No. 31088 BREL York 1991–1992. –/94. 39.4 t.

165 001	**CR**	A	*CR*	AL	58801	58834
165 002	**CR**	A	*CR*	AL	58802	58835
165 003	**CR**	A	*CR*	AL	58803	58836
165 004	**CR**	A	*CR*	AL	58804	58837
165 005	**CR**	A	*CR*	AL	58805	58838
165 006	**CR**	A	*CR*	AL	58806	58839
165 007	**CR**	A	*CR*	AL	58807	58840
165 008	**CR**	A	*CR*	AL	58808	58841

165 009	**CR**	A	*CR*	AL	58809		58842
165 010	**CR**	A	*CR*	AL	58810		58843
165 011	**CR**	A	*CR*	AL	58811		58844
165 012	**CR**	A	*CR*	AL	58812		58845
165 013	**CR**	A	*CR*	AL	58813		58846
165 014	**CR**	A	*CR*	AL	58814		58847
165 015	**CR**	A	*CR*	AL	58815		58848
165 016	**CR**	A	*CR*	AL	58816		58849
165 017	**CR**	A	*CR*	AL	58817		58850
165 018	**CR**	A	*CR*	AL	58818		58851
165 019	**CR**	A	*CR*	AL	58819		58852
165 020	**CR**	A	*CR*	AL	58820		58853
165 021	**CR**	A	*CR*	AL	58821		58854
165 022	**CR**	A	*CR*	AL	58822		58855
165 023	**CR**	A	*CR*	AL	58873		58867
165 024	**CR**	A	*CR*	AL	58874		58868
165 025	**CR**	A	*CR*	AL	58875		58869
165 026	**CR**	A	*CR*	AL	58876		58870
165 027	**CR**	A	*CR*	AL	58877		58871
165 028	**CR**	A	*CR*	AL	58878		58872
165 029	**CR**	A	*CR*	AL	58823	55404	58856
165 030	**CR**	A	*CR*	AL	58824	55405	58857
165 031	**CR**	A	*CR*	AL	58825	55406	58858
165 032	**CR**	A	*CR*	AL	58826	55407	58859
165 033	**CR**	A	*CR*	AL	58827	55408	58860
165 034	**CR**	A	*CR*	AL	58828	55409	58861
165 035	**CR**	A	*CR*	AL	58829	55410	58862
165 036	**CR**	A	*CR*	AL	58830	55411	58863
165 037	**CR**	A	*CR*	AL	58831	55412	58864
165 038	**CR**	A	*CR*	AL	58832	55413	58865
165 039	**CR**	A	*CR*	AL	58833	55414	58866

CLASS 165/1   NETWORK TURBO   BREL

First Great Western units. DMCL–MS–DMS or DMCL–DMS.

Construction: Welded aluminium.
Engines: One Perkins 2006-TWH of 260 kW (350 h.p.) at 1900 r.p.m.
Bogies: BREL P3-17 (powered), BREL T3-17 (non-powered).
Couplers: BSI at outer ends, bar within 3-car units.
Dimensions: 23.50/23.25 x 2.81 m.
Gangways: Within unit only.   **Wheel Arrangement:** 2-B (+ B-2) + B-2.
Doors: Twin-leaf swing plug.   **Maximum Speed:** 90 m.p.h.
Seating Layout: 1: 2+2 facing, 2: 3+2 facing/unidirectional.
Multiple Working: Within class and with Classes 166 and 168.

58953–58969. DMCL. Lot No. 31098 BREL York 1992. 16/66 1T. 38.0 t.
58879–58898. DMCL. Lot No. 31096 BREL York 1992. 16/72 1T. 38.0 t.
MS. Lot No. 31099 BREL 1992. –/106. 37.0 t.
DMS. Lot No. 31097 BREL 1992. –/98. 37.0 t.

Advertising livery: 165 136 – "Back the Bid" (London's Olympic Bid 2012) – blue with various images.

165 101	TT	A	GW	RG	58953	55415	58916
165 102	TT	A	GW	RG	58954	55416	58917
165 103	TT	A	GW	RG	58955	55417	58918
165 104	TT	A	GW	RG	58956	55418	58919
165 105	TT	A	GW	RG	58957	55419	58920
165 106	TT	A	GW	RG	58958	55420	58921
165 107	TT	A	GW	RG	58959	55421	58922
165 108	TT	A	GW	RG	58960	55422	58923
165 109	TT	A	GW	RG	58961	55423	58924
165 110	TT	A	GW	RG	58962	55424	58925
165 111	TT	A	GW	RG	58963	55425	58926
165 112	TT	A	GW	RG	58964	55426	58927
165 113	TT	A	GW	RG	58965	55427	58928
165 114	TT	A	GW	RG	58966	55428	58929
165 116	TT	A	GW	RG	58968	55430	58931
165 117	TT	A	GW	RG	58969	55431	58932
165 118	TT	A	GW	RG	58879		58933
165 119	TT	A	GW	RG	58880		58934
165 120	TT	A	GW	RG	58881		58935
165 121	TT	A	GW	RG	58882		58936
165 122	TT	A	GW	RG	58883		58937
165 123	TT	A	GW	RG	58884		58938
165 124	TT	A	GW	RG	58885		58939
165 125	TT	A	GW	RG	58886		58940
165 126	TT	A	GW	RG	58887		58941
165 127	TT	A	GW	RG	58888		58942
165 128	TT	A	GW	RG	58889		58943
165 129	TT	A	GW	RG	58890		58944
165 130	TT	A	GW	RG	58891		58945
165 131	TT	A	GW	RG	58892		58946
165 132	TT	A	GW	RG	58893		58947
165 133	TT	A	GW	RG	58894		58948
165 134	TT	A	GW	RG	58895		58949
165 135	TT	A	GW	RG	58896		58950
165 136	AL	A	GW	RG	58897		58951
165 137	TT	A	GW	RG	58898		58952

CLASS 166   NETWORK EXPRESS TURBO   ABB

DMCL(A)–MS–DMCL(B). First Great Western units, built for Paddington–Oxford/Newbury services. Air conditioned.

Construction: Welded aluminium.
Engines: One Perkins 2006-TWH of 260 kW (350 h.p.) at 1900 r.p.m.
Bogies: BREL P3-17 (powered), BREL T3-17 (non-powered).
Couplers: BSI.
Dimensions: 23.50 x 2.81 m.
Gangways: Within unit only.
Doors: Twin-leaf swing plug.
Wheel Arrangement: 2-B + B-2 + B-2.
Maximum Speed: 90 m.p.h.
Seating Layout: 1: 2+2 facing, 2: 3+2 facing/unidirectional. 20 standard class seats in 2+2 layout in DMCL(B).
Multiple Working: Within class and with Classes 165 and 168.

DMCL (A). Lot No. 31116 ABB York 1992–1993. 16/75 1T. 39.6 t.
MS. Lot No. 31117 ABB York 1992–1993. –/96. 38.0 t.
DMCL (B). Lot No. 31116 ABB York 1992–1993. 16/72 1T. 39.6 t.

166 201	**FD**	A	*GW*	RG	58101	58601	58122
166 202	**FD**	A	*GW*	RG	58102	58602	58123
166 203	**TT**	A	*GW*	RG	58103	58603	58124
166 204	**TT**	A	*GW*	RG	58104	58604	58125
166 205	**FD**	A	*GW*	RG	58105	58605	58126
166 206	**FD**	A	*GW*	RG	58106	58606	58127
166 207	**TT**	A	*GW*	RG	58107	58607	58128
166 208	**FD**	A	*GW*	RG	58108	58608	58129
166 209	**FD**	A	*GW*	RG	58109	58609	58130
166 210	**FD**	A	*GW*	RG	58110	58610	58131
166 211	**FD**	A	*GW*	RG	58111	58611	58132
166 212	**FD**	A	*GW*	RG	58112	58612	58133
166 213	**FD**	A	*GW*	RG	58113	58613	58134
166 214	**FD**	A	*GW*	RG	58114	58614	58135
166 215	**FD**	A	*GW*	RG	58115	58615	58136
166 216	**FD**	A	*GW*	RG	58116	58616	58137
166 217	**FD**	A	*GW*	RG	58117	58617	58138
166 218	**FD**	A	*GW*	RG	58118	58618	58139
166 219	**TT**	A	*GW*	RG	58119	58619	58140
166 220	**FD**	A	*GW*	RG	58120	58620	58141
166 221	**TT**	A	*GW*	RG	58121	58621	58142

CLASS 168 CLUBMAN ADTRANZ/BOMBARDIER

Air conditioned.

Construction: Welded aluminium bodies with bolt-on steel ends.
Engines: One MTU 6R183TD13H of 315 kW (422 h.p.) at 1900 r.p.m.
Transmission: Hydraulic. Voith T211rzze to ZF final drive.
Bogies: One Adtranz P3–23 and one BREL T3–23 per car.
Couplers: BSI at outer ends, bar within unit.
Dimensions: 24.10/23.61 x 2.70 m.
Gangways: Within unit only. **Wheel Arrangement:** 2-B (+ B-2 + B-2) + B-2.
Doors: Twin-leaf swing plug. **Maximum Speed:** 100 m.p.h.
Seating Layout: 2+2 facing/unidirectional.
Multiple Working: Within class and with Classes 165 and 166.

Fitted with tripcocks for working over London Underground tracks between Harrow-on-the-Hill and Amersham.

Class 168/0. Original Design. DMSL(A)–MSL–MS–DMSL(B).

58151–58155. DMSL(A). Adtranz Derby 1997–1998. –/60 1TD 1W. 43.7 t.
58651–58655. MSL. Adtranz Derby 1998. –/73 1T. 41.0 t.
58451–58455. MS. Adtranz Derby 1998. –/77. 40.5 t.
58251–58255. DMSL(B). Adtranz Derby 1998. –/68 1T. 43.6 t.

Note: 58451–58455 were numbered 58656–58660 for a time when used in 168 106–168 110.

168 001	**CR**	P	*CR*	AL	58151	58651	58451	58251
168 002	**CR**	P	*CR*	AL	58152	58652	58452	58252
168 003	**CR**	P	*CR*	AL	58153	58653	58453	58253
168 004	**CR**	P	*CR*	AL	58154	58654	58454	58254
168 005	**CR**	P	*CR*	AL	58155	58655	58455	58255

Class 168/1. These units are effectively Class 170s. DMSL(A)–MSL–MS–DMSL(B), DMSL(A)–MS–MSL–DMSL(B) or DMSL(A)–MS–DMSL(B).

58156–58163. DMSL(A). Adtranz Derby 2000. –/59 1TD 2W. 45.2 t.
58756–58757. MSL. Bombardier Derby 2002. –/73 1T. 42.9 t.
58456–58460. MS. Bombardier Derby 2002. –/76. 41.8 t.
58461–58463. MS. Adtranz Derby 2000. –/76. 42.4 t.
58256–58263. DMSL(B). Adtranz Derby 2000. –/69 1T. 45.2 t.

Notes: 58461–58463 have been renumbered from 58661–58663.

168 106	**CR**	P	*CR*	AL	58156	58756	58456	58256
168 107	**CR**	P	*CR*	AL	58157	58457	58757	58257
168 108	**CR**	P	*CR*	AL	58158		58458	58258
168 109	**CR**	P	*CR*	AL	58159		58459	58259
168 110	**CR**	P	*CR*	AL	58160		58460	58260
168 111	**CR**	H	*CR*	AL	58161		58461	58261
168 112	**CR**	H	*CR*	AL	58162		58462	58262
168 113	**CR**	H	*CR*	AL	58163		58463	58263

Class 168/2. These units are effectively Class 170s. DMSL(A)–MS–MS–DMSL(B) or DMSL(A)–MS–DMSL(B).

58164–58169. DMSL(A). Bombardier Derby 2003–2004. –/59 1TD 2W. 45.4 t.
58365–58367. MS. Bombardier Derby 2006. –/76. 43.3 t.
58464/58468/58469. MS. Bombardier Derby 2003–2004. –/76. 44.0 t.
58465–58467. MS. Bombardier Derby 2006. –/76. 43.3 t.
58264–58269. DMSL(B). Bombardier Derby 2003–2004. –/69 1T. 45.5 t.

168 214	**CR**	P	*CR*	AL	58164		58464	58264
168 215	**CR**	P	*CR*	AL	58165	58465	58365	58265
168 216	**CR**	P	*CR*	AL	58166	58366	58466	58266
168 217	**CR**	P	*CR*	AL	58167	58467	58367	58267
168 218	**CR**	P	*CR*	AL	58168		58468	58268
168 219	**CR**	P	*CR*	AL	58169		58469	58269

CLASS 170 TURBOSTAR ADTRANZ/BOMBARDIER

Various formations. Air conditioned.

Construction: Welded aluminium bodies with bolt-on steel ends.
Engines: One MTU 6R183TD13H of 315 kW (422 h.p.) at 1900 r.p.m.
Transmission: Hydraulic. Voith T211rzze to ZF final drive.
Bogies: One Adtranz P3–23 and one BREL T3–23 per car.
Couplers: BSI at outer ends, bar within later build units.
Dimensions: 24.10 x 2.70 m unless stated.
Gangways: Within unit only.   **Wheel Arrangement:** 2-B (+ B-2) + B-2.
Doors: Twin-leaf sliding plug.   **Maximum Speed:** 100 m.p.h.
Seating Layout: 1: 2+1 facing/unidirectional (2+2 in first class in Class 170/1 end cars). 2: 2+2 facing/unidirectional.
Multiple Working: Within class and with Classes 150, 153, 155, 156, 158 and 159.

Class 170/1. Central Trains units. Former Midland Mainline units, these now have their first class declassified. DMCL–MCRMB–DMCL or DMCL–DMCL.

DMCL (A). Adtranz Derby 1998–1999. 12/45 1TD 2W. 45.0 t.
MCRMB. Adtranz Derby 2001. 21/22 and bar. 43.0 t.
DMCL (B). Adtranz Derby 1998–1999. 12/52 1T. Catering point. 44.8 t

Note: 170 101 is currently out of traffic following collision damage, with 55101 operating in 170 117 at the time of writing.

170 101	**CM**	P		ZD (U)	50101		79101
170 102	**CM**	P	*CT*	TS	50102	55102	79102
170 103	**CM**	P	*CT*	TS	50103	55103	79103
170 104	**CM**	P	*CT*	TS	50104	55104	79104
170 105	**CM**	P	*CT*	TS	50105	55105	79105
170 106	**CM**	P	*CT*	TS	50106	55106	79106
170 107	**CM**	P	*CT*	TS	50107	55107	79107
170 108	**CM**	P	*CT*	TS	50108	55108	79108
170 109	**CM**	P	*CT*	TS	50109	55109	79109
170 110	**CM**	P	*CT*	TS	50110	55110	79110
170 111	**CM**	P	*CT*	TS	50111		79111
170 112	**CM**	P	*CT*	TS	50112		79112

170 113	**CM**	P	*CT*	TS	50113		79113
170 114	**CM**	P	*CT*	TS	50114		79114
170 115	**CM**	P	*CT*	TS	50115		79115
170 116	**CM**	P	*CT*	TS	50116		79116
170 117	**CM**	P	*CT*	TS	50117	55101	79117

Class 170/2. "One" 3-car units. DMCL–MSL–DMSL.

DMCL. Adtranz Derby 1999. 7/39 1TD 2W. 45.0 t.
MSL. Adtranz Derby 1999. –/68 1T. Guard's office. 45.3 t.
DMSL. Adtranz Derby 1999. –/66 1T. 43.4 t.

170 201	r	**1**	P	*1*	NC	50201	56201	79201
170 202	r	**1**	P	*1*	NC	50202	56202	79202
170 203	r	**1**	P	*1*	NC	50203	56203	79203
170 204	r	**1**	P	*1*	NC	50204	56204	79204
170 205	r	**1**	P	*1*	NC	50205	56205	79205
170 206	r	**1**	P	*1*	NC	50206	56206	79206
170 207	r	**1**	P	*1*	NC	50207	56207	79207
170 208	r	**1**	P	*1*	NC	50208	56208	79208

Class 170/2. "One" 2-car units. DMSL–DMCL.

DMSL. Bombardier Derby 2002. –/57 1TD 2W. 45.7 t.
DMCL. Bombardier Derby 2002. 9/53 1T. 45.7 t.

170 270	r	**1**	P	*1*	NC	50270	79270
170 271	r	**AN**	P	*1*	NC	50271	79271
170 272	r	**AN**	P	*1*	NC	50272	79272
170 273	r	**AN**	P	*1*	NC	50273	79273

Class 170/3. South West Trains units. DMCL–DMCL.

50301–50308. DMCL(A). Adtranz Derby 2000. 9/43 1TD 2W. 45.8 t.
50392. DMCL(A). Bombardier Derby 2003. 9/43 1TD 2W. 46.6 t.
79301–79308. DMCL(B). Adtranz Derby 2000. 9/53 1T. 45.8 t.
79392. DMCL(B). Bombardier Derby 2003. 9/53 1T. 46.5 t.

Note: 170 301–308 are due to transfer to Trans-Pennine Express during 2007, with 170 392 moving to Southern.

170 301	**SW**	P	*TP*	XW	50301	79301
170 302	**SW**	P	*TP*	XW	50302	79302
170 303	**SW**	P	*SW*	SA	50303	79303
170 304	**SW**	P	*TP*	XW	50304	79304
170 305	**SW**	P	*SW*	SA	50305	79305
170 306	**SW**	P	*SW*	SA	50306	79306
170 307	**SW**	P	*SW*	SA	50307	79307
170 308	**SW**	P	*SW*	SA	50308	79308
170 392	**SW**	P	*SW*	SA	50392	79392

Class 170/3. Units built for Hull Trains. Now in use with First ScotRail and dedicated to Edinburgh/Glasgow–Inverness services. DMCL–MSLRB–DMSL.
Dimensions: 23.62/23.61 x 2.75 m.

DMCL. Bombardier Derby 2004. 7/41 1TD 2W. 46.5 t.
MSLRB. Bombardier Derby 2004. –/60 1T. Buffet and guard's office 44.7 t.
DMSL. Bombardier Derby 2004. –/71 1T. 46.3 t.

170 393	**FS**	P	*SR*	HA	50393	56393	79393
170 394	**FS**	P	*SR*	HA	50394	56394	79394
170 395	**FS**	P	*SR*	HA	50395	56395	79395
170 396	**FS**	P	*SR*	HA	50396	56396	79396

Class 170/3. Porterbrook spot hire units. DMCL–MC–DMCL.

DMCL(A). Bombardier Derby 2002. 9/43 1TD 1W. 45.4 t.
MC. Bombardier Derby 2002. 22/36. 43.0 t.
DMCL(B). Bombardier Derby 2002. 9/53 1T. 45.8 t.

| 170 397 | **P** | P | *CT* | TS | 50397 | 56397 | 79397 |
| 170 398 | **P** | P | *CT* | TS | 50398 | 56398 | 79398 |

Class 170/3. Porterbrook spot hire unit. DMCL–DMCL.

DMCL(A). Bombardier Derby 2001. 9/43 1TD 2W. 45.8 t.
DMCL(B). Bombardier Derby 2001. 9/53 1T. 45.8 t.

| 170 399 | **P** | P | *CT* | TS | 50399 | | 79399 |

Class 170/4. First ScotRail "express" units. DMCL–MS–DMCL.
Dimensions: 23.62/23.61 x 2.75 m unless stated.

DMCL(A). Adtranz Derby 1999–2001. 9/43 1TD 2W. 45.2 t.
MS. Adtranz Derby 1999–2001. –/76. 42.5 t.
DMCL(B). Adtranz Derby 1999–2001. 9/53 1T. 45.2 t.

170 401	**FS**	P	*SR*	HA	50401	56401	79401
170 402	**FS**	P	*SR*	HA	50402	56402	79402
170 403	**SR**	P	*SR*	HA	50403	56403	79403
170 404	**FS**	P	*SR*	HA	50404	56404	79404
170 405	**FS**	P	*SR*	HA	50405	56405	79405
170 406	**FS**	P	*SR*	HA	50406	56406	79406
170 407	**SR**	P	*SR*	HA	50407	56407	79407
170 408	**FS**	P	*SR*	HA	50408	56408	79408
170 409	**FS**	P	*SR*	HA	50409	56409	79409
170 410	**FS**	P	*SR*	HA	50410	56410	79410
170 411	**FS**	P	*SR*	HA	50411	56411	79411
170 412	**FS**	P	*SR*	HA	50412	56412	79412
170 413	**FS**	P	*SR*	HA	50413	56413	79413
170 414	**FS**	P	*SR*	HA	50414	56414	79414
170 415	**FS**	P	*SR*	HA	50415	56415	79415
170 416	**FS**	H	*SR*	HA	50416	56416	79416
170 417	**FS**	H	*SR*	HA	50417	56417	79417
170 418	**FS**	H	*SR*	HA	50418	56418	79418
170 419	**FS**	H	*SR*	HA	50419	56419	79419
170 420	**SR**	H	*SR*	HA	50420	56420	79420
170 421	**SR**	H	*SR*	HA	50421	56421	79421
170 422	**SR**	H	*SR*	HA	50422	56422	79422
170 423	**SR**	H	*SR*	HA	50423	56423	79423
170 424	**SR**	H	*SR*	HA	50424	56424	79424

Class 170/4. First ScotRail "express" units. DMCL–MS–DMCL.
Dimensions: 23.62/23.61 x 2.75 m.

DMCL. Bombardier Derby 2003–2005. 9/43 1TD 2W. 46.8 t.
MS. Bombardier Derby 2003–2005. –/76. 43.7 t.
DMCL. Bombardier Derby 2003–2005. 9/53 1T. 46.5 t.

Notes: † 170 425 is running temporarily misformed to assess a new uprated engine fitted to 56431; an MTU 6H1800R83 of 360 kW (483 h.p.) at 1800 r.p.m.

* 170 431 is not currently formed. 50431 is out of traffic following collision damage.

170 425	†	**FS**	P	*SR*	HA	50425	56431	79425
170 426		**FS**	P	*SR*	HA	50426	56426	79426
170 427		**FS**	P	*SR*	HA	50427	56427	79427
170 428		**FS**	P	*SR*	HA	50428	56428	79428
170 429		**FS**	P	*SR*	HA	50429	56429	79429
170 430		**FS**	P	*SR*	HA	50430	56430	79430
170 431	*						
170 432		**FS**	P	*SR*	HA	50432	56432	79432
170 433		**FS**	P	*SR*	HA	50433	56433	79433
170 434		**FS**	P	*SR*	HA	50434	56434	79434
Spare		**FS**	P		ZC (U)	50431		
Spare		**FS**	P		ZD (U)		56425	

Class 170/4. First ScotRail "suburban" units. DMSL–MS–DMSL.
Dimensions: 23.62/23.61 x 2.75 m.

DMSL. Bombardier Derby 2004–2005. –/55 1TD 2W. 46.3 t.
MS. Bombardier Derby 2004–2005. –/76. 43.4 t.
DMSL. Bombardier Derby 2004–2005. –/67 1T. 46.4 t.

Note: 79460 is out of traffic following collision damage with 170 460 running with 79431 instead of 79460 at the time of writing.

170 450	**FS**	P	*SR*	HA	50450	56450	79450
170 451	**FS**	P	*SR*	HA	50451	56451	79451
170 452	**FS**	P	*SR*	HA	50452	56452	79452
170 453	**FS**	P	*SR*	HA	50453	56453	79453
170 454	**FS**	P	*SR*	HA	50454	56454	79454
170 455	**FS**	P	*SR*	HA	50455	56455	79455
170 456	**FS**	P	*SR*	HA	50456	56456	79456
170 457	**FS**	P	*SR*	HA	50457	56457	79457
170 458	**FS**	P	*SR*	HA	50458	56458	79458
170 459	**FS**	P	*SR*	HA	50459	56459	79459
170 460	**FS**	P	*SR*	HA	50460	56460	79431
170 461	**FS**	P	*SR*	HA	50461	56461	79461
Spare	**FS**	P		ZC (U)			79460

Class 170/4. First ScotRail units. Standard class only Strathclyde PTE units. DMSL–MS–DMSL.

50470–50471. DMSL(A). Adtranz Derby 2001. –/55 1TD 2W. 45.1 t.
50472–50478. DMSL(A). Bombardier Derby 2004–2005. –/57 1TD 2W. 46.3 t.
56470–56471. MS. Adtranz Derby 2001. –/76. 42.4 t.

56472–56478. MS. Bombardier Derby 2004–2005. –/76. 43.4 t.
79470–79471. DMSL(B). Adtranz Derby 2001. –/67 1T. 45.1 t.
79472–79478. DMSL(B). Bombardier Derby 2004–2005. –/67 1T. 46.4 t.

170 470	**SC**	P	*SR*	HA	50470	56470	79470
170 471	**SC**	P	*SR*	HA	50471	56471	79471
170 472	**SP**	P	*SR*	HA	50472	56472	79472
170 473	**SP**	P	*SR*	HA	50473	56473	79473
170 474	**SP**	P	*SR*	HA	50474	56474	79474
170 475	**SP**	P	*SR*	HA	50475	56475	79475
170 476	**SP**	P	*SR*	HA	50476	56476	79476
170 477	**SP**	P	*SR*	HA	50477	56477	79477
170 478	**SP**	P	*SR*	HA	50478	56478	79478

Class 170/5. Central Trains 2-car units. DMSL–DMSL.

DMSL(A). Adtranz Derby 1999–2000. –/55 1TD 2W. 45.8 t.
DMSL(B). Adtranz Derby 1999–2000. –/67 1T. 45.9 t.

170 501	**CT**	P	*CT*	TS	50501	79501
170 502	**CT**	P	*CT*	TS	50502	79502
170 503	**CT**	P	*CT*	TS	50503	79503
170 504	**CT**	P	*CT*	TS	50504	79504
170 505	**CT**	P	*CT*	TS	50505	79505
170 506	**CT**	P	*CT*	TS	50506	79506
170 507	**CT**	P	*CT*	TS	50507	79507
170 508	**CT**	P	*CT*	TS	50508	79508
170 509	**CT**	P	*CT*	TS	50509	79509
170 510	**CT**	P	*CT*	TS	50510	79510
170 511	**CT**	P	*CT*	TS	50511	79511
170 512	**CT**	P	*CT*	TS	50512	79512
170 513	**CT**	P	*CT*	TS	50513	79513
170 514	**CT**	P	*CT*	TS	50514	79514
170 515	**CT**	P	*CT*	TS	50515	79515
170 516	**CT**	P	*CT*	TS	50516	79516
170 517	**CT**	P	*CT*	TS	50517	79517
170 518	**CT**	P	*CT*	TS	50518	79518
170 519	**CT**	P	*CT*	TS	50519	79519
170 520	**CT**	P	*CT*	TS	50520	79520
170 521	**CT**	P	*CT*	TS	50521	79521
170 522	**CT**	P	*CT*	TS	50522	79522
170 523	**CT**	P	*CT*	TS	50523	79523

Class 170/6. Central Trains 3-car units. DMSL–MS–DMSL.

DMSL(A). Adtranz Derby 2000. –/55 1TD 2W. 45.8 t.
MS. Adtranz Derby 2000. –/74. 42.4 t.
DMSL(B). Adtranz Derby 2000. –/67 1T. 45.9 t.

170 630	**CT**	P	*CT*	TS	50630	56630	79630
170 631	**CT**	P	*CT*	TS	50631	56631	79631
170 632	**CT**	P	*CT*	TS	50632	56632	79632
170 633	**CT**	P	*CT*	TS	50633	56633	79633
170 634	**CT**	P	*CT*	TS	50634	56634	79634

170 635	**CT**	P	*CT*	TS	50635	56635	79635
170 636	**CT**	P	*CT*	TS	50636	56636	79636
170 637	**CT**	P	*CT*	TS	50637	56637	79637
170 638	**CT**	P	*CT*	TS	50638	56638	79638
170 639	**CT**	P	*CT*	TS	50639	56639	79639

CLASS 171　　TURBOSTAR　　BOMBARDIER

DMCL–DMSL or DMCL–MS–MS–DMCL. Southern units. Air conditioned.

Construction: Welded aluminium bodies with bolt-on steel ends.
Engines: One MTU 6R183TD13H of 315 kW (422 h.p.) at 1900 r.p.m.
Transmission: Hydraulic. Voith T211rzze to ZF final drive.
Bogies: One Adtranz P3–23 and one BREL T3–23 per car.
Couplers: Dellner 12 at outer ends, bar within unit (Class 171/8s).
Gangways: Within unit only.　　**Wheel Arrangement:** 2-B (+ B-2 + B-2) + B-2.
Doors: Twin-leaf swing plug.　　**Maximum Speed:** 100 m.p.h.
Seating Layout: 1: 2+1 facing/unidirectional. 2: 2+2 facing/unidirectional.
Multiple Working: Within class and with EMU Classes 375 and 377 in an emergency.

Class 171/7. Southern 2-car units. DMCL–DMSL.
Dimensions: 24.10 x 2.70 m (171 721–171 726). 23.70 x 2.75 m (171 727–171 729).

50721–50726. DMCL. Bombardier Derby 2003. 9/43 1TD 2W. 47.6 t.
50727–50729. DMCL. Bombardier Derby 2005. 9/43 1TD 2W. 46.3 t.
79721–79726. DMSL. Bombardier Derby 2003. –/64 1T. 47.8 t.
79727–79729. DMSL. Bombardier Derby 2005. –/64 1T. 46.2 t.

Note: 171 721–171 726 were built as Class 170s (170 721–170 726), but renumbered as 171s on fitting with Dellner couplers.

171 721	**SN**	P	*SN*	SU	50721	79721
171 722	**SN**	P	*SN*	SU	50722	79722
171 723	**SN**	P	*SN*	SU	50723	79723
171 724	**SN**	P	*SN*	SU	50724	79724
171 725	**SN**	P	*SN*	SU	50725	79725
171 726	**SN**	P	*SN*	SU	50726	79726
171 727	**SN**	P	*SN*	SU	50727	79727
171 728	**SN**	P	*SN*	SU	50728	79728
171 729	**SN**	P	*SN*	SU	50729	79729

Class 171/8. Southern 4-car units. DMCL(A)–MS–MS–DMCL(B).
Dimensions: 23.70/23.61 x 2.75 m.

DMCL(A). Bombardier Derby 2004. 9/43 1TD 2W. 46.5 t.
MS. Bombardier Derby 2004. –/74. 43.7 t.
DMCL(B). Bombardier Derby 2004. 9/50 1T. 46.5 t.

171 801	**SN**	P	*SN*	SU	50801	54801	56801	79801
171 802	**SN**	P	*SN*	SU	50802	54802	56802	79802
171 803	**SN**	P	*SN*	SU	50803	54803	56803	79803
171 804	**SN**	P	*SN*	SU	50804	54804	56804	79804
171 805	**SN**	P	*SN*	SU	50805	54805	56805	79805
171 806	**SN**	P	*SN*	SU	50806	54806	56806	79806

CLASS 175   CORADIA 1000   ALSTOM

Air conditioned.

Construction: Steel.
Engines: One Cummins N14 of 335 kW (450 h.p.).
Transmission: Hydraulic. Voith T211rzze to ZF Voith final drive.
Bogies: ACR (Alstom FBO) – LTB-MBS1, TB-MB1, MBS1-LTB.
Couplers: Scharfenberg outer ends and bar within unit (Class 175/1).
Dimensions: 23.06/23.93 x 2.80 m.
Gangways: Within unit only.   **Wheel Arrangement:** 2-B (+ B-2) + B-2.
Doors: Single-leaf swing plug.   **Maximum Speed:** 100 m.p.h.
Seating Layout: 2+2 facing/unidirectional.
Multiple Working: Within class and with Class 180.

Class 175/0. DMSL–DMSL. 2-car units.

DMSL(A). Alstom Birmingham 1999–2000. –/54 1TD 2W. 50.7 t.
DMSL(B). Alstom Birmingham 1999–2000. –/64 1T. 50.7 t.

175 001	**FS**	A	*AW*	CH	50701	79701
175 002	**FS**	A	*AW*	CH	50702	79702
175 003	**FS**	A	*AW*	CH	50703	79703
175 004	**FS**	A	*AW*	CH	50704	79704
175 005	**FS**	A	*AW*	CH	50705	79705
175 006	**FS**	A	*AW*	CH	50706	79706
175 007	**FS**	A	*AW*	CH	50707	79707
175 008	**AW**	A	*AW*	CH	50708	79708
175 009	**FS**	A	*AW*	CH	50709	79709
175 010	**FS**	A	*AW*	CH	50710	79710
175 011	**FS**	A	*AW*	CH	50711	79711

Names (carried on one side of each DMSL):

175 003	Eisteddfod Genedlaethol Cymru
175 004	MENCAP National Colleges Pengwern College
175 006	Brondyffryn Trust

Class 175/1. DMSL–MSL–DMSL. 3-car units.

DMSL(A). Alstom Birmingham 1999–2001. –/54 1TD 2W. 50.7 t.
MSL. Alstom Birmingham 1999–2001. –/68 1T. 47.5 t.
DMSL(B). Alstom Birmingham 1999–2001. –/64 1T. 50.7 t.

175 101	**FS**	A	*AW*	CH	50751	56751	79751
175 102	**FS**	A	*AW*	CH	50752	56752	79752
175 103	**FS**	A	*AW*	CH	50753	56753	79753
175 104	**FS**	A	*AW*	CH	50754	56754	79754
175 105	**FS**	A	*AW*	CH	50755	56755	79755
175 106	**FS**	A	*AW*	CH	50756	56756	79756
175 107	**FS**	A	*AW*	CH	50757	56757	79757
175 108	**FS**	A	*AW*	CH	50758	56758	79758
175 109	**FS**	A	*AW*	CH	50759	56759	79759
175 110	**AW**	A	*AW*	CH	50760	56760	79760

175 111	FS	A	AW	CH	50761	56761	79761
175 112	FS	A	AW	CH	50762	56762	79762
175 113	FS	A	AW	CH	50763	56763	79763
175 114	FS	A	AW	CH	50764	56764	79764
175 115	FS	A	AW	CH	50765	56765	79765
175 116	FS	A	AW	CH	50766	56766	79766

Names (carried on one side of each DMSL):

175 103	Mum
175 107	CORONATION ST. ROVERS RETURN
175 111	Brief Encounter
175 112	South Lakes Wild Animal Park SUMATRAN TIGER
175 114	Commonwealth Cruiser
175 116	PETER VL JONES Community Rail Officer – Conwy Valley Line

CLASS 180   ADELANTE   ALSTOM

Air conditioned.

Construction: Steel.
Engines: One Cummins QSK19 of 560 kW (750 h.p.) at 2100 r.p.m.
Transmission: Hydraulic. Voith T312br to Voith final drive.
Bogies: ACR (Alstom FBO) – LTB1-MBS2, TB1-MB2, TB1-MB2, TB2-MB2, MBS2-LTB1.
Couplers: Scharfenberg outer ends, bar within unit.
Dimensions: 23.71/23.03 x 2.80 m.
Gangways: Within unit only.
Wheel Arrangement: 2-B + B-2 + B-2 + B-2 + B-2.
Doors: Single-leaf swing plug.   **Maximum Speed:** 125 m.p.h.
Seating Layout: 1: 2+1 facing/unidirectional, 2: 2+2 facing/unidirectional.
Multiple Working: Within class and with Class 175.

DMSL(A). Alstom Birmingham 2000–2001. –/46 2W 1TD. 51.7 t.
MFL. Alstom Birmingham 2000–2001. 42/– 1T 1W + catering point. 49.6 t.
MSL. Alstom Birmingham 2000–2001. –/68 1T. 49.5 t.
MSLRB. Alstom Birmingham 2000–2001. –/56 1T. 50.3 t.
DMSL(B). Alstom Birmingham 2000–2001. –/56 1T. 51.4 t.

180 101	FG	A	GW	OO	50901	54901	55901	56901	59901
180 102	FG	A	GW	OO	50902	54902	55902	56902	59902
180 103	FG	A	GW	OO	50903	54903	55903	56903	59903
180 104	FG	A	GW	OO	50904	54904	55904	56904	59904
180 105	FG	A	GW	OO	50905	54905	55905	56905	59905
180 106	FG	A	GW	OO	50906	54906	55906	56906	59906
180 107	FG	A	GW	OO	50907	54907	55907	56907	59907
180 108	FG	A	GW	OO	50908	54908	55908	56908	59908
180 109	FG	A	GW	OO	50909	54909	55909	56909	59909
180 110	FG	A	GW	OO	50910	54910	55910	56910	59910
180 111	FG	A	GW	OO	50911	54911	55911	56911	59911
180 112	FG	A	GW	OO	50912	54912	55912	56912	59912
180 113	FG	A	GW	OO	50913	54913	55913	56913	59913
180 114	FG	A	GW	OO	50914	54914	55914	56914	59914

CLASS 185   DESIRO UK   SIEMENS

Air conditioned. New Trans-Pennine Express units.

Construction: Aluminium.
Engines: One Cummins QSK19 of 560 kW (750 h.p.) at 2100 r.p.m.
Transmission: Voith.
Bogies: Siemens.
Couplers: Dellner 12.
Dimensions: 23.76/23.75 x 2.66 m.
Gangways: Within unit only.   **Wheel Arrangement:** 2-B + 2-B + B-2.
Doors: Double-leaf sliding plug.   **Maximum Speed:** 100 m.p.h.
Seating Layout: 1: 2+1 facing/unidirectional, 2: 2+2 facing/unidirectional.
Multiple Working: Within class only.

DMCL. Siemens Uerdingen 2005–2006. 15/18(8) 2W 1TD + catering point. 55.4 t.
MSL. Siemens Uerdingen 2005–2006. –/72 1T. 52.7 t.
DMS. Siemens Uerdingen 2005–2006. –/64(4). 54.9 t.

185 101	**FT**	H	*TP*	AK	51101	53101	54101
185 102	**FT**	H	*TP*	AK	51102	53102	54102
185 103	**FT**	H	*TP*	AK	51103	53103	54103
185 104	**FT**	H	*TP*	AK	51104	53104	54104
185 105	**FT**	H	*TP*	AK	51105	53105	54105
185 106	**FT**	H	*TP*	AK	51106	53106	54106
185 107	**FT**	H	*TP*	AK	51107	53107	54107
185 108	**FT**	H	*TP*	AK	51108	53108	54108
185 109	**FT**	H	*TP*	AK	51109	53109	54109
185 110	**FT**	H	*TP*	AK	51110	53110	54110
185 111	**FT**	H	*TP*	AK	51111	53111	54111
185 112	**FT**	H	*TP*	AK	51112	53112	54112
185 113	**FT**	H	*TP*	AK	51113	53113	54113
185 114	**FT**	H	*TP*	AK	51114	53114	54114
185 115	**FT**	H	*TP*	AK	51115	53115	54115
185 116	**FT**	H	*TP*	AK	51116	53116	54116
185 117	**FT**	H	*TP*	AK	51117	53117	54117
185 118	**FT**	H	*TP*	AK	51118	53118	54118
185 119	**FT**	H	*TP*	AK	51119	53119	54119
185 120	**FT**	H	*TP*	AK	51120	53120	54120
185 121	**FT**	H	*TP*	AK	51121	53121	54121
185 122	**FT**	H	*TP*	AK	51122	53122	54122
185 123	**FT**	H	*TP*	AK	51123	53123	54123
185 124	**FT**	H	*TP*	AK	51124	53124	54124
185 125	**FT**	H	*TP*	AK	51125	53125	54125
185 126	**FT**	H	*TP*	AK	51126	53126	54126
185 127	**FT**	H	*TP*	AK	51127	53127	54127
185 128	**FT**	H	*TP*	AK	51128	53128	54128
185 129	**FT**	H	*TP*	AK	51129	53129	54129
185 130	**FT**	H	*TP*	AK	51130	53130	54130
185 131	**FT**	H	*TP*	AK	51131	53131	54131
185 132	**FT**	H	*TP*	AK	51132	53132	54132

185 133	**FT**	H	*TP*	AK	51133	53133	54133
185 134	**FT**	H	*TP*	AK	51134	53134	54134
185 135	**FT**	H	*TP*	AK	51135	53135	54135
185 136	**FT**	H	*TP*	AK	51136	53136	54136
185 137	**FT**	H	*TP*	AK	51137	53137	54137
185 138	**FT**	H	*TP*	AK	51138	53138	54138
185 139	**FT**	H	*TP*	AK	51139	53139	54139
185 140	**FT**	H	*TP*	AK	51140	53140	54140
185 141	**FT**	H	*TP*	AK	51141	53141	54141
185 142	**FT**	H	*TP*	AK	51142	53142	54142
185 143	**FT**	H	*TP*	AK	51143	53143	54143
185 144	**FT**	H	*TP*	AK	51144	53144	54144
185 145	**FT**	H	*TP*	AK	51145	53145	54145
185 146	**FT**	H	*TP*	AK	51146	53146	54146
185 147	**FT**	H	*TP*	AK	51147	53147	54147
185 148	**FT**	H	*TP*	AK	51148	53148	54148
185 149	**FT**	H	*TP*	AK	51149	53149	54149
185 150	**FT**	H	*TP*	AK	51150	53150	54150
185 151	**FT**	H	*TP*	AK	51151	53151	54151

3.2. DIESEL ELECTRIC UNITS

CLASS 201/202 PRESERVED "HASTINGS" UNIT BR

DMBS–TSL–TSL–TSRB–TSL–DMBS.

Preserved unit made up from two Class 201 short-frame cars and three Class 202 long-frame cars. The "Hastings" units were made with narrow body-profiles for use on the section between Tonbridge and Battle which had tunnels of restricted loading gauge. These tunnels were converted to single track operation in the 1980s thus allowing standard loading gauge stock to be used. The set also contains a Class 411 EMU trailer (not Hastings line gauge) and a Class 422 EMU buffet car.

Construction: Steel.
Engine: One English Electric 4SRKT Mk. 2 of 450 kW (600 h.p.) at 850 r.p.m.
Main Generator: English Electric EE824.
Traction Motors: Two English Electric EE507 mounted on the inner bogie.
Bogies: SR Mk. 4. (Former EMU TSL vehicles have Commonwealth bogies).
Couplers: Drophead buckeye.
Dimensions: 18.40 x 2.70 m (60000), 20.35 x 2.74 m (60116/60118/60529), 18.36 x 2.74 m (60501), 20.35 x 2.82 m (69337), 20.30 x 2.82 m (70262).
Gangways: Within unit only.
Doors: Manually operated slam.
Brakes: Electro-pneumatic and automatic air.
Maximum Speed: 75 m.p.h.
Seating Layout: 2+2 facing.
Multiple Working: Other ex-BR Southern Region DEMU vehicles.

60000. DMBS. Lot No. 30329 Eastleigh 1957. –/22. 55.0 t.
60116. DMBS (Spare). Lot No. 30395 Eastleigh 1957. –/31. 56.0 t.
60118. DMBS. Lot No. 30395 Eastleigh 1957. –/30. 56.0 t.
60501. TSL. Lot No. 30331 Hastings 1957. –/52 2T. 29.5 t.
60529. TSL. Lot No. 30397 Eastleigh 1957. –/60 2T. 30.5 t.
69337. TSRB (ex-Class 422 EMU). Lot No. 30805 York 1970. –/40. 35.0 t.
70262. TSL (ex-Class 411/5 EMU). Lot No. 30455 Eastleigh 1958. –/64 2T. 31.5 t.

201 001	**G**	HD *HD*	SE	60000	60529	70262	69337	60501	60118
Spare	**G**	HD *HD*	SE	60116					

Names:

60000 Hastings
60116 Mountfield
60118 Tunbridge Wells

CLASS 220   VOYAGER   BOMBARDIER

DMS–MSRMB–MS–DMF.

Construction: Steel.
Engine: Cummins QSK19 of 560 kW (750 h.p.) at 1800 r.p.m.
Transmission: Two Alstom Onix 800 three-phase traction motors of 275 kW.
Braking: Rheostatic and electro-pneumatic.
Bogies: Bombardier B5005.
Couplers: Dellner 12 at outer ends, bar within unit.
Dimensions: 23.67/23.00(602xx) x 2.73 m.
Gangways: Within unit only.
Wheel Arrangement: 1A-A1 + 1A-A1 + 1A-A1 + 1A-A1.
Doors: Single-leaf swing plug.
Maximum Speed: 125 m.p.h.
Seating Layout: 1: 2+1 facing/unidirectional, 2: 2+2 mainly unidirectional.
Multiple Working: Within class and with Classes 221 and 222. Also can be controlled from Class 57/3 locomotives.

DMS. Bombardier Brugge/Wakefield 2000–2001. –/42 1TD 1W. 48.0 t.
MSRMB. Bombardier Brugge/Wakefield 2000–2001. –/58. 45.0 t.
MS. Bombardier Brugge/Wakefield 2000–2001. –/60 1TD. 44.5 t.
DMF. Bombardier Brugge/Wakefield 2000–2001. 26/– 1TD 1W. 48.1 t.

220 001	**VT**	HX	*VX*	CZ	60301	60701	60201	60401
220 002	**VT**	HX	*VX*	CZ	60302	60702	60202	60402
220 003	**VT**	HX	*VX*	CZ	60303	60703	60203	60403
220 004	**VT**	HX	*VX*	CZ	60304	60704	60204	60404
220 005	**VT**	HX	*VX*	CZ	60305	60705	60205	60405
220 006	**VT**	HX	*VX*	CZ	60306	60706	60206	60406
220 007	**VT**	HX	*VX*	CZ	60307	60707	60207	60407
220 008	**VT**	HX	*VX*	CZ	60308	60708	60208	60408
220 009	**VT**	HX	*VX*	CZ	60309	60709	60209	60409
220 010	**VT**	HX	*VX*	CZ	60310	60710	60210	60410
220 011	**VT**	HX	*VX*	CZ	60311	60711	60211	60411
220 012	**VT**	HX	*VX*	CZ	60312	60712	60212	60412
220 013	**VT**	HX	*VX*	CZ	60313	60713	60213	60413
220 014	**VT**	HX	*VX*	CZ	60314	60714	60214	60414
220 015	**VT**	HX	*VX*	CZ	60315	60715	60215	60415
220 016	**VT**	HX	*VX*	CZ	60316	60716	60216	60416
220 017	**VT**	HX	*VX*	CZ	60317	60717	60217	60417
220 018	**VT**	HX	*VX*	CZ	60318	60718	60218	60418
220 019	**VT**	HX	*VX*	CZ	60319	60719	60219	60419
220 020	**VT**	HX	*VX*	CZ	60320	60720	60220	60420
220 021	**VT**	HX	*VX*	CZ	60321	60721	60221	60421
220 022	**VT**	HX	*VX*	CZ	60322	60722	60222	60422
220 023	**VT**	HX	*VX*	CZ	60323	60723	60223	60423
220 024	**VT**	HX	*VX*	CZ	60324	60724	60224	60424
220 025	**VT**	HX	*VX*	CZ	60325	60725	60225	60425
220 026	**VT**	HX	*VX*	CZ	60326	60726	60226	60426
220 027	**VT**	HX	*VX*	CZ	60327	60727	60227	60427
220 028	**VT**	HX	*VX*	CZ	60328	60728	60228	60428

220 029	**VT**	HX	*VX*	CZ	60329	60729	60229	60429
220 030	**VT**	HX	*VX*	CZ	60330	60730	60230	60430
220 031	**VT**	HX	*VX*	CZ	60331	60731	60231	60431
220 032	**VT**	HX	*VX*	CZ	60332	60732	60232	60432
220 033	**VT**	HX	*VX*	CZ	60333	60733	60233	60433
220 034	**VT**	HX	*VX*	CZ	60334	60734	60234	60434

Names (carried on MS):

220 001	Somerset Voyager	220 018	Dorset Voyager
220 002	Forth Voyager	220 019	Mersey Voyager
220 003	Solent Voyager	220 020	Wessex Voyager
220 004	Cumbrian Voyager	220 021	Staffordshire Voyager
220 005	Guildford Voyager	220 022	Brighton Voyager
220 006	Clyde Voyager	220 023	Mancunian Voyager
220 007	Thames Voyager	220 024	Sheffield Voyager
220 008	Draig Gymreig/Welsh Dragon	220 025	Severn Voyager
220 009	Gatwick Voyager	220 026	Stagecoach Voyager
220 010	Ribble Voyager	220 027	Avon Voyager
220 011	Tyne Voyager	220 028	Black Country Voyager
220 012	Lanarkshire Voyager	220 029	Vyajer Kernewek/Cornish Voyager
220 013	Gwibiwr De Cymru/South Wales Voyager	220 030	Devon Voyager
220 014	South Yorkshire Voyager	220 031	Tay Voyager
220 015	Solway Voyager	220 032	Grampian Voyager
220 016	Midland Voyager	220 033	Fife Voyager
220 017	BOMBARDIER Voyager	220 034	Yorkshire Voyager

CLASS 221   SUPER VOYAGER   BOMBARDIER

DMS–MSRMB–MS(–MS)–DMF. Tilting units.

Construction: Steel.
Engine: Cummins QSK19 of 560 kW (750 h.p.) at 1800 r.p.m.
Transmission: Two Alstom Onix 800 three-phase traction motors of 275 kW.
Braking: Rheostatic and electro-pneumatic.
Bogies: Bombardier HVP.
Couplers: Dellner 12 at outer ends, bar within unit.
Dimensions: 23.67 x 2.73 m.
Gangways: Within unit only.
Wheel Arrangement: 1A-A1 + 1A-A1 + 1A-A1 (+ 1A-A1) + 1A-A1.
Doors: Single-leaf swing plug.
Maximum Speed: 125 m.p.h.
Seating Layout: 1: 2+1 facing/unidirectional, 2: 2+2 mainly unidirectional.
Multiple Working: Within class and with Classes 221 and 222. Also can be controlled from Class 57/3 locomotives.

DMS. Bombardier Brugge/Wakefield 2001–2002. –/42 1TD 1W. 56.6 t.
MSRMB. Bombardier Brugge/Wakefield 2001–2002. –/58. 53.1 t.
60951–60994. MS. Bombardier Brugge/Wakefield 2001–2002. –/60 1TD. 56.6 t.
60851–60890. MS. Bombardier Brugge/Wakefield 2001–2002. –/60 1TD. 53.1 t.
DMF. Bombardier Brugge/Wakefield 2001–2002. 26/– 1TD 1W. 56.6 t.

221 101	**VT**	HX	*VX*	CZ	60351	60751	60951	60851	60451
221 102	**VT**	HX	*VX*	CZ	60352	60752	60952	60852	60452
221 103	**VT**	HX	*VX*	CZ	60353	60753	60953	60853	60453
221 104	**VT**	HX	*VX*	CZ	60354	60754	60954	60854	60454
221 105	**VT**	HX	*VX*	CZ	60355	60755	60955	60855	60455
221 106	**VT**	HX	*VX*	CZ	60356	60756	60956	60856	60456
221 107	**VT**	HX	*VX*	CZ	60357	60757	60957	60857	60457
221 108	**VT**	HX	*VX*	CZ	60358	60758	60958	60858	60458
221 109	**VT**	HX	*VX*	CZ	60359	60759	60959	60859	60459
221 110	**VT**	HX	*VX*	CZ	60360	60760	60960	60860	60460
221 111	**VT**	HX	*VX*	CZ	60361	60761	60961	60861	60461
221 112	**VT**	HX	*VX*	CZ	60362	60762	60962	60862	60462
221 113	**VT**	HX	*VX*	CZ	60363	60763	60963	60863	60463
221 114	**VT**	HX	*VX*	CZ	60364	60764	60964	60864	60464
221 115	**VT**	HX	*VX*	CZ	60365	60765	60965	60865	60465
221 116	**VT**	HX	*VX*	CZ	60366	60766	60966	60866	60466
221 117	**VT**	HX	*VX*	CZ	60367	60767	60967	60867	60467
221 118	**VT**	HX	*VX*	CZ	60368	60768	60968	60868	60468
221 119	**VT**	HX	*VX*	CZ	60369	60769	60969	60869	60469
221 120	**VT**	HX	*VX*	CZ	60370	60770	60970	60870	60470
221 121	**VT**	HX	*VX*	CZ	60371	60771	60971	60871	60471
221 122	**VT**	HX	*VX*	CZ	60372	60772	60972	60872	60472
221 123	**VT**	HX	*VX*	CZ	60373	60773	60973	60873	60473
221 124	**VT**	HX	*VX*	CZ	60374	60774	60974	60874	60474
221 125	**VT**	HX	*VX*	CZ	60375	60775	60975	60875	60475
221 126	**VT**	HX	*VX*	CZ	60376	60776	60976	60876	60476
221 127	**VT**	HX	*VX*	CZ	60377	60777	60977	60877	60477
221 128	**VT**	HX	*VX*	CZ	60378	60778	60978	60878	60478
221 129	**VT**	HX	*VX*	CZ	60379	60779	60979	60879	60479
221 130	**VT**	HX	*VX*	CZ	60380	60780	60980	60880	60480
221 131	**VT**	HX	*VX*	CZ	60381	60781	60981	60881	60481
221 132	**VT**	HX	*VX*	CZ	60382	60782	60982	60882	60482
221 133	**VT**	HX	*VX*	CZ	60383	60783	60983	60883	60483
221 134	**VT**	HX	*VX*	CZ	60384	60784	60984	60884	60484
221 135	**VT**	HX	*VX*	CZ	60385	60785	60985	60885	60485
221 136	**VT**	HX	*VX*	CZ	60386	60786	60986	60886	60486
221 137	**VT**	HX	*VX*	CZ	60387	60787	60987	60887	60487
221 138	**VT**	HX	*VX*	CZ	60388	60788	60988	60888	60488
221 139	**VT**	HX	*VX*	CZ	60389	60789	60989	60889	60489
221 140	**VT**	HX	*VX*	CZ	60390	60790	60990	60890	60490
221 141	**VT**	HX	*VX*	CZ	60391	60791	60991		60491
221 142	**VT**	HX	*VX*	CZ	60392	60792	60992		60492
221 143	**VT**	HX	*VX*	CZ	60393	60793	60993		60493
221 144	**VT**	HX	*VX*	CZ	60394	60794	60994		60494

Names (carried on MS No. 609xx):

221 101	Louis Bleriot	221 123	Henry Hudson
221 102	John Cabot	221 124	Charles Lindbergh
221 103	Christopher Columbus	221 125	Henry the Navigator
221 104	Sir John Franklin	221 126	Captain Robert Scott
221 105	William Baffin	221 127	Wright Brothers
221 106	Willem Barents	221 128	Captain John Smith
221 107	Sir Martin Frobisher	221 129	George Vancouver
221 108	Sir Ernest Shackleton	221 130	Michael Palin
221 109	Marco Polo	221 131	Edgar Evans
221 110	James Cook	221 132	William Speirs Bruce
221 111	Roald Amundsen	221 133	Alexander Selkirk
221 112	Ferdinand Magellan	221 134	Mary Kingsley
221 113	Sir Walter Raleigh	221 135	Donald Campbell
221 114	Sir Francis Drake	221 136	Yuri Gagarin
221 115	Sir Francis Chichester	221 137	Mayflower Pilgrims
221 116	David Livingstone	221 138	Thor Heyerdahl
221 117	Sir Henry Morton Stanley	221 139	Leif Erikson
221 118	Mungo Park	221 140	Vasco da Gama
221 119	Amelia Earhart	221 141	Amerigo Vespucci
221 120	Amy Johnson	221 142	Matthew Flinders
221 121	Charles Darwin	221 143	Auguste Picard
221 122	Doctor Who	221 144	Prince Madoc

CLASS 222 MERIDIAN/PIONEER BOMBARDIER

Construction: Steel.
Engine: Cummins QSK19 of 560 kW (750 h.p.) at 1800 r.p.m.
Transmission: Two Alstom Onix 800 three-phase traction motors of 275 kW.
Braking: Rheostatic and electro-pneumatic.
Bogies: Bombardier B5005.
Couplers: Dellner at outer ends, bar within unit.
Dimensions: 23.85/23.00 x 2.73 m.
Gangways: Within unit only.   **Wheel Arrangement:** All cars 1A-A1.
Doors: Single-leaf swing plug.   **Maximum Speed:** 125 m.p.h.
Seating Layout: 1: 2+1, 2: 2+2 facing/unidirectional.
Multiple Working: Within class and with Classes 220 and 221.

222 001–222 007. Midland Mainline Meridian. 8-car units. DMRFO–MFO–MFO–MSORMB–MSO–MSO–MSO–DMSO.

Note: The 8-car units were built as 9-car units, but in late 2006 one MSO (6053x series) was removed and used to augment 222 011–222 017 to 5-car sets.

DMRFO. Bombardier Brugge 2004–2005. 22/– 1TD 1W. 52.8 t.
MFO. Bombardier Brugge 2004–2005. 42/– 1T. 46.8 t.
MSO. Bombardier Brugge 2004–2005. –/68 1T. 47.0 t.
MSORMB. Bombardier Brugge 2004–2005. –/62. 48.0 t.
DMSO. Bombardier Brugge 2004–2005. –/38 1TD 1W. 49.4 t.

222 001	**MN**	H	*MM*	DY	60241	60441	60341	60621
					60561	60551	60541	60161

222 002	**MN**	H	*MM*	DY	60242	60442	60342	60622
					60562	60552	60542	60162
222 003	**MN**	H	*MM*	DY	60243	60443	60343	60623
					60563	60553	60543	60163
222 004	**MN**	H	*MM*	DY	60244	60444	60344	60624
					60564	60554	60544	60164
222 005	**MN**	H	*MM*	DY	60245	60445	60345	60625
					60565	60555	60545	60165
222 006	**MN**	H	*MM*	DY	60246	60446	60346	60626
					60566	60556	60546	60166
222 007	**MN**	H	*MM*	DY	60247	60447	60347	60627
					60567	60557	60547	60167

222 008–222 023. Midland Mainline Meridian. 4-car or 5-car units. DMRFO–MCO–MSORMB–(MSO)–DMSO.

DMRFO. Bombardier Brugge 2003–2004. 22/– 1TD 1W. 52.8 t.
MCO. Bombardier Brugge 2003–2004. 28/22 1T. 48.6 t.
MSORMB. Bombardier Brugge 2003–2004. –/62. 49.6 t.
MSO. Bombardier Brugge 2004–2005. –/68 1T. 47.0 t.
DMSO. Bombardier Brugge 2003–2004. –/40 1TD 1W. 51.0 t.

222 008	**MN**	H	*MM*	DY	60248	60918	60628		60168
222 009	**MN**	H	*MM*	DY	60249	60919	60629		60169
222 010	**MN**	H	*MM*	DY	60250	60920	60630		60170
222 011	**MN**	H	*MM*	DY	60251	60921	60631	60531	60171
222 012	**MN**	H	*MM*	DY	60252	60922	60632	60532	60172
222 013	**MN**	H	*MM*	DY	60253	60923	60633	60533	60173
222 014	**MN**	H	*MM*	DY	60254	60924	60634	60534	60174
222 015	**MN**	H	*MM*	DY	60255	60925	60635	60535	60175
222 016	**MN**	H	*MM*	DY	60256	60926	60636	60536	60176
222 017	**MN**	H	*MM*	DY	60257	60927	60637	60537	60177
222 018	**MN**	H	*MM*	DY	60258	60928	60638		60178
222 019	**MN**	H	*MM*	DY	60259	60929	60639		60179
222 020	**MN**	H	*MM*	DY	60260	60930	60640		60180
222 021	**MN**	H	*MM*	DY	60261	60931	60641		60181
222 022	**MN**	H	*MM*	DY	60262	60932	60642		60182
222 023	**MN**	H	*MM*	DY	60263	60933	60643		60183

222 101–222 104. Hull Trains Pioneer. DMRFO–MCO–MSORMB–DMSO.

DMRFO. Bombardier Brugge 2005. 22/– 1TD 1W. 52.8 t.
MCO. Bombardier Brugge 2005. 11/46 1T. 48.6 t.
MSORMB. Bombardier Brugge 2005. –/62. 49.6 t.
DMSO. Bombardier Brugge 2005. –/40 1TD 1W. 51.0 t.

222 101	**HT**	H	*HT*	XW	60271	60571	60681	60191
222 102	**HT**	H	*HT*	XW	60272	60572	60682	60192
222 103	**HT**	H	*HT*	XW	60273	60573	60683	60193
222 104	**HT**	H	*HT*	XW	60274	60574	60684	60194

Names (carried on end cars):

| 222 101 | Professor GEORGE GRAY | 222 103 | Dr JOHN GODBER |
| 222 102 | Professor STUART PALMER | 222 104 | Sir TERRY FARRELL |

3.3. SERVICE DMUS

This section lists vehicles not used for passenger-carrying purposes. Some vehicles are numbered in the special service stock number series.

CLASS 901   ULTRASONIC TEST UNIT

DM–DM. Converted 1986 from Class 101. Gangwayed within unit. Usually operates with 999602 (see below) as a centre car.

Construction: Aluminium alloy body on steel underframe.
Engines: Two Leyland 680/1 of 112 kW (150 h.p.) at 1800 r.p.m. per power car.
Transmission: Mechanical. Cardan shaft and freewheel to a four-speed epicyclic gearbox with a further cardan shaft to the final drive, each engine driving the inner axle of one bogie.
Brakes: Air.   **Bogies:** DD15 (motor) and DT11 (trailer).
Couplers: Screw couplings.   **Maximum Speed:** 70 m.p.h.
Dimensions: 18.50 x 2.82 m.
Doors: Manually-operated slam.
Multiple Working: "Blue Square" coupling code. First generation vehicles may be coupled together to work in multiple up to a maximum of 6 motor cars or 12 cars in total in a formation. First generation vehicles may not be coupled in multiple with second generation vehicles.

977391. DM. Lot No. 30500 Metro-Cammell. 1959. 32.5 t.
977392. DM. Lot No. 30254 Metro-Cammell. 1956. 32.5 t.

901 001	Y	NR *SO*	ZA	977391	(51433)	977392	(53167)

CLASS 901 ULTRASONIC TEST UNIT (EXTRA VEHICLE)

T. Converted 1986 from Class 432 EMU. Gangwayed. Operates with 977391/977392 (see above).

Construction: Steel.   **Maximum Speed:** 70 m.p.h.
Bogies: SR Mk. 6.   **Couplings:** Screw.
Brakes: Twin pipe vacuum.   **Multiple Working:** Blue Square.
Doors: Manually operated slam. **Dimensions:** 20.35 x 2.82 m.

999602. T. Lot No. 30862 York 1974. 55.5 t.

-	Y	NR *SO*	ZA	999602	(62483)

CLASS 901   TEST UNIT (Iris 2)

DM–DM. Converted 1991 from Class 101. Gangwayed within unit.

For details see above.

977693. DM. Lot No. 30261 Metro-Cammell. 1957. 32.5 t.
977694. DM. Lot No. 30276 Metro-Cammell. 1958. 32.5 t.

901 002	Y	NR *SO*	ZA	977693	(53222)	977694	(53338)

CLASS 930   SANDITE/DE-ICING UNIT

DMB–T–DMB. Converted 1993 from Class 205. Gangwayed within unit. Sandite Trailer 977870 is replaced by De-icing trailer 977364 (see below) as required.

Construction: Steel.
Engine: One English Electric 4SRKT Mk. 2 of 450 kW (600 h.p.) at 850 r.p.m.
Transmission: Electric. Two English Electric EE507 traction motors mounted on the bogie at the non-driving end of each power car.
Maximum Speed: 75 m.p.h.   **Bogies:** SR Mk. 4.
Brakes: Electro-pneumatic and automatic air.
Doors: Manually operated slam.   **Couplings:** Drophead buckeye.
Multiple Working: Classes 201–207.
Dimensions: 20.33 x 2.82 m. (DMB); 20.28 x 2.82 m.

977939–977940. DMB. Lot No. 30671 Eastleigh 1962. 56.0 t.
977870. T. Lot No. 30542 Eastleigh 1959. 30.5 t.

930 301	**RO**	NR	*SN*	SE	977939	(60145)	977870	(60660)
					977940	(60149)		

UNCLASSIFIED   DE-ICING TRAILER

T. Converted 1960 from 4-Sub EMU vehicle. Non gangwayed. Operates with 977939/977940 (see above) in place of Sandite Trailer 977870.

Construction: Steel.
Maximum Speed: 70 m.p.h.   **Couplings:** Drophead buckeye.
Bogies: Central 43 inch.   **Multiple Working:** SR system.
Brakes: Electro-pneumatic and automatic air.
Doors: Manually operated slam.   **Dimensions:** 19.99 x 2.74 m.

977364. T. Southern Railway Eastleigh 1946. 29.0 t.

-	**RO**	NR	*SN*	SU	977364	(10400)

CLASS 950   TRACK ASSESSMENT UNIT

DM–DM. Purpose built service unit based on the Class 150 design. Gangwayed within unit.

Construction: Steel.
Engine: One Cummins NT-855-RT5 of 213 kW (285 h.p.) at 2100 r.p.m. per power car.
Transmission: Hydraulic. Voith T211r with cardan shafts to Gmeinder GM190 final drive.
Maximum Speed: 75 m.p.h.   **Couplers:** BSI automatic.
Bogies: BP38 (powered), BT38 (non-powered).
Brakes: Electro-pneumatic.   **Dimensions:** 20.06 x 2.82 m.
Doors: Manually operated slam & power operated sliding.
Multiple Working: Classes 142, 143, 144, 150, 153, 155, 156, 158, 159 and 170.

999600. DM. Lot No. 4060 BREL York 1987. 35.0 t.
999601. DM. Lot No. 4061 BREL York 1987. 35.0 t.

950 001	**Y**	NR	*SO*	ZA	999600 999601

CLASS 960   SANDITE & SERVICE UNITS

DMB. Converted from Class 121s. Non gangwayed.

For details see Page 175.

960 011 is a Video Survey Unit.
960 012 is a South West Trains Route Learning Unit.
960 014 is a Chiltern Route Learning Unit.

977723. DMB. Lot No. 30518 Pressed Steel 1960. 38.0 t.
977858–60/66/73. DMB. Lot No. 30518 Pressed Steel 1960. 38.0 t.

960 010	**M**	NR	*CR*	AL	977858	(55024)	
960 011	**RK**	NR	*SO*	ZA	977859	(55025)	
960 012	**SD**	SW	*SW*	BM	977860	(55028)	John Cameron
960 013	**N**	NR		AL	977866	(55030)	
960 014	**BG**	CR	*CR*	AL	977873	(55022)	
960 021	**RO**	NR	*CR*	AL	977723	(55021)	

CLASS 960   SANDITE UNIT

DMB. Converted 1991 from Class 122. Non gangwayed.

Construction: Steel.
Engines: Two Leyland 1595 of 112 kW (150 h.p.) at 1800 r.p.m.
Transmission: Mechanical. Cardan shaft and freewheel to a four-speed epicyclic gearbox with a further cardan shaft to the final drive, each engine driving the inner axle of one bogie.
Maximum Speed: 70 m.p.h.
Bogies: DD10.
Brakes: Twin pipe vacuum.
Doors: Manually operated slam.
Couplings: Screw.
Multiple Working: Blue Square.
Dimensions: 20.45 x 2.82 m.

975042. DMB. Lot No. 30419 Gloucester 1958. 36.5 t.

960 015	**Y**	NR	*CR*	AL	975042	(55019)

CLASS 960   WATER-JETTING UNIT

DMB–IMV–DMB. Converted 2003/04 from Class 117. Non gangwayed.

Construction: Steel.
Engines: Two Leyland 1595 of 112 kW (150 h.p.) at 1800 r.p.m.
Transmission: Mechanical. Cardan shaft and freewheel to a four-speed epicyclic gearbox with a further cardan shaft to the final drive, each engine driving the inner axle of one bogie.
Maximum Speed: 70 m.p.h.
Bogies: DD10.
Brakes: Twin pipe vacuum.
Doors: Manually operated slam.
Couplings: Screw.
Multiple Working: Blue Square.
Dimensions: 20.45 x 2.84 m.

977987/977988. DMB. Lot No. 30546/30548 Pressed Steel 1959–1960. 36.5 t.
977992. IMV (Intermediate Motor Vehicle). Lot No. 30548 Pressed Steel 1959–1960. 36.5 t.

| 960 301 | **G** | CR *CR* | AL | 977987 | (51371) | 977992 (51375) |
| | | | | 977988 | (51413) | |

CLASS 960   DRIVER TRAINING UNIT

Converted from a Class 121.

For details see Page 175.

977968. DMB.

-	**Y**	CA *CA*	RU	977968	(55029)

CLASS 960 UNIVERSAL TRACK RECORDING UNIT

DM–DM. Universal track recording unit for video inspections, for measuring rail profiles and overhead line equipment testing etc. Plasser type UFM 160-1. Fitted with pantograph.

Construction: Steel.
Engine: MTU 12V183TD13 of 550 kW at 2100 r.p.m.
Transmission: Hydraulic, Voith.   **Bogies:** Plasser.
Maximum Speed: 100 m.p.h.   **Weight:** 68.0 t.
Brakes: **Dimensions:** 23.86 x 2.57 m.

999700. DM. Austria 2002.
999701. DM. Austria 2002.

-	**Y**	ES *CA*	Three Bridges	999700 999701

CLASS 960 TRACK ASSESSMENT/RECORDING UNIT

DM. Plasser & Theurer EM-SAT 100/RT Survey Cars. Full details awaited.

Construction: Steel.
Engine:
Transmission: Hydraulic, Voith.
Maximum Speed: 55 m.p.h.   **Weight:** 57 t.
Brakes: **Dimensions:** 17.70 x 2.75 m.

999800/1. DM. Austria 2003.

-	**Y**	NR *CA*	RU	999800	Richard Spoors
-	**Y**	NR *CA*	RU	999801	

3.4. DMUS AWAITING DISPOSAL

The list below comprises vehicles awaiting disposal which are stored on the Network Rail network.

IMPORTANT NOTE: DMUs still intact but already at scrapyards, unless specifically there for storage purposes, are not included in this list.

Class 101

Spare	**S**	A	SN	51500	
Spare	**RR**	X	SN	51432	51498
Spare	**S**	A	ZA	51231	

Class 117

Spare	**N**	DC	UKAEA Winfrith	51341	51356	51392	51398	
Spare	**RR**	DC	UKAEA Winfrith	51353	51395	59486	59492	59521
Spare	**N**	A	SN	51350	51366	51383	51408	
Spare	**RR**	CR	AL	51411				

Class 122

-	**LH**	X	TE	977941 (55012)

Class 960

Converted for use as Severn Tunnel Emergency Train units, but not actually used as such.

960 302	**Y**	NR	SJ	977975 (55027)
960 303	**Y**	NR	SJ	977976 (55031)

4. ELECTRIC MULTIPLE UNITS

INTRODUCTION

EMU CLASSES

Principal details and dimensions are quoted for each class in metric and/or imperial units as considered appropriate bearing in mind common UK usage.

All dimensions and weights are quoted for vehicles in an "as new" condition with all necessary supplies on board. Dimensions are quoted in the order length x overall width. All lengths quoted are over buffers or couplers as appropriate. Where two lengths are quoted, the first refers to outer vehicles in a set and the second to inner vehicles.

Bogie Types are quoted in the format motored/non-motored (e.g BP20/BT13 denotes BP20 motored bogies and BT non-motored bogies).

Unless noted to the contrary, all vehicles listed have bar couplers at non-driving ends.

Vehicles ordered under the auspices of BR were allocated a Lot (batch) number when ordered and these are quoted in class headings and sub-headings. Vehicles ordered since 1995 have no Lot Numbers, but the manufacturer and location that they were built is given.

NUMERICAL LISTINGS

25 kV AC 50 Hz overhead Electric Multiple Units (EMUs) and dual voltage EMUs are listed in numerical order of set numbers. Individual "loose" vehicles are listed in numerical order after vehicles formed into fixed formations.

750 V DC third rail EMUs are listed in numerical order of class number, then in numerical order of set number. Some of these use the former Southern Region four-digit set numbers. These are derived from theoretical six digit set numbers which are the four-digit set number prefixed by the first two numbers of the class.

Where sets or vehicles have been renumbered in recent years, former numbering detail is shown alongside current detail. Each entry is laid out as in the following example:

Set No.	Detail	Livery	Owner	Operator	Allocation	Formation			
5903	s	**SS**	P	*SW*	WD	77817	62828	71716	77818

Detail Differences. Only detail differences which currently affect the areas and types of train which vehicles may work are shown. All other detail differences are specifically excluded. Where such differences occur within a class or part class, these are shown alongside the individual set or vehicle number. Meaning of abbreviations are detailed in individual class headings.

Set Formations. Set formations shown are those normally maintained. Readers should note some set formations might be temporarily varied from time to time to suit maintenance and/or operational requirements. Vehicles shown as "Spare" are not formed in any regular set formation.

Codes. Codes are used to denote the livery, owner, operator and depot of each unit. Details of these will be found in section 7 of this book. Where a unit or spare car is off-lease, the operator column will be left blank.

Names. Only names carried with official sanction are listed. As far as possible names are shown in UPPER/lower case characters as actually shown on the name carried on the vehicle(s). Unless otherwise shown, complete units are regarded as named rather than just the individual car(s) which carry the name.

GENERAL INFORMATION

CLASSIFICATION AND NUMBERING

25 kV AC 50 Hz overhead and "Versatile" EMUs are classified in the series 300–399.

750 V DC third rail EMUs are classified in the series 400–599.

Service units are classified in the series 900–949.

EMU individual cars are numbered in the series 61000–78999, except for vehicles used on the Isle of Wight – which are numbered in a separate series, and for the new Class 395s, which will take up a new 39xxx series.

Any vehicle constructed or converted to replace another vehicle following accident damage and carrying the same number as the original vehicle is denoted by the suffix[II] in this publication.

OPERATING CODES

These codes are used by train operating company staff to describe the various different types of vehicles and normally appear on data panels on the inner (i.e. non driving) ends of vehicles.

A "B" prefix indicates a battery vehicle.
A "P" prefix indicates a trailer vehicle on which is mounted the pantograph, instead of the default case where the pantograph is mounted on a motor vehicle.

The first part of the code describes whether or not the car has a motor or a driving cab as follows:

DM Driving motor.
M Motor
DT Driving trailer
T Trailer

The next letter is a "B" for cars with a brake compartment.
This is followed by the saloon details:

F First
S Standard
C Composite

The next letter denotes the style of accommodation as follows:

O Open
K Side compartment with lavatory
so Semi-open (part compartments, part open). All other vehicles are
assumed   to consist solely of open saloons.

Finally vehicles with a buffet are suffixed RB or RMB for a miniature buffet.

Where two vehicles of the same type are formed within the same unit, the above codes may be suffixed by (A) and (B) to differentiate between the vehicles.

A composite is a vehicle containing both first and standard class accommodation, whilst a brake vehicle is a vehicle containing separate specific accommodation for the conductor.

Special Note: Where vehicles have been declassified, the correct operating code which describes the actual vehicle layout is quoted in this publication.

The following codes are used to denote special types of vehicle:

DMLF Driving Motor Lounge First
DMLV Driving Motor Luggage Van
MBRBS Motor buffet standard with luggage space and guard's compartment.
TFH   Trailer First with Handbrake

BUILD DETAILS

Lot Numbers

Vehicles ordered under the auspices of BR were allocated a Lot (batch) number when ordered and these are quoted in class headings and sub-headings.

Builders

These are shown in class headings. Abbreviations used are found in section 8.7.

Information on sub-contracting works which built parts of vehicles e.g. the underframes etc. is not shown.

ACCOMMODATION

The information given in class headings and sub-headings is in the form F/S nT (or TD) nW. For example 12/54 1T 1W denotes 12 first class and 54 standard class seats, one toilet and one space for a wheelchair. A number in brackets denotes tip-up seats (in addition to the fixed seats). Tip-up seats in vestibules do not count. The seating layout of open saloons is shown as 2+1, 2+2 or 3+2 as the case may be. Where units have first class accommodation as well as standard and the layout is different for each class then these are shown separately prefixed by "1:" and "2:". Compartments are three seats a side in first class and mostly four a side in standard class in EMUs. TD denotes a toilet suitable for use by a disabled person.

4.1. 25 kV AC 50 Hz OVERHEAD & DUAL VOLTAGE UNITS

Note: Except where otherwise stated, all units in this section operate on 25 kV AC 50 Hz overhead only.

CLASS 313   BREL YORK

First Capital Connect/Silverlink inner suburban units.

Formation: DMSO–PTSO–BDMSO.
Systems: 25 kV AC overhead/750 V DC third rail.
Construction: Steel underframe, aluminium alloy body and roof.
Traction Motors: Four GEC G310AZ of 82.125 kW.
Wheel Arrangement: Bo-Bo + 2-2 + Bo-Bo.
Braking: Disc & rheostatic.   **Dimensions:** 20.33/20.18 x 2.82 m.
Bogies: BX1.   **Couplers:** Tightlock.
Gangways: Within unit + end doors.   **Control System:** Camshaft.
Doors: Sliding.   **Maximum Speed:** 75 m.p.h.
Seating Layout: 3+2 low-back facing unless stated.
Multiple Working: Within class.

DMSO. Lot No. 30879 1976–1977. –/74. 36.0 t.
PTSO. Lot No. 30880 1976–1977. –/83 (313/0), –/80 (313/1). 31.0 t.
BDMSO. Lot No. 30885 1976–1977. –/74. 37.5 t.

Class 313/0. Standard Design. Refurbished with high back seats.

313 018	**FU**	H	*FC*	HE	62546	71230	62610
313 024	**FU**	H	*FC*	HE	62552	71236	62616
313 025	**WP**	H	*FC*	HE	62553	71237	62617
313 026	**WP**	H	*FC*	HE	62554	71238	62618
313 027	**WP**	H	*FC*	HE	62555	71239	62619
313 028	**FU**	H	*FC*	HE	62556	71240	62620
313 029	**FU**	H	*FC*	HE	62557	71241	62621
313 030	**WP**	H	*FC*	HE	62558	71242	62622
313 031	**FU**	H	*FC*	HE	62559	71243	62623
313 032	**FU**	H	*FC*	HE	62560	71244	62643
313 033	**WP**	H	*FC*	HE	62561	71245	62625
313 035	**FU**	H	*FC*	HE	62563	71247	62627
313 036	**FU**	H	*FC*	HE	62564	71248	62628
313 037	**WP**	H	*FC*	HE	62565	71249	62629
313 038	**FU**	H	*FC*	HE	62566	71250	62630
313 039	**FU**	H	*FC*	HE	62567	71251	62631
313 040	**FU**	H	*FC*	HE	62568	71252	62632
313 041	**U**	H	*FC*	HE	62569	71253	62633
313 042	**WP**	H	*FC*	HE	62570	71254	62634
313 043	**WP**	H	*FC*	HE	62571	71255	62635
313 044	**WP**	H	*FC*	HE	62572	71256	62636
313 045	**U**	H	*FC*	HE	62573	71257	62637

313 046	U	H	FC	HE	62574	71258	62638
313 047	FU	H	FC	HE	62575	71259	62639
313 048	FU	H	FC	HE	62576	71260	62640
313 049	U	H	FC	HE	62577	71261	62641
313 050	WP	H	FC	HE	62578	71262	62649
313 051	WP	H	FC	HE	62579	71263	62624
313 052	FU	H	FC	HE	62580	71264	62644
313 053	WP	H	FC	HE	62581	71265	62645
313 054	WP	H	FC	HE	62582	71266	62646
313 055	FU	H	FC	HE	62583	71267	62647
313 056	FU	H	FC	HE	62584	71268	62648
313 057	FU	H	FC	HE	62585	71269	62642
313 058	FU	H	FC	HE	62586	71270	62650
313 059	FU	H	FC	HE	62587	71271	62651
313 060	FU	H	FC	HE	62588	71272	62652
313 061	WP	H	FC	HE	62589	71273	62653
313 062	FU	H	FC	HE	62590	71274	62654
313 063	WP	H	FC	HE	62591	71275	62655
313 064	WP	H	FC	HE	62592	71276	62656

Class 313/1. Extra shoegear for Silverlink services.

313 101	SL	H	SL	WN	62529	71213	62593
313 102	SL	H	SL	WN	62530	71214	62594
313 103	SL	H	SL	WN	62531	71215	62595
313 104	SL	H	SL	WN	62532	71216	62596
313 105	SL	H	SL	WN	62533	71217	62597
313 106	SL	H	SL	WN	62534	71218	62598
313 107	SL	H	SL	WN	62535	71219	62599
313 108	SL	H	SL	WN	62536	71220	62600
313 109	SL	H	SL	WN	62537	71221	62601
313 110	SL	H	SL	WN	62538	71222	62602
313 111	SL	H	SL	WN	62539	71223	62603
313 112	SL	H	SL	WN	62540	71224	62604
313 113	SL	H	SL	WN	62541	71225	62605
313 114	SL	H	SL	WN	62542	71226	62606
313 115	SL	H	SL	WN	62543	71227	62607
313 116	SL	H	SL	WN	62544	71228	62608
313 117	SL	H	SL	WN	62545	71229	62609
313 119	SL	H	SL	WN	62547	71231	62611
313 120	SL	H	SL	WN	62548	71232	62612
313 121	SL	H	SL	WN	62549	71233	62613
313 122	SL	H	SL	WN	62550	71234	62614
313 123	SL	H	SL	WN	62551	71235	62615
313 134	SL	H	SL	WN	62562	71246	62626

Names (carried on PTSO):

313 101	Silvertown	313 109	Arnold Leah
313 111	London TravelWatch	313 116	Nikola Tesla
313 120	PARLIAMENT HILL	313 134	The Hackney Empire

CLASS 314   BREL YORK

First ScotRail inner suburban units.

Formation: DMSO–PTSO–DMSO.
Construction: Steel underframe, aluminium alloy body and roof.
Traction Motors: Four GEC G310AZ (* Brush TM61-53) of 82.125 kW.
Wheel Arrangement: Bo-Bo + 2-2 + Bo-Bo.
Braking: Disc & rheostatic.   **Dimensions:** 20.33/20.18 x 2.82 m.
Bogies: BX1.   **Couplers:** Tightlock.
Gangways: Within unit + end doors.   **Control System:** Thyristor.
Doors: Sliding.   **Maximum Speed:** 70 m.p.h.
Seating Layout: 3+2 low-back facing.
Multiple Working: Within class and with Class 315.

DMSO. Lot No. 30912 1979. –/68. 34.5 t.
64588^{II}. DMSO. Lot No. 30908 1978–1980. Rebuilt Railcare Glasgow 1996 from
Class 507 No. 64426. The original 64588 has been scrapped. This vehicle has
an experimental seating layout. –/74. 34.5 t.
PTSO. Lot No. 30913 1979. –/76. 33.0 t.

314 201	*	**SC**	A	*SR*	GW	64583	71450	64584
314 202	*	**SC**	A	*SR*	GW	64585	71451	64586
314 203	*	**SC**	A	*SR*	GW	64587	71452	64588^{II} European Union
314 204	*	**SC**	A	*SR*	GW	64589	71453	64590
314 205	*	**SC**	A	*SR*	GW	64591	71454	64592
314 206	*	**SC**	A	*SR*	GW	64593	71455	64594
314 207		**SC**	A	*SR*	GW	64595	71456	64596
314 208		**SC**	A	*SR*	GW	64597	71457	64598
314 209		**SC**	A	*SR*	GW	64599	71458	64600
314 210		**SC**	A	*SR*	GW	64601	71459	64602
314 211		**SC**	A	*SR*	GW	64603	71460	64604
314 212		**SC**	A	*SR*	GW	64605	71461	64606
314 213		**SC**	A	*SR*	GW	64607	71462	64608
314 214		**SC**	A	*SR*	GW	64609	71463	64610
314 215		**SC**	A	*SR*	GW	64611	71464	64612
314 216		**SC**	A	*SR*	GW	64613	71465	64614

CLASS 315   BREL YORK

"One" inner suburban units.

Formation: DMSO–TSO–PTSO–DMSO.
Construction: Steel underframe, aluminium alloy body and roof.
Traction Motors: Four Brush TM61-53 (* GEC G310AZ) of 82.125 kW.
Wheel Arrangement: Bo-Bo + 2-2 + 2-2 + Bo-Bo.
Braking: Disc & rheostatic.   **Dimensions:** 20.33/20.18 x 2.82 m.
Bogies: BX1.   **Couplers:** Tightlock.
Gangways: Within unit + end doors.   **Control System:** Thyristor.
Doors: Sliding.   **Maximum Speed:** 75 m.p.h.
Seating Layout: 3+2 low-back facing.
Multiple Working: Within class and with Class 314.

DMSO. Lot No. 30902 1980–1981. –/74. 35.0 t.
TSO. Lot No. 30904 1980–1981. –/86. 25.5 t.
PTSO. Lot No. 30903 1980–1981. –/84. 32.0 t.

Non-standard/Advertising liveries:

315 804, 315 806 and 315 809 All-over First Group blue.
315 812 "Back the bid" (London's Olympic bid 2012) – blue with various images.
315 844 Crime Prevention – White and red with various images.
315 845 WAGN Family Travelcard ("Go to town with WAGN") – White.
315 857 WAGN "Intalink" livery – White with yellow and green bodyside stripes.

315 801	1	H	1	IL	64461	71281	71389	64462
315 802	1	H	1	IL	64463	71282	71390	64464
315 803	1	H	1	IL	64465	71283	71391	64466
315 804	0	H	1	IL	64467	71284	71392	64468
315 805	1	H	1	IL	64469	71285	71393	64470
315 806	0	H	1	IL	64471	71286	71394	64472
315 807	1	H	1	IL	64473	71287	71395	64474
315 808	1	H	1	IL	64475	71288	71396	64476
315 809	0	H	1	IL	64477	71289	71397	64478
315 810	1	H	1	IL	64479	71290	71398	64480
315 811	1	H	1	IL	64481	71291	71399	64482
315 812	AL	H	1	IL	64483	71292	71400	64484
315 813	1	H	1	IL	64485	71293	71401	64486
315 814	1	H	1	IL	64487	71294	71402	64488
315 815	1	H	1	IL	64489	71295	71403	64490
315 816	1	H	1	IL	64491	71296	71404	64492
315 817	1	H	1	IL	64493	71297	71405	64494
315 818	1	H	1	IL	64495	71298	71406	64496
315 819	1	H	1	IL	64497	71299	71407	64498
315 820	1	H	1	IL	64499	71300	71408	64500
315 821	1	H	1	IL	64501	71301	71409	64502
315 822	1	H	1	IL	64503	71302	71410	64504
315 823	1	H	1	IL	64505	71303	71411	64506
315 824	1	H	1	IL	64507	71304	71412	64508
315 825	1	H	1	IL	64509	71305	71413	64510
315 826	1	H	1	IL	64511	71306	71414	64512
315 827	1	H	1	IL	64513	71307	71415	64514
315 828	GE	H	1	IL	64515	71308	71416	64516
315 829	1	H	1	IL	64517	71309	71417	64518
315 830	1	H	1	IL	64519	71310	71418	64520
315 831	1	H	1	IL	64521	71311	71419	64522
315 832	1	H	1	IL	64523	71312	71420	64524
315 833	1	H	1	IL	64525	71313	71421	64526
315 834	GE	H	1	IL	64527	71314	71422	64528
315 835	1	H	1	IL	64529	71315	71423	64530
315 836	GE	H	1	IL	64531	71316	71424	64532
315 837	GE	H	1	IL	64533	71317	71425	64534
315 838	GE	H	1	IL	64535	71318	71426	64536
315 839	1	H	1	IL	64537	71319	71427	64538
315 840	GE	H	1	IL	64539	71320	71428	64540

315 841		1	H	1	IL	64541	71321	71429	64542
315 842	*	GE	H	1	IL	64543	71322	71430	64544
315 843	*	GE	H	1	IL	64545	71323	71431	64546
315 844	*	AL	H	1	IL	64547	71324	71432	64548
315 845	*	AL	H	1	IL	64549	71325	71433	64550
315 846	*	U	H	1	IL	64551	71326	71434	64552
315 847	*	U	H	1	IL	64553	71327	71435	64554
315 848	*	U	H	1	IL	64555	71328	71436	64556
315 849	*	U	H	1	IL	64557	71329	71437	64558
315 850	*	U	H	1	IL	64559	71330	71438	64560
315 851	*	U	H	1	IL	64561	71331	71439	64562
315 852	*	U	H	1	IL	64563	71332	71440	64564
315 853	*	U	H	1	IL	64565	71333	71441	64566
315 854	*	U	H	1	IL	64567	71334	71442	64568
315 855	*	U	H	1	IL	64569	71335	71443	64570
315 856	*	U	H	1	IL	64571	71336	71444	64572
315 857	*	AL	H	1	IL	64573	71337	71445	64574
315 858	*	WP	H	1	IL	64575	71338	71446	64576
315 859	*	WP	H	1	IL	64577	71339	71447	64578
315 860	*	WP	H	1	IL	64579	71340	71448	64580
315 861	*	WP	H	1	IL	64581	71341	71449	64582

Names (carried on DMSO):

315 812	London Borough of Newham Host Borough 2012 Olympics Bid
315 817	Transport for London
315 829	London Borough of Havering Celebrating 40 years

CLASS 317   BREL

"One" and First Capital Connect outer suburban units.

Formation: Various, see sub-class headings.
Construction: Steel.
Traction Motors: Four GEC G315BZ of 247.5 kW.
Wheel Arrangement: 2-2 + Bo-Bo + 2-2 + 2-2.
Braking: Disc.   **Dimensions:** 20.13/20.18 x 2.82 m.
Bogies: BP20 (MSO), BT13 (others).   **Couplers:** Tightlock.
Gangways: Throughout   **Control System:** Thyristor.
Doors: Sliding.   **Maximum Speed:** 100 m.p.h.
Seating Layout: Various, see sub-class headings.
Multiple Working: Within class and with Classes 318, 319, 320, 321, 322 and 323.

Class 317/1. Pressure ventilated.

Formation: DTSO–MSO–TCO–DTSO.
Seating Layout: 1: 2+2 facing, 2: 3+2 facing.

DTSO(A) Lot No. 30955 York 1981–1982. –/74. 29.5 t.
MSO. Lot No. 30958 York 1981–1982. –/79. 49.0 t.
TCO. Lot No. 30957 Derby 1981–1982. 22/46 2T. 29.0 t.
DTSO(B) Lot No. 30956 York 1981–1982. –/71. 29.5 t.

317 337	**WP**	A	*FC*	HE	77036	62671	71613	77084
317 338	**WP**	A	*FC*	HE	77037	62698	71614	77085
317 339	**WP**	A	*FC*	HE	77038	62699	71615	77086
317 340	**WP**	A	*FC*	HE	77039	62700	71616	77087
317 341	**WP**	A	*FC*	HE	77040	62701	71617	77088
317 342	**WP**	A	*FC*	HE	77041	62702	71618	77089
317 343	**WP**	A	*FC*	HE	77042	62703	71619	77090
317 344	**WP**	A	*FC*	HE	77029	62690	71620	77091
317 345	**WP**	A	*FC*	HE	77044	62705	71621	77092
317 346	**WP**	A	*FC*	HE	77045	62706	71622	77093
317 347	**WP**	A	*FC*	HE	77046	62707	71623	77094
317 348	**WP**	A	*FC*	HE	77047	62708	71624	77095

Names (carried on TCO):

317 345   Driver John Webb | 317 348   Richard A Jenner

Class 317/5. Pressure ventilated. Units renumbered from Class 317/1 in 2005 for "One" Metro services in the West Anglia area. Refurbished with new upholstery and Passenger Information Systems. Details as Class 317/1.

317 501	(317 301)	**1**	A	*1*	IL	77024	62661	71577	77048
317 502	(317 302)	**1**	A	*1*	IL	77001	62662	71578	77049
317 503	(317 303)	**1**	A	*1*	IL	77002	62663	71579	77050
317 504	(317 304)	**1**	A	*1*	IL	77003	62664	71580	77051
317 505	(317 305)	**1**	A	*1*	IL	77004	62665	71581	77052
317 506	(317 306)	**1**	A	*1*	IL	77005	62666	71582	77053
317 507	(317 307)	**1**	A	*1*	IL	77006	62667	71583	77054
317 508	(317 311)	**WP**	A	*1*	IL	77010	62697	71587	77058
317 509	(317 312)	**1**	A	*1*	IL	77011	62672	71588	77059
317 510	(317 313)	**1**	A	*1*	IL	77012	62673	71589	77060
317 511	(317 315)	**1**	A	*1*	IL	77014	62675	71591	77062
317 512	(317 316)	**1**	A	*1*	IL	77015	62676	71592	77063
317 513	(317 317)	**1**	A	*1*	IL	77016	62677	71593	77064
317 514	(317 318)	**1**	A	*1*	IL	77017	62678	71594	77065
317 515	(317 320)	**1**	A	*1*	IL	77019	62680	71596	77067

Class 317/6. Convection heating. Units converted from Class 317/2 by Railcare Wolverton 1998–99 with new seating layouts.

Formation: DTSO–MSO–TSO–DTCO.
Seating Layout: 2+2 facing.

77200–77219. DTSO. Lot No. 30994 York 1985–1986. –/64. 29.5 t.
77280–77283. DTSO. Lot No. 31007 York 1987. –/64. 29.5 t.
62846–62865. MSO. Lot No. 30996 York 1985–1986. –/70. 49.0 t.
62886–62889. MSO. Lot No. 31009 York 1987. –/70. 49.0 t.
71734–71753. TSO. Lot No. 30997 York 1985–1986. –/62 2T. 29.0 t.
71762–71765. TSO. Lot No. 31010 York 1987. –/62 2T. 29.0 t.
77220–77239. DTCO. Lot No. 30995 York 1985–1986. 24/48. 29.5 t.
77284–77287. DTCO. Lot No. 31008 York 1987. 24/48. 29.5 t.

317 649	**WN**	A	*1*	IL	77200	62846	71734	77220
317 650	**WN**	A	*1*	IL	77201	62847	71735	77221
317 651	**WN**	A	*1*	IL	77202	62848	71736	77222

317 652	1	A	1	IL	77203	62849	71739	77223
317 653	1	A	1	IL	77204	62850	71738	77224
317 654	1	A	1	IL	77205	62851	71737	77225
317 655	1	A	1	IL	77206	62852	71740	77226
317 656	1	A	1	IL	77207	62853	71742	77227
317 657	1	A	1	IL	77208	62854	71741	77228
317 658	1	A	1	IL	77209	62855	71743	77229
317 659	1	A	1	IL	77210	62856	71744	77230
317 660	1	A	1	IL	77211	62857	71745	77231
317 661	1	A	1	IL	77212	62858	71746	77232
317 662	1	A	1	IL	77213	62859	71747	77233
317 663	1	A	1	IL	77214	62860	71748	77234
317 664	1	A	1	IL	77215	62861	71749	77235
317 665	1	A	1	IL	77216	62862	71750	77236
317 666	1	A	1	IL	77217	62863	71752	77237
317 667	1	A	1	IL	77218	62864	71751	77238
317 668	1	A	1	IL	77219	62865	71753	77239
317 669	1	A	1	IL	77280	62886	71762	77284
317 670	1	A	1	IL	77281	62887	71763	77285
317 671	1	A	1	IL	77282	62888	71764	77286
317 672	1	A	1	IL	77283	62889	71765	77287

Name (carried on TCO):

317 654   Richard Wells

Class 317/7. Units converted from Class 317/1 by Railcare Wolverton 2000 for Stansted Express services between London Liverpool Street and Stansted. Air conditioning. Fitted with luggage stacks.

Formation: DTSO–MSO–TSO–DTCO.
Seating Layout: 1: 2+1 facing, 2: 2+2 facing.

DTSO Lot No. 30955 York 1981–1982. –/52 + catering point. 31.4 t.
MSO. Lot No. 30958 York 1981–1982. –/62. 51.3 t.
TSO. Lot No. 30957 Derby 1981–1982. –/42 1W 1T 1TD. 30.2 t.
DTCO Lot No. 30956 York 1981–1982. 22/16 + catering point. 31.6 t.

Advertising livery: Vehicles 77055 of 317 708, 77066 of 317 719, 77069 of 317 722 and 77079 of 317 732 – Finspreads (white, blue and orange with various images).

317 708	(317 308)	SX	A	1	IL	77007	62668	71584	77055
317 709	(317 309)	SX	A	1	IL	77008	62669	71585	77056
317 710	(317 310)	SX	A	1	IL	77009	62670	71586	77057
317 714	(317 314)	SX	A	1	IL	77013	62674	71590	77061
317 719	(317 319)	SX	A	1	IL	77018	62679	71595	77066
317 722	(317 392)	SX	A	1	IL	77021	62682	71598	77069
317 723	(317 393)	SX	A	1	IL	77022	62683	71599	77070
317 729	(317 329)	1S	A	1	IL	77028	62689	71605	77076
317 732	(317 332)	SX	A	1	IL	77031	62692	71608	77079

Names (carried on DTCO):

317 709   Len Camp | 317 723   The Tottenham Flyer

Class 317/8. Pressure Ventilated. Units refurbished and renumbered from Class 317/1 in 2005–2006 at Wabtec, Doncaster for use on Stansted Express services. Fitted with luggage stacks.

Formation: DTSO–MSO–TCO–DTSO.
Seating Layout: 1: 2+2 facing, 2: 3+2 facing.

DTSO(A) Lot No. 30955 York 1981–1982. –/66. 29.5 t.
MSO. Lot No. 30958 York 1981–1982. –/71. 49.0 t.
TCO. Lot No. 30957 Derby 1981–1982. 20/42 2T. 29.0 t.
DTSO(B) Lot No. 30956 York 1981–1982. –/66. 29.5 t.

317 881	(317 321)	**SU**	A	1	IL	77020	62681	71597	77068
317 882	(317 324)	**SU**	A	1	IL	77023	62684	71600	77071
317 883	(317 325)	**SU**	A	1	IL	77000	62685	71601	77072
317 884	(317 326)	**SU**	A	1	IL	77025	62686	71602	77073
317 885	(317 327)	**SU**	A	1	IL	77026	62687	71603	77074
317 886	(317 328)	**SU**	A	1	IL	77027	62688	71604	77075
317 887	(317 330)	**SU**	A	1	IL	77043	62704	71606	77077
317 888	(317 331)	**SU**	A	1	IL	77030	62691	71607	77078
317 889	(317 333)	**SU**	A	1	IL	77032	62693	71609	77080
317 890	(317 334)	**SU**	A	1	IL	77033	62694	71610	77081
317 891	(317 335)	**SU**	A	1	IL	77034	62695	71611	77082
317 892	(317 336)	**SU**	A	1	IL	77035	62696	71612	77083

Name (carried on TCO):

317 892   Ilford Depot

CLASS 318   BREL YORK

First ScotRail outer suburban units.

Formation: DTSO–MSO–DTSO.
Construction: Steel.
Traction Motors: Four Brush TM 2141 of 268 kW.
Wheel Arrangement: 2-2 + Bo-Bo + 2-2.

Braking: Disc.	**Dimensions:** 20.86 x 2.82 m.
Bogies: BP20 (MSO), BT13 (others).	**Couplers:** Tightlock.
Gangways: Throughout (not *).	**Control System:** Thyristor.
Doors: Sliding.	**Maximum Speed:** 90 m.p.h.

Seating Layout: 3+2 facing.
Multiple Working: Within class and with Classes 317, 319, 320, 321, 322 and 323.

77240–77259. DTSO. Lot No. 30999 1985–1986. –/66 1T (* –/64 1T). 30.0 t.
77288. DTSO. Lot No. 31020 1987. –/64 1T. 30.0 t.
62866–62885. MSO. Lot No. 30998 1985–1986. –/79 (* –/77). 50.9 t.
62890. MSO. Lot No. 31019 1987. –/77. 50.9 t.
77260–77279. DTSO. Lot No. 31000 1985–1986. –/71 (* –/72). 29.6 t.
77289. DTSO. Lot No. 31021 1987. –/72. 29.6 t.

Note: * Refurbished – end gangway sealed.

318 250		**SC**	H	*SR*	GW	77240	62866	77260
318 251	*	**SC**	H	*SR*	GW	77241	62867	77261
318 252		**SC**	H	*SR*	GW	77242	62868	77262
318 253		**SC**	H	*SR*	GW	77243	62869	77263
318 254	*	**SC**	H	*SR*	GW	77244	62870	77264
318 255		**SC**	H	*SR*	GW	77245	62871	77265
318 256		**SC**	H	*SR*	GW	77246	62872	77266
318 257	*	**SC**	H	*SR*	GW	77247	62873	77267
318 258	*	**SC**	H	*SR*	GW	77248	62874	77268
318 259	*	**SC**	H	*SR*	GW	77249	62875	77269
318 260		**SC**	H	*SR*	GW	77250	62876	77270
318 261		**SC**	H	*SR*	GW	77251	62877	77271
318 262	*	**SC**	H	*SR*	GW	77252	62878	77272
318 263	*	**SC**	H	*SR*	GW	77253	62879	77273
318 264	*	**SC**	H	*SR*	GW	77254	62880	77274
318 265	*	**SC**	H	*SR*	GW	77255	62881	77275
318 266	*	**SC**	H	*SR*	GW	77256	62882	77276
318 267		**SC**	H	*SR*	GW	77257	62883	77277
318 268		**SC**	H	*SR*	GW	77258	62884	77278
318 269		**SC**	H	*SR*	GW	77259	62885	77279
318 270	*	**SC**	H	*SR*	GW	77288	62890	77289

Names (carried on MSO):

318 259   Citizens' Network | 318 266   STRATHCLYDER

CLASS 319 BREL YORK

First Capital Connect and Southern express and outer suburban units.

Formation: Various, see sub-class headings.
Systems: 25 kV AC overhead/750 V DC third rail.
Construction: Steel.
Traction Motors: Four GEC G315BZ of 268 kW.
Wheel Arrangement: 2-2 + Bo-Bo + 2-2 + 2-2.
Braking: Disc. **Dimensions:** 20.17/20.16 x 2.82 m.
Bogies: P7-4 (MSO), T3-7 (others). **Couplers:** Tightlock.
Gangways: Within unit + end doors. **Control System:** GTO chopper.
Doors: Sliding. **Maximum Speed:** 100 m.p.h.
Seating Layout: Various, see sub-class headings.
Multiple Working: Within class and with Classes 317, 318, 320, 321, 322 and 323.

Class 319/0. DTSO–MSO–TSO–DTSO.

Seating Layout: 3+2 facing.

DTSO(A). Lot No. 31022 (odd nos.) 1987–1988. –/82. 28.2 t.
MSO. Lot No. 31023 1987–1988. –/82. 49.2 t.
TSO. Lot No. 31024 1987–1988. –/77 2T. 31.0 t.
DTSO(B). Lot No. 31025 (even nos.) 1987–1988. –/78. 28.1 t.

Non-standard liveries: 319 001 White with blue doors.
319 010 Mid blue with yellow doors.

319 001	**0**	P	*FC*	SU	77291	62891	71772	77290
319 002	**SN**	P	*SN*	SU	77293	62892	71773	77292
319 003	**SN**	P	*FC*	SU	77295	62893	71774	77294
319 004	**SN**	P	*FC*	SU	77297	62894	71775	77296
319 005	**SN**	P	*FC*	SU	77299	62895	71776	77298
319 006	**SN**	P	*FC*	SU	77301	62896	71777	77300
319 007	**SN**	P	*FC*	SU	77303	62897	71778	77302
319 008	**SN**	P	*FC*	SU	77305	62898	71779	77304
319 009	**SN**	P	*SN*	SU	77307	62899	71780	77306
319 010	**0**	P	*FC*	SU	77309	62900	71781	77308
319 011	**SN**	P	*SN*	SU	77311	62901	71782	77310
319 012	**SN**	P	*SN*	SU	77313	62902	71783	77312
319 013	**SN**	P	*SN*	SU	77315	62903	71784	77314

Names (carried on TSO):

319 008	Cheriton	319 011	John Ruskin College
319 009	Coquelles	319 013	The Surrey Hills

Class 319/2. DTSO–MSO–TSO–DTCO. Units converted from Class 319/0 for express services from London to Brighton. Now used by Southern on outer suburban services.

Seating Layout: 1: 2+1 facing, 2: 2+2 facing.

DTSO. Lot No. 31022 (odd nos.) 1987–1988. –/64. 28.2 t.
MSO. Lot No. 31023 1987–1988. –/60 2T. (including 12 seats in a "snug" under the pantograph area). External sliding doors sealed adjacent to this area. 49.2 t.
TSO. Lot No. 31024 1987–1988. –/52 1T 1TD. 31.0 t.
DTCO. Lot No. 31025 (even nos.) 1987–1988. 18/36. 28.1 t.

Advertising livery:
319 215 Connex Days out/"Family Zone" (Yellow, green and red with various images).

319 214	**SN**	P	*SN*	SU	77317	62904	71785	77316
319 215	**AL**	P	*SN*	SU	77319	62905	71786	77318
319 216	**CX**	P	*SN*	SU	77321	62906	71787	77320
319 217	**CX**	P	*SN*	SU	77323	62907	71788	77322
319 218	**SN**	P	*SN*	SU	77325	62908	71789	77324
319 219	**CX**	P	*SN*	SU	77327	62909	71790	77326
319 220	**SN**	P	*SN*	SU	77329	62910	71791	77328

Names (carried on TSO):

319 215	London	319 218	Croydon
319 217	Brighton		

Class 319/3. DTSO–MSO–TSO–DTSO. Converted from Class 319/1 by replacing first class seats with standard class seats. Used mainly on the Luton–Sutton/Wimbledon routes.

Seating Layout: 3+2 facing.
Dimensions: 19.33 x 2.82 m.

DTSO(A). Lot No. 31063 1990. –/70. 29.0 t.
MSO. Lot No. 31064 1990. –/78. 50.6 t.
TSO. Lot No. 31065 1990. –/74 2T. 31.0 t.
DTSO(B). Lot No. 31066 1990. –/78. 29.7 t.

319 361	**TW**	P	*FC*	BF	77459	63043	71929	77458
319 362	**TR**	P	*FC*	BF	77461	63044	71930	77460
319 363	**TW**	P	*FC*	BF	77463	63045	71931	77462
319 364	**TW**	P	*FC*	BF	77465	63046	71932	77464
319 365	**TW**	P	*FC*	BF	77467	63047	71933	77466
319 366	**TW**	P	*FC*	BF	77469	63048	71934	77468
319 367	**TW**	P	*FC*	BF	77471	63049	71935	77470
319 368	**TR**	P	*FC*	BF	77473	63050	71936	77472
319 369	**TW**	P	*FC*	BF	77475	63051	71937	77474
319 370	**TW**	P	*FC*	BF	77477	63052	71938	77476
319 371	**TW**	P	*FC*	BF	77479	63053	71939	77478
319 372	**FU**	P	*FC*	BF	77481	63054	71940	77480
319 373	**TL**	P	*FC*	BF	77483	63055	71941	77482
319 374	**TW**	P	*FC*	BF	77485	63056	71942	77484
319 375	**TW**	P	*FC*	BF	77487	63057	71943	77486
319 376	**TW**	P	*FC*	BF	77489	63058	71944	77488
319 377	**TW**	P	*FC*	BF	77491	63059	71945	77490
319 378	**TW**	P	*FC*	BF	77493	63060	71946	77492
319 379	**TW**	P	*FC*	BF	77495	63061	71947	77494
319 380	**TW**	P	*FC*	BF	77497	63062	71948	77496
319 381	**TW**	P	*FC*	BF	77973	63093	71979	77974
319 382	**TW**	P	*FC*	BF	77975	63094	71980	77976
319 383	**TW**	P	*FC*	BF	77977	63095	71981	77978
319 384	**TW**	P	*FC*	BF	77979	63096	71982	77980
319 385	**TW**	P	*FC*	BF	77981	63097	71983	77982
319 386	**TR**	P	*FC*	BF	77983	63098	71984	77984

Class 319/4. DTCO–MSO–TSO–DTSO. Converted from Class 319/0. Refurbished with carpets. DTSO(A) converted to composite. Used mainly on the Bedford–Gatwick–Brighton route.

Seating Layout: 1: 2+1 facing 2: 2+2/3+2 facing.

* Sets refurbished by First Capital Connect with some seats removed for additional luggage space. This programme is ongoing.

77331–77381. DTCO. Lot No. 31022 (odd nos.) 1987–1988. 12/54 (* 12/51). 28.2 t.
77431–77457. DTCO. Lot No. 31038 (odd nos.) 1988. 12/54 (* 12/51). 28.2 t.
62911–62936. MSO. Lot No. 31023 1987–1988. –/77 (* –/74). 49.2 t.
62961–62974. MSO. Lot No. 31039 1988. –/77 (* –/74). 49.2 t.
71792–71817. TSO. Lot No. 31024 1987–1988. –/72 2T. 31.0 t.
71866–71879. TSO. Lot No. 31040 1988. –/72 2T. 31.0 t.

77330–77380. DTSO. Lot No. 31025 (even nos.) 1987–1988. –/74 (* –/71 1W). 28.1 t.
77430–77456. DTSO. Lot No. 31041 (even nos.) 1988. –/74 (* –/71 1W). 28.1 t.

Advertising livery:
319 456 Continental Airlines (mid blue with gold and yellow script).

319 421	*	FU	P	*FC*	BF	77331	62911	71792	77330
319 422	*	FU	P	*FC*	BF	77333	62912	71793	77332
319 423	*	FU	P	*FC*	BF	77335	62913	71794	77334
319 424		TW	P	*FC*	BF	77337	62914	71795	77336
319 425	*	FU	P	*FC*	BF	77339	62915	71796	77338
319 426		TW	P	*FC*	BF	77341	62916	71797	77340
319 427		TL	P	*FC*	BF	77343	62917	71798	77342
319 428		TW	P	*FC*	BF	77345	62918	71799	77344
319 429		FU	P	*FC*	BF	77347	62919	71800	77346
319 430		TL	P	*FC*	BF	77349	62920	71801	77348
319 431		FU	P	*FC*	BF	77351	62921	71802	77350
319 432		TW	P	*FC*	BF	77353	62922	71803	77352
319 433		TW	P	*FC*	BF	77355	62923	71804	77354
319 434		TW	P	*FC*	BF	77357	62924	71805	77356
319 435	*	FU	P	*FC*	BF	77359	62925	71806	77358
319 436		TW	P	*FC*	BF	77361	62926	71807	77360
319 437		TW	P	*FC*	BF	77363	62927	71808	77362
319 438		TL	P	*FC*	BF	77365	62928	71809	77364
319 439		FU	P	*FC*	BF	77367	62929	71810	77366
319 440		TL	P	*FC*	BF	77369	62930	71811	77368
319 441		TW	P	*FC*	BF	77371	62931	71812	77370
319 442		TW	P	*FC*	BF	77373	62932	71813	77372
319 443		TL	P	*FC*	BF	77375	62933	71814	77374
319 444		TL	P	*FC*	BF	77377	62934	71815	77376
319 445		FU	P	*FC*	BF	77379	62935	71816	77378
319 446		TW	P	*FC*	BF	77381	62936	71817	77380
319 447		FU	P	*FC*	BF	77431	62961	71866	77430
319 448		TW	P	*FC*	BF	77433	62962	71867	77432
319 449		TL	P	*FC*	BF	77435	62963	71868	77434
319 450		TW	P	*FC*	BF	77437	62964	71869	77436
319 451		TW	P	*FC*	BF	77439	62965	71870	77438
319 452		TW	P	*FC*	BF	77441	62966	71871	77440
319 453		TW	P	*FC*	BF	77443	62967	71872	77442
319 454		TW	P	*FC*	BF	77445	62968	71873	77444
319 455		TL	P	*FC*	BF	77447	62969	71874	77446
319 456		AL	P	*FC*	BF	77449	62970	71875	77448
319 457		TW	P	*FC*	BF	77451	62971	71876	77450
319 458		TL	P	*FC*	BF	77453	62972	71877	77452
319 459	*	FU	P	*FC*	BF	77455	62973	71878	77454
319 460	*	FU	P	*FC*	BF	77457	62974	71879	77456

Name (carried on TSO):

319 425   Transforming Travel

CLASS 320   BREL YORK

First ScotRail suburban units.

Formation: DTSO–MSO–DTSO.
Construction: Steel
Traction Motors: Four Brush TM2141B of 268 kW.
Wheel Arrangement: 2-2 + Bo-Bo + 2-2.
Braking: Disc.   **Dimensions:** 19.33 x 2.82 m.
Bogies: P7-4 (MSO), T3-7 (others).   **Couplers:** Tightlock.
Gangways: Within unit.   **Control System:** Thyristor.
Doors: Sliding.   **Maximum Speed:** 75 m.p.h.
Seating Layout: 3+2 facing.
Multiple Working: Within class and with Classes 317, 318, 319, 321, 322 and 323.

DTSO (A). Lot No. 31060 1990. –/76 1W. 30.7 t.
MSO. Lot No. 31062 1990. –/76 1W. 52.1 t.
DTSO (B). Lot No. 31061 1990. –/75. 31.7 t.

320 301	**SC**	H	*SR*	GW	77899	63021	77921
320 302	**SC**	H	*SR*	GW	77900	63022	77922
320 303	**SC**	H	*SR*	GW	77901	63023	77923
320 304	**SC**	H	*SR*	GW	77902	63024	77924
320 305	**SC**	H	*SR*	GW	77903	63025	77925
320 306	**SC**	H	*SR*	GW	77904	63026	77926
320 307	**SC**	H	*SR*	GW	77905	63027	77927
320 308	**SC**	H	*SR*	GW	77906	63028	77928
320 309	**SC**	H	*SR*	GW	77907	63029	77929
320 310	**SC**	H	*SR*	GW	77908	63030	77930
320 311	**SC**	H	*SR*	GW	77909	63031	77931
320 312	**SC**	H	*SR*	GW	77910	63032	77932
320 313	**SC**	H	*SR*	GW	77911	63033	77933
320 314	**SC**	H	*SR*	GW	77912	63034	77934
320 315	**SC**	H	*SR*	GW	77913	63035	77935
320 316	**SC**	H	*SR*	GW	77914	63036	77936
320 317	**SC**	H	*SR*	GW	77915	63037	77937
320 318	**SC**	H	*SR*	GW	77916	63038	77938
320 319	**SC**	H	*SR*	GW	77917	63039	77939
320 320	**SC**	H	*SR*	GW	77918	63040	77940
320 321	**SC**	H	*SR*	GW	77919	63041	77941
320 322	**SC**	H	*SR*	GW	77920	63042	77942

Names (carried on MSO):

320 305	GLASGOW SCHOOL OF ART 1845 150 1995
320 306	Model Rail Scotland
320 308	High Road 20th Anniversary 2000
320 309	Radio Clyde 25th Anniversary
320 311	Royal College of Physicians and Surgeons of Glasgow
320 312	Sir William A Smith Founder of the Boys' Brigade
320 321	The Rt. Hon. John Smith, QC, MP
320 322	Festive Glasgow Orchid

CLASS 321   BREL YORK

Formation: DTCO (DTSO on Class 321/9)–MSO–TSO–DTSO.
Construction: Steel.
Traction Motors: Four Brush TM2141C (268 kW).
Wheel Arrangement: 2-2 + Bo-Bo + 2-2 + 2-2.
Braking: Disc.   **Dimensions:** 19.95 x 2.82 m.
Bogies: P7-4 (MSO), T3-7 (others).   **Couplers:** Tightlock.
Gangways: Within unit.   **Control System:** Thyristor.
Doors: Sliding.   **Maximum Speed:** 100 m.p.h..
Seating Layout: 1: 2+2 facing, 2: 3+2 facing.
Multiple Working: Within class and with Classes 317, 318, 319, 320, 322 and 323.

Class 321/3. "One" units.

DTCO. Lot No. 31053 1988–1990. 16/57. 29.7 t.
MSO. Lot No. 31054 1988–1990. –/82. 51.5 t.
TSO. Lot No. 31055 1988–1990. –/75 2T. 29.1 t.
DTSO. Lot No. 31056 1988–1990. –/78. 29.7 t.

321 301	GE	H	1	IL	78049	62975	71880	77853
321 302	GE	H	1	IL	78050	62976	71881	77854
321 303	GE	H	1	IL	78051	62977	71882	77855
321 304	GE	H	1	IL	78052	62978	71883	77856
321 305	GE	H	1	IL	78053	62979	71884	77857
321 306	GE	H	1	IL	78054	62980	71885	77858
321 307	GE	H	1	IL	78055	62981	71886	77859
321 308	GE	H	1	IL	78056	62982	71887	77860
321 309	GE	H	1	IL	78057	62983	71888	77861
321 310	GE	H	1	IL	78058	62984	71889	77862
321 311	GE	H	1	IL	78059	62985	71890	77863
321 312	GE	H	1	IL	78060	62986	71891	77864
321 313	GE	H	1	IL	78061	62987	71892	77865
321 314	GE	H	1	IL	78062	62988	71893	77866
321 315	GE	H	1	IL	78063	62989	71894	77867
321 316	GE	H	1	IL	78064	62990	71895	77868
321 317	GE	H	1	IL	78065	62991	71896	77869
321 318	GE	H	1	IL	78066	62992	71897	77870
321 319	GE	H	1	IL	78067	62993	71898	77871
321 320	GE	H	1	IL	78068	62994	71899	77872
321 321	GE	H	1	IL	78069	62995	71900	77873
321 322	GE	H	1	IL	78070	62996	71901	77874
321 323	GE	H	1	IL	78071	62997	71902	77875
321 324	GE	H	1	IL	78072	62998	71903	77876
321 325	GE	H	1	IL	78073	62999	71904	77877
321 326	GE	H	1	IL	78074	63000	71905	77878
321 327	GE	H	1	IL	78075	63001	71906	77879
321 328	GE	H	1	IL	78076	63002	71907	77880
321 329	GE	H	1	IL	78077	63003	71908	77881
321 330	GE	H	1	IL	78078	63004	71909	77882
321 331	GE	H	1	IL	78079	63005	71910	77883

321 332	**GE**	H	*1*	IL	78080	63006	71911	77884
321 333	**GE**	H	*1*	IL	78081	63007	71912	77885
321 334	**GE**	H	*1*	IL	78082	63008	71913	77886
321 335	**GE**	H	*1*	IL	78083	63009	71914	77887
321 336	**GE**	H	*1*	IL	78084	63010	71915	77888
321 337	**GE**	H	*1*	IL	78085	63011	71916	77889
321 338	**GE**	H	*1*	IL	78086	63012	71917	77890
321 339	**GE**	H	*1*	IL	78087	63013	71918	77891
321 340	**GE**	H	*1*	IL	78088	63014	71919	77892
321 341	**GE**	H	*1*	IL	78089	63015	71920	77893
321 342	**GE**	H	*1*	IL	78090	63016	71921	77894
321 343	**GE**	H	*1*	IL	78091	63017	71922	77895
321 344	**GE**	H	*1*	IL	78092	63018	71923	77896
321 345	**GE**	H	*1*	IL	78093	63019	71924	77897
321 346	**GE**	H	*1*	IL	78094	63020	71925	77898
321 347	**GE**	H	*1*	IL	78131	63105	71991	78280
321 348	**GE**	H	*1*	IL	78132	63106	71992	78281
321 349	**GE**	H	*1*	IL	78133	63107	71993	78282
321 350	**GE**	H	*1*	IL	78134	63108	71994	78283
321 351	**GE**	H	*1*	IL	78135	63109	71995	78284
321 352	**GE**	H	*1*	IL	78136	63110	71996	78285
321 353	**GE**	H	*1*	IL	78137	63111	71997	78286
321 354	**GE**	H	*1*	IL	78138	63112	71998	78287
321 355	**GE**	H	*1*	IL	78139	63113	71999	78288
321 356	**GE**	H	*1*	IL	78140	63114	72000	78289
321 357	**GE**	H	*1*	IL	78141	63115	72001	78290
321 358	**GE**	H	*1*	IL	78142	63116	72002	78291
321 359	**GE**	H	*1*	IL	78143	63117	72003	78292
321 360	**GE**	H	*1*	IL	78144	63118	72004	78293
321 361	**GE**	H	*1*	IL	78145	63119	72005	78294
321 362	**GE**	H	*1*	IL	78146	63120	72006	78295
321 363	**GE**	H	*1*	IL	78147	63121	72007	78296
321 364	**GE**	H	*1*	IL	78148	63122	72008	78297
321 365	**GE**	H	*1*	IL	78149	63123	72009	78298
321 366	**GE**	H	*1*	IL	78150	63124	72010	78299

Names (carried on TSO):

321 312	Southend-on-Sea
321 321	NSPCC ESSEX FULL STOP
321 334	Amsterdam
321 336	GEOFFREY FREEMAN ALLEN
321 343	RSA RAILWAY STUDY ASSOCIATION
321 351	GURKHA

Class 321/4. Silverlink/"One" units (plus two on hire to c2c and one on hire to Northern).

DTCO. Lot No. 31067 1989–1990. 28/40. 29.8 t.
MSO. Lot No. 31068 1989–1990. –/79. 51.6 t.
TSO. Lot No. 31069 1989–1990. –/74 2T. 29.2 t.
DTSO. Lot No. 31070 1989–1990. –/78. 29.8 t.

Note: The DTCOs of the "One" units have had 12 first class seats declassified.

321 401	**SL**	H	*SL*	BY	78095	63063	71949	77943
321 402	**SL**	H	*SL*	BY	78096	63064	71950	77944
321 403	**SL**	H	*SL*	BY	78097	63065	71951	77945
321 404	**SL**	H	*SL*	BY	78098	63066	71952	77946
321 405	**SL**	H	*SL*	BY	78099	63067	71953	77947
321 406	**SL**	H	*SL*	BY	78100	63068	71954	77948
321 407	**SL**	H	*SL*	BY	78101	63069	71955	77949
321 408	**SL**	H	*C2*	EM	78102	63070	71956	77950
321 409	**SL**	H	*SL*	BY	78103	63071	71957	77951
321 410	**SL**	H	*SL*	BY	78104	63072	71958	77952
321 411	**SL**	H	*SL*	BY	78105	63073	71959	77953
321 412	**SL**	H	*SL*	BY	78106	63074	71960	77954
321 413	**SL**	H	*SL*	BY	78107	63075	71961	77955
321 414	**SL**	H	*SL*	BY	78108	63076	71962	77956
321 415	**SL**	H	*SL*	BY	78109	63077	71963	77957
321 416	**SL**	H	*SL*	BY	78110	63078	71964	77958
321 417	**SL**	H	*SL*	BY	78111	63079	71965	77959
321 418	**SL**	H	*SL*	BY	78112	63080	71968	77962
321 419	**SL**	H	*SL*	BY	78113	63081	71967	77961
321 420	**SL**	H	*SL*	BY	78114	63082	71966	77960
321 421	**SL**	H	*SL*	BY	78115	63083	71969	77963
321 422	**SL**	H	*SL*	BY	78116	63084	71970	77964
321 423	**SL**	H	*NO*	NL	78117	63085	71971	77965
321 424	**SL**	H	*SL*	BY	78118	63086	71972	77966
321 425	**SL**	H	*SL*	BY	78119	63087	71973	77967
321 426	**SL**	H	*SL*	BY	78120	63088	71974	77968
321 427	**SL**	H	*SL*	BY	78121	63089	71975	77969
321 428	**SL**	H	*C2*	EM	78122	63090	71976	77970
321 429	**SL**	H	*SL*	BY	78123	63091	71977	77971
321 430	**SL**	H	*SL*	BY	78124	63092	71978	77972
321 431	**SL**	H	*SL*	BY	78151	63125	72011	78300
321 432	**SL**	H	*SL*	BY	78152	63126	72012	78301
321 433	**SL**	H	*SL*	BY	78153	63127	72013	78302
321 434	**SL**	H	*SL*	BY	78154	63128	72014	78303
321 435	**SL**	H	*SL*	BY	78155	63129	72015	78304
321 436	**SL**	H	*SL*	BY	78156	63130	72016	78305
321 437	**SL**	H	*SL*	BY	78157	63131	72017	78306
321 438	**GE**	H	*1*	IL	78158	63132	72018	78307
321 439	**GE**	H	*1*	IL	78159	63133	72019	78308
321 440	**GE**	H	*1*	IL	78160	63134	72020	78309
321 441	**GE**	H	*1*	IL	78161	63135	72021	78310
321 442	**GE**	H	*1*	IL	78162	63136	72022	78311
321 443	**GE**	H	*1*	IL	78125	63099	71985	78274
321 444	**GE**	H	*1*	IL	78126	63100	71986	78275
321 445	**GE**	H	*1*	IL	78127	63101	71987	78276
321 446	**1**	H	*1*	IL	78128	63102	71988	78277
321 447	**GE**	H	*1*	IL	78129	63103	71989	78278
321 448	**GE**	H	*1*	IL	78130	63104	71990	78279

Names (carried on TSO):

321 407	HERTFORDSHIRE WRVS
321 413	Bill Green
321 425	Bletchley Pride
321 427	Major Tim Warr
321 444	Essex Lifeboats
321 446	George Mullings

Class 321/9. DTSO(A)–MSO–TSO–DTSO(B).

DTSO(A). Lot No. 31108 1991. –/70(8). 29.0 t.
MSO. Lot No. 31109 1991. –/79. 51.0 t.
TSO. Lot No. 31110 1991. –/74 2T. 29.0 t.
DTSO(B). Dia. EE277. Lot No. 31111 1991. –/70(7) 1W. 29.0 t.

321 901	**YR**	H	*NO*	NL	77990	63153	72128	77993
321 902	**YR**	H	*NO*	NL	77991	63154	72129	77994
321 903	**YR**	H	*NO*	NL	77992	63155	72130	77995

CLASS 322 — BREL YORK

Units built for use on Stansted Airport services, now in use with First ScotRail.

Formation: DTSO–MSO–TSO–DTSO.
Construction: Steel.
Traction Motors: Four Brush TM2141C (268 kW).
Wheel Arrangement: 2-2 + Bo-Bo + 2-2 + 2-2.
Braking: Disc.   **Dimensions:** 19.95/19.92 x 2.82 m.
Bogies: P7-4 (MSO), T3-7 (others).   **Couplers:** Tightlock.
Gangways: Within unit.   **Control System:** Thyristor.
Doors: Sliding.   **Maximum Speed:** 100 m.p.h.
Seating Layout: 3+2 facing.
Multiple Working: Within class and with Classes 317, 318, 319, 320, 321 and 323.

DTSO(A). Lot No. 31094 1990. –/58. 29.3 t.
MSO. Lot No. 31092 1990. –/83. 51.5 t.
TSO. Lot No. 31093 1990. –/76 2T. 28.8 t.
DTSO(B). Lot No. 31091 1990. –/74(2) 1W. 29.1 t.

322 481	**FS**	H	*SR*	GW	78163	63137	72023	77985
322 482	**FS**	H	*SR*	GW	78164	63138	72024	77986
322 483	**FS**	H	*SR*	GW	78165	63139	72025	77987
322 484	**FS**	H	*SR*	GW	78166	63140	72026	77988
322 485	**FS**	H	*SR*	GW	78167	63141	72027	77989

Name (carried on DTSO(A)):

322 481	North Berwick Flyer 1850–2000

CLASS 323 HUNSLET TRANSPORTATION PROJECTS

Birmingham and Greater Manchester area suburban units.

Formation: DMSO–PTSO–DMSO.
Construction: Welded aluminium alloy.
Traction Motors: Four Holec DMKT 52/24 asynchronous of 146 kW.
Wheel Arrangement: Bo-Bo + 2-2 + Bo-Bo.
Braking: Disc.   **Dimensions:** 23.37/23.44 x 2.80 m.
Bogies: SRP BP62 (DMSO), BT52 (PTSO).   **Couplers:** Tightlock.
Gangways: Within unit.   **Control System:** GTO Inverter.
Doors: Sliding plug.   **Maximum Speed:** 90 m.p.h.
Seating Layout: 3+2 facing/unidirectional.
Multiple Working: Within class and with Classes 317, 318, 319, 320, 321 and 322.

DMSO(A). Lot No. 31112 Hunslet 1992–1993. –/98 (* –/82). 39.1 t.
TSO. Lot No. 31113 Hunslet 1992–1993. –/88 1T. (* –/80 1T). 36.5 t.
DMSO(B). Lot No. 31114 Hunslet 1992–1993. –/98 (* –/82). 39.1 t.

323 201		**CO**	P	*CT*	SI	64001	72201	65001
323 202		**CO**	P	*CT*	SI	64002	72202	65002
323 203		**CO**	P	*CT*	SI	64003	72203	65003
323 204		**CO**	P	*CT*	SI	64004	72204	65004
323 205		**CO**	P	*CT*	SI	64005	72205	65005
323 206		**CO**	P	*CT*	SI	64006	72206	65006
323 207		**CO**	P	*CT*	SI	64007	72207	65007
323 208		**CO**	P	*CT*	SI	64008	72208	65008
323 209		**CO**	P	*CT*	SI	64009	72209	65009
323 210		**CO**	P	*CT*	SI	64010	72210	65010
323 211		**CO**	P	*CT*	SI	64011	72211	65011
323 212		**CO**	P	*CT*	SI	64012	72212	65012
323 213		**CO**	P	*CT*	SI	64013	72213	65013
323 214		**CO**	P	*CT*	SI	64014	72214	65014
323 215		**CO**	P	*CT*	SI	64015	72215	65015
323 216		**CO**	P	*CT*	SI	64016	72216	65016
323 217		**CO**	P	*CT*	SI	64017	72217	65017
323 218		**CO**	P	*CT*	SI	64018	72218	65018
323 219		**CO**	P	*CT*	SI	64019	72219	65019
323 220		**CO**	P	*CT*	SI	64020	72220	65020
323 221		**CO**	P	*CT*	SI	64021	72221	65021
323 222		**CO**	P	*CT*	SI	64022	72222	65022
323 223	*	**FS**	P	*NO*	LG	64023	72223	65023
323 224	*	**FS**	P	*NO*	LG	64024	72224	65024
323 225	*	**FS**	P	*NO*	LG	64025	72225	65025
323 226		**FS**	P	*NO*	LG	64026	72226	65026
323 227		**FS**	P	*NO*	LG	64027	72227	65027
323 228		**FS**	P	*NO*	LG	64028	72228	65028
323 229		**FS**	P	*NO*	LG	64029	72229	65029
323 230		**FS**	P	*NO*	LG	64030	72230	65030
323 231		**FS**	P	*NO*	LG	64031	72231	65031
323 232		**FS**	P	*NO*	LG	64032	72232	65032

323 233	**FS**	P	*NO*	LG	64033	72233	65033
323 234	**FS**	P	*NO*	LG	64034	72234	65034
323 235	**FS**	P	*NO*	LG	64035	72235	65035
323 236	**FS**	P	*NO*	LG	64036	72236	65036
323 237	**FS**	P	*NO*	LG	64037	72237	65037
323 238	**FS**	P	*NO*	LG	64038	72238	65038
323 239	**FS**	P	*NO*	LG	64039	72239	65039
323 240	**CO**	P	*CT*	SI	64040	72240	65040
323 241	**CO**	P	*CT*	SI	64041	72241	65041
323 242	**CO**	P	*CT*	SI	64042	72242	65042
323 243	**CO**	P	*CT*	SI	64043	72243	65043

CLASS 325   ABB DERBY

Postal units based on Class 319s. Compatible with diesel or electric locomotive haulage.

Formation: DTPMV–MPMV–TPMV–DTPMV.
System: 25 kV AC overhead/750 V DC third rail.
Construction: Steel.
Traction Motors: Four GEC G315BZ of 268 kW.
Wheel Arrangement: 2-2 + Bo-Bo + 2-2 + 2-2.
Braking: Disc.   **Dimensions:** 19.33 x 2.82 m.
Bogies: P7-4 (MSO), T3-7 (others).   **Couplers:** Drop-head buckeye.
Gangways: None.   **Control System:** GTO Chopper.
Doors: Roller shutter.   **Maximum Speed:** 100 m.p.h.
Multiple Working: Within class.

DTPMV. Lot No. 31144 1995. 29.1 t.
MPMV. Lot No. 31145 1995. 49.5 t.
TPMV. Lot No. 31146 1995. 30.7 t.

Note: 325 009 and 325 010 are currently disbanded, and one "good unit" has been made from the two – 325 017.

325 001	**RM**	RM	*GB*	WB	68300	68340	68360	68301
325 002	**RM**	RM	*GB*	WB	68302	68341	68361	68303
325 003	**RM**	RM	*GB*	WB	68304	68342	68362	68305
325 004	**RM**	RM	*GB*	WB	68306	68343	68363	68307
325 005	**RM**	RM	*GB*	WB	68308	68344	68364	68309
325 006	**RM**	RM	*GB*	WB	68310	68345	68365	68311
325 007	**RM**	RM	*GB*	WB	68312	68346	68366	68313
325 008	**RM**	RM	*GB*	WB	68314	68347	68367	68315
325 011	**RM**	RM	*GB*	WB	68320	68350	68370	68321
325 012	**RM**	RM	*GB*	WB	68322	68351	68371	68323
325 013	**RM**	RM	*GB*	WB	68324	68352	68372	68325
325 014	**RM**	RM	*GB*	WB	68326	68353	68373	68327
325 015	**RM**	RM	*GB*	WB	68328	68354	68374	68329
325 016	**RM**	RM	*GB*	WB	68330	68355	68375	68331
325 017	**RM**	RM	*GB*	WB	68316	68349	68368	68317
Spare	**RM**	RM		WN	68318		68369	68319
Spare	**RM**	RM		WB		68348		

Names (carried on one side of each DTPMV):

325 002	Royal Mail North Wales & North West
325 006	John Grierson
325 008	Peter Howarth C.B.E.

CLASS 332   HEATHROW EXPRESS   SIEMENS

Dedicated Heathrow Express units. Five units were increased from 4-car to 5-car in 2002. Usually operate in coupled pairs.

Formations: Various.
Construction: Steel.
Traction Motors: Two Siemens monomotors asynchronous of 350 kW.
Wheel Arrangement: B-B + 2-2 + 2-2 (+ 2-2) + B-B.
Braking: Disc.   **Dimensions:** 23.63/23.35 x 2.75 m.
Bogies: CAF.   **Couplers:** Scharfenberg 10L.
Gangways: Within unit.   **Control System:** IGBT Inverter.
Doors: Sliding plug.   **Maximum Speed:** 100 m.p.h.
Heating & ventilation: Air conditioning.
Seating Layout: 1: 2+1 facing, 2: 2+2 mainly unidirectional.
Multiple Working: Within class and with Class 333.

332 001–332 007. DMFO–TSO–PTSO–(TSO)–DMSO.

DMFO. CAF 1997–1998. 26/–. 48.8 t.
72400–72413. TSO. CAF 1997–1998. –/56 35.8 t.
72414–72418. TSO. CAF 2002. –/56 35.8 t.
PTSO. CAF 1997–1998. –/44 1TD 1W. 45.6 t.
DMSO. CAF 1997–1998. –/48. 48.8 t.
DMLFO. CAF 1997–1998. 14/– 1W. 48.8 t.

Advertising livery: Vehicles 78401, 78402, 78405, 78406, 78408, 78410, 78412 carry Royal Bank of Scotland advertising livery (deep blue).

332 001	**HE**	HE *HE*	OH	78400	72412	63400		78401
332 002	**HE**	HE *HE*	OH	78402	72409	63401		78403
332 003	**HE**	HE *HE*	OH	78404	72407	63402		78405
332 004	**HE**	HE *HE*	OH	78406	72405	63403		78407
332 005	**HE**	HE *HE*	OH	78408	72411	63404	72417	78409
332 006	**HE**	HE *HE*	OH	78410	72410	63405	72415	78411
332 007	**HE**	HE *HE*	OH	78412	72401	63406	72414	78413

332 008–332 014. DMSO–TSO–PTSO–(TSO)–DMLFO.

Advertising livery: Vehicles 78414, 78416, 78419, 78421, 78423, 78425, 78427 carry Royal Bank of Scotland advertising livery (deep blue).

332 008	**HE**	HE *HE*	OH	78414	72413	63407	72418	78415
332 009	**HE**	HE *HE*	OH	78416	72400	63408	72416	78417
332 010	**HE**	HE *HE*	OH	78418	72402	63409		78419
332 011	**HE**	HE *HE*	OH	78420	72403	63410		78421
332 012	**HE**	HE *HE*	OH	78422	72404	63411		78423
332 013	**HE**	HE *HE*	OH	78424	72408	63412		78425
332 014	**HE**	HE *HE*	OH	78426	72406	63413		78427

CLASS 333   SIEMENS

West Yorkshire area suburban units.

Formation: DMSO–PTSO–TSO–DMSO.
Construction: Steel.
Traction Motors: Two Siemens monomotors asynchronous of 350 kW.
Wheel Arrangement: B-B + 2-2 + 2-2 + B-B.
Braking: Disc.
Dimensions: 22.95 (outer ends)/22.90 (PTSO)/23.35 (TSO) x 2.57 m.
Bogies: CAF.   **Couplers:** Dellner 10L.
Gangways: Within unit.   **Control System:** IGBT Inverter.
Doors: Sliding plug.   **Maximum Speed:** 100 m.p.h.
Heating & ventilation: Air conditioning.
Seating Layout: 3+2 facing/unidirectional.
Multiple Working: Within class and with Class 332.

DMSO(A). (Odd Nos.) CAF 2001. –/90. 50.6 t.
PTSO. CAF 2001. –/63(7) 1TD 2W. 46.7 t.
TSO. CAF 2002–2003. –/100. 38.5 t.
DMSO(B). (Even Nos.) CAF 2001. –/90. 50.6 t.

Notes: 333 001–333 008 were made up to 4-car units from 3-car units in 2002.

333 009–333 016 were made up to 4-car units from 3-car units in 2003.

333 001	**YN**	A	*NO*	NL	78451	74461	74477	78452
333 002	**YN**	A	*NO*	NL	78453	74462	74478	78454
333 003	**YN**	A	*NO*	NL	78455	74463	74479	78456
333 004	**YN**	A	*NO*	NL	78457	74464	74480	78458
333 005	**YN**	A	*NO*	NL	78459	74465	74481	78460
333 006	**YN**	A	*NO*	NL	78461	74466	74482	78462
333 007	**YN**	A	*NO*	NL	78463	74467	74483	78464
333 008	**YN**	A	*NO*	NL	78465	74468	74484	78466
333 009	**YN**	A	*NO*	NL	78467	74469	74485	78468
333 010	**YN**	A	*NO*	NL	78469	74470	74486	78470
333 011	**YN**	A	*NO*	NL	78471	74471	74487	78472
333 012	**YN**	A	*NO*	NL	78473	74472	74488	78474
333 013	**YN**	A	*NO*	NL	78475	74473	74489	78476
333 014	**YN**	A	*NO*	NL	78477	74474	74490	78478
333 015	**YN**	A	*NO*	NL	78479	74475	74491	78480
333 016	**YN**	A	*NO*	NL	78481	74476	74492	78482

CLASS 334 JUNIPER ALSTOM BIRMINGHAM

First ScotRail outer suburban units.

Formation: DMSO–PTSO–DMSO.
Construction: Steel.
Traction Motors: Two Alstom ONIX 800 asynchronous of 270 kW.
Wheel Arrangement: 2-Bo + 2-2 + Bo-2.
Braking: Disc.   **Dimensions:** 21.01/19.94 x 2.80 m.
Bogies: Alstom LTB3/TBP3.   **Couplers:** Tightlock.

Gangways: Within unit.   **Control System:** IGBT Inverter.
Doors: Sliding plug.   **Maximum Speed:** 90 m.p.h.
Heating & ventilation: Pressure heating and ventilation.
Seating Layout: 2+2 facing/unidirectional (3+2 in PTSO).
Multiple Working: Within class.

64101–64140. DMSO. Alstom Birmingham 1999–2001. –/64. 42.6 t.
PTSO. Alstom Birmingham 1999–2001. –/55 1TD 1W. 39.4 t.
65101–65140. DMSO. Alstom Birmingham 1999–2001. –/64. 42.6 t.

334 001	**SP**	H	*SR*	GW	64101	74301	65101	Donald Dewar
334 002	**SP**	H	*SR*	GW	64102	74302	65102	
334 003	**SP**	H	*SR*	GW	64103	74303	65103	
334 004	**SP**	H	*SR*	GW	64104	74304	65104	
334 005	**SP**	H	*SR*	GW	64105	74305	65105	
334 006	**SP**	H	*SR*	GW	64106	74306	65106	
334 007	**SP**	H	*SR*	GW	64107	74307	65107	
334 008	**SP**	H	*SR*	GW	64108	74308	65108	
334 009	**SP**	H	*SR*	GW	64109	74309	65109	
334 010	**SP**	H	*SR*	GW	64110	74310	65110	
334 011	**SP**	H	*SR*	GW	64111	74311	65111	
334 012	**SP**	H	*SR*	GW	64112	74312	65112	
334 013	**SP**	H	*SR*	GW	64113	74313	65113	
334 014	**SP**	H	*SR*	GW	64114	74314	65114	
334 015	**SP**	H	*SR*	GW	64115	74315	65115	
334 016	**SP**	H	*SR*	GW	64116	74316	65116	
334 017	**SP**	H	*SR*	GW	64117	74317	65117	
334 018	**SP**	H	*SR*	GW	64118	74318	65118	
334 019	**SP**	H	*SR*	GW	64119	74319	65119	
334 020	**SP**	H	*SR*	GW	64120	74320	65120	
334 021	**SP**	H	*SR*	GW	64121	74321	65121	Larkhall
334 022	**SP**	H	*SR*	GW	64122	74322	65122	
334 023	**SP**	H	*SR*	GW	64123	74323	65123	
334 024	**SP**	H	*SR*	GW	64124	74324	65124	
334 025	**SP**	H	*SR*	GW	64125	74325	65125	
334 026	**SP**	H	*SR*	GW	64126	74326	65126	
334 027	**SP**	H	*SR*	GW	64127	74327	65127	
334 028	**SP**	H	*SR*	GW	64128	74328	65128	
334 029	**SP**	H	*SR*	GW	64129	74329	65129	
334 030	**SP**	H	*SR*	GW	64130	74330	65130	
334 031	**SP**	H	*SR*	GW	64131	74331	65131	
334 032	**SP**	H	*SR*	GW	64132	74332	65132	
334 033	**SP**	H	*SR*	GW	64133	74333	65133	
334 034	**SP**	H	*SR*	GW	64134	74334	65134	
334 035	**SP**	H	*SR*	GW	64135	74335	65135	
334 036	**SP**	H	*SR*	GW	64136	74336	65136	
334 037	**SP**	H	*SR*	GW	64137	74337	65137	
334 038	**SP**	H	*SR*	GW	64138	74338	65138	
334 039	**SP**	H	*SR*	GW	64139	74339	65139	
334 040	**SP**	H	*SR*	GW	64140	74340	65140	

CLASS 350   DESIRO UK   SIEMENS

"West Coast" units for use by Silverlink and Central Trains. Formerly part of an aborted South West Trains 5-car Class 450/2 order.

Formation: DMCO–TCO–PTSO–DMCO.
Systems: 25 kV AC overhead (also 750 V DC if required).
Construction: Welded aluminium.
Traction Motors: 4 Siemens 1TB2016-0GB02 asynchronous of 250 kW.
Wheel Arrangement: Bo-Bo + 2-2 + 2-2 + Bo-Bo.
Braking: Disc & regenerative.   **Dimensions:** 20.34 x 2.80 m.
Bogies: SGP SF5000.   **Couplers:** Dellner 12.
Gangways: Throughout.   **Control System:** IGBT Inverter.
Doors: Sliding plug.   **Maximum Speed:** 100 m.p.h.
Heating & ventilation: Air conditioning.
Seating Layout: 1: 2+2 facing, 2: 2+2 facing/unidirectional.
Multiple Working: Within class.

DMSO(A). Siemens Uerdingen 2004–2005. –/60. 48.7 t.
TCO. Siemens Wien 2004–2005. 24/32 1T. 36.2 t.
PTSO. Siemens Wien 2004–2005. –/48(9) 1TD 2W. 45.2 t.
DMSO(B). Siemens Uerdingen 2004–2005. –/60. 49.2 t.

Note: 350 103/105/108 were all running misformed at the time of writing.

350 101	**WD**	A	*SL/CT*	NN	63761	66811	66861	63711
350 102	**WD**	A	*SL/CT*	NN	63762	66812	66862	63712
350 103	**WD**	A	*SL/CT*	NN	63765	66813	66863	63713
350 104	**WD**	A	*SL/CT*	NN	63764	66814	66864	63714
350 105	**WD**	A	*SL/CT*	NN	63763	66815	66868	63715
350 106	**WD**	A	*SL/CT*	NN	63766	66816	66866	63716
350 107	**WD**	A	*SL/CT*	NN	63767	66817	66867	63717
350 108	**WD**	A	*SL/CT*	NN	63768	66818	66865	63718
350 109	**WD**	A	*SL/CT*	NN	63769	66819	66869	63719
350 110	**WD**	A	*SL/CT*	NN	63770	66820	66870	63720
350 111	**WD**	A	*SL/CT*	NN	63771	66821	66871	63721
350 112	**WD**	A	*SL/CT*	NN	63772	66822	66872	63722
350 113	**WD**	A	*SL/CT*	NN	63773	66823	66873	63723
350 114	**WD**	A	*SL/CT*	NN	63774	66824	66874	63724
350 115	**WD**	A	*SL/CT*	NN	63775	66825	66875	63725
350 116	**WD**	A	*SL/CT*	NN	63776	66826	66876	63726
350 117	**WD**	A	*SL/CT*	NN	63777	66827	66877	63727
350 118	**WD**	A	*SL/CT*	NN	63778	66828	66878	63728
350 119	**WD**	A	*SL/CT*	NN	63779	66829	66879	63729
350 120	**WD**	A	*SL/CT*	NN	63780	66830	66880	63730
350 121	**WD**	A	*SL/CT*	NN	63781	66831	66881	63731
350 122	**WD**	A	*SL/CT*	NN	63782	66832	66882	63732
350 123	**WD**	A	*SL/CT*	NN	63783	66833	66883	63733
350 124	**WD**	A	*SL/CT*	NN	63784	66834	66884	63734
350 125	**WD**	A	*SL/CT*	NN	63785	66835	66885	63735
350 126	**WD**	A	*SL/CT*	NN	63786	66836	66886	63736
350 127	**WD**	A	*SL/CT*	NN	63787	66837	66887	63737

350 128	**WD**	A	*SL/CT*	NN	63788	66838	66888	63738
350 129	**WD**	A	*SL/CT*	NN	63789	66839	66889	63739
350 130	**WD**	A	*SL/CT*	NN	63790	66840	66890	63740

Names (carried on one side of each TCO):

| 350 111 | Apollo |
| 350 115 | Archimedes |

CLASS 357 ELECTROSTAR
ADTRANZ/BOMBARDIER DERBY

c2c units. Provision for 750 V DC supply if required.

Formation: DMSO–MSO–PTSO–DMSO.
Construction: Welded aluminium alloy underframe, sides and roof with steel ends. All sections bolted together.
Traction Motors: Two Adtranz asynchronous of 250 kW.
Wheel Arrangement: 2-Bo + 2-Bo + 2-2 + Bo-2.
Braking: Disc & regenerative.   **Dimensions:** 20.40/19.99 x 2.80 m.
Bogies: Adtranz P3-25/T3-25.   **Couplers:** Tightlock.
Gangways: Within unit.   **Control System:** IGBT Inverter.
Doors: Sliding plug.   **Maximum Speed:** 100 m.p.h.
Heating & ventilation: Air conditioning.
Seating Layout: 3+2 facing/unidirectional.
Multiple Working: Within class.

Class 357/0. Owned by Porterbrook Leasing.

DMSO(A). Adtranz Derby 1999–2001. –/71. 40.7 t.
MSO. Adtranz Derby 1999–2001. –/78. 36.7 t.
PTSO. Adtranz Derby 1999–2001. –/58(4) 1TD 2W. 39.5 t.
DMSO(B). Adtranz Derby 1999–2001. –/71. 40.7 t.

Note. * Due to accident damage 357 002/043 are temporarily misformed as 357 098/099, at the time of writing.

357 001	**C2**	P	*C2*	EM	67651	74151	74051	67751
357 002	*							
357 003	**C2**	P	*C2*	EM	67653	74153	74053	67753
357 004	**C2**	P	*C2*	EM	67654	74154	74054	67754
357 005	**C2**	P	*C2*	EM	67655	74155	74055	67755
357 006	**C2**	P	*C2*	EM	67656	74156	74056	67756
357 007	**C2**	P	*C2*	EM	67657	74157	74057	67757
357 008	**C2**	P	*C2*	EM	67658	74158	74058	67758
357 009	**C2**	P	*C2*	EM	67659	74159	74059	67759
357 010	**C2**	P	*C2*	EM	67660	74160	74060	67760
357 011	**C2**	P	*C2*	EM	67661	74161	74061	67761
357 012	**C2**	P	*C2*	EM	67662	74162	74062	67762
357 013	**C2**	P	*C2*	EM	67663	74163	74063	67763
357 014	**C2**	P	*C2*	EM	67664	74164	74064	67764
357 015	**C2**	P	*C2*	EM	67665	74165	74065	67765
357 016	**C2**	P	*C2*	EM	67666	74166	74066	67766

357 017	**C2**	P	*C2*	EM	67667	74167	74067	67767
357 018	**C2**	P	*C2*	EM	67668	74168	74068	67768
357 019	**C2**	P	*C2*	EM	67669	74169	74069	67769
357 020	**C2**	P	*C2*	EM	67670	74170	74070	67770
357 021	**C2**	P	*C2*	EM	67671	74171	74071	67771
357 022	**C2**	P	*C2*	EM	67672	74172	74072	67772
357 023	**C2**	P	*C2*	EM	67673	74173	74073	67773
357 024	**C2**	P	*C2*	EM	67674	74174	74074	67774
357 025	**C2**	P	*C2*	EM	67675	74175	74075	67775
357 026	**C2**	P	*C2*	EM	67676	74176	74076	67776
357 027	**C2**	P	*C2*	EM	67677	74177	74077	67777
357 028	**C2**	P	*C2*	EM	67678	74178	74078	67778
357 029	**C2**	P	*C2*	EM	67679	74179	74079	67779
357 030	**C2**	P	*C2*	EM	67680	74180	74080	67780
357 031	**C2**	P	*C2*	EM	67681	74181	74081	67781
357 032	**C2**	P	*C2*	EM	67682	74182	74082	67782
357 033	**C2**	P	*C2*	EM	67683	74183	74083	67783
357 034	**C2**	P	*C2*	EM	67684	74184	74084	67784
357 035	**C2**	P	*C2*	EM	67685	74185	74085	67785
357 036	**C2**	P	*C2*	EM	67686	74186	74086	67786
357 037	**C2**	P	*C2*	EM	67687	74187	74087	67787
357 038	**C2**	P	*C2*	EM	67688	74188	74088	67788
357 039	**C2**	P	*C2*	EM	67689	74189	74089	67789
357 040	**C2**	P	*C2*	EM	67690	74190	74090	67790
357 041	**C2**	P	*C2*	EM	67691	74191	74091	67791
357 042	**C2**	P	*C2*	EM	67692	74192	74092	67792
357 043	*							
357 044	**C2**	P	*C2*	EM	67694	74194	74094	67794
357 045	**C2**	P	*C2*	EM	67695	74195	74095	67795
357 046	**C2**	P	*C2*	EM	67696	74196	74096	67796
357 098	**C2**	P		ZC	67793	74152	74052	67752
357 099	**C2**	P	*C2*	EM	67652	74193	74093	67693

Names (carried on DMSO(A) and DMSO(B) (one plate on each)):

357 001	BARRY FLAXMAN
357 003	JASON LEONARD
357 004	TONY AMOS
357 011	JOHN LOWING
357 028	London, Tilbury & Southend Railway 1854–2004
357 029	THOMAS WHITELEGG 1840–1922
357 030	ROBERT HARBEN WHITELEGG 1871–1957

Class 357/2. Owned by Angel Trains.

DMSO(A). Bombardier Derby 2001–2002. –/71. 40.7 t.
MSO. Bombardier Derby 2001–2002. –/78. 36.7 t.
PTSO. Bombardier Derby 2001–2002. –/62 1TD 2W. 39.5 t.
DMSO(B). Bombardier Derby 2001–2002. –/71. 40.7 t.

357 201	**C2**	A	*C2*	EM	68601	74701	74601	68701
357 202	**C2**	A	*C2*	EM	68602	74702	74602	68702
357 203	**C2**	A	*C2*	EM	68603	74703	74603	68703

357 204	C2	A	C2	EM	68604	74704	74604	68704
357 205	C2	A	C2	EM	68605	74705	74605	68705
357 206	C2	A	C2	EM	68606	74706	74606	68706
357 207	C2	A	C2	EM	68607	74707	74607	68707
357 208	C2	A	C2	EM	68608	74708	74608	68708
357 209	C2	A	C2	EM	68609	74709	74609	68709
357 210	C2	A	C2	EM	68610	74710	74610	68710
357 211	C2	A	C2	EM	68611	74711	74611	68711
357 212	C2	A	C2	EM	68612	74712	74612	68712
357 213	C2	A	C2	EM	68613	74713	74613	68713
357 214	C2	A	C2	EM	68614	74714	74614	68714
357 215	C2	A	C2	EM	68615	74715	74615	68715
357 216	C2	A	C2	EM	68616	74716	74616	68716
357 217	C2	A	C2	EM	68617	74717	74617	68717
357 218	C2	A	C2	EM	68618	74718	74618	68718
357 219	C2	A	C2	EM	68619	74719	74619	68719
357 220	C2	A	C2	EM	68620	74720	74620	68720
357 221	C2	A	C2	EM	68621	74721	74621	68721
357 222	C2	A	C2	EM	68622	74722	74622	68722
357 223	C2	A	C2	EM	68623	74723	74623	68723
357 224	C2	A	C2	EM	68624	74724	74624	68724
357 225	C2	A	C2	EM	68625	74725	74625	68725
357 226	C2	A	C2	EM	68626	74726	74626	68726
357 227	C2	A	C2	EM	68627	74727	74627	68727
357 228	C2	A	C2	EM	68628	74728	74628	68728

Names (carried on DMSO(A) and DMSO(B) (one plate on each)):

357 201	KEN BIRD
357 202	KENNY MITCHELL
357 203	HENRY PUMFRETT
357 204	DEREK FOWERS
357 208	DAVE DAVIS
357 209	JAMES SNELLING
357 213	UPMINSTER I.E.C.C.

CLASS 360/0   DESIRO UK   SIEMENS

"One" units.

Formation: DMCO–PTSO–TSO–DMCO.
Construction: Welded aluminium.
Traction Motors: 4 Siemens 1TB2016-0GB02 asynchronous of 250 kW.
Wheel Arrangement: Bo-Bo + 2-2 + 2-2 + Bo-Bo.

Braking: Disc & regenerative.	**Dimensions:** 20.34 x 2.80 m.
Bogies: SGP SF5000.	**Couplers:** Dellner 12.
Gangways: Within unit.	**Control System:** IGBT Inverter.
Doors: Sliding plug.	**Maximum Speed:** 100 m.p.h.

Heating & ventilation: Air conditioning.
Seating Layout: 1: 2+2 facing, 2: 3+2 facing/unidirectional.
Multiple Working: Within class.

DMCO(A). Siemens Uerdingen 2002–2003. 8/59. 45.0 t.
PTSO. Siemens Wien 2002–2003. –/60(9) 1TD 2W. 43.0 t.
TSO. Siemens Wien 2002–2003. –/78. 35.0 t.
DMCO(B). Siemens Uerdingen 2002–2003. 8/59. 45.0 t.

360 101	**FS**	A	*1*	IL	65551	72551	74551	68551
360 102	**FS**	A	*1*	IL	65552	72552	74552	68552
360 103	**FS**	A	*1*	IL	65553	72553	74553	68553
360 104	**FS**	A	*1*	IL	65554	72554	74554	68554
360 105	**FS**	A	*1*	IL	65555	72555	74555	68555
360 106	**FS**	A	*1*	IL	65556	72556	74556	68556
360 107	**FS**	A	*1*	IL	65557	72557	74557	68557
360 108	**FS**	A	*1*	IL	65558	72558	74558	68558
360 109	**FS**	A	*1*	IL	65559	72559	74559	68559
360 110	**FS**	A	*1*	IL	65560	72560	74560	68560
360 111	**FS**	A	*1*	IL	65561	72561	74561	68561
360 112	**FS**	A	*1*	IL	65562	72562	74562	68562
360 113	**FS**	A	*1*	IL	65563	72563	74563	68563
360 114	**FS**	A	*1*	IL	65564	72564	74564	68564
360 115	**FS**	A	*1*	IL	65565	72565	74565	68565
360 116	**FS**	A	*1*	IL	65566	72566	74566	68566
360 117	**FS**	A	*1*	IL	65567	72567	74567	68567
360 118	**FS**	A	*1*	IL	65568	72568	74568	68568
360 119	**FS**	A	*1*	IL	65569	72569	74569	68569
360 120	**FS**	A	*1*	IL	65570	72570	74570	68570
360 121	**FS**	A	*1*	IL	65571	72571	74571	68571

CLASS 360/2   DESIRO UK   SIEMENS

Original 4-car Class 350 testbed units rebuilt for use by Heathrow Express on Paddington–Heathrow Airport stopping services ("Heathrow Connect").

All units to be made up to 5-car during 2007 (72431–72434 will be inserted into 360 201–360 204, these cars are shown in the sets below in *italics*). A fifth unit (360 205) was delivered in late 2005 as a 5-car set.

Formation: DMSO–PTSO–(TSO)–TSO–DMSO.
Construction: Welded aluminium.
Traction Motors: 4 Siemens 1TB2016-0GB02 asynchronous of 250 kW.
Wheel Arrangement: Bo-Bo + 2-2 + 2-2 + 2-2 + Bo-Bo.
Braking: Disc & regenerative.   **Dimensions:** 20.34 x 2.80 m.
Bogies: SGP SF5000.   **Couplers:** Dellner 12.
Gangways: Within unit.   **Control System:** IGBT Inverter.
Doors: Sliding plug.   **Maximum Speed:** 100 m.p.h.
Heating & ventilation: Air conditioning.
Seating Layout: 3+2 facing/unidirectional.
Multiple Working: Within class.

DMSO(A). Siemens Uerdingen 2002–2006. –/63. 44.8 t.
PTSO. Siemens Uerdingen 2002–2006. –/57(9) 1TD 2W. 44.2 t.
TSO. Siemens Uerdingen 2005–2006. –/74. 34.8 t.
TSO. Siemens Uerdingen 2002–2006. –/74. 34.8 t.
DMSO(B). Siemens Uerdingen 2002–2006. –/63. 44.4 t.

IMPORTANT NOTE: Vehicles 72431–72434 are additional fifth vehicles for 360 201–360 204, not yet formed in these sets at the time of writing.

360 201	**HC**	HE *HC*	OH	78431	63421	*72431*	72421	78441
360 202	**HC**	HE *HC*	OH	78432	63422	*72432*	72422	78442
360 203	**HC**	HE *HC*	OH	78433	63423	*72433*	72423	78443
360 204	**HC**	HE *HC*	OH	78434	63424	*72434*	72424	78444
360 205	**HC**	HE *HC*	OH	78435	63425	72435	72425	78445

CLASS 365   NETWORKER EXPRESS   ABB YORK

First Capital Connect outer suburban units.

Formations: DMCO–TSO–PTSO–DMCO.
Construction: Welded aluminium alloy.
Traction Motors: Four GEC-Alsthom G354CX asynchronous of 157 kW.
Wheel Arrangement: Bo-Bo + 2-2 + 2-2 + Bo-Bo.
Braking: Disc, rheostatic & regenerative.
Dimensions: 20.89/20.06 x 2.81 m.
Bogies: ABB P3-16/T3-16.
Gangways: Within unit.
Doors: Sliding plug.
Couplers: Tightlock.
Control System: GTO Inverter.
Maximum Speed: 100 m.p.h.
Seating Layout: 1: 2+2 facing, 2: 2+2 facing.
Multiple Working: Within class only.

DMCO(A). Lot No. 31133 1994–1995. 12/56. 41.7 t.
TSO. Lot No. 31134 1994–1995. –/59 1TD. 32.9 t.
PTSO. Lot No. 31135 1994–1995. –/68 1T. 34.6 t.
DMCO(B). Lot No. 31136 1994–1995. 12/56. 41.7 t.

Advertising liveries:
365 510 Cambridge & Ely; Cathedral cities (blue & white with various images).
365 519 Peterborough; environment capital (blue & white with various images).
365 531 Nelson's County; Norfolk (blue & white with various images).
365 540 Garden cities of Hertfordshire (blue & white with various images).

365 501	**FU**	H	*FC*	HE	65894	72241	72240	65935
365 502	**FU**	H	*FC*	HE	65895	72243	72242	65936
365 503	**NT**	H	*FC*	HE	65896	72245	72244	65937
365 504	**NT**	H	*FC*	HE	65897	72247	72246	65938
365 505	**FU**	H	*FC*	HE	65898	72249	72248	65939
365 506	**FU**	H	*FC*	HE	65899	72251	72250	65940
365 507	**FU**	H	*FC*	HE	65900	72253	72252	65941
365 508	**FU**	H	*FC*	HE	65901	72255	72254	65942
365 509	**FU**	H	*FC*	HE	65902	72257	72256	65943
365 510	**AL**	H	*FC*	HE	65903	72259	72258	65944
365 511	**FU**	H	*FC*	HE	65904	72261	72260	65945
365 512	**FU**	H	*FC*	HE	65905	72263	72262	65946
365 513	**NT**	H	*FC*	HE	65906	72265	72264	65947
365 514	**NT**	H	*FC*	HE	65907	72267	72266	65948
365 515	**NT**	H	*FC*	HE	65908	72269	72268	65949
365 516	**NT**	H	*FC*	HE	65909	72271	72270	65950
365 517	**FU**	H	*FC*	HE	65910	72273	72272	65951

365 518	**FU**	H	*FC*	HE	65911	72275	72274	65952
365 519	**AL**	H	*FC*	HE	65912	72277	72276	65953
365 520	**NT**	H	*FC*	HE	65913	72279	72278	65954
365 521	**FU**	H	*FC*	HE	65914	72281	72280	65955
365 522	**FU**	H	*FC*	HE	65915	72283	72282	65956
365 523	**FU**	H	*FC*	HE	65916	72285	72284	65957
365 524	**FU**	H	*FC*	HE	65917	72287	72286	65958
365 525	**FU**	H	*FC*	HE	65918	72289	72288	65959
365 526	**NT**	H		ZC	65919	72291	72290	65960
365 527	**FU**	H	*FC*	HE	65920	72293	72292	65961
365 528	**FU**	H	*FC*	HE	65921	72295	72294	65962
365 529	**NT**	H	*FC*	HE	65922	72297	72296	65963
365 530	**FU**	H	*FC*	HE	65923	72299	72298	65964
365 531	**AL**	H	*FC*	HE	65924	72301	72300	65965
365 532	**FU**	H	*FC*	HE	65925	72303	72302	65966
365 533	**FU**	H	*FC*	HE	65926	72305	72304	65967
365 534	**FU**	H	*FC*	HE	65927	72307	72306	65968
365 535	**FU**	H	*FC*	HE	65928	72309	72308	65969
365 536	**NT**	H	*FC*	HE	65929	72311	72310	65970
365 537	**NT**	H	*FC*	HE	65930	72313	72312	65971
365 538	**NT**	H	*FC*	HE	65931	72315	72314	65972
365 539	**FU**	H	*FC*	HE	65932	72317	72316	65973
365 540	**AL**	H	*FC*	HE	65933	72319	72318	65974
365 541	**FU**	H	*FC*	HE	65934	72321	72320	65975

Names (carried on one DMCO):

| 365 518 | The Fenman |
| 365 527 | Robert Stripe Passenger's Champion |

CLASS 375 ELECTROSTAR
ADTRANZ/BOMBARDIER DERBY

Southeastern express and outer suburban units.

Formations: Various.
Systems: 25 kV AC overhead/750 V DC third rail (some third rail only with provision for retro-fitting of AC equipment).
Construction: Welded aluminium alloy underframe, sides and roof with steel ends. All sections bolted together.
Traction Motors: Two Adtranz asynchronous of 250 kW.
Wheel Arrangement: 2-Bo (+ 2-Bo) + 2-2 + Bo-2.
Braking: Disc & regenerative.   **Dimensions:** 20.40/19.99 x 2.80 m.
Bogies: Adtranz P3-25/T3-25.   **Couplers:** Dellner 12.
Gangways: Throughout.   **Control System:** IGBT Inverter.
Doors: Sliding plug.   **Maximum Speed:** 100 m.p.h.
Heating & ventilation: Air conditioning.
Seating Layout: 1: 2+2 facing/unidirectional (seats behind drivers cab in each DMCO). 2: 2+2 facing/unidirectional (375/3, 375/6, 375/7 and 375/8), 3+2 facing/unidirectional (375/9).
Multiple Working: Within class and with Classes 376 and 377.

Class 375/3. Express units. 750 V DC only. DMCO–TSO–DMCO.

DMCO(A). Bombardier Derby 2001–2002. 12/48. 43.8 t.
TSO. Bombardier Derby 2001–2002. –/56 1TD 2W. 35.5 t.
DMCO(B). Bombardier Derby 2001–2002. 12/48. 43.8 t.

Name (carried on TSO):

375 304   Medway Valley Line 1856–2006

375 301	**CN**	H	*SE*	RM	67921	74351	67931
375 302	**CN**	H	*SE*	RM	67922	74352	67932
375 303	**CN**	H	*SE*	RM	67923	74353	67933
375 304	**CN**	H	*SE*	RM	67924	74354	67934
375 305	**CN**	H	*SE*	RM	67925	74355	67935
375 306	**CN**	H	*SE*	RM	67926	74356	67936
375 307	**CN**	H	*SE*	RM	67927	74357	67937
375 308	**CN**	H	*SE*	RM	67928	74358	67938
375 309	**CN**	H	*SE*	RM	67929	74359	67939
375 310	**CN**	H	*SE*	RM	67930	74360	67940

Class 375/6. Express units. 25 kV AC/750 V DC. DMCO–MSO–PTSO–DMCO.

DMCO(A). Adtranz Derby 1999–2001. 12/48. 46.2 t.
MSO. Adtranz Derby 1999–2001. –/66 1T. 40.5 t.
PTSO. Adtranz Derby 1999–2001. –/56 1TD 2W. 40.7 t.
DMCO(B). Adtranz Derby 1999–2001. 12/48. 46.2 t.

Non-standard livery: 375 610 is as **CN** but with blue doors instead of yellow and a gold band instead of a grey band on the lower bodyside (a special "Golden Jubilee" livery).

375 601	**CN**	H	*SE*	RM	67801	74251	74201	67851
375 602	**CN**	H	*SE*	RM	67802	74252	74202	67852
375 603	**CN**	H	*SE*	RM	67803	74253	74203	67853
375 604	**CN**	H	*SE*	RM	67804	74254	74204	67854
375 605	**CN**	H	*SE*	RM	67805	74255	74205	67855
375 606	**CN**	H	*SE*	RM	67806	74256	74206	67856
375 607	**CN**	H	*SE*	RM	67807	74257	74207	67857
375 608	**CN**	H	*SE*	RM	67808	74258	74208	67858
375 609	**CN**	H	*SE*	RM	67809	74259	74209	67859
375 610	**0**	H	*SE*	RM	67810	74260	74210	67860
375 611	**CN**	H	*SE*	RM	67811	74261	74211	67861
375 612	**CN**	H	*SE*	RM	67812	74262	74212	67862
375 613	**CN**	H	*SE*	RM	67813	74263	74213	67863
375 614	**CN**	H	*SE*	RM	67814	74264	74214	67864
375 615	**CN**	H	*SE*	RM	67815	74265	74215	67865
375 616	**CN**	H	*SE*	RM	67816	74266	74216	67866
375 617	**CN**	H	*SE*	RM	67817	74267	74217	67867
375 618	**CN**	H	*SE*	RM	67818	74268	74218	67868
375 619	**CN**	H	*SE*	RM	67819	74269	74219	67869
375 620	**CN**	H	*SE*	RM	67820	74270	74220	67870
375 621	**CN**	H	*SE*	RM	67821	74271	74221	67871
375 622	**CN**	H	*SE*	RM	67822	74272	74222	67872
375 623	**CN**	H	*SE*	RM	67823	74273	74223	67873

375 624	**CN**	H	*SE*	RM	67824	74274	74224	67874
375 625	**CN**	H	*SE*	RM	67825	74275	74225	67875
375 626	**CN**	H	*SE*	RM	67826	74276	74226	67876
375 627	**CN**	H	*SE*	RM	67827	74277	74227	67877
375 628	**CN**	H	*SE*	RM	67828	74278	74228	67878
375 629	**CN**	H	*SE*	RM	67829	74279	74229	67879
375 630	**CN**	H	*SE*	RM	67830	74280	74230	67880

Names (carried on one side of each MSO or PTSO):

375 608	Bromley Travelwise	375 610	Royal Tunbridge Wells
375 611	Dr. William Harvey	375 619	Driver John Neve
375 623	Hospice in the Weald	375 624	White Cliffs Country

Class 375/7. Express units. 750 V DC only. DMCO–MSO–TSO–DMCO.

DMCO(A). Bombardier Derby 2001–2002. 12/48. 43.8 t.
MSO. Bombardier Derby 2001–2002. –/66 1T. 36.4 t.
TSO. Bombardier Derby 2001–2002. –/56 1TD 2W. 34.1 t.
DMCO(B). Bombardier Derby 2001–2002. 12/48. 43.8 t.

375 701	**CN**	H	*SE*	RM	67831	74281	74231	67881
375 702	**CN**	H	*SE*	RM	67832	74282	74232	67882
375 703	**CN**	H	*SE*	RM	67833	74283	74233	67883
375 704	**CN**	H	*SE*	RM	67834	74284	74234	67884
375 705	**CN**	H	*SE*	RM	67835	74285	74235	67885
375 706	**CN**	H	*SE*	RM	67836	74286	74236	67886
375 707	**CN**	H	*SE*	RM	67837	74287	74237	67887
375 708	**CN**	H	*SE*	RM	67838	74288	74238	67888
375 709	**CN**	H	*SE*	RM	67839	74289	74239	67889
375 710	**CN**	H	*SE*	RM	67840	74290	74240	67890
375 711	**CN**	H	*SE*	RM	67841	74291	74241	67891
375 712	**CN**	H	*SE*	RM	67842	74292	74242	67892
375 713	**CN**	H	*SE*	RM	67843	74293	74243	67893
375 714	**CN**	H	*SE*	RM	67844	74294	74244	67894
375 715	**CN**	H	*SE*	RM	67845	74295	74245	67895

Names (carried on one side of each MSO or TSO):

375 701   Kent Air Ambulance Explorer
375 703   Dickens Traveller

Class 375/8. Express units. 750 V DC only. DMCO–MSO–TSO–DMCO.

DMCO(A). Bombardier Derby 2004. 12/48. 43.3 t.
MSO. Bombardier Derby 2004. –/66 1T. 39.8 t.
TSO. Bombardier Derby 2004. –/52 1TD 2W. 35.9 t.
DMCO(B). Bombardier Derby 2004. 12/52. 43.3 t.

375 801	**CN**	H	*SE*	RM	73301	79001	78201	73701
375 802	**CN**	H	*SE*	RM	73302	79002	78202	73702
375 803	**CN**	H	*SE*	RM	73303	79003	78203	73703
375 804	**CN**	H	*SE*	RM	73304	79004	78204	73704
375 805	**CN**	H	*SE*	RM	73305	79005	78205	73705
375 806	**CN**	H	*SE*	RM	73306	79006	78206	73706
375 807	**CN**	H	*SE*	RM	73307	79007	78207	73707

375 808	CN	H	SE	RM	73308	79008	78208	73708
375 809	CN	H	SE	RM	73309	79009	78209	73709
375 810	CN	H	SE	RM	73310	79010	78210	73710
375 811	CN	H	SE	RM	73311	79011	78211	73711
375 812	CN	H	SE	RM	73312	79012	78212	73712
375 813	CN	H	SE	RM	73313	79013	78213	73713
375 814	CN	H	SE	RM	73314	79014	78214	73714
375 815	CN	H	SE	RM	73315	79015	78215	73715
375 816	CN	H	SE	RM	73316	79016	78216	73716
375 817	CN	H	SE	RM	73317	79017	78217	73717
375 818	CN	H	SE	RM	73318	79018	78218	73718
375 819	CN	H	SE	RM	73319	79019	78219	73719
375 820	CN	H	SE	RM	73320	79020	78220	73720
375 821	CN	H	SE	RM	73321	79021	78221	73721
375 822	CN	H	SE	RM	73322	79022	78222	73722
375 823	CN	H	SE	RM	73323	79023	78223	73723
375 824	CN	H	SE	RM	73324	79024	78224	73724
375 825	CN	H	SE	RM	73325	79025	78225	73725
375 826	CN	H	SE	RM	73326	79026	78226	73726
375 827	CN	H	SE	RM	73327	79027	78227	73727
375 828	CN	H	SE	RM	73328	79028	78228	73728
375 829	CN	H	SE	RM	73329	79029	78229	73729
375 830	CN	H	SE	RM	73330	79030	78230	73730

Name (carried on one side of each MSO or TSO):

375 830   City of London

Class 375/9. Outer suburban units. 750 V DC only. DMCO–MSO–TSO–DMCO.

DMCO(A). Bombardier Derby 2003–2004. 12/59. 43.4 t.
MSO. Bombardier Derby 2003–2004. –/73 1T. 39.3 t.
TSO. Bombardier Derby 2003–2004. –/59 1TD 2W. 35.6 t.
DMCO(B). Bombardier Derby 2003–2004. 12/59. 43.4 t.

375 901	CN	H	SE	RM	73331	79031	79061	73731
375 902	CN	H	SE	RM	73332	79032	79062	73732
375 903	CN	H	SE	RM	73333	79033	79063	73733
375 904	CN	H	SE	RM	73334	79034	79064	73734
375 905	CN	H	SE	RM	73335	79035	79065	73735
375 906	CN	H	SE	RM	73336	79036	79066	73736
375 907	CN	H	SE	RM	73337	79037	79067	73737
375 908	CN	H	SE	RM	73338	79038	79068	73738
375 909	CN	H	SE	RM	73339	79039	79069	73739
375 910	CN	H	SE	RM	73340	79040	79070	73740
375 911	CN	H	SE	RM	73341	79041	79071	73741
375 912	CN	H	SE	RM	73342	79042	79072	73742
375 913	CN	H	SE	RM	73343	79043	79073	73743
375 914	CN	H	SE	RM	73344	79044	79074	73744
375 915	CN	H	SE	RM	73345	79045	79075	73745
375 916	CN	H	SE	RM	73346	79046	79076	73746
375 917	CN	H	SE	RM	73347	79047	79077	73747
375 918	CN	H	SE	RM	73348	79048	79078	73748

375 919	**CN**	H	*SE*	RM	73349	79049	79079	73749
375 920	**CN**	H	*SE*	RM	73350	79050	79080	73750
375 921	**CN**	H	*SE*	RM	73351	79051	79081	73751
375 922	**CN**	H	*SE*	RM	73352	79052	79082	73752
375 923	**CN**	H	*SE*	RM	73353	79053	79083	73753
375 924	**CN**	H	*SE*	RM	73354	79054	79084	73754
375 925	**CN**	H	*SE*	RM	73355	79055	79085	73755
375 926	**CN**	H	*SE*	RM	73356	79056	79086	73756
375 927	**CN**	H	*SE*	RM	73357	79057	79087	73757

CLASS 376 ELECTROSTAR BOMBARDIER DERBY

Southeastern inner suburban units.

Formation: DMSO–MSO–TSO–MSO–DMSO.
System: 750 V DC third rail.
Construction: Welded aluminium alloy underframe, sides and roof with steel ends. All sections bolted together.
Traction Motors: Two Bombardier asynchronous of 250 kW.
Wheel Arrangement: 2-Bo + 2-Bo + 2-2 + Bo-2 + Bo-2.
Braking: Disc & regenerative.   **Dimensions:** 20.40/19.99 x 2.80 m.
Bogies: Adtranz P3-25/T3-25.   **Couplers:** Dellner 12.
Gangways: Within unit.   **Control System:** IGBT Inverter.
Doors: Sliding.   **Maximum Speed:** 75 m.p.h.
Heating & ventilation: Pressure heating and ventilation.
Seating Layout: 2+2 low density facing.
Multiple Working: Within class and with Classes 375 and 377.

DMSO(A). Bombardier Derby 2004–2005. –/42 1W. 42.1 t.
MSO. Bombardier Derby 2004–2005. –/48. 36.2 t.
TSO. Bombardier Derby 2004–2005. –/48. 36.3 t.
DMSO(B). Bombardier Derby 2004–2005. –/42 1W. 42.1 t.

376 001	**CN**	H	*SE*	SG	61101	63301	64301	63501	61601
376 002	**CN**	H	*SE*	SG	61102	63302	64302	63502	61602
376 003	**CN**	H	*SE*	SG	61103	63303	64303	63503	61603
376 004	**CN**	H	*SE*	SG	61104	63304	64304	63504	61604
376 005	**CN**	H	*SE*	SG	61105	63305	64305	63505	61605
376 006	**CN**	H	*SE*	SG	61106	63306	64306	63506	61606
376 007	**CN**	H	*SE*	SG	61107	63307	64307	63507	61607
376 008	**CN**	H	*SE*	SG	61108	63308	64308	63508	61608
376 009	**CN**	H	*SE*	SG	61109	63309	64309	63509	61609
376 010	**CN**	H	*SE*	SG	61110	63310	64310	63510	61610
376 011	**CN**	H	*SE*	SG	61111	63311	64311	63511	61611
376 012	**CN**	H	*SE*	SG	61112	63312	64312	63512	61612
376 013	**CN**	H	*SE*	SG	61113	63313	64313	63513	61613
376 014	**CN**	H	*SE*	SG	61114	63314	64314	63514	61614
376 015	**CN**	H	*SE*	SG	61115	63315	64315	63515	61615
376 016	**CN**	H	*SE*	SG	61116	63316	64316	63516	61616
376 017	**CN**	H	*SE*	SG	61117	63317	64317	63517	61617
376 018	**CN**	H	*SE*	SG	61118	63318	64318	63518	61618
376 019	**CN**	H	*SE*	SG	61119	63319	64319	63519	61619

376 020	**CN**	H	*SE*	SG	61120	63320	64320	63520	61620
376 021	**CN**	H	*SE*	SG	61121	63321	64321	63521	61621
376 022	**CN**	H	*SE*	SG	61122	63322	64322	63522	61622
376 023	**CN**	H	*SE*	SG	61123	63323	64323	63523	61623
376 024	**CN**	H	*SE*	SG	61124	63324	64324	63524	61624
376 025	**CN**	H	*SE*	SG	61125	63325	64325	63525	61625
376 026	**CN**	H	*SE*	SG	61126	63326	64326	63526	61626
376 027	**CN**	H	*SE*	SG	61127	63327	64327	63527	61627
376 028	**CN**	H	*SE*	SG	61128	63328	64328	63528	61628
376 029	**CN**	H	*SE*	SG	61129	63329	64329	63529	61629
376 030	**CN**	H	*SE*	SG	61130	63330	64330	63530	61630
376 031	**CN**	H	*SE*	SG	61131	63331	64331	63531	61631
376 032	**CN**	H	*SE*	SG	61132	63332	64332	63532	61632
376 033	**CN**	H	*SE*	SG	61133	63333	64333	63533	61633
376 034	**CN**	H	*SE*	SG	61134	63334	64334	63534	61634
376 035	**CN**	H	*SE*	SG	61135	63335	64335	63535	61635
376 036	**CN**	H	*SE*	SG	61136	63336	64336	63536	61636

CLASS 377   ELECTROSTAR   BOMBARDIER DERBY

Southern express and outer suburban units.

Formations: Various.
Systems: 25 kV AC overhead/750 V DC third rail or third rail only with provision for retro-fitting of AC equipment.
Construction: Welded aluminium alloy underframe, sides and roof with steel ends. All sections bolted together.
Traction Motors: Two Bombardier asynchronous of 250 kW.
Wheel Arrangement: 2-Bo (+ 2-Bo) + 2-2 + Bo-2.
Braking: Disc & regenerative.   **Dimensions:** 20.40/19.99 x 2.80 m.
Bogies: Bombardier P3-25/T3-25.   **Couplers:** Dellner 12.
Gangways: Throughout.   **Control System:** IGBT Inverter.
Doors: Sliding plug.   **Maximum Speed:** 100 m.p.h.
Heating & ventilation: Air conditioning.
Seating Layout: Various.
Multiple Working: Within class and with Classes 375 and 376.

Class 377/1. 750 V DC only. DMCO–MSO–TSO–DMCO.
Seating layout: 1: 2+2 facing/unidirectional, 2: 2+2 facing/unidirectional (377 101–377 119), 3+2 and 2+2 facing/unidirectional (377 120–377 164) (3+2 seating in middle cars only 377 140–377 164).

DMCO(A). Bombardier Derby 2002–2003. 12/48 (s 12/56). 43.4 t.
MSO. Bombardier Derby 2002–2003. –/62 (s –/70, t –/69). 1T. 39.0 t.
TSO. Bombardier Derby 2002–2003. –/52 (s –/60, t –/57). 1TD 2W. 35.4 t.
DMCO(B). Bombardier Derby 2002–2003. 12/48 (s 12/56). 43.4 t.

377 101	**SN**	P	*SN*	Bl	78501	77101	78901	78701
377 102	**SN**	P	*SN*	Bl	78502	77102	78902	78702
377 103	**SN**	P	*SN*	Bl	78503	77103	78903	78703
377 104	**SN**	P	*SN*	Bl	78504	77104	78904	78704
377 105	**SN**	P	*SN*	Bl	78505	77105	78905	78705

377 106		**SN**	P	*SN*	BI	78506	77106	78906	78706
377 107		**SN**	P	*SN*	BI	78507	77107	78907	78707
377 108		**SN**	P	*SN*	BI	78508	77108	78908	78708
377 109		**SN**	P	*SN*	BI	78509	77109	78909	78709
377 110		**SN**	P	*SN*	BI	78510	77110	78910	78710
377 111		**SN**	P	*SN*	BI	78511	77111	78911	78711
377 112		**SN**	P	*SN*	BI	78512	77112	78912	78712
377 113		**SN**	P	*SN*	BI	78513	77113	78913	78713
377 114		**SN**	P	*SN*	BI	78514	77114	78914	78714
377 115		**SN**	P	*SN*	BI	78515	77115	78915	78715
377 116		**SN**	P	*SN*	BI	78516	77116	78916	78716
377 117		**SN**	P	*SN*	BI	78517	77117	78917	78717
377 118		**SN**	P	*SN*	BI	78518	77118	78918	78718
377 119		**SN**	P	*SN*	BI	78519	77119	78919	78719
377 120	s	**SN**	P	*SN*	SU	78520	77120	78920	78720
377 121	s	**SN**	P	*SN*	SU	78521	77121	78921	78721
377 122	s	**SN**	P	*SN*	SU	78522	77122	78922	78722
377 123	s	**SN**	P	*SN*	SU	78523	77123	78923	78723
377 124	s	**SN**	P	*SN*	SU	78524	77124	78924	78724
377 125	s	**SN**	P	*SN*	SU	78525	77125	78925	78725
377 126	s	**SN**	P	*SN*	SU	78526	77126	78926	78726
377 127	s	**SN**	P	*SN*	SU	78527	77127	78927	78727
377 128	s	**SN**	P	*SN*	SU	78528	77128	78928	78728
377 129	s	**SN**	P	*SN*	SU	78529	77129	78929	78729
377 130	s	**SN**	P	*SN*	SU	78530	77130	78930	78730
377 131	s	**SN**	P	*SN*	SU	78531	77131	78931	78731
377 132	s	**SN**	P	*SN*	SU	78532	77132	78932	78732
377 133	s	**SN**	P	*SN*	SU	78533	77133	78933	78733
377 134	s	**SN**	P	*SN*	SU	78534	77134	78934	78734
377 135	s	**SN**	P	*SN*	SU	78535	77135	78935	78735
377 136	s	**SN**	P	*SN*	SU	78536	77136	78936	78736
377 137	s	**SN**	P	*SN*	SU	78537	77137	78937	78737
377 138	s	**SN**	P	*SN*	SU	78538	77138	78938	78738
377 139	s	**SN**	P	*SN*	SU	78539	77139	78939	78739
377 140	t	**SN**	P	*SN*	SU	78540	77140	78940	78740
377 141	t	**SN**	P	*SN*	SU	78541	77141	78941	78741
377 142	t	**SN**	P	*SN*	SU	78542	77142	78942	78742
377 143	t	**SN**	P	*SN*	SU	78543	77143	78943	78743
377 144	t	**SN**	P	*SN*	SU	78544	77144	78944	78744
377 145	t	**SN**	P	*SN*	SU	78545	77145	78945	78745
377 146	t	**SN**	P	*SN*	SU	78546	77146	78946	78746
377 147	t	**SN**	P	*SN*	SU	78547	77147	78947	78747
377 148	t	**SN**	P	*SN*	SU	78548	77148	78948	78748
377 149	t	**SN**	P	*SN*	SU	78549	77149	78949	78749
377 150	t	**SN**	P	*SN*	SU	78550	77150	78950	78750
377 151	t	**SN**	P	*SN*	SU	78551	77151	78951	78751
377 152	t	**SN**	P	*SN*	SU	78552	77152	78952	78752
377 153	t	**SN**	P	*SN*	SU	78553	77153	78953	78753
377 154	t	**SN**	P	*SN*	BI	78554	77154	78954	78754
377 155	t	**SN**	P	*SN*	BI	78555	77155	78955	78755
377 156	t	**SN**	P	*SN*	BI	78556	77156	78956	78756

377 157	t	**SN**	P	*SN*	Bl	78557	77157	78957	78757
377 158	t	**SN**	P	*SN*	Bl	78558	77158	78958	78758
377 159	t	**SN**	P	*SN*	Bl	78559	77159	78959	78759
377 160	t	**SN**	P	*SN*	Bl	78560	77160	78960	78760
377 161	t	**SN**	P	*SN*	Bl	78561	77161	78961	78761
377 162	t	**SN**	P	*SN*	Bl	78562	77162	78962	78762
377 163	t	**SN**	P	*SN*	Bl	78563	77163	78963	78763
377 164	t	**SN**	P	*SN*	Bl	78564	77164	78964	78764

Class 377/2. 25 kV AC/750 V DC. DMCO–MSO–PTSO–DMCO. These dual-voltage units are used on the Watford Junction–Gatwick Airport/Brighton services.
Seating layout: 1: 2+2 facing/unidirectional, 2: 2+2 and 3+2 facing/unidirectional (3+2 seating in middle cars only).

DMCO(A). Bombardier Derby 2003–2004. 12/48. 44.2 t.
MSO. Bombardier Derby 2003–2004. –/69 1T. 39.8 t.
PTSO. Bombardier Derby 2003–2004. –/57 1TD 2W. 40.1 t.
DMCO(B). Bombardier Derby 2003–2004. 12/48. 44.2 t.

377 201	**SN**	P	*SN*	SU	78571	77171	78971	78771
377 203	**SN**	P	*SN*	SU	78572	77172	78972	78772
377 203	**SN**	P	*SN*	SU	78573	77173	78973	78773
377 204	**SN**	P	*SN*	SU	78574	77174	78974	78774
377 205	**SN**	P	*SN*	SU	78575	77175	78975	78775
377 206	**SN**	P	*SN*	SU	78576	77176	78976	78776
377 207	**SN**	P	*SN*	SU	78577	77177	78977	78777
377 208	**SN**	P	*SN*	SU	78578	77178	78978	78778
377 209	**SN**	P	*SN*	SU	78579	77179	78979	78779
377 210	**SN**	P	*SN*	SU	78580	77180	78980	78780
377 211	**SN**	P	*SN*	SU	78581	77181	78981	78781
377 212	**SN**	P	*SN*	SU	78582	77182	78982	78782
377 213	**SN**	P	*SN*	SU	78583	77183	78983	78783
377 214	**SN**	P	*SN*	SU	78584	77184	78984	78784
377 215	**SN**	P	*SN*	SU	78585	77185	78985	78785

Class 377/3. 750 V DC only. DMCO–TSO–DMCO.
Seating Layout: 1: 2+2 facing/unidirectional, 2: 2+2 facing/unidirectional.

Notes: Units built as Class 375, but renumbered in the Class 377/3 range when fitted with Dellner couplers.

† Wi-fi high-speed internet connection equipment fitted. Units generally used on Victoria–Brighton fast services.

DMCO(A). Bombardier Derby 2001–2002. 12/48. 43.5 t.
TSO. Bombardier Derby 2001–2002. –/56 1TD 2W. 35.4 t.
DMCO(B). Bombardier Derby 2001–2002. 12/48. 43.5 t.

377 301	(375 311)		**SN**	P	*SN*	Bl	68201	74801	68401
377 302	(375 312)		**SN**	P	*SN*	Bl	68202	74802	68402
377 303	(375 313)		**SN**	P	*SN*	Bl	68203	74803	68403
377 304	(375 314)	†	**SN**	P	*SN*	Bl	68204	74804	68404
377 305	(375 315)	†	**SN**	P	*SN*	Bl	68205	74805	68405
377 306	(375 316)		**SN**	P	*SN*	Bl	68206	74806	68406
377 307	(375 317)		**SN**	P	*SN*	Bl	68207	74807	68407

377 308	(375 318)		**SN**	P	*SN*	BI	68208	74808	68408
377 309	(375 319)		**SN**	P	*SN*	BI	68209	74809	68409
377 310	(375 320)		**SN**	P	*SN*	BI	68210	74810	68410
377 311	(375 321)		**SN**	P	*SN*	BI	68211	74811	68411
377 312	(375 322)		**SN**	P	*SN*	BI	68212	74812	68412
377 313	(375 323)	†	**SN**	P	*SN*	BI	68213	74813	68413
377 314	(375 324)		**SN**	P	*SN*	BI	68214	74814	68414
377 315	(375 325)	†	**SN**	P	*SN*	BI	68215	74815	68415
377 316	(375 326)		**SN**	P	*SN*	BI	68216	74816	68416
377 317	(375 327)	†	**SN**	P	*SN*	BI	68217	74817	68417
377 318	(375 328)		**SN**	P	*SN*	BI	68218	74818	68418
377 319	(375 329)		**SN**	P	*SN*	BI	68219	74819	68419
377 320	(375 330)	†	**SN**	P	*SN*	BI	68220	74820	68420
377 321	(375 331)	†	**SN**	P	*SN*	BI	68221	74821	68421
377 322	(375 332)	†	**SN**	P	*SN*	BI	68222	74822	68422
377 323	(375 333)		**SN**	P	*SN*	BI	68223	74823	68423
377 324	(375 334)		**SN**	P	*SN*	BI	68224	74824	68424
377 325	(375 335)	†	**SN**	P	*SN*	BI	68225	74825	68425
377 326	(375 336)	†	**SN**	P	*SN*	BI	68226	74826	68426
377 327	(375 337)	†	**SN**	P	*SN*	BI	68227	74827	68427
377 328	(375 338)		**SN**	P	*SN*	BI	68228	74828	68428

Class 377/4. 750 V DC only. DMCO–MSO–TSO–DMCO.
Seating Layout: 1: 2+2 facing/two seats longitudinal, 2: 2+2 and 3+2 facing/unidirectional (3+2 seating in middle cars only).

DMCO(A). Bombardier Derby 2004–2005. 10/48. 43.1 t.
MSO. Bombardier Derby 2004–2005. –/69 1T. 39.3 t.
TSO. Bombardier Derby 2004–2005. –/56 1TD 2W. 35.3 t.
DMCO(B). Bombardier Derby 2004–2005. 10/48. 43.1 t.

377 401	**SN**	P	*SN*	BI	73401	78801	78601	73801
377 402	**SN**	P	*SN*	BI	73402	78802	78602	73802
377 403	**SN**	P	*SN*	BI	73403	78803	78603	73803
377 404	**SN**	P	*SN*	BI	73404	78804	78604	73804
377 405	**SN**	P	*SN*	BI	73405	78805	78605	73805
377 406	**SN**	P	*SN*	BI	73406	78806	78606	73806
377 407	**SN**	P	*SN*	BI	73407	78807	78607	73807
377 408	**SN**	P	*SN*	BI	73408	78808	78608	73808
377 409	**SN**	P	*SN*	BI	73409	78809	78609	73809
377 410	**SN**	P	*SN*	BI	73410	78810	78610	73810
377 411	**SN**	P	*SN*	BI	73411	78811	78611	73811
377 412	**SN**	P	*SN*	BI	73412	78812	78612	73812
377 413	**SN**	P	*SN*	BI	73413	78813	78613	73813
377 414	**SN**	P	*SN*	BI	73414	78814	78614	73814
377 415	**SN**	P	*SN*	BI	73415	78815	78615	73815
377 416	**SN**	P	*SN*	BI	73416	78816	78616	73816
377 417	**SN**	P	*SN*	BI	73417	78817	78617	73817
377 418	**SN**	P	*SN*	BI	73418	78818	78618	73818
377 419	**SN**	P	*SN*	BI	73419	78819	78619	73819
377 420	**SN**	P	*SN*	BI	73420	78820	78620	73820
377 421	**SN**	P	*SN*	BI	73421	78821	78621	73821

377 422	**SN**	P	*SN*	BI	73422	78822	78622	73822
377 423	**SN**	P	*SN*	BI	73423	78823	78623	73823
377 424	**SN**	P	*SN*	BI	73424	78824	78624	73824
377 425	**SN**	P	*SN*	BI	73425	78825	78625	73825
377 426	**SN**	P	*SN*	BI	73426	78826	78626	73826
377 427	**SN**	P	*SN*	BI	73427	78827	78627	73827
377 428	**SN**	P	*SN*	BI	73428	78828	78628	73828
377 429	**SN**	P	*SN*	BI	73429	78829	78629	73829
377 430	**SN**	P	*SN*	BI	73430	78830	78630	73830
377 431	**SN**	P	*SN*	BI	73431	78831	78631	73831
377 432	**SN**	P	*SN*	BI	73432	78832	78632	73832
377 433	**SN**	P	*SN*	BI	73433	78833	78633	73833
377 434	**SN**	P	*SN*	BI	73434	78834	78634	73834
377 435	**SN**	P	*SN*	BI	73435	78835	78635	73835
377 436	**SN**	P	*SN*	BI	73436	78836	78636	73836
377 437	**SN**	P	*SN*	BI	73437	78837	78637	73837
377 438	**SN**	P	*SN*	BI	73438	78838	78638	73838
377 439	**SN**	P	*SN*	BI	73439	78839	78639	73839
377 440	**SN**	P	*SN*	BI	73440	78840	78640	73840
377 441	**SN**	P	*SN*	BI	73441	78841	78641	73841
377 442	**SN**	P	*SN*	BI	73442	78842	78642	73842
377 443	**SN**	P	*SN*	BI	73443	78843	78643	73843
377 444	**SN**	P	*SN*	BI	73444	78844	78644	73844
377 445	**SN**	P	*SN*	BI	73445	78845	78645	73845
377 446	**SN**	P	*SN*	BI	73446	78846	78646	73846
377 447	**SN**	P	*SN*	BI	73447	78847	78647	73847
377 448	**SN**	P	*SN*	BI	73448	78848	78648	73848
377 449	**SN**	P	*SN*	BI	73449	78849	78649	73849
377 450	**SN**	P	*SN*	BI	73450	78850	78650	73850
377 451	**SN**	P	*SN*	BI	73451	78851	78651	73851
377 452	**SN**	P	*SN*	BI	73452	78852	78652	73852
377 453	**SN**	P	*SN*	BI	73453	78853	78653	73853
377 454	**SN**	P	*SN*	BI	73454	78854	78654	73854
377 455	**SN**	P	*SN*	BI	73455	78855	78655	73855
377 456	**SN**	P	*SN*	BI	73456	78856	78656	73856
377 457	**SN**	P	*SN*	BI	73457	78857	78657	73857
377 458	**SN**	P	*SN*	BI	73458	78858	78658	73858
377 459	**SN**	P	*SN*	BI	73459	78859	78659	73859
377 460	**SN**	P	*SN*	BI	73460	78860	78660	73860
377 461	**SN**	P	*SN*	BI	73461	78861	78661	73861
377 462	**SN**	P	*SN*	BI	73462	78862	78662	73862
377 463	**SN**	P	*SN*	BI	73463	78863	78663	73863
377 464	**SN**	P	*SN*	BI	73464	78864	78664	73864
377 465	**SN**	P	*SN*	BI	73465	78865	78665	73865
377 466	**SN**	P	*SN*	BI	73466	78866	78666	73866
377 467	**SN**	P	*SN*	BI	73467	78867	78667	73867
377 468	**SN**	P	*SN*	BI	73468	78868	78668	73868
377 469	**SN**	P	*SN*	BI	73469	78869	78669	73869
377 470	**SN**	P	*SN*	BI	73470	78870	78670	73870
377 471	**SN**	P	*SN*	BI	73471	78871	78671	73871
377 472	**SN**	P	*SN*	BI	73472	78872	78672	73872

377 473	**SN**	P	*SN*	BI	73473	78873	78673	73873
377 474	**SN**	P	*SN*	BI	73474	78874	78674	73874
377 475	**SN**	P	*SN*	BI	73475	78875	78675	73875

CLASS 378 ELECTROSTAR BOMBARDIER DERBY

44 new Class 378 suburban Electrostars (similar to the Class 376s) are on order for the new Transport for London "London Rail" franchise. There will be 24 dual voltage 3-car units (Class 378/0) and 20 third rail only 4-car units (Class 378/1). The first is due for completion in 2008. These units will be owned by TfL. Numbering details awaited.

CLASS 390 PENDOLINO ALSTOM BIRMINGHAM

Tilting Virgin West Coast units.

Formation: DMRFO–MFO–PTFO–MFO–TSO–MSO–PTSRMB–MSO–DMSO.
Construction: Welded aluminium alloy.
Traction Motors: Two Alstom ONIX 800 of 425 kW.
Wheel Arrangement: 1A-A1 + 1A-A1 + 2-2 + 1A-A1 + 2-2 + 1A-A1 + 2-2 + 1A-A1 + 1A-A1.
Braking: Disc, rheostatic & regenerative.
Dimensions: 24.80/23.90 x 2.73 m.

Bogies: Fiat-SIG.	**Couplers:** Dellner 12.
Gangways: Within unit.	**Control System:** IGBT Inverter.
Doors: Sliding plug.	**Maximum Speed:** 125 m.p.h.

Heating & ventilation: Air conditioning.
Seating Layout: 1: 2+1 facing/unidirectional, 2: 2+2 facing/unidirectional.
Multiple Working: Within class. Can also be controlled from Class 57/3 locomotives.

DMRFO: Alstom Birmingham 2001–2005. 18/–. 55.6 t.
MFO(A): Alstom Birmingham 2001–2005. 37/–(2) 1TD 1W. 52.0 t.
PTFO: Alstom Birmingham 2001–2005. 44/– 1T. 50.1 t.
MFO(B): Alstom Birmingham 2001–2005. 46/– 1T. 51.8 t.
TSO: Alstom Birmingham 2001–2005. –/76 1T. 45.5 t.
MSO(A): Alstom Birmingham 2001–2005. –/62(4) 1TD 1W. 50.0 t.
PTSRMB: Alstom Birmingham 2001–2005. –/48. 52.0 t.
MSO(B): Alstom Birmingham 2001–2005. –/62(2) 1TD 1W. 51.7 t.
DMSO: Alstom Birmingham 2001–2005. –/46 1T. 51.0 t.

Note: Units up to 390 034 were delivered as 8-car sets, without the TSO (688xx). During 2004 and early 2005 these units had their 9th cars added.

390 001	**VT**	A	*VW*	MA	69101	69401	69501	69601	68801
					69701	69801	69901	69201	
390 002	**VT**	A	*VW*	MA	69102	69402	69502	69602	68802
					69702	69802	69902	69202	
390 003	**VT**	A	*VW*	MA	69103	69403	69503	69603	68803
					69703	69803	69903	69203	
390 004	**VT**	A	*VW*	MA	69104	69404	69504	69604	68804
					69704	69804	69904	69204	

390 005	**VT**	A	*VW*	MA	69105	69405	69505	69605	68805
					69705	69805	69905	69205	
390 006	**VT**	A	*VW*	MA	69106	69406	69506	69606	68806
					69706	69806	69906	69206	
390 007	**VT**	A	*VW*	MA	69107	69407	69507	69607	68807
					69707	69807	69907	69207	
390 008	**VT**	A	*VW*	MA	69108	69408	69508	69608	68808
					69708	69808	69908	69208	
390 009	**VT**	A	*VW*	MA	69109	69409	69509	69609	68809
					69709	69809	69909	69209	
390 010	**VT**	A	*VW*	MA	69110	69410	69510	69610	68810
					69710	69810	69910	69210	
390 011	**VT**	A	*VW*	MA	69111	69411	69511	69611	68811
					69711	69811	69911	69211	
390 012	**VT**	A	*VW*	MA	69112	69412	69512	69612	68812
					69712	69812	69912	69212	
390 013	**VT**	A	*VW*	MA	69113	69413	69513	69613	68813
					69713	69813	69913	69213	
390 014	**VT**	A	*VW*	MA	69114	69414	69514	69614	68814
					69714	69814	69914	69214	
390 015	**VT**	A	*VW*	MA	69115	69415	69515	69615	68815
					69715	69815	69915	69215	
390 016	**VT**	A	*VW*	MA	69116	69416	69516	69616	68816
					69716	69816	69916	69216	
390 017	**VT**	A	*VW*	MA	69117	69417	69517	69617	68817
					69717	69817	69917	69217	
390 018	**VT**	A	*VW*	MA	69118	69418	69518	69618	68818
					69718	69818	69918	69218	
390 019	**VT**	A	*VW*	MA	69119	69419	69519	69619	68819
					69719	69819	69919	69219	
390 020	**VT**	A	*VW*	MA	69120	69420	69520	69620	68820
					69720	69820	69920	69220	
390 021	**VT**	A	*VW*	MA	69121	69421	69521	69621	68821
					69721	69821	69921	69221	
390 022	**VT**	A	*VW*	MA	69122	69422	69522	69622	68822
					69722	69822	69922	69222	
390 023	**VT**	A	*VW*	MA	69123	69423	69523	69623	68823
					69723	69823	69923	69223	
390 024	**VT**	A	*VW*	MA	69124	69424	69524	69624	68824
					69724	69824	69924	69224	
390 025	**VT**	A	*VW*	MA	69125	69425	69525	69625	68825
					69725	69825	69925	69225	
390 026	**VT**	A	*VW*	MA	69126	69426	69526	69626	68826
					69726	69826	69926	69226	
390 027	**VT**	A	*VW*	MA	69127	69427	69527	69627	68827
					69727	69827	69927	69227	
390 028	**VT**	A	*VW*	MA	69128	69428	69528	69628	68828
					69728	69828	69928	69228	
390 029	**VT**	A	*VW*	MA	69129	69429	69529	69629	68829
					69729	69829	69929	69229	

390 030	**VT**	A	*VW*	MA	69130	69430	69530	69630	68830
					69730	69830	69930	69230	
390 031	**VT**	A	*VW*	MA	69131	69431	69531	69631	68831
					69731	69831	69931	69231	
390 032	**VT**	A	*VW*	MA	69132	69432	69532	69632	68832
					69732	69832	69932	69232	
390 033	**VT**	A	*VW*	MA	69133	69433	69533	69633	68833
					69733	69833	69933	69233	
390 034	**VT**	A	*VW*	MA	69134	69434	69534	69634	68834
					69734	69834	69934	69234	
390 035	**VT**	A	*VW*	MA	69135	69435	69535	69635	68835
					69735	69835	69935	69235	
390 036	**VT**	A	*VW*	MA	69136	69436	69536	69636	68836
					69736	69836	69936	69236	
390 037	**VT**	A	*VW*	MA	69137	69437	69537	69637	68837
					69737	69837	69937	69237	
390 038	**VT**	A	*VW*	MA	69138	69438	69538	69638	68838
					69738	69838	69938	69238	
390 039	**VT**	A	*VW*	MA	69139	69439	69539	69639	68839
					69739	69839	69939	69239	
390 040	**VT**	A	*VW*	MA	69140	69440	69540	69640	68840
					69740	69840	69940	69240	
390 041	**VT**	A	*VW*	MA	69141	69441	69541	69641	68841
					69741	69841	69941	69241	
390 042	**VT**	A	*VW*	MA	69142	69442	69542	69642	68842
					69742	69842	69942	69242	
390 043	**VT**	A	*VW*	MA	69143	69443	69543	69643	68843
					69743	69843	69943	69243	
390 044	**VT**	A	*VW*	MA	69144	69444	69544	69644	68844
					69744	69844	69944	69244	
390 045	**VT**	A	*VW*	MA	69145	69445	69545	69645	68845
					69745	69845	69945	69245	
390 046	**VT**	A	*VW*	MA	69146	69446	69546	69646	68846
					69746	69846	69946	69246	
390 047	**VT**	A	*VW*	MA	69147	69447	69547	69647	68847
					69747	69847	69947	69247	
390 048	**VT**	A	*VW*	MA	69148	69448	69548	69648	68848
					69748	69848	69948	69248	
390 049	**VT**	A	*VW*	MA	69149	69449	69549	69649	68849
					69749	69849	69949	69249	
390 050	**VT**	A	*VW*	MA	69150	69450	69550	69650	68850
					69750	69850	69950	69250	
390 051	**VT**	A	*VW*	MA	69151	69451	69551	69651	68851
					69751	69851	69951	69251	
390 052	**VT**	A	*VW*	MA	69152	69452	69552	69652	68852
					69752	69852	69952	69252	
390 053	**VT**	A	*VW*	MA	69153	69453	69553	69653	68853
					69753	69853	69953	69253	

Names (carried on MFO No. 696xx):

390 001	Virgin Pioneer	390 028	City of Preston
390 002	Virgin Angel	390 029	City of Stoke-on-Trent
390 003	Virgin Hero	390 030	City of Edinburgh
390 004	Virgin Scot	390 031	City of Liverpool
390 005	City of Wolverhampton	390 032	City of Birmingham
390 006	Virgin Sun	390 033	City of Glasgow
390 007	Virgin Lady	390 034	City of Carlisle
390 008	Virgin King	390 035	City of Lancaster
390 009	Virgin Queen	390 036	City of Coventry
390 010	Chris Green	390 037	Virgin Difference
390 011	City of Lichfield	390 038	City of London
390 012	Virgin Star	390 039	Virgin Quest
390 013	Virgin Spirit	390 040	Virgin Pathfinder
390 014	City of Manchester	390 041	City of Chester
390 015	Virgin Crusader	390 042	City of Bangor/Dinas Bangor
390 016	Virgin Champion	390 043	Virgin Explorer
390 017	Virgin Prince	390 044	Virgin Lionheart
390 018	Virgin Princess	390 045	Virgin Valiant
390 019	Virgin Warrior	390 046	Virgin Soldiers
390 020	Virgin Cavalier	390 047	Heaven's Angels
390 021	Virgin Dream	390 048	Virgin Harrier
390 022	Virgin Hope	390 049	Virgin Express
390 023	Virgin Glory	390 050	Virgin Invader
390 024	Virgin Venturer	390 051	Virgin Ambassador
390 025	Virgin Stagecoach	390 052	Virgin Knight
390 026	Virgin Enterprise	390 053	Mission Accomplished
390 027	Virgin Buccaneer		

CLASS 395 CTRL DOMESTIC SETS HITACHI JAPAN

New 6-car dual-voltage units on order for Channel Tunnel Rail Link domestic services from London St. Pancras International to Ashford, Dover, Ramsgate and Margate, to be operated by Southeastern. The first unit is due to arrive for testing in summer 2007. Details given below are provisional, full details awaited.

Formation: DTSO–MSO–MSO–MSO–MSO–DTSO.
Systems: 25 kV AC overhead/750 V DC third rail.
Construction: Aluminium.

Traction Motors:	**Wheel Arrangement:**
Braking:	**Dimensions:** 20.65/20.00 × 2.81.
Bogies:	**Couplers:** Scharfenberg.
Gangways: Within unit.	**Control System:** IGBT Inverter.
Doors: Single-leaf sliding.	**Maximum Speed:** 140 m.p.h.

Heating & ventilation: Air conditioning.
Seating Layout: 2+2 facing/unidirectional (mainly unidirectional).
Multiple Working: Within class only.

DTSO(A): Hitachi Kasado, Japan 2006–2008. –/28(13) 1TD 2W.   . t.
MSO: Hitachi Kasado, Japan 2006–2008. –/68.   . t.
DTSO(B): Hitachi Kasado, Japan 2006–2008. –/48 1T.   . t.

395 001	H	39011	39012	39013	39014	39015	39016
395 002	H	39021	39022	39023	39024	39025	39026
395 003	H	39031	39032	39033	39034	39035	39036
395 004	H	39041	39042	39043	39044	39045	39046
395 005	H	39051	39052	39053	39054	39055	39056
395 006	H	39061	39062	39063	39064	39065	39066
395 007	H	39071	39072	39073	39074	39075	39076
395 008	H	39081	39082	39083	39084	39085	39086
395 009	H	39091	39092	39093	39094	39095	39096
395 010	H	39101	39102	39103	39104	39105	39106
395 011	H	39111	39112	39113	39114	39115	39116
395 012	H	39121	39122	39123	39124	39125	39126
395 013	H	39131	39132	39133	39134	39135	39136
395 014	H	39141	39142	39143	39144	39145	39146
395 015	H	39151	39152	39153	39154	39155	39156
395 016	H	39161	39162	39163	39164	39165	39166
395 017	H	39171	39172	39173	39174	39175	39176
395 018	H	39181	39182	39183	39184	39185	39186
395 019	H	39191	39192	39193	39194	39195	39196
395 020	H	39201	39202	39203	39204	39205	39206
395 021	H	39211	39212	39213	39214	39215	39216
395 022	H	39221	39222	39223	39224	39225	39226
395 023	H	39231	39232	39233	39234	39235	39236
395 024	H	39241	39242	39243	39244	39245	39246
395 025	H	39251	39252	39253	39254	39255	39256
395 026	H	39261	39262	39263	39264	39265	39266
395 027	H	39271	39272	39273	39274	39275	39276
395 028	H	39281	39282	39283	39284	39285	39286
395 029	H	39291	39292	39293	39294	39295	39296

4.2. 750 V DC THIRD RAIL EMUs

These classes use the third rail system at 750 V DC (unless stated). Outer couplers are buckeyes on units built before 1982 with bar couplers within the units. Newer units generally have Dellner outer couplers.

CLASS 421   BR YORK

Units built for Portsmouth and Brighton lines. Facelifted with new trim and fluorescent lighting in saloons.

Formation: DTCso–MBSO–DTCso.
Construction: Steel.
Traction Motors: Four EE507 of 185 kW.
SR designation: 3 Cig.
Wheel Arrangement: 2-2 + Bo-Bo + 2-2.
Braking: Tread.
Bogies: Mark 6 motor bogies (MBSO). B5 (SR) bogies (trailer cars).
Gangways: Throughout.
Seating Layout: 1: Compartments, 2: 2+2 facing (plus one four-a-side compartment per DTC).

Couplers: Buckeye.
Dimensions: 20.18 x 2.82 m.
Control System: 1963-type.
Maximum Speed: 90 m.p.h.
Multiple Working: Not required.
Doors: Slam.

Class 421/7. Phase 2 sets. Specially converted 3-car units for use on the Lymington branch line. Central Door Locking system fitted and wheelchair space created. Toilets removed.

76764/76773. DTCso(A). Lot No. 30814 1971. 18/36. 35.5 t.
62402/62411. MBSO. Lot No. 30816 1971. –/56 1W + 3 tip-up seats. 49 t.
76835/76844. DTCso(B). Lot No. 30815 1971. 18/36. 35 t.

| 1497 | (1883) | **BG** | SW | *SW* | BM | 76764 | 62402 | 76835 | Freshwater |
| 1498 | (1888) | **G** | SW | *SW* | BM | 76773 | 62411 | 76844 | Farringford |

CLASS 442   WESSEX EXPRESS   BREL DERBY

Stock built for Waterloo–Bournemouth–Weymouth services. Can be hauled and heated by any ETH-fitted locomotive. Withdrawn from service with South West Trains in early 2007.

Formation: DTFso–TSO–MBRMB–TSO–DTSO.
Construction: Steel.
Traction Motors: Four EE546 of 300 kW recovered from Class 432s.
SR designation: 5 Wes.
Wheel Arrangement: 2-2 + 2-2 + Bo-Bo + 2-2 + 2-2.
Braking: Disc.
Bogies: Two BREL P7 motor bogies (MBSO). T4 bogies (trailer cars).
Couplers: Buckeye.
Gangways: Throughout.
Doors: Sliding plug.
Heating & Ventilation: Air conditioning.
Seating Layout: 1: 2+2 facing/compartments, 2: 2+2 facing/unidirectional.

Dimensions: 22.15 x 2.74 m.

Control System: 1986-type.
Maximum Speed: 100 m.p.h.

Multiple Working: Within class and with locos of Classes 33/1 & 73 in an emergency.

DTFso. Lot No. 31030 Derby 1988–1989. 50/– 1T. (36 in six compartments and 14 in one saloon). 39.0 t.
TSO (A). Lot No. 31032 Derby 1988–1989. –/80 2T. 35.3 t.
MBRMB. Lot No. 31034 Derby 1988–1989. –/30+17 ("snug") 1W. 54.7 t.
TSO (B). Lot No. 31033 Derby 1988–1989. –/76(2) 2T 1W. 35.4 t.
DTSO. Lot No. 31031 Derby 1988–1989. –/78 1T. 35.7 t.

2401	**SW**	A	ZG	77382	71818	62937	71842	77406
2402	**SW**	A	BM	77383	71819	62938	71843	77407
2403	**SW**	A	ZG	77384	71820	62941	71844	77408
2404	**SW**	A	ZG	77385	71821	62939	71845	77409
2405	**SW**	A	BM	77386	71822	62944	71846	77410
2406	**SW**	A	ZG	77389	71823	62942	71847	77411
2407	**SW**	A	ZG	77388	71824	62943	71848	77412
2408	**SW**	A	ZG	77387	71825	62945	71849	77413
2409	**SW**	A	ZG	77390	71826	62946	71850	77414
2410	**SW**	A	BM	77391	71827	62948	71851	77415
2411	**SW**	A	ZG	77392	71828	62940	71858	77422
2412	**SW**	A	BM	77393	71829	62947	71853	77417
2413	**SW**	A	ZG	77394	71830	62949	71854	77418
2414	**U**	A	ZG	77395	71831	62950	71855	77419
2415	**SW**	A	ZG	77396	71832	62951	71856	77420
2416	**SW**	A	BM	77397	71833	62952	71857	77421
2417	**SW**	A	ZG	77398	71834	62953	71852	77416
2418	**SW**	A	BM	77399	71835	62954	71859	77423
2419	**SW**	A	BM	77400	71836	62955	71860	77424
2420	**SW**	A	ZG	77401	71837	62956	71861	77425
2421	**U**	A	ZG	77402	71838	62957	71862	77426
2422	**SW**	A	ZG	77403	71839	62958	71863	77427
2423	**SW**	A	BM	77404	71840	62959	71864	77428
2424	**SW**	A	ZI	77405	71841	62960	71865	77429

CLASS 444   DESIRO UK   SIEMENS

South West Trains express units.

Formation: DMCO–TSO–TSO–TSORMB–DMSO.
Construction: Aluminium.
Traction Motors: 4 Siemens 1TB2016-0GB02 asynchronous of 250 kW.
Wheel Arrangement: Bo-Bo + 2-2 + 2-2 + 2-2 + Bo-Bo.
Braking: Disc & rheostatic.   **Dimensions:** 23.57 x 2.80 m.
Bogies: SGP SF5000.   **Couplers:** Dellner 12.
Gangways: Throughout.   **Control System:** IGBT Inverter.
Doors: Single-leaf sliding plug.   **Maximum Speed:** 100 m.p.h.
Heating & Ventilation: Air conditioning.
Seating Layout: 1: 2+1 facing/unidirectional, 2: 2+2 facing/unidirectional.
Multiple Working: Within class and with Class 450.

DMSO. Siemens Wien/Uerdingen 2003–2004. –/76. 51.3 t.
TSO 67101–67145. Siemens Wien/Uerdingen 2003–2004. –/76 1T. 40.3 t.
TSO 67151–67195. Siemens Wien/Uerdingen 2003–2004. –/76 1T. 36.8 t.

TSORMB. Siemens Wien/Uerdingen 2003–2004. –/47 1T 1TD 2W. 42.1 t.
DMCO. Siemens Wien/Uerdingen 2003–2004. 35/24. 51.3 t.

444 001	**SW**	A	*SW*	NT	63801	67101	67151	67201	63851
444 002	**SW**	A	*SW*	NT	63802	67102	67152	67202	63852
444 003	**SW**	A	*SW*	NT	63803	67103	67153	67203	63853
444 004	**SW**	A	*SW*	NT	63804	67104	67154	67204	63854
444 005	**SW**	A	*SW*	NT	63805	67105	67155	67205	63855
444 006	**SW**	A	*SW*	NT	63806	67106	67156	67206	63856
444 007	**SW**	A	*SW*	NT	63807	67107	67157	67207	63857
444 008	**SW**	A	*SW*	NT	63808	67108	67158	67208	63858
444 009	**SW**	A	*SW*	NT	63809	67109	67159	67209	63859
444 010	**SW**	A	*SW*	NT	63810	67110	67160	67210	63860
444 011	**SW**	A	*SW*	NT	63811	67111	67161	67211	63861
444 012	**SW**	A	*SW*	NT	63812	67112	67162	67212	63862
444 013	**SW**	A	*SW*	NT	63813	67113	67163	67213	63863
444 014	**SW**	A	*SW*	NT	63814	67114	67164	67214	63864
444 015	**SW**	A	*SW*	NT	63815	67115	67165	67215	63865
444 016	**SW**	A	*SW*	NT	63816	67116	67166	67216	63866
444 017	**SW**	A	*SW*	NT	63817	67117	67167	67217	63867
444 018	**SW**	A	*SW*	NT	63818	67118	67168	67218	63868
444 019	**SW**	A	*SW*	NT	63819	67119	67169	67219	63869
444 020	**SW**	A	*SW*	NT	63820	67120	67170	67220	63870
444 021	**SW**	A	*SW*	NT	63821	67121	67171	67221	63871
444 022	**SW**	A	*SW*	NT	63822	67122	67172	67222	63872
444 023	**SW**	A	*SW*	NT	63823	67123	67173	67223	63873
444 024	**SW**	A	*SW*	NT	63824	67124	67174	67224	63874
444 025	**SW**	A	*SW*	NT	63825	67125	67175	67225	63875
444 026	**SW**	A	*SW*	NT	63826	67126	67176	67226	63876
444 027	**SW**	A	*SW*	NT	63827	67127	67177	67227	63877
444 028	**SW**	A	*SW*	NT	63828	67128	67178	67228	63878
444 029	**SW**	A	*SW*	NT	63829	67129	67179	67229	63879
444 030	**SW**	A	*SW*	NT	63830	67130	67180	67230	63880
444 031	**SW**	A	*SW*	NT	63831	67131	67181	67231	63881
444 032	**SW**	A	*SW*	NT	63832	67132	67182	67232	63882
444 033	**SW**	A	*SW*	NT	63833	67133	67183	67233	63883
444 034	**SW**	A	*SW*	NT	63834	67134	67184	67234	63884
444 035	**SW**	A	*SW*	NT	63835	67135	67185	67235	63885
444 036	**SW**	A	*SW*	NT	63836	67136	67186	67236	63886
444 037	**SW**	A	*SW*	NT	63837	67137	67187	67237	63887
444 038	**SW**	A	*SW*	NT	63838	67138	67188	67238	63888
444 039	**SW**	A	*SW*	NT	63839	67139	67189	67239	63889
444 040	**SW**	A	*SW*	NT	63840	67140	67190	67240	63890
444 041	**SW**	A	*SW*	NT	63841	67141	67191	67241	63891
444 042	**SW**	A	*SW*	NT	63842	67142	67192	67242	63892
444 043	**SW**	A	*SW*	NT	63843	67143	67193	67243	63893
444 044	**SW**	A	*SW*	NT	63844	67144	67194	67244	63894
444 045	**SW**	A	*SW*	NT	63845	67145	67195	67245	63895

Name (carried on TSORMB):

444 018 THE FAB 444

CLASS 450   DESIRO UK   SIEMENS

South West Trains outer suburban units.

Formation: DMSO–TCO–TSO–DMSO. (DMSO–TSO–TCO–DMSO for 450 111–127).
Construction: Aluminium.
Traction Motors: 4 Siemens 1TB2016-0GB02 asynchronous of 250 kW.
Wheel Arrangement: Bo-Bo + 2-2 + 2-2 + Bo-Bo.
Braking: Disc & rheostatic.   **Dimensions:** 20.34 x 2.79 m.
Bogies: SGP SF5000.   **Couplers:** Dellner 12.
Gangways: Throughout.   **Control System:** IGBT Inverter.
Doors: Sliding plug.   **Maximum Speed:** 100 m.p.h.
Heating & Ventilation: Air conditioning.
Seating Layout: 1: 2+2 facing/unidirectional, 2: 3+2 facing/unidirectional.
Multiple Working: Within class and with Class 444.

DMSO(A). Siemens Uerdingen/Wien 2002–2006. –/70. 48.0 t.
TCO. Siemens Uerdingen/Wien 2002–2006. 24/32(4) 1T. 35.8 t.
TSO. Siemens Uerdingen/Wien 2002–2006. –/61(9) 1TD 2W. 39.8 t.
DMSO(B). Siemens Uerdingen/Wien 2002–2006. –/70. 48.6 t.

450 001	**SD**	A	*SW*	NT	63201	64201	68101	63601
450 002	**SD**	A	*SW*	NT	63202	64202	68102	63602
450 003	**SD**	A	*SW*	NT	63203	64203	68103	63603
450 004	**SD**	A	*SW*	NT	63204	64204	68104	63604
450 005	**SD**	A	*SW*	NT	63205	64205	68105	63605
450 006	**SD**	A	*SW*	NT	63206	64206	68106	63606
450 007	**SD**	A	*SW*	NT	63207	64207	68107	63607
450 008	**SD**	A	*SW*	NT	63208	64208	68108	63608
450 009	**SD**	A	*SW*	NT	63209	64209	68109	63609
450 010	**SD**	A	*SW*	NT	63210	64210	68110	63610
450 011	**SD**	A	*SW*	NT	63211	64211	68111	63611
450 012	**SD**	A	*SW*	NT	63212	64212	68112	63612
450 013	**SD**	A	*SW*	NT	63213	64213	68113	63613
450 014	**SD**	A	*SW*	NT	63214	64214	68114	63614
450 015	**SD**	A	*SW*	NT	63215	64215	68115	63615
450 016	**SD**	A	*SW*	NT	63216	64216	68116	63616
450 017	**SD**	A	*SW*	NT	63217	64217	68117	63617
450 018	**SD**	A	*SW*	NT	63218	64218	68118	63618
450 019	**SD**	A	*SW*	NT	63219	64219	68119	63619
450 020	**SD**	A	*SW*	NT	63220	64220	68120	63620
450 021	**SD**	A	*SW*	NT	63221	64221	68121	63621
450 022	**SD**	A	*SW*	NT	63222	64222	68122	63622
450 023	**SD**	A	*SW*	NT	63223	64223	68123	63623
450 024	**SD**	A	*SW*	NT	63224	64224	68124	63624
450 025	**SD**	A	*SW*	NT	63225	64225	68125	63625
450 026	**SD**	A	*SW*	NT	63226	64226	68126	63626
450 027	**SD**	A	*SW*	NT	63227	64227	68127	63627
450 028	**SD**	A	*SW*	NT	63228	64228	68128	63628
450 029	**SD**	A	*SW*	NT	63229	64229	68129	63629
450 030	**SD**	A	*SW*	NT	63230	64230	68130	63630

450 031	**SD**	A	*SW*	NT	63231	64231	68131	63631
450 032	**SD**	A	*SW*	NT	63232	64232	68132	63632
450 033	**SD**	A	*SW*	NT	63233	64233	68133	63633
450 034	**SD**	A	*SW*	NT	63234	64234	68134	63634
450 035	**SD**	A	*SW*	NT	63235	64235	68135	63635
450 036	**SD**	A	*SW*	NT	63236	64236	68136	63636
450 037	**SD**	A	*SW*	NT	63237	64237	68137	63637
450 038	**SD**	A	*SW*	NT	63238	64238	68138	63638
450 039	**SD**	A	*SW*	NT	63239	64239	68139	63639
450 040	**SD**	A	*SW*	NT	63240	64240	68140	63640
450 041	**SD**	A	*SW*	NT	63241	64241	68141	63641
450 042	**SD**	A	*SW*	NT	63242	64242	68142	63642
450 043	**SD**	A	*SW*	NT	63243	64243	68143	63643
450 044	**SD**	A	*SW*	NT	63244	64244	68144	63644
450 045	**SD**	A	*SW*	NT	63245	64245	68145	63645
450 046	**SD**	A	*SW*	NT	63246	64246	68146	63646
450 047	**SD**	A	*SW*	NT	63247	64247	68147	63647
450 048	**SD**	A	*SW*	NT	63248	64248	68148	63648
450 049	**SD**	A	*SW*	NT	63249	64249	68149	63649
450 050	**SD**	A	*SW*	NT	63250	64250	68150	63650
450 051	**SD**	A	*SW*	NT	63251	64251	68151	63651
450 052	**SD**	A	*SW*	NT	63252	64252	68152	63652
450 053	**SD**	A	*SW*	NT	63253	64253	68153	63653
450 054	**SD**	A	*SW*	NT	63254	64254	68154	63654
450 055	**SD**	A	*SW*	NT	63255	64255	68155	63655
450 056	**SD**	A	*SW*	NT	63256	64256	68156	63656
450 057	**SD**	A	*SW*	NT	63257	64257	68157	63657
450 058	**SD**	A	*SW*	NT	63258	64258	68158	63658
450 059	**SD**	A	*SW*	NT	63259	64259	68159	63659
450 060	**SD**	A	*SW*	NT	63260	64260	68160	63660
450 061	**SD**	A	*SW*	NT	63261	64261	68161	63661
450 062	**SD**	A	*SW*	NT	63262	64262	68162	63662
450 063	**SD**	A	*SW*	NT	63263	64263	68163	63663
450 064	**SD**	A	*SW*	NT	63264	64264	68164	63664
450 065	**SD**	A	*SW*	NT	63265	64265	68165	63665
450 066	**SD**	A	*SW*	NT	63266	64266	68166	63666
450 067	**SD**	A	*SW*	NT	63267	64267	68167	63667
450 068	**SD**	A	*SW*	NT	63268	64268	68168	63668
450 069	**SD**	A	*SW*	NT	63269	64269	68169	63669
450 070	**SD**	A	*SW*	NT	63270	64270	68170	63670
450 071	**SD**	A	*SW*	NT	63271	64271	68171	63671
450 072	**SD**	A	*SW*	NT	63272	64272	68172	63672
450 073	**SD**	A	*SW*	NT	63273	64273	68173	63673
450 074	**SD**	A	*SW*	NT	63274	64274	68174	63674
450 075	**SD**	A	*SW*	NT	63275	64275	68175	63675
450 076	**SD**	A	*SW*	NT	63276	64276	68176	63676
450 077	**SD**	A	*SW*	NT	63277	64277	68177	63677
450 078	**SD**	A	*SW*	NT	63278	64278	68178	63678
450 079	**SD**	A	*SW*	NT	63279	64279	68179	63679
450 080	**SD**	A	*SW*	NT	63280	64280	68180	63680
450 081	**SD**	A	*SW*	NT	63281	64281	68181	63681

450 082	**SD**	A	*SW*	NT	63282	64282	68182	63682
450 083	**SD**	A	*SW*	NT	63283	64283	68183	63683
450 084	**SD**	A	*SW*	NT	63284	64284	68184	63684
450 085	**SD**	A	*SW*	NT	63285	64285	68185	63685
450 086	**SD**	A	*SW*	NT	63286	64286	68186	63686
450 087	**SD**	A	*SW*	NT	63287	64287	68187	63687
450 088	**SD**	A	*SW*	NT	63288	64288	68188	63688
450 089	**SD**	A	*SW*	NT	63289	64289	68189	63689
450 090	**SD**	A	*SW*	NT	63290	64290	68190	63690
450 091	**SD**	A	*SW*	NT	63291	64291	68191	63691
450 092	**SD**	A	*SW*	NT	63292	64292	68192	63692
450 093	**SD**	A	*SW*	NT	63293	64293	68193	63693
450 094	**SD**	A	*SW*	NT	63294	64294	68194	63694
450 095	**SD**	A	*SW*	NT	63295	64295	68195	63695
450 096	**SD**	A	*SW*	NT	63296	64296	68196	63696
450 097	**SD**	A	*SW*	NT	63297	64297	68197	63697
450 098	**SD**	A	*SW*	NT	63298	64298	68198	63698
450 099	**SD**	A	*SW*	NT	63299	64299	68199	63699
450 100	**SD**	A	*SW*	NT	63300	64300	68200	63700
450 101	**SD**	A	*SW*	NT	63701	66851	66801	63751
450 102	**SD**	A	*SW*	NT	63702	66852	66802	63752
450 103	**SD**	A	*SW*	NT	63703	66853	66803	63753
450 104	**SD**	A	*SW*	NT	63704	66854	66804	63754
450 105	**SD**	A	*SW*	NT	63705	66855	66805	63755
450 106	**SD**	A	*SW*	NT	63706	66856	66806	63756
450 107	**SD**	A	*SW*	NT	63707	66857	66807	63757
450 108	**SD**	A	*SW*	NT	63708	66858	66808	63758
450 109	**SD**	A	*SW*	NT	63709	66859	66809	63759
450 110	**SD**	A	*SW*	NT	63710	66860	66810	63760
450 111	**SD**	A	*SW*	NT	63901	66921	66901	63921
450 112	**SD**	A	*SW*	NT	63902	66922	66902	63922
450 113	**SD**	A	*SW*	NT	63903	66923	66903	63923
450 114	**SD**	A	*SW*	NT	63904	66924	66904	63924
450 115	**SD**	A	*SW*	NT	63905	66925	66905	63925
450 116	**SD**	A	*SW*	NT	63906	66926	66906	63926
450 117	**SD**	A	*SW*	NT	63907	66927	66907	63927
450 118	**SD**	A	*SW*	NT	63908	66928	66908	63928
450 119	**SD**	A	*SW*	NT	63909	66929	66909	63929
450 120	**SD**	A	*SW*	NT	63910	66930	66910	63930
450 121	**SD**	A	*SW*	NT	63911	66931	66911	63931
450 122	**SD**	A	*SW*	NT	63912	66932	66912	63932
450 123	**SD**	A	*SW*	NT	63913	66933	66913	63933
450 124	**SD**	A	*SW*	NT	63914	66934	66914	63934
450 125	**SD**	A	*SW*	NT	63915	66935	66915	63935
450 126	**SD**	A	*SW*	NT	63916	66936	66916	63936
450 127	**SD**	A	*SW*	NT	63917	66937	66917	63937

Names (carried on DMSO(B)):

450 015   DESIRO
450 042   TRELOAR COLLEGE
450 114   FAIRBRIDGE investing in the future

CLASS 455   BR YORK

South West Trains/Southern inner suburban units.

Formation: DTSO–MSO–TSO–DTSO.
Construction: Steel. Class 455/7 TSO have a steel underframe and an aluminium alloy body & roof.
Traction Motors: Four GEC507-20J of 185 kW, some recovered from Class 405s.
Wheel Arrangement: 2-2 + Bo-Bo + 2-2 + 2-2.
Braking: Disc.   **Dimensions:** 20.28/20.18 x 2.82 m.
Bogies: P7 (motor) and T3 (455/8 & 455/9) BX1 (455/7) trailer.
Gangways: Within unit + end doors (sealed on Southern units).
Couplers: Tightlock.   **Control System:** 1982-type, camshaft.
Doors: Sliding.   **Maximum Speed:** 75 m.p.h.
Heating & Ventilation: Various.
Seating Layout: 3+2 low-back facing unless shown.
Multiple Working: Within class and with Class 456.

South West Trains refurbished units (livery **SS**) have been fitted with 2+2 facing/unidirectional high-back seating, with some tip-up and "perch" seating.

Class 455/7. Refurbished South West Trains units. Second series with TSOs originally in Class 508s. Pressure heating & ventilation.

DTSO. Lot No. 30976 1984–1985. –/50(4) 1W. 30.3 t.
MSO. Lot No. 30975 1984–1985. –/68. 45.7 t.
TSO. Lot No. 30944 1979–1980. –/68. 26.1 t.

5701	SS	P	*SW*	WD	77727	62783	71545	77728
5702	SS	P	*SW*	WD	77729	62784	71547	77730
5703	SS	P	*SW*	WD	77731	62785	71540	77732
5704	SS	P	*SW*	WD	77733	62786	71548	77734
5705	SS	P	*SW*	WD	77735	62787	71565	77736
5706	SS	P	*SW*	WD	77737	62788	71534	77738
5707	SS	P	*SW*	WD	77739	62789	71536	77740
5708	SS	P	*SW*	WD	77741	62790	71560	77742
5709	SS	P	*SW*	WD	77743	62791	71532	77744
5710	SS	P	*SW*	WD	77745	62792	71566	77746
5711	SS	P	*SW*	WD	77747	62793	71542	77748
5712	SS	P	*SW*	WD	77749	62794	71546	77750
5713	SS	P	*SW*	WD	77751	62795	71567	77752
5714	SS	P	*SW*	WD	77753	62796	71539	77754
5715	SS	P	*SW*	WD	77755	62797	71535	77756
5716	SS	P	*SW*	WD	77757	62798	71564	77758
5717	SS	P	*SW*	WD	77759	62799	71528	77760
5718	SS	P	*SW*	WD	77761	62800	71557	77762
5719	SS	P	*SW*	WD	77763	62801	71558	77764
5720	SS	P	*SW*	WD	77765	62802	71568	77766
5721	SS	P	*SW*	WD	77767	62803	71553	77768
5722	SS	P	*SW*	WD	77769	62804	71533	77770
5723	SS	P	*SW*	WD	77771	62805	71526	77772
5724	SS	P	*SW*	WD	77773	62806	71561	77774

5725	**SS**	P	*SW*	WD	77775	62807	71541	77776
5726	**SS**	P	*SW*	WD	77777	62808	71556	77778
5727	**SS**	P	*SW*	WD	77779	62809	71562	77780
5728	**SS**	P	*SW*	WD	77781	62810	71527	77782
5729	**SS**	P	*SW*	WD	77783	62811	71550	77784
5730	**SS**	P	*SW*	WD	77785	62812	71557	77786
5731	**SS**	P	*SW*	WD	77787	62813	71555	77788
5732	**SS**	P	*SW*	WD	77789	62814	71552	77790
5733	**SS**	P	*SW*	WD	77791	62815	71549	77792
5734	**SS**	P	*SW*	WD	77793	62816	71531	77794
5735	**SS**	P	*SW*	WD	77795	62817	71563	77796
5736	**SS**	P	*SW*	WD	77797	62818	71554	77798
5737	**SS**	P	*SW*	WD	77799	62819	71544	77800
5738	**SS**	P	*SW*	WD	77801	62820	71529	77802
5739	**SS**	P	*SW*	WD	77803	62821	71537	77804
5740	**SS**	P	*SW*	WD	77805	62822	71530	77806
5741	**SS**	P	*SW*	WD	77807	62823	71559	77808
5742	**SS**	P	*SW*	WD	77809	62824	71543	77810
5750	**SS**	P	*SW*	WD	77811	62825	71538	77812

Class 455/8. Southern units. First series. Pressure heating & ventilation.

All units refurbished with 3+2 high-back seating. Fitted with in-cab air-conditioning systems meaning that the end door has been sealed.

DTSO. Lot No. 30972 York 1982–1984. –/74. 33.6 t.
MSO. Lot No. 30973 York 1982–1984. –/84. 37.9 t.
TSO. Lot No. 30974 York 1982–1984. –/75(3) 2W. 34.0 t.

455 801	**SN**	H	*SN*	SU	77627	62709	71657	77580
455 802	**SN**	H	*SN*	SU	77581	62710	71664	77582
455 803	**SN**	H	*SN*	SU	77583	62711	71639	77584
455 804	**SN**	H	*SN*	SU	77585	62712	71640	77586
455 805	**SN**	H	*SN*	SU	77587	62713	71641	77588
455 806	**SN**	H	*SN*	SU	77589	62714	71642	77590
455 807	**SN**	H	*SN*	SU	77591	62715	71643	77592
455 808	**SN**	H	*SN*	SU	77637	62716	71644	77594
455 809	**SN**	H	*SN*	SU	77623	62717	71648	77602
455 810	**SN**	H	*SN*	SU	77597	62718	71646	77598
455 811	**SN**	H	*SN*	SU	77599	62719	71647	77600
455 812	**SN**	H	*SN*	SU	77595	62720	71645	77626
455 813	**SN**	H	*SN*	SU	77603	62721	71649	77604
455 814	**SN**	H	*SN*	SU	77605	62722	71650	77606
455 815	**SN**	H	*SN*	SU	77607	62723	71651	77608
455 816	**SN**	H	*SN*	SU	77609	62724	71652	77633
455 817	**SN**	H	*SN*	SU	77611	62725	71653	77612
455 818	**SN**	H	*SN*	SU	77613	62726	71654	77632
455 819	**SN**	H	*SN*	SU	77615	62727	71637	77616
455 820	**SN**	H	*SN*	SU	77617	62728	71656	77618
455 821	**SN**	H	*SN*	SU	77619	62729	71655	77620
455 822	**SN**	H	*SN*	SU	77621	62730	71658	77622
455 823	**SN**	H	*SN*	SU	77601	62731	71659	77596
455 824	**SN**	H	*SN*	SU	77593	62732	71660	77624

455 825	**SN**	H	*SN*	SU	77579	62733	71661	77628
455 826	**SN**	H	*SN*	SU	77630	62734	71662	77629
455 827	**SN**	H	*SN*	SU	77610	62735	71663	77614
455 828	**SN**	H	*SN*	SU	77631	62736	71638	77634
455 829	**SN**	H	*SN*	SU	77635	62737	71665	77636
455 830	**SN**	H	*SN*	SU	77625	62743	71666	77638
455 831	**SN**	H	*SN*	SU	77639	62739	71667	77640
455 832	**SN**	H	*SN*	SU	77641	62740	71668	77642
455 833	**SN**	H	*SN*	SU	77643	62741	71669	77644
455 834	**SN**	H	*SN*	SU	77645	62742	71670	77646
455 835	**SN**	H	*SN*	SU	77647	62738	71671	77648
455 836	**SN**	H	*SN*	SU	77649	62744	71672	77650
455 837	**SN**	H	*SN*	SU	77651	62745	71673	77652
455 838	**SN**	H	*SN*	SU	77653	62746	71674	77654
455 839	**SN**	H	*SN*	SU	77655	62747	71675	77656
455 840	**SN**	H	*SN*	SU	77657	62748	71676	77658
455 841	**SN**	H	*SN*	SU	77659	62749	71677	77660
455 842	**SN**	H	*SN*	SU	77661	62750	71678	77662
455 843	**SN**	H	*SN*	SU	77663	62751	71679	77664
455 844	**SN**	H	*SN*	SU	77665	62752	71680	77666
455 845	**SN**	H	*SN*	SU	77667	62753	71681	77668
455 846	**SN**	H	*SN*	SU	77669	62754	71682	77670

Class 455/8. South West Trains units. First series. Pressure heating & ventilation.

DTSO. Lot No. 30972 York 1982–1984. –/74. 29.5 t.
MSO. Lot No. 30973 York 1982–1984. –/84. 45.6 t.
TSO. Lot No. 30974 York 1982–1984. –/84. 27.1 t.

Advertising liveries:
5853 Cotes du Rhone wine (All over deep red with various images).
5856 Legoland Windsor (Yellow, blue and red with various images).
5868 Golden Jubilee/Hampton Court Palace (Gold with various images).
5869 Royal British Legion poppy appeal (white with poppy images).

5847	**ST**	P	*SW*	WD	77671	62755	71683	77672
5848	**ST**	P	*SW*	WD	77673	62756	71684	77674
5849	**ST**	P	*SW*	WD	77675	62757	71685	77676
5850	**ST**	P	*SW*	WD	77677	62758	71686	77678
5851	**ST**	P	*SW*	WD	77679	62759	71687	77680
5852	**ST**	P	*SW*	WD	77681	62760	71688	77682
5853	**AL**	P	*SW*	WD	77683	62761	71689	77684
5854	**ST**	P	*SW*	WD	77685	62762	71690	77686
5855	**ST**	P	*SW*	WD	77687	62763	71691	77688
5856	**AL**	P	*SW*	WD	77689	62764	71692	77690
5857	**ST**	P	*SW*	WD	77691	62765	71693	77692
5858	**ST**	P	*SW*	WD	77693	62766	71694	77694
5859	**ST**	P	*SW*	WD	77695	62767	71695	77696
5860	**ST**	P	*SW*	WD	77697	62768	71696	77698
5861	**ST**	P	*SW*	WD	77699	62769	71697	77700
5862	**ST**	P	*SW*	WD	77701	62770	71698	77702
5863	**ST**	P	*SW*	WD	77703	62771	71699	77704
5864	**ST**	P	*SW*	WD	77705	62772	71700	77706

5865	**ST**		P	*SW*	WD	77707	62773	71701	77708
5866	**ST**		P	*SW*	WD	77709	62774	71702	77710
5867	**ST**		P	*SW*	WD	77711	62775	71703	77712
5868	**AL**		P	*SW*	WD	77713	62776	71704	77714
5869	**AL**		P	*SW*	WD	77715	62777	71705	77716
5870	**ST**		P	*SW*	WD	77717	62778	71706	77718
5871	**ST**		P	*SW*	WD	77719	62779	71707	77720
5872	**ST**		P	*SW*	WD	77721	62780	71708	77722
5873	**ST**		P	*SW*	WD	77723	62781	71709	77724
5874	**ST**		P	*SW*	WD	77725	62782	71710	77726

Class 455/9. South West Trains units. Third series. Convection heating.
Dimensions: 19.96/20.18 x 2.82 m.

DTSO. Lot No. 30991 York 1985. –/74 (s –/50(4) 1W). 29.0 t.
MSO. Lot No. 30992 York 1985. –/84 (s –/68). 46.3 t.
TSO. Lot No. 30993 York 1985. –/84 (s –/68). 28.3 t.
TSO†. Lot No. 30932 Derby 1981. –/68. 26.5 t.

Note: † Prototype vehicle 67400 converted from a Class 210 DEMU.

5901	s	**SS**	P	*SW*	WD	77813	62826	71714	77814
5902	s	**SS**	P	*SW*	WD	77815	62827	71715	77816
5903	s	**SS**	P	*SW*	WD	77817	62828	71716	77818
5904	s	**SS**	P	*SW*	WD	77819	62829	71717	77820
5905	s	**SS**	P	*SW*	WD	77821	62830	71725	77822
5906	s	**SS**	P	*SW*	WD	77823	62831	71719	77824
5907	s	**SS**	P	*SW*	WD	77825	62832	71720	77826
5908	s	**SS**	P	*SW*	WD	77827	62833	71721	77828
5909	s	**SS**	P	*SW*	WD	77829	62834	71722	77830
5910	s	**SS**	P	*SW*	WD	77831	62835	71723	77832
5911	s	**SS**	P	*SW*	WD	77833	62836	71724	77834
5912	†s	**SS**	P	*SW*	WD	77835	62837	67400	77836
5913	s	**SS**	P	*SW*	WD	77837	62838	71726	77838
5914	s	**SS**	P	*SW*	WD	77839	62839	71727	77840
5915	s	**SS**	P	*SW*	WD	77841	62840	71728	77842
5916	s	**SS**	P	*SW*	WD	77843	62841	71729	77844
5917	s	**SS**	P	*SW*	WD	77845	62842	71730	77846
5918		**ST**	P	*SW*	WD	77847	62843	71732	77848
5919	s	**SS**	P	*SW*	WD	77849	62844	71718	77850
5920	s	**SS**	P	*SW*	WD	77851	62845	71733	77852

CLASS 456 BREL YORK

Southern inner suburban units.

Formation: DMSO–DTSO.
Construction: Steel underframe, aluminium alloy body & roof.
Traction Motors: Two GEC507-20J of 185 kW, some recovered from Class 405s.
Wheel Arrangement: 2-Bo + 2-2.

Braking: Disc.	**Dimensions:** 20.61 x 2.82 m.
Bogies: P7 (motor) and T3 (trailer).	**Couplers:** Tightlock.
Gangways: Within unit.	**Control System:** GTO Chopper.

Doors: Sliding.   **Maximum Speed:** 75 m.p.h.
Heating & Ventilation: Convection heating.
Seating Layout: 3+2 facing.
Multiple Working: Within class and with Class 455.

DMSO. Lot No. 31073 1990–1991. –/79. 41.1 t.
DTSO. Lot No. 31074 1990–1991. –/73 1T. 31.4 t.

456 001	N	P	*SN*	SU	64735	78250	
456 002	SN	P	*SN*	SU	64736	78251	
456 003	N	P	*SN*	SU	64737	78252	
456 004	SN	P	*SN*	SU	64738	78253	
456 005	N	P	*SN*	SU	64739	78254	
456 006	U	P	*SN*	SU	64740	78255	
456 007	N	P	*SN*	SU	64741	78256	
456 008	N	P	*SN*	SU	64742	78257	
456 009	N	P	*SN*	SU	64743	78258	
456 010	N	P	*SN*	SU	64744	78259	
456 011	N	P	*SN*	SU	64745	78260	
456 012	SN	P	*SN*	SU	64746	78261	
456 013	N	P	*SN*	SU	64747	78262	
456 014	SN	P	*SN*	SU	64748	78263	
456 015	SN	P	*SN*	SU	64749	78264	
456 016	N	P	*SN*	SU	64750	78265	
456 017	SN	P	*SN*	SU	64751	78266	
456 018	SN	P	*SN*	SU	64752	78267	
456 019	SN	P	*SN*	SU	64753	78268	
456 020	N	P	*SN*	SU	64754	78269	
456 021	N	P	*SN*	SU	64755	78270	
456 022	N	P	*SN*	SU	64756	78271	
456 023	N	P	*SN*	SU	64757	78272	
456 024	SN	P	*SN*	SU	64758	78273	Sir Cosmo Bonsor

CLASS 458   JUNIPER   ALSTOM BIRMINGHAM

South West Trains outer suburban units.

Formation: DMCO–TSO–MSO–DMCO.
Construction: Steel.
Traction Motors: Two Alstom ONIX 800 asynchronous of 270 kW.
Wheel Arrangement: 2-Bo + 2-2 + Bo-2 + Bo-2.
Braking: Disc & regenerative.   **Dimensions:** 21.16/19.94 x 2.80 m.
Bogies: ACR.   **Couplers:** Scharfenberg AAR.
Gangways: Throughout (not in use).   **Control System:** IGBT Inverter.
Doors: Sliding plug.   **Maximum Speed:** 100 m.p.h.
Heating & Ventilation: Air conditioning.
Seating Layout: 1: 2+2 facing, 2: 3+2 facing/unidirectional.
Multiple Working: Within class.

DMCO(A). Alstom 1998–2000. 12/63. 46.4 t.
TSO. Alstom 1998–2000. –/38(11) 1TD 2W. 34.6 t.
MSO. Alstom 1998–2000. –/75 1T. 42.1 t.
DMCO(B). Alstom 1998–2000. 12/63. 46.4 t.

8001	**SW**	P		WD	67601	74001	74101	67701
8002	**SW**	P		WD	67602	74002	74102	67702
8003	**SW**	P	*SW*	WD	67603	74003	74103	67703
8004	**SW**	P		WD	67604	74004	74104	67704
8005	**SW**	P	*SW*	WD	67605	74005	74105	67705
8006	**SW**	P	*SW*	WD	67606	74006	74106	67706
8007	**SW**	P	*SW*	WD	67607	74007	74107	67707
8008	**SW**	P	*SW*	WD	67608	74008	74108	67708
8009	**SW**	P	*SW*	WD	67609	74009	74109	67709
8010	**SW**	P	*SW*	WD	67610	74010	74110	67710
8011	**SW**	P		WD	67611	74011	74111	67711
8012	**SW**	P	*SW*	WD	67612	74012	74112	67712
8013	**SW**	P	*SW*	WD	67613	74013	74113	67713
8014	**SW**	P	*SW*	WD	67614	74014	74114	67714
8015	**SW**	P	*SW*	WD	67615	74015	74115	67715
8016	**SW**	P	*SW*	WD	67616	74016	74116	67716
8017	**SW**	P	*SW*	WD	67617	74017	74117	67717
8018	**SW**	P	*SW*	WD	67618	74018	74118	67718
8019	**SW**	P	*SW*	WD	67619	74019	74119	67719
8020	**SW**	P	*SW*	WD	67620	74020	74120	67720
8021	**SW**	P	*SW*	WD	67621	74021	74121	67721
8022	**SW**	P	*SW*	WD	67622	74022	74122	67722
8023	**SW**	P	*SW*	WD	67623	74023	74123	67723
8024	**SW**	P	*SW*	WD	67624	74024	74124	67724
8025	**SW**	P	*SW*	WD	67625	74025	74125	67725
8026	**SW**	P	*SW*	WD	67626	74026	74126	67726
8027	**SW**	P	*SW*	WD	67627	74027	74127	67727
8028	**SW**	P	*SW*	WD	67628	74028	74128	67728
8029	**SW**	P	*SW*	WD	67629	74029	74129	67729
8030	**SW**	P	*SW*	WD	67630	74030	74130	67730

CLASS 460   GEC-ALSTHOM JUNIPER

Gatwick Express units. Only the last two digits of the unit number are carried on the front ends of these units.

Formation: DMLFO–TFO–TCO–MSO–MSO–TSO–MSO–DMSO.
Construction: Steel.
Traction Motors: Two Alstom ONIX 800 asynchronous of 270 kW.
Wheel Arrangement: 2-Bo + 2-2 + 2-2 +Bo-2 + 2-Bo + 2-2 + Bo-2 + Bo-2.
Braking: Disc & regenerative.   **Dimensions:** 21.01/19.94 x 2.80 m.
Bogies: ACR.
Couplers: Scharfenberg 330 at outer ends and between cars 4 and 5.
Gangways: Within unit.   **Control System:** IGBT Inverter.
Doors: Sliding plug.   **Maximum Speed:** 100 m.p.h.
Heating & Ventilation: Air conditioning.
Seating Layout: 1: 2+1 facing, 2: 2+2 facing/unidirectional.
Multiple Working: Within class.

DMLFO. Alstom 1998–1999. 10/– 42.6 t.
TFO. Alstom 1998–1999. 28/– 1TD 1W. 33.5 t.
TCO. Alstom 1998–1999. 9/42 1T. 34.9 t.

MSO(A). Alstom 1998–1999. –/60. 42.5 t.
MSO(B). Alstom 1998–1999. –/60. 42.5 t.
TSO. Alstom 1998–1999. –/38 1TD 1W. 35.2 t.
MSO(C). Alstom 1998–1999. –/56. 40.5 t.
DMSO. Alstom 1998–1999. –/56. 45.3 t.

Advertising livery:
Delta Airlines (blue, white & red).

460 001	**AL**	P	*GX*	SL	67901	74401	74411	74421
					74431	74441	74451	67911
460 002	**AL**	P	*GX*	SL	67902	74402	74412	74422
					74432	74442	74452	67912
460 003	**AL**	P	*GX*	SL	67903	74403	74413	74423
					74433	74443	74453	67913
460 004	**AL**	P	*GX*	SL	67904	74404	74414	74424
					74434	74444	74454	67914
460 005	**AL**	P	*GX*	SL	67905	74405	74415	74425
					74435	74445	74455	67915
460 006	**AL**	P	*GX*	SL	67906	74406	74416	74426
					74436	74446	74456	67916
460 007	**AL**	P	*GX*	SL	67907	74407	74417	74427
					74437	74447	74457	67917
460 008	**AL**	P	*GX*	SL	67908	74408	74418	74428
					74438	74448	74458	67918

CLASS 465   NETWORKER

Southeastern suburban units.

Formation: DMSO–TSO–TSO–DMSO.
Construction: Welded aluminium alloy.
Traction Motors: Four Brush TIM970 (Classes 465/0 and 465/1) or GEC-Alsthom G352BY (Classes 465/2 and 465/9) asynchronous of 280 kW.
Wheel Arrangement: Bo-Bo + 2-2 + 2-2 + Bo-Bo.
Braking: Disc, rheostatic & regenerative.
Dimensions: 20.89/20.06 x 2.81 m.
Bogies: BREL P3/T3 (Classes 465/0 and 465/1), SRP BP62/BT52 (Classes 465/2 and 465/9).
Couplers: Tightlock.
Gangways: Within unit.   **Control System:** 1992-type GTO Inverter.
Doors: Sliding plug.   **Maximum Speed:** 75 m.p.h.
Seating Layout: 3+2 facing/unidirectional.
Multiple Working: Within class and with Class 466.

64759–64808. DMSO(A). Lot No. 31100 BREL York 1991–1993. –/86. 39.2 t.
64809–64858. DMSO(B). Lot No. 31100 BREL York 1991–1993. –/86. 39.2 t.
65734–65749. DMSO(A). Lot No. 31103 Metro-Cammell 1991–1993. –/86. 39.2 t.
65784–65799. DMSO(B). Lot No. 31103 Metro-Cammell 1991–1993. –/86. 39.2 t.
65800–65846. DMSO(A). Lot No. 31130 ABB York 1993–1994. –/86. 39.2 t.
65847–65893. DMSO(B). Lot No. 31130 ABB York 1993–1994. –/86. 39.2 t.
72028–72126 (even nos.) TSO. Lot No. 31102 BREL York 1991–1993. –/90. 27.2 t.

72029–72127 **(odd nos.) TSO**. Lot No. 31101 BREL York 1991–1993. –/86 1T. 28.0 t.
72787–72817 **(odd nos.) TSO**. Lot No. 31104 Metro-Cammell 1991–1992. –/86 1T. 28.0 t.
72788–72818 **(even nos.) TSO**. Lot No. 31105 Metro-Cammell 1991–1992. –/90. 27.2 t.
72900–72992 **(even nos.) TSO**. Lot No. 31102 ABB York 1993–1994. –/90. 27.2 t.
72901–72993 **(odd nos.) TSO**. Lot No. 31101 ABB York 1993–1994. –/86 1T. 28.0 t.

Class 465/0. Built by BREL/ABB.

465 001	**CN**	H	*SE*	SG	64759	72028	72029	64809
465 002	**CN**	H	*SE*	SG	64760	72030	72031	64810
465 003	**CN**	H	*SE*	SG	64761	72032	72033	64811
465 004	**CN**	H	*SE*	SG	64762	72034	72035	64812
465 005	**CN**	H	*SE*	SG	64763	72036	72037	64813
465 006	**CN**	H	*SE*	SG	64764	72038	72039	64814
465 007	**CN**	H	*SE*	SG	64765	72040	72041	64815
465 008	**CN**	H	*SE*	SG	64766	72042	72043	64816
465 009	**CN**	H	*SE*	SG	64767	72044	72045	64817
465 010	**CN**	H	*SE*	SG	64768	72046	72047	64818
465 011	**CN**	H	*SE*	SG	64769	72048	72049	64819
465 012	**CN**	H	*SE*	SG	64770	72050	72051	64820
465 013	**CN**	H	*SE*	SG	64771	72052	72053	64821
465 014	**CN**	H	*SE*	SG	64772	72054	72055	64822
465 015	**CN**	H	*SE*	SG	64773	72056	72057	64823
465 016	**CN**	H	*SE*	SG	64774	72058	72059	64824
465 017	**CN**	H	*SE*	SG	64775	72060	72061	64825
465 018	**CN**	H	*SE*	SG	64776	72062	72063	64826
465 019	**CN**	H	*SE*	SG	64777	72064	72065	64827
465 020	**CN**	H	*SE*	SG	64778	72066	72067	64828
465 021	**CN**	H	*SE*	SG	64779	72068	72069	64829
465 022	**CN**	H	*SE*	SG	64780	72070	72071	64830
465 023	**CN**	H	*SE*	SG	64781	72072	72073	64831
465 024	**CN**	H	*SE*	SG	64782	72074	72075	64832
465 025	**CN**	H	*SE*	SG	64783	72076	72077	64833
465 026	**CN**	H	*SE*	SG	64784	72078	72079	64834
465 027	**NT**	H	*SE*	SG	64785	72080	72081	64835
465 028	**CN**	H	*SE*	SG	64786	72082	72083	64836
465 029	**CN**	H	*SE*	SG	64787	72084	72085	64837
465 030	**NT**	H	*SE*	SG	64788	72086	72087	64838
465 031	**NT**	H	*SE*	SG	64789	72088	72089	64839
465 032	**CN**	H	*SE*	SG	64790	72090	72091	64840
465 033	**CN**	H	*SE*	SG	64791	72092	72093	64841
465 034	**CN**	H	*SE*	SG	64792	72094	72095	64842
465 035	**CN**	H	*SE*	SG	64793	72096	72097	64843
465 036	**CN**	H	*SE*	SG	64794	72098	72099	64844
465 037	**CN**	H	*SE*	SG	64795	72100	72101	64845
465 038	**NT**	H	*SE*	SG	64796	72102	72103	64846
465 039	**CN**	H	*SE*	SG	64797	72104	72105	64847
465 040	**CN**	H	*SE*	SG	64798	72106	72107	64848
465 041	**CN**	H	*SE*	SG	64799	72108	72109	64849

465 042	CN	H	*SE*	SG	64800	72110	72111	64850
465 043	CN	H	*SE*	SG	64801	72112	72113	64851
465 044	CN	H	*SE*	SG	64802	72114	72115	64852
465 045	CN	H	*SE*	SG	64803	72116	72117	64853
465 046	CN	H	*SE*	SG	64804	72118	72119	64854
465 047	NT	H	*SE*	SG	64805	72120	72121	64855
465 048	CN	H	*SE*	SG	64806	72122	72123	64856
465 049	CN	H	*SE*	SG	64807	72124	72125	64857
465 050	CN	H	*SE*	SG	64808	72126	72127	64858

Class 465/1. Built by BREL/ABB. Similar to Class 465/0 but with detail differences.

465 151	NT	H	*SE*	SG	65800	72900	72901	65847
465 152	CN	H	*SE*	SG	65801	72902	72903	65848
465 153	NT	H	*SE*	SG	65802	72904	72905	65849
465 154	NT	H	*SE*	SG	65803	72906	72907	65850
465 155	CN	H	*SE*	SG	65804	72908	72909	65851
465 156	CN	H	*SE*	SG	65805	72910	72911	65852
465 157	NT	H	*SE*	SG	65806	72912	72913	65853
465 158	CN	H	*SE*	SG	65807	72914	72915	65854
465 159	NT	H	*SE*	SG	65808	72916	72917	65855
465 160	CN	H	*SE*	SG	65809	72918	72919	65856
465 161	CN	H	*SE*	SG	65810	72920	72921	65857
465 162	NT	H	*SE*	SG	65811	72922	72923	65858
465 163	NT	H	*SE*	SG	65812	72924	72925	65859
465 164	CN	H	*SE*	SG	65813	72926	72927	65860
465 165	CN	H	*SE*	SG	65814	72928	72929	65861
465 166	CN	H	*SE*	SG	65815	72930	72931	65862
465 167	NT	H	*SE*	SG	65816	72932	72933	65863
465 168	NT	H	*SE*	SG	65817	72934	72935	65864
465 169	CN	H	*SE*	SG	65818	72936	72937	65865
465 170	CN	H	*SE*	SG	65819	72938	72939	65866
465 171	CN	H	*SE*	SG	65820	72940	72941	65867
465 172	CN	H	*SE*	SG	65821	72942	72943	65868
465 173	NT	H	*SE*	SG	65822	72944	72945	65869
465 174	NT	H	*SE*	SG	65823	72946	72947	65870
465 175	NT	H	*SE*	SG	65824	72948	72949	65871
465 176	NT	H	*SE*	SG	65825	72950	72951	65872
465 177	NT	H	*SE*	SG	65826	72952	72953	65873
465 178	NT	H	*SE*	SG	65827	72954	72955	65874
465 179	NT	H	*SE*	SG	65828	72956	72957	65875
465 180	CN	H	*SE*	SG	65829	72958	72959	65876
465 181	NT	H	*SE*	SG	65830	72960	72961	65877
465 182	CN	H	*SE*	SG	65831	72962	72963	65878
465 183	CN	H	*SE*	SG	65832	72964	72965	65879
465 184	NT	H	*SE*	SG	65833	72966	72967	65880
465 185	NT	H	*SE*	SG	65834	72968	72969	65881
465 186	CN	H	*SE*	SG	65835	72970	72971	65882
465 187	CN	H	*SE*	SG	65836	72972	72973	65883
465 188	NT	H	*SE*	SG	65837	72974	72975	65884
465 189	CN	H	*SE*	SG	65838	72976	72977	65885
465 190	CN	H	*SE*	SG	65839	72978	72979	65886

465 191	NT	H	*SE*	SG	65840	72980	72981	65887
465 192	NT	H	*SE*	SG	65841	72982	72983	65888
465 193	NT	H	*SE*	SG	65842	72984	72985	65889
465 194	NT	H	*SE*	SG	65843	72986	72987	65890
465 195	NT	H	*SE*	SG	65844	72988	72989	65891
465 196	NT	H	*SE*	SG	65845	72990	72991	65892
465 197	NT	H	*SE*	SG	65846	72992	72993	65893

Class 465/2. Built by Metro-Cammell.
Dimensions: 20.80/20.15 x 2.81 m.

465 235	CN	A	*SE*	SG	65734	72787	72788	65784
465 236	CN	A	*SE*	SG	65735	72789	72790	65785
465 237	CN	A	*SE*	SG	65736	72791	72792	65786
465 238	CN	A	*SE*	SG	65737	72793	72794	65787
465 239	CN	A	*SE*	SG	65738	72795	72796	65788
465 240	CN	A	*SE*	SG	65739	72797	72798	65789
465 241	CN	A	*SE*	SG	65740	72799	72800	65790
465 242	CN	A	*SE*	SG	65741	72801	72802	65791
465 243	CN	A	*SE*	SG	65742	72803	72804	65792
465 244	CN	A	*SE*	SG	65743	72805	72806	65793
465 245	CN	A	*SE*	SG	65744	72807	72808	65794
465 246	CN	A	*SE*	SG	65745	72809	72810	65795
465 247	CN	A	*SE*	SG	65746	72811	72812	65796
465 248	CN	A	*SE*	SG	65747	72813	72814	65797
465 249	CN	A	*SE*	SG	65748	72815	72816	65798
465 250	CN	A	*SE*	SG	65749	72817	72818	65799

Class 465/9. Built by Metro-Cammell. Refurbished at Wabtec, Doncaster in 2005 for longer distance services, with the addition of first class seating areas and wheelchair spaces. Details as Class 465/0 unless stated.

Formation: DMCO–TSO(A)–TSO(B)–DMCO.
Seating Layout: 1: 2+2 facing/unidirectional, 2: 3+2 facing/unidirectional.

65700–65733. DMCO(A). Lot No. 31103 Metro-Cammell 1991–1993. 12/68. 39.2 t.
72719–72785 (odd nos.) TSO(A). Lot No. 31104 Metro-Cammell 1991–1992. –/76 1T 2W. 30.3 t.
72720–72786 (even nos.) TSO(B). Lot No. 31105 Metro-Cammell 1991–1992. –/90. 29.5 t.
65750–65783. DMCO(B). Lot No. 31103 Metro-Cammell 1991–1993. 12/68. 39.2 t.

465 901	(465 201)	CN	A	*SE*	SG	65700	72719	72720	65750
465 902	(465 202)	CN	A	*SE*	SG	65701	72721	72722	65751
465 903	(465 203)	CN	A	*SE*	SG	65702	72723	72724	65752
465 904	(465 204)	CN	A	*SE*	SG	65703	72725	72726	65753
465 905	(465 205)	CN	A	*SE*	SG	65704	72727	72728	65754
465 906	(465 206)	CN	A	*SE*	SG	65705	72729	72730	65755
465 907	(465 207)	CN	A	*SE*	SG	65706	72731	72732	65756
465 908	(465 208)	CN	A	*SE*	SG	65707	72733	72734	65757
465 909	(465 209)	CN	A	*SE*	SG	65708	72735	72736	65758
465 910	(465 210)	CN	A	*SE*	SG	65709	72737	72738	65759
465 911	(465 211)	CN	A	*SE*	SG	65710	72739	72740	65760
465 912	(465 212)	CN	A	*SE*	SG	65711	72741	72742	65761

465 913	(465 213)	**CN**	A	*SE*	SG	65712	72743	72744	65762
465 914	(465 214)	**CN**	A	*SE*	SG	65713	72745	72746	65763
465 915	(465 215)	**CN**	A	*SE*	SG	65714	72747	72748	65764
465 916	(465 216)	**CN**	A	*SE*	SG	65715	72749	72750	65765
465 917	(465 217)	**CN**	A	*SE*	SG	65716	72751	72752	65766
465 918	(465 218)	**CN**	A	*SE*	SG	65717	72753	72754	65767
465 919	(465 219)	**CN**	A	*SE*	SG	65718	72755	72756	65768
465 920	(465 220)	**CN**	A	*SE*	SG	65719	72757	72758	65769
465 921	(465 221)	**CN**	A	*SE*	SG	65720	72759	72760	65770
465 922	(465 222)	**CN**	A	*SE*	SG	65721	72761	72762	65771
465 923	(465 223)	**CN**	A	*SE*	SG	65722	72763	72764	65772
465 924	(465 224)	**CN**	A	*SE*	SG	65723	72765	72766	65773
465 925	(465 225)	**CN**	A	*SE*	SG	65724	72767	72768	65774
465 926	(465 226)	**CN**	A	*SE*	SG	65725	72769	72770	65775
465 927	(465 227)	**CN**	A	*SE*	SG	65726	72771	72772	65776
465 928	(465 228)	**CN**	A	*SE*	SG	65727	72773	72774	65777
465 929	(465 229)	**CN**	A	*SE*	SG	65728	72775	72776	65778
465 930	(465 230)	**CN**	A	*SE*	SG	65729	72777	72778	65779
465 931	(465 231)	**CN**	A	*SE*	SG	65730	72779	72780	65780
465 932	(465 232)	**CN**	A	*SE*	SG	65731	72781	72782	65781
465 933	(465 233)	**CN**	A	*SE*	SG	65732	72783	72784	65782
465 934	(465 234)	**CN**	A	*SE*	SG	65733	72785	72786	65783

Name: 465 903   Remembrance

CLASS 466   NETWORKER   GEC-ALSTHOM

Southeastern suburban units.

Formation: DMSO–DTSO.
Construction: Welded aluminium alloy.
Traction Motors: Four GEC-Alsthom G352AY asynchronous of 280 kW.
Wheel Arrangement: Bo-Bo + 2-2.
Braking: Disc, rheostatic & regenerative.
Dimensions: 20.80 x 2.80 m.
Bogies: BREL P3/T3.   **Couplers:** Tightlock.
Gangways: Within unit.   **Control System:** 1992-type GTO Inverter
Doors: Sliding plug.   **Maximum Speed:** 75 m.p.h.
Seating Layout: 3+2 facing/unidirectional.
Multiple Working: Within class and with Class 465.

DMSO. Lot No. 31128 Birmingham 1993–1994. –/86. 40.6 t.
DTSO. Lot No. 31129 Birmingham 1993–1994. –/82 1T. 31.4 t.

466 001	**CN**	A	*SE*	SG	64860	78312
466 002	**CN**	A	*SE*	SG	64861	78313
466 003	**CN**	A	*SE*	SG	64862	78314
466 004	**CN**	A	*SE*	SG	64863	78315
466 005	**CN**	A	*SE*	SG	64864	78316
466 006	**CN**	A	*SE*	SG	64865	78317
466 007	**CN**	A	*SE*	SG	64866	78318

466 008	**CN**	A	*SE*	SG	64867	78319
466 009	**CN**	A	*SE*	SG	64868	78320
466 010	**CN**	A	*SE*	SG	64869	78321
466 011	**CN**	A	*SE*	SG	64870	78322
466 012	**CN**	A	*SE*	SG	64871	78323
466 013	**CN**	A	*SE*	SG	64872	78324
466 014	**CN**	A	*SE*	SG	64873	78325
466 015	**CN**	A	*SE*	SG	64874	78326
466 016	**CN**	A	*SE*	SG	64875	78327
466 017	**CN**	A	*SE*	SG	64876	78328
466 018	**CN**	A	*SE*	SG	64877	78329
466 019	**CN**	A	*SE*	SG	64878	78330
466 020	**CN**	A	*SE*	SG	64879	78331
466 021	**CN**	A	*SE*	SG	64880	78332
466 022	**CN**	A	*SE*	SG	64881	78333
466 023	**CN**	A	*SE*	SG	64882	78334
466 024	**CN**	A	*SE*	SG	64883	78335
466 025	**CN**	A	*SE*	SG	64884	78336
466 026	**CN**	A	*SE*	SG	64885	78337
466 027	**CN**	A	*SE*	SG	64886	78338
466 028	**CN**	A	*SE*	SG	64887	78339
466 029	**CN**	A	*SE*	SG	64888	78340
466 030	**CN**	A	*SE*	SG	64889	78341
466 031	**CN**	A	*SE*	SG	64890	78342
466 032	**CN**	A	*SE*	SG	64891	78343
466 033	**CN**	A	*SE*	SG	64892	78344
466 034	**CN**	A	*SE*	SG	64893	78345
466 035	**CN**	A	*SE*	SG	64894	78346
466 036	**CN**	A	*SE*	SG	64895	78347
466 037	**CN**	A	*SE*	SG	64896	78348
466 038	**CN**	A	*SE*	SG	64897	78349
466 039	**CN**	A	*SE*	SG	64898	78350
466 040	**CN**	A	*SE*	SG	64899	78351
466 041	**CN**	A	*SE*	SG	64900	78352
466 042	**CN**	A	*SE*	SG	64901	78353
466 043	**CN**	A	*SE*	SG	64902	78354

CLASS 483   METRO-CAMMELL

Built 1938 onwards for LTE. Converted 1989–1990 for the Isle of Wight Line.

Formation: DMSO–DMSO.
System: 660 V DC third rail.
Construction: Steel.
Traction Motors: Two Crompton Parkinson/GEC/BTH LT100 of 125 kW.
Braking: Tread.   **Dimensions:** 16.15 x 2.69 m.
Bogies: LT design.   **Couplers:** Wedglock.
Gangways: None. End doors.   **Control System:** IGBT Inverter.
Doors: Sliding.   **Maximum Speed:** 45 m.p.h.
Seating Layout: Longitudinal or 2+2 facing/unidirectional.
Multiple Working: Within class.

Notes: The last three numbers of the unit number only are carried.

Former London Underground numbers are shown in parentheses.

DMSO (A). Lot No. 31071. –/40. 27.4 t.
DMSO (B). Lot No. 31072. –/42. 27.4 t.

483 002	IL	H	SW	RY	122	(10221)	225	(11142)
483 004	IL	H	SW	RY	124	(10205)	224	(11205)
483 006	IL	H	SW	RY	126	(10297)	226	(11297)
483 007	LM	H	SW	RY	127	(10291)	227	(11291)
483 008	IL	H	SW	RY	128	(10255)	228	(11255)
483 009	LM	H	SW	RY	129	(10289)	229	(11229)

CLASS 507   BREL YORK

Merseyrail suburban units.

Formation: BDMSO–TSO–DMSO.
Construction: Steel underframe, aluminium alloy body and roof.
Traction Motors: Four GEC G310AZ of 82.125 kW.
Wheel Arrangement: Bo-Bo + 2-2 + Bo-Bo.
Braking: Disc & rheostatic.   **Dimensions:** 20.33/20.18 x 2.82 m.
Bogies: BX1.   **Couplers:** Tightlock.
Gangways: Within unit + end doors.   **Control System:** Camshaft.
Doors: Sliding.   **Maximum Speed:** 75 m.p.h.
Seating Layout: All refurbished with 2+2 high-back facing seating.
Multiple Working: Within class and with Class 508.

BDMSO. Lot No. 30906 1978–1980. –/59 1W. 37.0 t.
TSO. Lot No. 30907 1978–1980. –/74. 25.5 t.
DMSO. Lot No. 30908 1978–1980. –/59 1W. 35.5 t.

507 001	ME	A	ME	BD	64367	71342	64405
507 002	ME	A	ME	BD	64368	71343	64406
507 003	ME	A	ME	BD	64369	71344	64407
507 004	ME	A	ME	BD	64388	71345	64408
507 005	ME	A	ME	BD	64371	71346	64409
507 006	ME	A	ME	BD	64372	71347	64410

507 007	**ME**	A	*ME*	BD	64373	71348	64411	
507 008	**ME**	A	*ME*	BD	64374	71349	64412	
507 009	**ME**	A	*ME*	BD	64375	71350	64413	
507 010	**ME**	A	*ME*	BD	64376	71351	64414	
507 011	**ME**	A	*ME*	BD	64377	71352	64415	
507 012	**ME**	A	*ME*	BD	64378	71353	64416	
507 013	**ME**	A	*ME*	BD	64379	71354	64417	
507 014	**ME**	A	*ME*	BD	64380	71355	64418	
507 015	**ME**	A	*ME*	BD	64381	71356	64419	
507 016	**ME**	A	*ME*	BD	64382	71357	64420	
507 017	**ME**	A	*ME*	BD	64383	71358	64421	
507 018	**ME**	A	*ME*	BD	64384	71359	64422	
507 019	**ME**	A	*ME*	BD	64385	71360	64423	
507 020	**ME**	A	*ME*	BD	64386	71361	64424	
507 021	**ME**	A	*ME*	BD	64387	71362	64425	
507 023	**ME**	A	*ME*	BD	64389	71364	64427	
507 024	**ME**	A	*ME*	BD	64390	71365	64428	
507 025	**ME**	A	*ME*	BD	64391	71366	64429	
507 026	**ME**	A	*ME*	BD	64392	71367	64430	
507 027	**ME**	A	*ME*	BD	64393	71368	64431	
507 028	**ME**	A	*ME*	BD	64394	71369	64432	
507 029	**ME**	A	*ME*	BD	64395	71370	64433	
507 030	**ME**	A	*ME*	BD	64396	71371	64434	
507 031	**ME**	A	*ME*	BD	64397	71372	64435	
507 032	**ME**	A	*ME*	BD	64398	71373	64436	
507 033	**ME**	A	*ME*	BD	64399	71374	64437	Cllr George Howard

CLASS 508   BREL YORK

Merseyrail/Southeastern/Silverlink suburban units.

Formation: DMSO–TSO–BDMSO.
Construction: Steel underframe, aluminium alloy body and roof.
Traction Motors: Four GEC G310AZ of 82.125 kW.
Wheel Arrangement: Bo-Bo + 2-2 + Bo-Bo.
Braking: Disc & rheostatic.   **Dimensions:** 20.33/20.18 x 2.82 m.
Bogies: BX1.   **Couplers:** Tightlock.
Gangways: Within unit + end doors.   **Control System:** Camshaft.
Doors: Sliding.   **Maximum Speed:** 75 m.p.h.
Seating Layout: All Merseyrail units have been refurbished with 2+2 high-back facing seating. SE and Silverlink units have 3+2 low-back facing seating.
Multiple Working: Within class and with Class 507.

DMSO. Lot No. 30979 1979–1980. –/59 1W. 36.0 t.
TSO. Lot No. 30980 1979–1980. –/74. 26.5 t.
BDMSO. Lot No. 30981 1979–1980. –/59 1W. 36.5 t.

Class 508/1. Merseyrail units.

508 103	**ME**	A	*ME*	BD	64651	71485	64694
508 104	**ME**	A	*ME*	BD	64652	71486	64695
508 108	**ME**	A	*ME*	BD	64656	71490	64699
508 110	**ME**	A	*ME*	BD	64658	71492	64701

508 111	**ME**	A	*ME*	BD	64659	71493	64702	
508 112	**ME**	A	*ME*	BD	64660	71494	64703	
508 114	**ME**	A	*ME*	BD	64662	71496	64705	
508 115	**ME**	A	*ME*	BD	64663	71497	64706	
508 117	**ME**	A	*ME*	BD	64665	71499	64708	
508 120	**ME**	A	*ME*	BD	64668	71502	64711	
508 122	**ME**	A	*ME*	BD	64670	71504	64713	
508 123	**ME**	A	*ME*	BD	64671	71505	64714	
508 124	**ME**	A	*ME*	BD	64672	71506	64715	
508 125	**ME**	A	*ME*	BD	64673	71507	64716	
508 126	**ME**	A	*ME*	BD	64674	71508	64717	
508 127	**ME**	A	*ME*	BD	64675	71509	64718	
508 128	**ME**	A	*ME*	BD	64676	71510	64719	
508 130	**ME**	A	*ME*	BD	64678	71512	64721	
508 131	**ME**	A	*ME*	BD	64679	71513	64722	
508 134	**ME**	A	*ME*	BD	64682	71516	64725	
508 136	**ME**	A	*ME*	BD	64684	71518	64727	Capital of Culture
508 137	**ME**	A	*ME*	BD	64685	71519	64728	
508 138	**ME**	A	*ME*	BD	64686	71520	64729	
508 139	**ME**	A	*ME*	BD	64687	71521	64730	
508 140	**ME**	A	*ME*	BD	64688	71522	64731	
508 141	**ME**	A	*ME*	BD	64689	71523	64732	
508 143	**ME**	A	*ME*	BD	64691	71525	64734	

Class 508/2. Units facelifted for the South Eastern lines by Wessex Traincare/Alstom, Eastleigh 1998–1999.

DMSO. Lot No. 30979 1979–1980. –/66. 36.0 t.
TSO. Lot No. 30980 1979–1980. –/79 1W. 26.5 t.
BDMSO. Lot No. 30981 1979–1980. –/74. 36.5 t.

508 201	(508 101)	**CX**	A		AF	64649	71483	64692
508 202	(508 105)	**CX**	A		AF	64653	71487	64696
508 203	(508 106)	**CX**	A	*SE*	GI	64654	71488	64697
508 204	(508 107)	**CX**	A	*SE*	GI	64655	71489	64698
508 205	(508 109)	**CX**	A		AF	64657	71491	64700
508 206	(508 113)	**CX**	A		AF	64661	71495	64704
508 207	(508 116)	**CX**	A	*SE*	GI	64664	71498	64707
508 208	(508 119)	**CN**	A	*SE*	GI	64667	71501	64710
508 209	(508 121)	**CX**	A		AF	64669	71503	64712
508 210	(508 129)	**CX**	A	*SE*	GI	64677	71511	64720
508 211	(508 132)	**CX**	A	*SE*	GI	64680	71514	64723
508 212	(508 133)	**CX**	A		GI	64681	71515	64724

Class 508/3. Units facelifted units for Silverlink for use on Euston–Watford Junction services by Alstom, Eastleigh 2002–2003.

DMSO. Lot No. 30979 1979–1980. –/68 1W. 36.0 t.
TSO. Lot No. 30980 1979–1980. –/86. 26.5 t.
BDMSO. Lot No. 30981 1979–1980. –/68 1W. 36.5 t.

508 301	(508 102)	**SL**	A	*SL*	WN	64650	71484	64693
508 302	(508 135)	**SL**	A	*SL*	WN	64683	71517	64726
508 303	(508 142)	**SL**	A	*SL*	WN	64690	71524	64733

▲ Silverlink-liveried 313 121 approaches Headstone Lane on 26/05/05 with the 13.42 Watford Junction–London Euston service.   **Gavin Morrison**

▼ "One"-liveried 315 811 is seen at Romford with the 14.12 London Liverpool Street–Shenfield on 03/06/06.   **Mark Beal**

▲ Refurbished 318 257 (with end doors sealed) is seen on the 3 mile Lanark branch with the 17.42 from Milngavie on 01/07/06. **Robin Ralston**

▼ 319 007, in Southern livery but on lease to First Capital Connect, is seen at St. Albans on 10/06/06 after arriving with a service from Sutton. **Keith Fender**

First Group-liveried 322 481 "North Berwick Flyer 1850–2000" crosses Slateford Viaduct, Edinburgh with the 07.05 Glasgow Central–North Berwick on 28/06/06.　　**Robin Ralston**

▲ Still in First Group livery, Northern's 323 228 passes Dinting Lane with the 11.17 Manchester Piccadilly–Glossop/Hadfield on 13/05/05. **Andrew Wills**

▼ Royal Mail-liveried 325 012 leads 325 011 and 325 016 at Norton Bridge with the 16.26 Willesden–Shieldmuir mail train on 23/06/06. These services are operated by GB Railfreight. **Hugh Ballantyne**

▲ West Yorkshire PTE-liveried 333 002 approaches Bingley with a Skipton–Leeds service on 07/06/06.   **Andrew Wills**

▼ Strathclyde PTE Carmine & Cream-liveried 334 006 pauses at Westerton with the 13.12 Milngavie–Motherwell on 11/05/06.   **Adrian Sumner**

▲ Carrying a special "neutral" grey and blue livery 350 124 passes Dudswell, near Tring, with the 14.53 London Euston–Northampton on 14/07/06.
Rodney Lissenden

▼ c2c-liveried 357 028 "London Tilbury & Southend Railway 1854–2004" arrives at Limehouse with a Shoeburyness–London Fenchurch Street service on 28/06/06.
Iain Scotchman

▲ First Group-liveried 360 101 and 360 111 pass Pudding Mill Lane with a London Liverpool Street–Ilford e.c.s. on 08/09/06 as refurbished Docklands cars 10+75 arrive with a Lewisham–Stratford service. **Robert Pritchard**

▼ Southeastern have retained the Connex-inspired white, black and yellow livery for their units. On 05/06/06 375 806 leaves Ashford with the 18.00 to London Victoria. **Rodney Lissenden**

▲ Southern's 377 466 arrives at Southampton Central with a service from London Victoria via the "Coastway" route on 16/07/05.　　**John Chalcraft**

▲ Inner suburban units 376 004 and 376 001 pass New Cross at speed with a Dartford service on 17/08/05. **Darren Ford**

▼ Virgin-liveried 390 002 "Virgin Angel" is seen at Wandelmill, north of Abington, with the 17.40 Glasgow Central–London Euston on 14/07/06. **Robin Ralston**

▲ Two Class 421 "Cig" units dating from the early 1970s are used by South West Trains on the Brockenhurst–Lymington branch. 1497, carrying BR Blue & Grey livery, is seen at Lymington Pier on 03/09/05. **Darren Ford**

▼ Carrying the South West Trains white "long distance" livery Class 442s 2407 and 2417 are seen near Basingstoke with the 06.54 Weymouth–Waterloo on 04/05/06. **Alex Dasi-Sutton**

▲ 444 034 and 444 002 pass Battledown, west of Basingstoke, with the 11.30 London Waterloo–Portsmouth Harbour on 01/03/06. **Brian Denton**

▼ In lovely early morning sunshine 450 008 and 450 009 pass Egham with the 07.33 Weybridge–London Waterloo on 29/06/06. **Chris Wilson**

◀ Around half of the 91-strong SWT Class 455 fleet had been refurbished and painted in the new red livery as this book went to press, with the programme due for completion in 2008. On 29/06/06 5735 leads an 8-car set near Twickenham with the 09.27 Waterloo–Waterloo via the Hounslow Loop.
Alex Dasi-Sutton

▼ Still in NSE livery, 456 017 leaves London Bridge with the 09.24 to London Victoria (showing Epsom on the destination in error) on 19/11/05.
Robert Pritchard

▲ Class 458 8021 leads an 8-car formation on the approaches to Barnes station with the 11.41 Reading–London Waterloo on 22/06/06. **Rodney Lissenden**

▼ Gatwick Express-liveried 460 002 passes Redhill with the 18.15 London Victoria–Gatwick Airport on 17/06/05. **Robert Pritchard**

▲ 466 025 and 465 924 arrive at Paddock Wood with the 10.00 London Charing Cross–Ashford International on 03/09/05.   **Alex Dasi-Sutton**

▼ Merseyrail-liveried 507 019 calls at the new Liverpool South Parkway station with the 11.43 Southport–Hunts Cross on 17/07/06.   **Doug Birmingham**

▲ Eurostar set 3208/07 approaches Fawkham Junction, on the CTRL, with the 15.19 Paris Nord–London Waterloo on 06/06/06.　　**Rodney Lissenden**

▼ Refurbished Sheffield Tram 119 leaves Woodbourn Road with the 18.43 Meadowhall Interchange–Middlewood service on 24/07/06.　　**Robert Pritchard**

▲ Unrefurbished Blackpool "Balloon" car 702 is seen at North Pier with an evening Starr Gate–Cleveleys service on 23/07/06. **Robert Pritchard**

4.3. EUROSTAR UNITS (CLASS 373)

Eurostar units were built for and are normally used on services between Britain and Continental Europe via the Channel Tunnel. Apart from such workings units may be used as follows:

- SNCF-owned units 3203/04, 3225/26 and 3227/28 have been removed from the Eurostar pool and only operate SNCF-internal services between Paris and Lille.

Each train consists of two 10-car units coupled, with a motor car at each driving end (the sets built for Regional Eurostar services are 8-car). All units are articulated with an extra motor bogie on the coach adjacent to the motor car.

Sets marked "r" have been refurbished. This now includes all sets used by Eurostar, but not 3101/02 (in store) or the sets used by SNCF.

Formation: DM–MSO–4TSO–RB–2TFO–TBFO or DM–MSO–3TSO–RB–TFO–TBFO. Gangwayed within pair of units. Air conditioned.
Construction: Steel.
Supply Systems: 25 kV AC 50 Hz overhead or 3000 V DC overhead or 750 V DC third rail (* also equipped for 1500 V DC overhead operation).
Control System: GTO–GTO Inverter on UK 750 V DC and 25 kV AC, GTO Chopper on SNCB 3000 V DC.
Wheel Arrangement: Bo–Bo + Bo–2–2–2–2–2–2–2–2–2.
Length: 22.15 m (DM), 21.85 m (MS & TBF), 18.70 m (other cars).
Couplers: Schaku 10S at outer ends, Schaku 10L at inner end of each DM and outer ends of each sub set.
Maximum Speed: 186 m.p.h. (300 km/h.)
Built: 1992–1993 by GEC-Alsthom/Brush/ANF/De Dietrich/BN Construction/ACEC.
Note: DM vehicles carry the set numbers indicated below.

Class 373/0. 10-Car sets. Built for services starting from/terminating at London Waterloo. Individual vehicles in each set are allocated numbers 373xxx0 + 373xxx1 + 373xxx2 + 373xxx3 + 373xxx4 + 373xxx5 + 373xxx6 + 373xxx7 + 373xxx8 + 373xxx9, where 3xxx denotes the set number.

Non-standard livery (0): Grey with silver ends, TGV symbol & green/blue doors.

373xxx0 series. DM. Lot No. 31118 1992–1995. 68.5 t.
373xxx1 series. MSO. Lot No. 31119 1992–1995. –/48 2T. 44.6 t.
373xxx2 series. TSO. Lot No. 31120 1992–1995. –/58 1T (r –/56 1T). 28.1 t.
373xxx3 series. TSO. Lot No. 31121 1992–1995. –/58 2T (r –/56 2T). 29.7 t.
373xxx4 series. TSO. Lot No. 31122 1992–1995. –/58 1T (r –/56 1T). 28.3 t.
373xxx5 series. TSO. Lot No. 31123 1992–1995. –/58 2T (r –/56 2T). 29.2 t.
373xxx6 series. RB. Lot No.31124 1992–1995. 31.1 t.
373xxx7 series. TFO. Lot No. 31125 1992–1995. 39/– 1T. 29.6 t.
373xxx8 series. TFO. Lot No. 31126 1992–1995. 39/– 1T. 32.2 t.
373xxx9 series. TBFO. Lot No. 31127 1992–1995. 25/– 1TD. 39.4 t.

3001	r	**EU**	EU	*EU*	NP	3006	r	**EU**	EU	*EU*	NP
3002	r	**EU**	EU	*EU*	NP	3007	r	**EU**	EU	*EU*	NP
3003	r	**EU**	EU	*EU*	NP	3008	r	**EU**	EU	*EU*	NP
3004	r	**EU**	EU	*EU*	NP	3009	r	**EU**	EU	*EU*	NP
3005	r	**EU**	EU	*EU*	NP	3010	r	**EU**	EU	*EU*	NP

3011	r **EU**	EU	*EU*	NP		3207	r* **EU**	SF	*EU*	LY MICHEL HOLLARD
3012	r **EU**	EU	*EU*	NP		3208	r* **EU**	SF	*EU*	LY MICHEL HOLLARD
3013	r **EU**	EU	*EU*	NP LONDON 2012		3209	r* **EU**	SF	*EU*	LY The Da Vinci Code
3014	r **EU**	EU	*EU*	NP LONDON 2012		3210	r* **EU**	SF	*EU*	LY The Da Vinci Code
3015	r **EU**	EU	*EU*	NP		3211	r **EU**	SF	*EU*	LY
3016	r **EU**	EU	*EU*	NP		3212	r **EU**	SF	*EU*	LY
3017	r **EU**	EU	*EU*	NP		3213	r* **EU**	SF	*EU*	LY
3018	r **EU**	EU	*EU*	NP		3214	r* **EU**	SF	*EU*	LY
3019	r **EU**	EU	*EU*	NP		3215	r **EU**	SF	*EU*	LY
3020	r **EU**	EU	*EU*	NP		3216	r* **EU**	SF	*EU*	LY
3021	r **EU**	EU	*EU*	NP		3217	r* **EU**	SF	*EU*	LY
3022	r **EU**	EU	*EU*	NP		3218	r* **EU**	SF	*EU*	LY
3101	**EU**	SB		FF		3219	r **EU**	SF	*EU*	LY
3102	**EU**	SB		FF		3220	r **EU**	SF	*EU*	LY
3103	r **EU**	SB	*EU*	FF		3221	r* **EU**	SF	*EU*	LY
3104	r **EU**	SB	*EU*	FF		3222	r* **EU**	SF	*EU*	LY
3105	r **EU**	SB	*EU*	FF		3223	r* **EU**	SF	*EU*	LY
3106	r **EU**	SB	*EU*	FF		3224	r* **EU**	SF	*EU*	LY
3107	r **EU**	SB	*EU*	FF		3225	**0**	SF	*SF*	LY
3108	r **EU**	SB	*EU*	FF		3226	**0**	SF	*SF*	LY
3201	r* **EU**	SF	*EU*	LY		3227	**0**	SF	*SF*	LY
3202	r* **EU**	SF	*EU*	LY		3228	**0**	SF	*SF*	LY
3203	**0**	SF	*SF*	LY		3229	r* **EU**	SF	*EU*	LY
3204	**0**	SF	*SF*	LY		3230	r* **EU**	SF	*EU*	LY
3205	r **EU**	SF	*EU*	LY		3231	r **EU**	SF	*EU*	LY
3206	r **EU**	SF	*EU*	LY		3232	r **EU**	SF	*EU*	LY

Class 373/2. 8-Car sets. Built for Regional Eurostar services. Individual vehicles in each set are allocated numbers 373xxx0 + 373xxx1 + 373xxx2 + 373xxx3 + 373xxx5 + 373xxx6 + 373xxx7 + 373xxx9, where 3xxx denotes the set number. Set 3313/14 is used by Eurostar for special workings.

3733xx0 series. DM. 68.5 t.
3733xx1 series. MSO. –/48 1T. 44.6 t.
3733xx2 series. TSO. –/58 2T. 28.1 t.
3733xx3 series. TSO. –/58 1T. 29.7 t.
3733xx5 series. TSO. –/58 1T. 29.2 t.
3733xx6 series. RB. 31.1 t.
3733xx7 series. TFO. 39/– 1T. 29.6 t.
3733xx9 series. TBFO. 18/– 1TD. 39.4 t.

3301	**EU**	EU		NP		3308	**EU**	EU		NP
3302	**EU**	EU		NP		3309	**EU**	EU		NP
3303	**EU**	EU		NP		3310	**EU**	EU		NP
3304	**EU**	EU		NP		3311	**EU**	EU		NP
3305	**EU**	EU		NP		3312	**EU**	EU		NP
3306	**EU**	EU		NP		3313	**EU**	EU	*EU*	NP
3307	**EU**	EU		NP		3314	**EU**	EU	*EU*	NP

Spare DM:

3999	**EU**	EU	*EU*	NP

Other names: 3313 and 3314   ENTENTE CORDIALE

4.4. SERVICE/INTERNAL USE EMUS

SERVICE UNIT

Very few EMUs are still in what can be classed as "Service Stock" although are few can be considererd to be Internal Users.

Class 423 "Vep" Service Unit

The following unit is used by South West Trains for staff training.

| 3417 | **B** | SW | BM | 76262 | 62236 | 70797 | 76263 | Gordon Pettitt |

EMUS IN INTERNAL USE

Class 423 "Vep" Service Units

The following units are used by Bombardier Transportation as tractor units at Chart Leacon. They have been fitted with special couplers for moving intermediate EMU vehicles.

| 3905 | **CX** | BT | AF | 76398 | 62266 | 70904 | 76397 |
| 3918 | **CX** | BT | AF | 76528 | 62321 | 70950 | 76527 |

Class 930 (converted from Class 405)

The following unit is in use by Maintrain at Derby as a Staff Coach (975600) and as a Training Room (975601).

| 930 010 | **RK** | MA | DY | 975600 | (10988) | 975601 | (10843) |

4.5. EMUS AWAITING DISPOSAL

The list below comprises vehicles awaiting disposal which are stored on the Network Rail network.

IMPORTANT NOTE: EMUs still intact but already at scrapyards, unless specifically there for storage purposes, are not included in this list.

25 kV AC 50 Hz OVERHEAD UNITS:

Non-standard livery: 960 101 and 960 102 – Light blue & white.

310 046	**N**	H	SN	76130	62071	70731	76180
310 047	**N**	H	SN	76131	62072	70732	76181
310 049	**N**	H	KT	76133	62074	70734	76183
310 050	**N**	H	SN	76134	62075	70735	76184
310 051	**N**	H	SN	76135	62076	70736	76185
310 058	**N**	H	SN	76142	62083	70743	76192

310 059	**N**	H	SN	76143	62084	70744	76205
310 060	**N**	H	SN	76144	62085	70745	76194
310 064	**N**	H	SN	76148	62089		76198
310 067	**N**	H	SN	76151	62092	70752	76201
310 069	**N**	H	SN	76153	62094	70754	76203
310 070	**N**	H	SN	76154	62095	70755	76204
310 101	**RR**	H	SN	76157	62098		76207
310 102	**RR**	H	SN	76139	62080		76189
310 108	**RR**	H	SN	76132	62073		76182
310 110	**RR**	H	SN	76138	62079		76188
310 111	**RR**	H	SN	76147	62088		76197

960 101	**O**	A	SN	977962 (75642)	977963 (61937)	977964 (75981)	
960 102	**O**	A	SN	977965 (75965)	977966 (61928)	977967 (75972)	

Spare cars:

Cl. 310	**RR**	H	SN	62086	62087	76140	76156	76190	76193
	N	H	SN	62077	62091	70751	76145	76200	76206
Cl. 312	**N**	A	SN	71205	78037				

750 V DC THIRD RAIL UNITS:

Non-standard liveries: 930 101 – Used for paint trials.
960 201 – Deep green & black.

1304	**ST**	H	SN	76583	62289	70969	76613
1312	**ST**	H	CT	76562	62278	71928	76572
1881	**ST**	H	SN	76762	62400	71080	76833
1884	**ST**	H	SN	76767	62405	71085	76838
3536	**ST**	H	SN	76384	62207	70897	76383

930 101	**O**	NR	AF	977207 (61658)	977609 (65414)	
930 204	**RK**	SN	SU	977874 (65302)	977875 (65304)	
930 206	**RK**	SN	SU	977924 (65382)	977925 (65379)	
960 201	**O**	X	SN	977977 (76137)	977978 (62090)	
				977979 (62078)	977980 (76187)	

Spare cars:

Non-standard liveries: 70293 – Used for paint trials (61390 is **N**).
76112 – Silver (prototype Class 424 "Networker Classic" conversion).
64709 – Old Merseytravel (yellow & white with grey & black stripes).

Cl. 411	**O**	H	ZI	61390	70293		
Cl. 421	**ST**	H	SN	76765	76775	76836	76846
Cl. 424	**O**	BT	ZD	76112			
Cl. 507	**O**	A	IR	64709			
Cl. 930	**RO**	NR	AF	975598 (10989)		975605 (10940)	

5.1. NON-PASSENGER-CARRYING COACHING STOCK

The notes shown for locomotive-hauled passenger stock generally apply also to non-passenger-carrying coaching stock (often abbreviated to NPCCS).

TOPS TYPE CODES

TOPS type codes for NPCCS are made up as follows:

(1) Two letters denoting the type of the vehicle:

AX	Nightstar generator van
AY	Eurostar barrier vehicle
NA	Propelling control vehicle.
NB	High security brake van (100 m.p.h.).
ND	Gangwayed brake van (90 m.p.h.).
NI	High security brake van (110 m.p.h.).
NJ	General utility van (90 m.p.h.).
NK	High security general utility van (100 m.p.h.).
NN	Courier vehicle.
NO	General utility van (100 m.p.h. e.t.h. wired).
NQ	High security brake van (110 m.p.h.).
NR	BAA container van (100 m.p.h.).
NZ	Driving brake van (also known as driving van trailer).
YR	Ferry van (special Southern Region version of NJ with two pairs of side doors instead of three).

(2) A third letter denoting the brake type:

A	Air braked
V	Vacuum braked
X	Dual braked

OPERATING CODES

The normal operating codes are given in parentheses after the TOPS type codes. These are as follows:

BG	Gangwayed brake van.
BV	Barrier vehicle.
DLV	Driving brake van (also known as driving van trailer – DVT).
GUV	General utility van.
PCV	Propelling control van.

AK51 (RK)   KITCHEN CAR

Mark 1. Converted 1989/2006 from RBR. Buffet and seating area replaced with additional kitchen and food preparation area. Fluorescent lighting. Commonwealth bogies. ETH 2X.

Lot No. 30628 Pressed Steel 1960–61. 39 t.

Note: Kitchen cars have traditionally been numbered in the NPCCS series, but have passenger coach diagram numbers!

Non-standard livery: 80042 Nanking blue.

80041	(1690)	x	**M**	E	*E*	OM
80042	(1646)		**0**	FM	*VI*	EM

NNX   COURIER VEHICLE

Mark 1. Converted 1986–7 from BSKs. One compartment and toilet retained for courier use. One set of roller shutter doors inserted on each side. ETH 2.

80204/17/23. Lot No. 30699 Wolverton 1962. Commonwealth bogies. 37 t.
80220. Lot No. 30573 Gloucester 1960. B4 bogies. 33 t.

Note: 80223 has been converted to a bar car with the former stowage area becoming an open saloon with a bar.

80204	(35297)	**M**	WC	*LS*	CS
80217	(35299)	**M**	WC	*LS*	CS
80220	(35276)	**M**	NE	*LS*	NY
80223	(35331)	**G**	MH	*MH*	RL

ND (BG)   GANGWAYED BRAKE VAN (90 m.p.h.)

Mark 1. Short frames (57'). Load 10t. All vehicles were built with BR Mark 1 bogies. ETH 1. Vehicles numbered 81xxx had 3000 added to the original numbers to avoid confusion with Class 81 locomotives. The full lot number list is listed here for reference purposes with renumbered vehicles. No unmodified vehicles remain in service.

80621. Lot No. 30046 York 1954. 31.5 t.
80826. Lot No. 30144 Cravens 1955. 31.5 t.
80858–80959. Lot No. 30162 Pressed Steel 1956–57. 32 t.
80980–81001. Lot No. 30173 York 1956. 31.5 t.
81025–81026. Lot No. 30224 Cravens 1956. 31.5 t.
81083–81154. Lot No. 30228 Metro-Cammell 1957–58. 31.5 t.
81205–81265. Lot No. 30163 Pressed Steel 1957. 31.5 t.
81266–81289. Lot No. 30323 Pressed Steel 1957. 32 t.
81325–81497. Lot No. 30400 Pressed Steel 1957–58. 32 t.
81501–81550. Lot No. 30484 Pressed Steel 1958. 32 t.

Non-standard livery: 81025 British racing green with gold lining.

The following vehicle is an ND rebogied with Commonwealth bogies and adapted for use as exhibition van 1998 at Lancastrian Carriage & Wagon Co. Ltd. 33 t.

81025	(81025, 84025)	**0**	RA	*RA*	CP	VALIANT

NZ (DLV)   DRIVING BRAKE VAN (110 m.p.h.)

Mark 3B. Air conditioned. T4 bogies. dg. ETH 5X.

Lot No. 31042 Derby 1988. 45.18 t.

Non-standard livery: 82146 EWS silver.

82101	**V**	P		WB		82128	**V**	P	*E*	OM
82102	**1**	P	*1*	NC		82129	**V**	P		LM
82103	**1**	P	*1*	NC		82130	**V**	P		LM
82104	**V**	P		NC		82131	**V**	P	*1*	NC
82105	**1**	P	*1*	NC		82132	**1**	P	*1*	NC
82106	**V**	P		ZB		82133	**1**	P	*1*	NC
82107	**1**	P	*1*	NC		82134	**V**	P		OY
82108	**V**	P		LM		82135	**V**	P		LM
82109	**V**	P		ZB		82136	**1**	P	*1*	NC
82110	**V**	P		LM		82137	**V**	P		LM
82111	**V**	P		LM		82138	**V**	P		LM
82112	**1**	P	*1*	NC		82139	**1**	P	*1*	NC
82113	**V**	P		LM		82140	**V**	P		LM
82114	**1**	P	*1*	NC		82141	**V**	P		LM
82115	**V**	P		LM		82142	**V**	P		LM
82116	**V**	P		LM		82143	**1**	P	*1*	NC
82117	**V**	P		LM		82144	**V**	P		LM
82118	**1**	P	*1*	NC		82145	**V**	P	*E*	OM
82120	**V**	P		LM		82146	**0**	E	*E*	TO
82121	**1**	P	*1*	NC		82147	**V**	P		LM
82122	**V**	P		LM		82148	**V**	P		LM
82123	**V**	P		LM		82149	**V**	P		LM
82124	**V**	P		LM		82150	**V**	P		LM
82125	**V**	P		LM		82151	**V**	P	*E*	OM
82126	**V**	P		WB		82152	**1**	P	*1*	NC
82127	**1**	P	*1*	NC						

Names:

82101	101 Squadron
82126	Wembley Traincare Centre

NZ (DLV)   DRIVING BRAKE VAN (140 m.p.h.)

Mark 4. Air conditioned. Swiss-built (SIG) bogies. dg. ETH 6X.

Fitted with transceiver "domes" for wi-fi.

Lot No. 31043 Metro-Cammell 1988. 45.18 t.

82200	**GN**	H	*GN*	BN		82202	**GN**	H	*GN*	BN
82201	**GN**	H	*GN*	BN		82203	**GN**	H	*GN*	BN

82204	**GN**	H	*GN*	BN		82218	**GN**	H	*GN*	BN
82205	**GN**	H	*GN*	BN		82219	**GN**	H	*GN*	BN
82206	**GN**	H	*GN*	BN		82220	**GN**	H	*GN*	BN
82207	**GN**	H	*GN*	BN		82222	**GN**	H	*GN*	BN
82208	**GN**	H	*GN*	BN		82223	**GN**	H	*GN*	BN
82209	**GN**	H	*GN*	BN		82224	**GN**	H	*GN*	BN
82210	**GN**	H	*GN*	BN		82225	**GN**	H	*GN*	BN
82211	**GN**	H	*GN*	BN		82226	**GN**	H	*GN*	BN
82212	**GN**	H	*GN*	BN		82227	**GN**	H	*GN*	BN
82213	**GN**	H	*GN*	BN		82228	**GN**	H	*GN*	BN
82214	**GN**	H	*GN*	BN		82229	**GN**	H	*GN*	BN
82215	**GN**	H	*GN*	BN		82230	**GN**	H	*GN*	BN
82216	**GN**	H	*GN*	BN		82231	**GN**	H	*GN*	BN
82217	**GN**	H	*GN*	BN						

Names:

82217	OFF TO THE RACES
82219	Duke of Edinburgh

NJ (GUV)   GENERAL UTILITY VAN

Mark 1. Short frames. Load 14 t. Screw couplings. These vehicles had 7000 added to the original numbers to avoid confusion with Class 86 locomotives. The full lot number list is listed here for reference purposes with renumbered vehicles. No unmodified vehicles remain in service. All vehicles were built with BR Mark 2 bogies. ETH 0 or 0X*.

86084–86499. Lot No. 30417 Pressed Steel 1958–59. 30 t.
86508. Lot No. 30343 York 1957. 30 t.
86529–86624. Lot No. 30403 York/Glasgow 1958–60. 30 t.
86656–86820. Lot No. 30565 Pressed Steel 1959. 30 t.
86849–86956. Lot No. 30616 Pressed Steel 1959–60. 30 t.

NKA   HIGH SECURITY GENERAL UTILITY VAN

Mark 1. These vehicles are GUVs further modified with new floors, three roller shutter doors per side and the end doors removed. For lot Nos. see original number series. Commonwealth bogies. Add 2 t to weight. ETH0X.

94101	(86142, 95101)	**RX**	E		GL
94103	(86956, 95103)	**RX**	E		SD
94104	(86942, 95104)	**RX**	E		OM
94106	(86353, 95106)	**RX**	E		ML
94111	(86578, 95111)	**RX**	E	*E*	ML
94113	(86235, 95113)	**RX**	E		OM
94116	(86426, 95116)	**RX**	E		TY
94118	(86675, 95118)	**RX**	E		EN
94132	(86607, 95132)	**RX**	E		ML
94133	(86604, 95133)	**RX**	E		ML
94137	(86610, 95137)	**RX**	E	*E*	ML
94147	(86091, 95147)	**RX**	E		ML
94150	(86560, 95150)	**RX**	E	*E*	ML

94153	(86798, 95153)	**RX**	E		WE
94155	(86820, 95155)	**RX**	E		ML
94160	(86581, 95160)	**RX**	E		ML
94164	(86104, 95164)	**RX**	E		ML
94166	(86112, 95166)	**RX**	E		ML
94168	(86914, 95168)	**RX**	E	*E*	ML
94170	(86395, 95170)	**RX**	E		ML
94172	(86429, 95172)	**RX**	E		ML
94176	(86210, 95176)	**RX**	E	*E*	ML
94177	(86411, 95177)	**RX**	E		SM
94180	(86362, 95141)	**RX**	E		ML
94190	(86624, 95350)	**RX**	E		BK
94191	(86596, 95351)	**RX**	E	*E*	ML
94192	(86727, 95352)	**RX**	E	*E*	ML
94195	(86375, 95355)	**RX**	E		ML
94196	(86478, 95356)	**RX**	E		ML
94197	(86508, 95357)	**RX**	E	*E*	ML
94198	(86195, 95358)	**RX**	E		ML
94199	(86854, 95359)	**RX**	E	*E*	ML
94203	(86345, 95363)	**RX**	E		ML
94204	(86715, 95364)	**RX**	E		ER
94207	(86529, 95367)	**RX**	E		OM
94208	(86656, 95368)	**RX**	E		SM
94209	(86390, 95369)	**RX**	E		SD
94213	(86258, 95373)	**RX**	E	*E*	ML
94214	(86367, 95374)	**RX**	E	*E*	ML
94217	(86131, 93131)	**RX**	E		ML
94221	(86905, 93905)	**RX**	E		ML
94222	(86474, 93474)	**RX**	E		ML
94224	(86273, 93273)	**RX**	E		CD
94225	(86849, 93849)	**RX**	E		ML
94227	(86585, 93585)	**RX**	E		TE
94229	(86720, 93720)	**RX**	E		ML

NAA   PROPELLING CONTROL VEHICLE

Mark 1. Class 307 driving trailers converted for use in propelling mail trains out of termini. Fitted with roller shutter doors. Equipment fitted for communication between cab of PCV and locomotive. B5 bogies. ETH 2X.

Lot No. 30206 Eastleigh 1954–56. Converted at Hunslet-Barclay, Kilmarnock 1994–96.

94302	(75124)	**RX**	E	TY		94311	(75105)	**RX**	E	WE
94303	(75131)	**RX**	E	TY		94312	(75126)	**RX**	E	MG
94304	(75107)	**RX**	E	ML		94313	(75129)	**RX**	E	WE
94305	(75104)	**RX**	E	EN		94314	(75106)	**RX**	E	MG
94306	(75112)	**RX**	E	TY		94316	(75108)	**RX**	E	SM
94307	(75127)	**RX**	E	SD		94317	(75117)	**RX**	E	OM
94308	(75125)	**RX**	E	ML		94318	(75115)	**RX**	E	SD
94309	(75130)	**RX**	E	EN		94319	(75128)	**RX**	E	EN
94310	(75119)	**RX**	E	WE		94320	(75120)	**RX**	E	Norwich

94321	(75122)	**RX** E	EN	94335	(75032)	**RX** E	TY
94322	(75111)	**RX** E	ML	94336	(75031)	**RX** E	TY
94323	(75110)	**RX** E	ML	94337	(75029)	**RX** E	WE
94324	(75103)	**RX** E	MG	94338	(75008)	**RX** E	WE
94325	(75113)	**RX** E	EN	94340	(75012)	**RX** E	CD
94326	(75123)	**RX** E	TY	94341	(75007)	**RX** E	EN
94327	(75116)	**RX** E	EN	94342	(75005)	**RX** E	EN
94331	(75022)	**RX** E	SD	94343	(75027)	**RX** E	ML
94332	(75011)	**RX** E	TY	94344	(75014)	**RX** E	SM
94333	(75016)	**RX** E	TY	94345	(75004)	**RX** E	EN
94334	(75017)	**RX** E	CD				

NBA HIGH SECURITY BRAKE VAN (100 m.p.h.)

Mark 1. These vehicles are NEs further modified with sealed gangways, new
floors, built-in tail lights and roller shutter doors. For lot Nos. see original number
series. B4 bogies. 31.4 t. ETH 1X.

94400	(81224, 92954)	**RX**	E		SD
94401	(81277, 92224)	**RX**	E	*E*	ML
94405	(80890, 92233)	**RX**	E		EN
94406	(81226, 92956)	**RX**	E	*E*	ML
94408	(81264, 92981)	**RX**	E		TY
94410	(81205, 92941)	**RX**	E		WE
94411	(81378, 92997)	**RX**	E		SD
94412	(81210, 92945)	**RX**	E	*E*	ML
94413	(80909, 92236)	**RX**	E		ML
94414	(81377, 92996)	**RX**	E		EN
94416	(80929, 92746)	**RX**	E		TY
94418	(81248, 92244)	**RX**	E		EN
94420	(81325, 92263)	**RX**	E		ML
94422	(81516, 92651)	**RX**	E		OM
94423	(80923, 92914)	**RX**	E		ML
94424	(81400, 92103)	**RX**	E		ML
94427	(80894, 92754)	**RX**	E		WE
94428	(81550, 92166)	**RX**	E	*E*	ML
94429	(80870, 92232)	**RX**	E		TE
94431	(81401, 92604)	**RX**	E		ML
94432	(81383, 92999)	**RX**	E		TY
94433	(81495, 92643)	**RX**	E		AC
94434	(81268, 92584)	**RX**	E		TY
94435	(81485, 92134)	**RX**	E		OM
94436	(81237, 92565)	**RX**	E		EN
94437	(81403, 92208)	**RX**	E		EN
94438	(81425, 92251)	**RX**	E		TO
94439	(81480, 92130)	**RX**	E		ER
94440	(81497, 92645)	**RX**	E		TY
94443	(81473, 92127)	**RX**	E		ML
94444	(81484, 92133)	**RX**	E		ML
94445	(81444, 92615)	**RX**	E		WE
94451	(80955, 92257)	**RX**	E		WE

94458	(81255, 92974)		**RX**	E		SD
94462	(81289, 92270)		**RX**	E		CD
94463	(81375, 92995)		**RX**	E		TY
94467	(81245, 92969)		**RX**	E		EN
94470	(81442, 92113)		**RX**	E		OM
94474	(81452, 92618)		**RX**	E		ML
94476	(81209, 92944)		**RX**	E		CD
94479	(81482, 92132)		**RX**	E		OM
94480	(81411, 92608)		**RX**	E		ML
94481	(81493, 92641)		**RX**	E		SD
94482	(81491, 92639)		**RX**	E		ML
94484	(81426, 92110)		**RX**	E		EN
94488	(81405, 92105)		**RX**	E		CD
94490	(81409, 92606)		**RX**	E		ML
94492	(80888, 92721)		**RX**	E		WE
94494	(81451, 92617)		**RX**	E		EN
94495	(80871, 92755)		**RX**	E		ML
94496	(81514, 92650)		**RX**	E		EN
94497	(80877, 92717)		**RX**	E		ML
94498	(81225, 92555)		**RX**	E	*E*	ML
94499	(81258, 92577)		**RX**	E		CD

NBA/NIA/NQA
HIGH SECURITY BRAKE VAN (100/110 m.p.h.)

Mark 1. These vehicles are NEs further modified with sealed gangways, new floors, built-in tail lights and roller shutter doors. For lot Nos. see original number series. B4 bogies. 31.4 t. ETH 1X.

These vehicles are identical to the 94400–94499 series. Certain vehicles were given a special maintenance regime whereby tyres were reprofiled more frequently than normal and were then allowed to run at 110 m.p.h. Vehicles from the 94400 series upgraded to 110 m.p.h. were renumbered in this series. Vehicles are NBA (100 m.p.h.) unless marked NIA or NQA (100 m.p.h., previously 110 m.p.h.). NQA are vehicles which were modified for haulage by Class 90/2 locos, which were fitted with composition brake blocks.

94501	(80891, 92725)		**RX**	E		OM
94502	(80924, 92720)	NQA	**RX**	E		ML
94504	(80935, 92748)	NQA	**RX**	E		ML
94512	(81265, 92582)		**RX**	E		TY
94514	(81459, 92122)	NIA	**RX**	E	*E*	ML
94515	(80916, 92513)	NQA	**RX**	E		ML
94517	(81489, 92243)	NIA	**RX**	E		CD
94518	(81346, 92258)		**RX**	E	*E*	ML
94519	(80930, 92916)	NQA	**RX**	E	*E*	ML
94520	(80940, 92917)	NQA	**RX**	E		TY
94521	(80900, 92510)	NIA	**RX**	E		CD
94522	(80880, 92907)	NIA	**RX**	E		ML
94523	(81509, 92649)	NIA	**RX**	E		EN
94525	(80902, 92229)	NIA	**RX**	E		ML

94526	(80941, 92518)	NIA	**RX**	E		TY
94527	(80921, 92728)	NQA	**RX**	E		TY
94528	(81404, 92267)		**RX**	E		ML
94529	(80959, 92252)	NQA	**RX**	E		CD
94530	(81511, 94409)	NIA	**RX**	E	*E*	ML
94531	(80879, 94456)	NQA	**RX**	E		TY
94532	(81423, 94489)	NQA	**RX**	E		OM
94534	(80908, 94430)	NIA	**RX**	E	*E*	ML
94535	(80858, 94419)	NIA	**RX**	E		EN
94536	(80936, 94491)	NIA	**RX**	E		ML
94537	(81230, 94421)	NIA	**RX**	E		MG
94538	(81283, 94426)	NQA	**RX**	E		ML

NBA HIGH SECURITY BRAKE VAN (100 m.p.h.)

Mark 1. Details as for 94400–99 but fitted with Commonwealth bogies. 34.4 t. ETH 1X.

94539	(81501, 92302)	**RX**	E		ML
94540	(81431, 92860)	**RX**	E		TJ
94541	(80980, 92316)	**RX**	E	*E*	ML
94542	(80995, 92330)	**RX**	E		TY
94543	(81026, 92389)	**RX**	E	*E*	ML
94544	(81083, 92345)	**RX**	E		ML
94545	(81001, 92329)	**RX**	E		TE
94546	(81339, 92804)	**RX**	E		TY
94547	(80861, 92392)	**RX**	E		ML
94548	(81154, 92344)	**RX**	E		TY

NRA   BAA CONTAINER VAN (100 m.p.h.)

Mark 1. Modified for carriage of British Airports Authority containers with roller shutter doors and roller floors and gangways removed. Now used for general parcels traffic. For lot Nos. see original number series. Commonwealth bogies. Add 2 t to weight. ETH3.

95400	(80621, 95203)	**E**	E	ML
95410	(80826, 95213)	**E**	E	ML

NOA   HIGH SECURITY GENERAL UTILITY VAN

Mark 1. These vehicles are GUVs further modified with new floors, two roller shutter doors per side, middle doors sealed and end doors removed. For lot Nos. see original number series. Commonwealth bogies. Add 2 t to weight. ETH 0X.

95727	(86323, 95127)	**R**	E	WE
95734	(86462, 95134)	**R**	E	EN
95743	(86485, 95143)	**R**	E	EN

95754	(86897, 95154)	**R**	E		TY
95758	(86499, 95158)	**R**	E		ML
95759	(86084, 95159)	**R**	E		EN
95761	(86205, 95161)	**R**	E		WE
95763	(86407, 95163)	**R**	E	*E*	ML

AX5G   NIGHTSTAR GENERATOR VAN

Mark 3A. Generator vans converted from sleeping cars for use on "Nightstar" services. Designed to operate between two Class 37/6 locomotives. Gangways removed. Two Cummins diesel generator groups providing a 1500 V train supply. Hydraulic parking brake. 61-way ENS interface jumpers. BT10 bogies.

Lot No. 30960 Derby 1981–83. 46.01 t.

96371	(10545, 6371)	**EP**	EU		NP
96372	(10564, 6372)	**EP**	EU		NP
96373	(10568, 6373)	**EP**	EU		NP
96374	(10585, 6374)	**EP**	EU		NP
96375	(10587, 6375)	**EP**	EU		NP

AY5 (BV)   EUROSTAR BARRIER VEHICLE

Mark 1. Converted from GUVs. Bodies removed. B4 bogies.

96380–96382. Lot No. 30417 Pressed Steel 1958–59. 40 t.
96383. Lot No. 30565 Pressed Steel 1959. 40 t.
96384. Lot No. 30616 Pressed Steel 1959–60. 40 t.

96380	(86386, 6380)	**B**	EU	*EU*	NP
96381	(86187, 6381)	**B**	EU	*EU*	NP
96382	(86295, 6382)	**B**	EU	*EU*	NP
96383	(86664, 6383)	**B**	EU	*EU*	NP
96384	(86955, 6384)	**B**	EU	*EU*	NP

YR   FERRY VAN

This vehicle was built to a wagon lot although the design closely resembles that of NJ except it only has two sets of doors per side. Short Frames (57'). Load 14 t. Commonwealth bogies.

Built Eastleigh 1958. Wagon Lot. No. 2849. 30 t.

Non-standard livery: Pullman Car umber with gold lining and lettering.

889202	**0**	VS		SL

Name: 889202 is branded "BAGGAGE CAR No.8".

5.2. NPCCS AWAITING DISPOSAL

68504	BH	80428	EN	93180	Derby South Dock Siding
68505	BH	80429	WE	93723	BY
80211	DY	80432	TO	93930	CD
80320	EN	80433	EN	94450	WE
80323	EN	80434	TO	95228	NC
80331	EN	80435	EN	95300	ML
80337	EN	80437	EN	95301	ML
80339	EN	80438	WE	96100	TM
80344	EN	80456	EN	96101	SN
80345	EN	80458	EN	96110	CS
80349	EN	84364	DW	96132	CS
80350	EN	84519	CD	96135	CS
80356	EN	92100	CP	96164	CS
80358	EN	92111	CP	96165	CS
80360	EN	92114	DY	96170	CS
80361	EN	92146	ZA	96175	CS
80365	EN	92159	KT	96177	CS
80367	EN	92174	SN	96178	CS
80373	EN	92175	CD	96181	KT
80375	EN	92193	Preston CS	96182	CS
80377	EN	92194	SN	96191	CS
80378	EN	92198	ZB	96192	CS
80380	EN	92303	OM	96210	CS
80382	WE	92314	CD	96218	CS
80385	EN	92350	OM	96452	BR
80394	EN	92384	OM	96453	BR
80395	EN	92400	CD	96602	LM
80401	TO	92530	OM	96603	LM
80402	EN	92908	CS	96604	LM
80403	CS	92929	CP	96605	LM
80404	CS	92931	SN	96606	LM
80414	EN	92935	SN	96607	LM
80417	EN	92936	CD	96608	LM
80423	EN	92938	SN	96609	LM
80426	EN	92939	ZA	99646	SL
80427	EN				

6. SERVICE STOCK

Most vehicles in this section are numbered in the former BR departmental number series. They are used for internal purposes within the railway industry, i.e. they do not generate revenue from outside the industry.

EMU TRANSLATOR VEHICLES

These vehicles are used to move EMU vehicles around the National Rail system in the same way as other vehicles included in this book. Similar vehicles numbered in the BR capital stock series are included elsewhere in this book. Converted from Mark 1 TSO, RSOs, RUOs, BSKs and GUVs (NP/NL).

975864. Lot No. 30054 Eastleigh 1951–54. Commonwealth bogies.
975867. Lot No. 30014 York 1950–51. Commonwealth bogies.
975875. Lot No. 30143 Charles Roberts 1954–55. Commonwealth bogies.
975974–975978. Lot No. 30647 Wolverton 1959–61. Commonwealth bogies.
977087. Lot No. 30229 Metro–Cammell 1955–57. Commonwealth bogies.
977942/948. Lot No. 30417 Pressed Steel 1958–59. B5 bogies.
977943/949. Lot No. 30565 Pressed Steel 1959. B5 bogies.

Non-standard livery: 975974 and 975978 Plain grey.

975864	(3849)	**HB** H	*FL*	ZJ
975867	(1006)	**HB** H	*FL*	ZJ
975875	(34643)	**HB** H	*FL*	ZJ
975974	(1030)	**0** A	*ME*	BD
975976	(1033)	**N** A		KT
975977	(1023)	**N** A		KT
975978	(1025)	**0** A	*ME*	BD
977087	(34971)	**HB** H	*FL*	ZJ
977942	(86467, 80251)	**E** E	*E*	TO
977943	(86718, 80252)	**E** E	*E*	TO
977948	(86733, 94028)	**E** E	*E*	TO
977949	(86377, 94025)	**E** E	*E*	TO

LABORATORY, TESTING & INSPECTION COACHES

These coaches are used for research, development, testing and inspection on the National Rail system. Many are fitted with sophisticated technical equipment.

Generator Vans. Mark 1. Converted from BR Mark 1 BGs. B5 bogies.

6260. Lot No. 30400 Pressed Steel 1957–58.
6261. Lot No. 30323 Pressed Steel 1957.
6262. Lot No. 30228 Metro-Cammell 1957–58.
6263. Lot No. 30163 Pressed Steel 1957.
6264. Lot No. 30173 York 1956.

6260	(81450, 92116)	**NR**	NR		LU
6261	(81284, 92988)	**NR**	NR		OM
6262	(81064, 92928)	**Y**	NR		LU
6263	(81231, 92961)	**Y**	NR	*SO*	ZA
6264	(80971, 92923)	**Y**	NR	*SO*	ZA

Ultrasonic Test Coach. Converted from Class 432 EMU MSO. Lot No. 30862 York 1974. SR Mk. 6 bogies.

62482		**RK**	NR	*SO*	ZA

Ultrasonic Test Coach. Converted from BR Mark 2E FO then converted to exhibition van. Lot No. 30843 Derby 1972–73. B4 bogies.

99666	(3250)	**RK**	NR	*SO*	ZA

Network Rail Inspection Saloon. Converted from Class 202 DEMU TRB at Stewarts Lane for use as a BR Southern Region General Manager's Saloon. Overhauled by FM Rail in 2004/05 for use as a Network Rail New Trains Project Saloon. Can be used in push-pull mode with suitably equipped locomotives such as a Class 33/1. Eastleigh 1958. SR Mk. 4 bogies.

975025	(60755)	**G**	NR	*SO*	ZA	CAROLINE

Structure Gauging Driving Trailer Coach. Converted from BR Mark 1 BSK. Lot No. 30699 Wolverton 1961–63. B4 bogies.

975081	(35313)	**Y**	NR	*SO*	ZA

Overhead Line Equipment Test Coach ("MENTOR"). Can either be locomotive-hauled or included between DMU vehicles 977391/2. Converted from BR Mark 1 BSK Lot No. 30142 Gloucester 1954–5. Fitted with pantograph. B4 bogies.

975091	(34615)	**Y**	NR	*SO*	ZA

Structure Gauging Train Dormitory and Generator Coach. Converted from BR Mark 1 BCK Lot No. 30732 Derby 1962–4. B4 bogies.

975280	(21263)	**Y**	NR	*SO*	ZA

Test Coach. Converted from BR Mark 2 FK Lot No. 30734 Derby 1962–64. B4 bogies.

975290	(13396)	**SO**	SO	*SO*	ZA

Test Coach. Converted from BR Mark 1 BSK Lot No. 30699 Wolverton 1961–63. Commonwealth bogies.

| 975397 | (35386) | **SO** | SO | *SO* | ZA |

Test Coach. Converted from BR Mark 1 BSK Lot No. 30223 Charles Roberts 1955–56. BT5 bogies.

| 975422 | (34875) | **SO** | SO | *SO* | ZA |

New Measurement Train Conference Coach. Converted from prototype HST TF Lot No. 30848 Derby 1972. BT10 bogies.

| 975814 | (11000,41000) | **Y** | NR | *SO* | EC |

New Measurement Train Lecture Coach. Converted from prototype HST TRUB Lot No. 30849 Derby 1972–3. BT10 bogies.

| 975984 | (10000, 40000) | **Y** | NR | *SO* | EC |

Track Recording Train Dormitory Coach. Converted from BR Mark 2 BSO. Lot No 30757 Derby 1965–66. B4 bogies.

| 977337 | (9395) | **Y** | NR | *SO* | ZA |

Test Train Brake & Stores Coach. Converted from Mark 2 BSO. Lot No. 30757 Derby 1965–66. B4 bogies.

| 977338 | (9387) | **SO** | SO | *SO* | ZA |

Radio Equipment Survey Coaches. Converted from BR Mark 2E TSO. Lot No. 30844 Derby 1972–73. B4 bogies.

| 977868 | (5846) | **Y** | NR | *SO* | ZA |
| 977869 | (5858) | **Y** | NR | *SO* | ZA |

Ultrasonic Test Train Staff Coach. Converted from Royal Household couchette Lot No. 30889, which in turn had been converted from BR Mark 2B BFK Lot No. 30790 Derby 1969. B5 bogies.

| 977969 | (14112, 2906) | **Y** | NR | *SO* | ZA |

Laboratory Coach. Converted from BR Mark 2E TSO. Lot No. 30844 Derby 1972–73. B4 bogies.

| 977974 | (5854) | **Y** | AE | *SO* | ZA |

Hot Box Detection Coach. Converted from BR Mark 2F FO converted to Class 488/2 EMU TFOH. Lot No. 30859 Derby 1973–74. B4 bogies.

| 977983 | (3407, 72503) | **RK** | NR | *SO* | ZA |

New Measurement Train Staff Coach. Converted from HST TRFK. Lot No. 30884 Derby 1976–77. BT10 bogies.

| 977984 | (40501) | **Y** | P | *SO* | EC |

Structure Gauging Train Coach. Converted from BR Mark 2F TSO converted to Class 488/3 EMU TSO. Lot No. 30860 Derby 1973–74. B4 bogies.

| 977985 | (6019, 72715) | **Y** | NR | *SO* | ZA |

Track Recording Train Coach. Converted from BR Mark 2D FO subsequently declassified to SO and then converted to exhibition van. Lot No. 30821 Derby 1971.

977986 (3189, 99664)   **Y**   NR   *SO*   ZA

New Measurement Train Overhead Line Equipment Test Coach. Converted from HST TGS. Lot No. 30949 Derby 1982. Fitted with pantograph. BT10 bogies.

977993 (44053)   **Y**   P   *SO*   EC

New Measurement Train Track Recording Coach. Converted from HST TGS. Lot No. 30949 Derby 1982. BT10 bogies.

977994 (44087)   **Y**   P   *SO*   EC

New Measurement Train Coach. Converted from HST TRFM. Lot No. 30921 Derby 1978–79. BT10 bogies. Fitted with generator.

977995 (40719, 40619)   **Y**   P   *SO*   EC

New Measurement Train Coach. Undergoing conversion at Brush, Loughborough from HST TGS for Network Rail. Lot No. 30949 Derby 1982. BT10 bogies.

977996 (44062)   **Y**   P   LB

Inspection Coach. Converted from BR Inspection Saloon. BR Wagon Lot No. 3095. Swindon 1957. B4 bogies.

999506 AMANDA   **M**   NR   *SO*   ZA

Track Recording Coach. Converted from BR Inspection Saloon. BR Wagon Lot No. 3379. Swindon 1960. B4 bogies.

999508   **SO**   SO   *SO*   ZA

Track Recording Coach. Purpose built Mark 2. B4 bogies.

999550   **Y**   NR   *SO*   ZA

Ultrasonic Test Coach. Converted from a Class 421 EMU MBSO. Lot No. 30816. York 1970. ? bogies.

999606 (62356)   **Y**   NR   *SO*   ZA

TEST TRAIN BRAKE FORCE RUNNER SETS

Converted from Class 488/3 ex-Gatwick Express locomotive hauled stock
(formerly Mark 2 coaches). These sets of vehicles are included in test trains to
provide brake force and are not used for any other purposes.

72612–72616/72630/72631/72639. Lot No. 30860 Derby 1973–74. 33.5 t.
72708. Lot No. 30860 Derby 1973–74. 33.5 t.

910 001	**RK**	NR	*SO*	ZA	72616 (6007)	72708 (6095)	72639 (6070)
910 002	**RK**	NR	*SO*	ZA	72612 (6156)		72613 (6126)
-	**Y**	NR	*SO*	ZA	72630 (6094)		72631 (6096)

BREAKDOWN TRAIN COACHES

These coaches are formed in trains used for the recovery of derailed railway
vehicles and were converted from BR Mark 1 BCK, BG, BSK and SK. The current
use of each vehicle is given. 975611–613 were previously converted to trailer
luggage vans in 1968. BR Mark 1 bogies.

975080. Lot No. 30155 Wolverton 1955–56.
975087. Lot No. 30032 Wolverton 1951–52.
975463/573. Lot No. 30156 Wolverton 1954–55.
975465/477/494. Lot No. 30233 GRCW 1955–57.
975471. Lot No. 30095 Wolverton 1953–55.
975481/482/574. Lot No. 30141 GRCW 1954–55.
975498. Lot No. 30074 Wolverton 1953–54.
975611–613. Lot No. 30162 Pressed Steel 1954–57.
977088/235. Lot No. 30229 Metro-Cammell 1955–57.
977107. Lot No. 30425 Metro-Cammell 1956–58.

r refurbished

975080	(25079)	r	**Y**	NR	*E*	OM	Tool Van
975087	(34289)	r	**NR**	NR	*E*	OM	Generator Van
975463	(34721)	r	**Y**	NR	*E*	TE	Staff Coach
975465	(35109)	r	**Y**	NR	*E*	OM	Staff Coach
975471	(34543)	r	**NR**	NR	*E*	OM	Staff & Tool Coach
975477	(35108)	r	**NR**	NR	*E*	OM	Staff Coach
975481	(34606)	r	**Y**	NR	*E*	OM	Generator Van
975482	(34602)	r	**Y**	NR	*E*	TE	Generator Van
975494	(35082)	r	**Y**	NR	*E*	MG	Generator Van
975498	(34367)	r	**Y**	NR	*E*	TE	Tool Van
975573	(34729)	r	**Y**	NR	*E*	MG	Staff Coach
975574	(34599)	r	**Y**	NR	*E*	OM	Staff Coach
975611	(80915, 68201)	r	**Y**	NR	*E*	OM	Generator Van
975612	(80922, 68203)	r	**Y**	NR	*E*	MG	Tool Van
975613	(80918, 68202)	r	**Y**	NR	*E*	OM	Tool Van
977088	(34990)		**Y**	NR	*E*	CE	Generator Van
977107	(21202)		**Y**	NR	*E*	CE	Staff Coach
977235	(34989, 083172)		**Y**	NR	*E*	CE	Tool Van

INFRASTRUCTURE MAINTENANCE COACHES

Overhead Line Maintenance Coaches

These coaches are formed in a train used for the maintenance, repair and renewal of overhead lines and were converted from BR Mark 1 BSK, CK and SK. The current use of each vehicle is given. All have been refurbished.

Non-standard livery: Light grey with a blue stripe.

975699. Lot No. 30233 GRCW 1955–57. BR Mark 1 bogies.
975700. Lot No. 30025 Wolverton 1950–52. BR Mark 1 bogies.
975714. Lot No. 30374. York 1958. Commonwealth bogies.
975724. Lot No. 30471 Metro-Cammell 1957–59. Commonwealth bogies.
975734. Lot No. 30426 Wolverton 1956–58. BR Mark 1 Bogies.
975744. Lot No. 30350 Wolverton 1956–57.BR Mark 1 bogies.

975699	(35105)	**0**	NR	*CA*	Preston	Pantograph coach
975700	(34138)	**0**	NR	*CA*	Preston	Pantograph coach
975714	(25466)	**0**	NR	*CA*	Preston	Stores van
975724	(16079)	**0**	NR	*CA*	Preston	Stores & generator van
975734	(25695)	**0**	NR	*CA*	Preston	Stores & roof access coach
975744	(25440)	**0**	NR	*CA*	Preston	Staff & office coach

Snowblower Train Coaches

These coaches worked with Snowblower ADB 968501. They were converted from BR Mark 1 BSK. The current use of each vehicle is given. Commonwealth bogies.

975464. Lot No. 30386 Charles Roberts 1956–58.
975486. Lot No. 30025 Wolverton 1950–52.

| 975464 | (35171) | **Y** | NR | ZR | Staff & dormitory coach |
| 975486 | (34100) | **Y** | NR | ZR | Tool van |

Snowblower Train Tool Vans

These vans worked with Snowblower ADB 968500.

200715. Wagon Lot No. 3855 Ashford 1976. 4-wheeled.
787395. Wagon Lot No. 3567 Eastleigh 1966. 4-wheeled.

| 200715 | **Y** | NR | IS |
| 787395 | **Y** | NR | IS |

Spray Coaches

These coaches are used to spray various concoctions onto the rails or trackbed. In addition to spraying equipment they contain storage tanks. They were converted from BR Mark 1 RMB & GUV.

99019. Lot No. 30702 Wolverton 1961–62. Commonwealth bogies.
99025/26. Lot No. 30565 Pressed Steel 1959. B5 bogies.
99027. Lot No. 30417 Pressed Steel 1958–59. B5 bogies.

| 99019 | (1870) | **NR** | NR | ZR |
| 99025 | (86744, 96103) | **RK** | NR | KT |

| 99026 | (86745, 96211) | **RK** | NR | | KT |
| 99027 | (86331, 96214) | **RK** | NR | | KT |

De-Icing Coaches

These coaches are used for removing ice from the conductor rail of DC lines. They were converted from Class 489 DMLVs that had originally been Class 414/3 DMBSOs.

68501/508. Lot No. 30452 Ashford/Eastleigh 1959. Mk 4 bogies.

| 68501 | (61281) | **Y** | NR | *GB* | TN |
| 68508 | (61272) | **Y** | NR | *GB* | TN |

Miscellaneous Infrastructure Coaches

These coaches are used for various infrastructure projects on the National Railway network. They were converted from BR Mark 1 BSK & BG and BR Mark 3 SLEP. The current use of each vehicle is given.

977163/165/166. Lot No. 30721 Wolverton 1961–63. Commonwealth bogies.
977167. Lot No. 30699 Wolverton 1961–63. Commonwealth bogies.
977168. Lot No. 30573 GRCW 1959–60. B4 bogies.
977989. Lot No. 30960 Derby 1981–83. BT 10 bogies.
977990. Lot No. 30228 Metro-Cammell 1957-58. B4 bogies.
977991. Lot No. 30323 Pressed steel 1957. B4 bogies.

Non-standard liveries:

977163 and 977167 White with a blue stripe.
977165, 975166 and 975168 All over white.

977163	(35487)	**O**	BB	*BB*	AP	Staff & generator coach
977165	(35408)	**O**	BB	*BB*	AP	Staff & generator coach
977166	(35419)	**O**	BB	*BB*	AP	Staff & generator coach
977167	(35400)	**O**	BB	*BB*	AP	Staff & generator coach
977168	(35289)	**O**	BB	*BB*	AP	Staff & generator coach
977989	(10536)	**M**	J		Leeman Road EY, York	Staff & Dormitory Coach
977990	(81165, 92937)	**NR**	NR		OM	Tool Van
977991	(81308, 92991)	**NR**	NR		OM	Tool Van

INTERNAL USER VEHICLES

These vehicles are confined to yards and depots or do not normally move at all. Details are given of the internal user number (if allocated), type and former identity, current use and location. Many of those listed no longer see regular use.

024877	BR CCT 94698	Stores van	Wavertree Yard, Edge Hill
024909	BR BSOT 9106	Staff accommodation	Preston Station
025000	BR BSO 9423	Staff accommodation	Preston Station
025026	BR TSO 5259	Staff accommodation	Wavertree Yard, Edge Hill
041379	LMS CCT 35527	Stores van	Leeman Road EY, York
041898	BR BG 84608	Stores van	Leeman Road EY, York
041947	BR GUV 93425	Stores van	IL
041963	LMS milk tank 44047	Storage tank	DR
042154	BR GUV 93975	Stores van	Ipswich Upper Yard
061061	BR CCT 94135	Stores van	Oxford station
061171	BR GUV 93480	Stores van	RG
061223	BR GUV 93714	Stores van	Oxford station
083439	BR CCT 94752	Stores van	WD
083602	BR CCT 94494	Stores van	Three Bridges station
083633	BR GUV 93724	Stores van	BI
083644	BR Ferry Van 889201	Stores van	EH
083664	BR Ferry Van 889203	Stores van	EH
095020	LNER BG 70170	Stores van	Inverness Yard
095030	BR GUV 96140	Stores van	EC
-	BR FO 3186	Instruction Coach	DY
-	BR FO 3381	Instruction Coach	HE
-	BR TSO 5636	Instruction Coach	PM
-	BR BFK 17156	Instruction Coach	DY
-	BR TSOLH 72614	Instruction Coach	DY
-	BR TSOLH 72615	Instruction Coach	DY
-	BR TSOL 72707	Instruction Coach	DY
-	BR BG 92901	Stores van	WB
-	BR NL 94003	Stores van	OO
-	BR NL 94006	Stores van	OO
-	BR NK 84121	Stores van	TO
-	BR GUV 96139	Stores van	MA
-	BR TSO 975403	Cinema Coach	PM

Notes: CCT = Covered Carriage Truck (a 4-wheeled van similar to a GUV).

NL = Newspaper Van (converted from a GUV).

LOCO-HAULED NETWORK RAIL TEST TRAIN FORMATIONS

Correct at the time of going to press. Locos used are generally Network Rail Class 31s or DRS Class 37s.

Train	Formation				
Track Recording Train	6264	977337	999550	977986	
New Measurement Train (HST)	977995	977984	977994	977993	975984
Structure Gauging Train	975280	975081	DC460000*	977985	
Ultrasonic Test Train 3	99666	62482	977969	6263	
Ultrasonic Test Train 4	72630	999606	72631		
Radio Survey Train 1	977868	975091	72639	72708	72616
Radio Survey Train 2	977983	72613	72612	999508	977869

* This vehicle is an optical measurement wagon.

SERVICE STOCK AWAITING DISPOSAL

This list contains the last known locations of service vehicles awaiting disposal. The definition of which vehicles are "awaiting disposal" is somewhat vague, but generally speaking these are vehicles of types not now in normal service or vehicles which have been damaged by fire, vandalism or collision.

70220	Western Trading Estate Siding, North Acton	977077	Ripple Lane Yard
		977085	BH
99014	Horsham Yard	977095	CS
99015	Horsham Yard	977111	Ripple Lane Yard
320645	Leeman Road EY, York	977112	Ripple Lane Yard
975000	ZA	977193	BH
975051	CD	977359	ZN
975379	Leeman Road EY, York	977390	CD
975454	TO	977399	NL
975484	CS	977449	CD
975491	TH	977526	SJ
975497	Sudbrook	977595	CD
975535	Carnforth Bottom End Sidings	977618	BY
975554	DW	977787	TH
975555	DW	977789	LU
975615	SJ	977790	LU
975639	CS	977791	LU
975681	Portobello	977793	LU
975682	Portobello	977794	LU
975685	Portobello	977855	ZA
975686	Portobello	977905	EH
975687	Portobello	977944	TO
975688	Portobello	977945	TO
975721	DW	977946	TO
975991	CD	977947	TO

PLATFORM 5 MAIL ORDER

FREIGHTMASTER
Freightmaster Publishing

Freightmaster is the Great Britain National Railfreight Timetable. It contains full timetable listings for over 70 key locations around the country, including dates of operation, train type and booked motive power for every train. Most locations feature 0700-2300 listings, with full 24 hour timetables for busy locations. Also includes a separate analysis of national freight flows. Well illustrated by a series of detailed maps.160 pages. **£12.95.**

Note: Freightmaster is published 4 times a year in January, April, July and October. Customers ordering this title will be supplied with the latest edition available unless requested otherwise.

LINE BY LINE
Freightmaster Publishing

Line by Line is a series of excellent guidebooks tracing the route of Britain's main line railways. Each page covers a five-mile section of route with gradient profiles, track layout diagrams and a black & white illustration provided for each section. Also includes a general overview of the line, a gallery section of colour photographs, several OS map reproductions and a table of distances in miles & chains. The following volumes are currently available:

Line by Line: The Scottish Highland Lines **£17.95**
Line by Line: The Great Western Main Line **£14.95**
Line by Line: The East Coast Main Line **£14.95**
Line by Line: The Midland Route **£14.95**

Please add postage: 10% UK, 20% Europe, 30% Rest of World.

Telephone, fax or send your order to the Platform 5 Mail Order Department. See page 384 of this book for details.

7. UK LIGHT RAIL & METRO SYSTEMS

From this edition we are pleased to be able to provide full fleet listings of the Light Rail and Metro systems of the UK. Updates to the list will appear in the Light Rail News section of the Platform 5 magazine **Today's Railways UK**. This listing covers passenger carrying vehicles only (not works vehicles).

This listing does not cover the underground systems of London or Glasgow.

7.1. BLACKPOOL & FLEETWOOD TRAMWAY

Until the opening of Manchester Metrolink, the Blackpool Tramway was the only urban/inter-urban tramway system left in Britain. The infrastructure is owned by the local authorities and the tramway is operated by Blackpool Transport Services Ltd., using a mixture of trams dating back to the 1930s, as well as some newer vehicles dating from the 1980s. The line runs for 11½ miles from Fleetwood in the north to Starr Gate in the south. There is an extensive summer service between North Pier and Pleasure Beach.
System: 550 V DC overhead.
Depot & Workshops: Rigby Road, Blackpool.
Standard livery: Cream & green except where stated otherwise.

All cars are single-deck unless stated otherwise. For advertising liveries predominate colours are given.

(S) – Stored out of service. At the end of the 2004 season several trams were stood down (or "mothballed") at Rigby Road depot as surplus to requirements.

OPEN BOAT CARS   A1-1A

Used mainly during the summer months!
Built: 1934 by English Electric. 12 built.
Traction Motors: Two EE327 of 30 kW.
Seats: 56 (* 52).

600	604 *	607 (S) **Yellow & Green**
602 * **Yellow & Black**	605 * **Green & Cream**	

BRUSH RAILCOACHES   A1-1A

Most of the Brush Railcoaches are now mothballed and only four remained in use for the 2006 season.
Built: 1937 by Brush, Loughborough. 20 built.
Traction Motors: Two EE305 of 40 kW.
Seats: 48 (* 46).
Note: 636 has been withdrawn for testing of new traction equipment.
Advertising liveries:

621 – Hot Ice Show, Pleasure Beach (blue)
622 – Pontins (blue & yellow)
623 – Mystique Show, Pleasure Beach (black, pink & white)

626 – Blackpool Zoo & Dinosaur Safari (white, black & green)
627 – Buccaneer Family Bar (black)
630 – Karting 2000 (yellow & purple)
631 – Laughing Donkey Bar, South Pier (blue & white)
632 – Blackpool Sealife Centre (blue)
634 – Cala Gran Holiday Park (blue)
636 – Metro Coastlines – Blackpool Tramway (green & yellow)
637 – Blackpool Zoo (green & white)

621 (S)	**AL**	626 *	**AL**	632 (S)	**AL**
622	**AL**	627 (S)	**AL**	634 (S)	**AL**
623 (S)	**AL**	630	**AL**	636 (S)	**AL**
625 (S)		631	**AL**	637 (S)	**AL**

CENTENARY CLASS   A1-1A

The newest trams in use, these are used all year round.
Built: 1984–1987. Body by East Lancs. Coachbuilders, Blackburn. Driver-only operated.
Traction Motors: Two EE305 of 40 kW.
Seats: 52 (*53).   † Rebuilt from GEC car 651.
Advertising liveries:

641 – Orion Bingo, Cleveleys (blue, yellow & pink)
643 – Grosvenor Casinos (purple)
644 – Farmer Parrs Animal World (yellow)
645 – Palm Beach Hotel (blue)
646 – Paul Gaunt Furniture (cream & blue)
647 – Tiffany's Hotel (pink & white)
648 – Vue Cinema, Cleveleys (blue)

641 *	**AL**	643	**AL**	645	**AL**	647	**AL**
642 *	**Yellow**	644	**AL**	646 *	**AL**	648 †	**AL**

PROGRESS TWIN CARS   A1-1A + 2-2

These cars mainly see use during the "illuminations" season.
Built: Motor cars (671–677) rebuilt 1958–1960 from English Electric Railcoaches by Blackpool Corporation Transport. Driving trailers (681–687) built 1960 by Metro-Cammell.
Traction Motors: Two EE305 of 40 kW.   **Seats:** 53 + 61.
Advertising liveries:

671+681 – Metro Coastlines – Blackpool Tramway (green & yellow)
672+682 – Metro Coastlines – Blackpool Tramway (orange & yellow)
673+683 – Metro Coastlines – Blackpool Tramway (turquoise & yellow)
674+684 – Metro Coastlines – Blackpool Tramway (blue & yellow)
675+685 – Metro Coastlines – Blackpool Tramway (red & yellow)

671+681	**AL**	674+684	**AL**	676+686	(S)
672+682	**AL**	675+685	**AL**	677+687	(S)
673+683	**AL**				

ENGLISH ELECTRIC RAILCOACHES　　　　A1-1A

Built: Rebuilt 1958–1960 from EE Railcoaches. Originally ran with trailers.
Traction Motors: Two EE305 of 40 kW.　　**Seats:** 48.
Advertising liveries:

678 – Radiowave (black & blue)
680 – Merrie England Bar, North Pier (blue & red)

678	**AL**	679	(S)	680	**AL**

"BALLOON" DOUBLE DECKERS　　　　A1-1A

The "Balloon" cars are still the mainstay of the fleet during the summer months and are also used in lesser numbers during the winter.
Built: 1934–1935 by English Electric. 700–712 were originally built with open tops and 706 has now reverted to that condition.
Traction Motors: Two EE305 of 40 kW.　　**Seats:** 94 (*† 92, ‡ 90, ¶ 88).

Notes:

717 is undergoing an overhaul to return it to original condition.
* Rebuilt with a new flat front end design and air-conditioned cabs. Known as "Millennium Class".
o Rebuilt as an open-topped double-decker seating 82. Named "PRINCESS ALICE". Also carries original number 243.
§ Converted to an "ice cream tram" in 1996 with an ice cream sales area in the lower saloon. This has since been removed. Seats 78.

Advertising liveries:

701 – Palm Beach Hotel (gold & purple)
704 – Eclipse at the Globe, Pleasure Beach (black & orange)
707 – Buccaneer Family Bar (black)
709 – Blackpool Sealife Centre (blue)
710 – Metro Coastlines (Blackpool Tramway) (yellow & purple)
711 – Lambrini at Brannigans (gold)
713 – Asda, Fleetwood (green & white)
718 – Vodka Kick (various)
719 – Walls Ice Cream (yellow, blue & red)
720 – Eclipse at the Globe, Pleasure Beach (black)
722 – Transport & General Workers Union (white)
723 – McDonalds (red & orange)
724 – Metro Coastlines (Blackpool Tramway) (red & yellow)
726 – Thwaites Bitter (green & cream)

700		**Green & Cream**	709	*	**AL**	718	*	**AL**
701	‡	**AL**	710		**AL**	719	§	**AL**
702	¶		711	†	**AL**	720		**AL**
703			712			721		**White**
704	(S)	**AL**	713		**AL**	722	‡	**AL**
706	o		715		**White**	723	†	**AL**
707	*	**AL**	716	(S)		724	*	**AL**
708	(S)	‡	717	(S)		726		**AL**

JUBILEE CLASS DOUBLE DECKERS

Built: Rebuilt 1979/1982 from Balloon cars 725 and 714 respectively. Standard bus ends, thyristor control and stairs at each end. 761 has one door per side whereas 762 has two. Suitable for driver-only operation.
Traction Motors: Two EE305 of 40 kW.   **Seats:** 104 (*90).
Advertising liveries:
761 – Isle of Man (purple & cream)
762 – Unison (yellow)

761   **AL** | 762 * **AL**

ILLUMINATED CARS

633	Illuminated Trawler – "Fisherman's Friend"	Built: 1937	Seats: 48
732 (S)	The Rocket	Built: 1961	Seats: 47
733 (S)	Western Train loco & tender	Built: 1962	Seats: 35
734 (S)	Western Train coach	Built: 1962	Seats: 60
735 (S)	The Hovertram	Built: 1963	Seats: 99
736	HMS Blackpool	Built: 1965	Seats: 71

VINTAGE CARS

These trams are used for special services as well as for occasional normal services, particularly during the "illuminations" season.

Notes: 147 is named "MICHAEL AIREY"
304 is on loan from the Lancastrian Transport Trust.

Stockport 5	Open-top double-decker	Built: 1901
Blackpool & Fleetwood 40	Single deck "box car"	Built: 1914
Bolton 66	Bogie double-decker	Built: 1901
Blackpool 147	Standard double-decker	Built: 1924
Blackpool 304	Coronation Class single decker	Built: 1952
Sheffield "Roberts Car" 513	Double-decker	Built: 1950
Blackpool 619	Single deck Replica Vanguard	Built: 1987
Blackpool 660	Coronation Class single decker	Built: 1953

"TRAM POWER" CAR

This rebuilt articulated car is currently at Blackpool for evaluation but is not in regular service. Seats 200.

Tram Power 611	"City Class" articulated tram	Built: 1998

7.2. SHEFFIELD SUPERTRAM

This system opened in 1994 and has three lines radiating from Sheffield City Centre. These run to Halfway in the south east, with a spur from Gleadless Townend to Herdings Park, to Middlewood in the north with a spur from Hillsborough to Malin Bridge and to Meadowhall Interchange in the north east, adjacent to the large shopping complex. The total route mileage is 18 miles. The system is a mixture of on-street and segregated running.

The cars are owned by South Yorkshire Light Rail Ltd., a subsidiary of South Yorkshire PTE. The operating company, South Yorkshire Supertram Ltd. is leased to Stagecoach who operate the system as Stagecoach Supertram.

Because of severe gradients in Sheffield (up to 1 in 10) all axles are powered on the vehicles.

System: 750 DC overhead.
Depot & Workshops: Nunnery.
Standard livery: White with orange, red & blue stripes.
SM – New Sheffield Supertram livery (blue, red and orange, similar to the South West Trains "Desiro" livery, but with yellow doors).

Cars are currently being refurbished at Nunnery depot. These are shown as "r".

Advertising liveries:

106 – Thomsonfly.com (blue).
116 – Meadowhall Shopping Centre (purple).

EIGHT-AXLE ARTICLUATED UNITS   B–B–B–B

Built: 1993–1994 by Duewag, Dusseldorf, Germany.
Traction Motors: Four monomotors.
Seats: 88 (r 80 + 6 tip-up).
Weight: 52 t.
Dimensions: 34.75 x 2.65 m.
Couplers: Not equipped.
Doors: Sliding plug.
Braking: Rheostatic, regenerative, disc and emergency track.
Max. Speed: 50 m.p.h.

101 **SM** r	106 **AL**	110	114	118	122 **SM** r
102	107 **SM** r	111	115 **SM** r	119 **SM** r	123
103	108	112	116 **AL**	120 **SM** r	124
104 **SM** r	109	113	117	121 **SM** r	125
105 **SM** r					

7.3. DOCKLANDS LIGHT RAILWAY

This system now runs for a total of 19 route miles, with more extensions in the pipeline. Lines run from termini at Bank and Tower Gateway, central London to Lewisham, Stratford, Beckton and King George V (on the new London City Airport line). Future extensions are planned from King George V under the Thames to Woolwich Arsenal and from Stratford to Canning Town. The first line was opened in 1987 from Tower Gateway to Island Gardens.

Originally owned by London Transport, it is now owned by DLR Ltd. and operated by Serco Docklands. Cars are normally "driven" automatically using the Alcatel "Seltrack" moving block signalling system.

Notes: Original P86 and P89 Class vehicles 01–21 were withdrawn from service in 1991 (01–11) and 1995 (12–21) and sold for use in Essen, Germany.

24 cars were ordered from Bombardier in 2005, to be built at their Bautzen plant, Germany for delivery 2007–08. 31 extra cars were ordered in 2006 in prospect of the "London 2012" Olympic Games. These are due for delivery in 2009. The numbering series for these vehicles has not yet been announced.

System: 750 V DC third rail (bottom contact).
Depots: Poplar and Beckton.
Workshops: Poplar.
Standard livery: Red with a curving blue stripe to represent the River Thames. Refurbished cars (shown as "r") carry this livery. Other cars carry the original blue livery with a red stripe on the lower bodyside. The refurbishment programme was due for completion by the end of 2006.

CLASS B90   B–2–B

Built: 1991–1992 by BN Construction, Brugge, Belgium. Chopper control.
Traction Motors: Two Brush of 140 kW.

Seats: r 52 + 4 tip-up.		**Weight:** 36 t.
Dimensions: 28.80 x 2.65 m.		**Braking:** Rheostatic.
Couplers: Scharfenberg.		**Max. Speed:** 50 m.p.h.

Doors: Sliding. End doors for staff use.

22 r	26 r	30 r	34 r	38 r	42 r
23 r	27 r	31 r	35 r	39 r	43 r
24 r	28 r	32 r	36 r	40 r	44 r
25 r	29 r	33 r	37 r	41 r	

CLASS B92   B–2–B

Built: 1992–1995 by BN Construction, Brugge, Belgium. Chopper control.
Traction Motors: Two Brush of 140 kW.

Seats: r 52 + 4 tip-up.		**Weight:** 36 t.
Dimensions: 28.80 x 2.65 m.		**Braking:** Rheostatic.
Couplers: Scharfenberg.		**Max. Speed:** 50 m.p.h.

Doors: Sliding. End doors for staff use.

45	r	53	r	61	r	69	r	77	r	85	r
46	r	54	r	62	r	70	r	78	r	86	r
47	r	55	r	63	r	71	r	79	r	87	r
48	r	56	r	64	r	72	r	80	r	88	r
49	r	57	r	65	r	73	r	81	r	89	r
50	r	58	r	66	r	74	r	82	r	90	r
51	r	59	r	67	r	75	r	83	r	91	r
52	r	60	r	68	r	76	r	84	r		

CLASS B2K   B–2–B

Built: 2002–2003 by Bombardier Transportation, Brugge, Belgium.
Traction Motors: Two Brush of 140 kW.
Seats: 64 + 4 tip-up (r 52 + 4 tip-up). **Weight:** 36 t.
Dimensions: 28.80 x 2.65 m. **Braking:** Rheostatic.
Couplers: Scharfenberg. **Max. Speed:** 50 m.p.h.
Doors: Sliding. End doors for staff use.
Non-standard liveries:

92 & 08 Blue & yellow.

92	**0**	96		01		05		09		13	r
93		97	r	02		06	r	10	r	14	r
94	r	98	r	03	r	07		11	r	15	r
95		99	r	04	r	08	**0**	12	r	16	r

7.4. CROYDON TRAMLINK

This system runs through central Croydon via a one-way loop, with lines radiating out to Wimbledon, New Addington and Beckenham Junction/ Elmers End with the total route mileage being 18½ miles. The system opened in 2000 and is operated by Tramlink Croydon Ltd. (owned by First Group).

System: 750 V DC overhead.
Depot & Workshops: Therapia Lane, Croydon.

SIX AXLE ARTICULATED CARS   Bo–2–Bo

Built: 1998–1999 by Bombardier-Wien Schienenfahrzeuge, Austria.
Traction Motors: Four of 120 kW each.
Seats: 70. **Dimensions:** 30.1 x 2.65 m.
Couplers: Scharfenberg. **Doors:** Sliding plug.
Weight: 36.3 t. **Max. Speed:** 50 m.p.h.
Braking: Disc, regenerative and magnetic track.

Standard livery: Red & white unless stated.
AL Advertising livery:

2552 – Grants Entertainment Centre (black & brown).

2530	2534	2538	2542	2546	2550	
2531	2535	2539	2543	2547	2551	
2532	2536	2540	2544	2548	2552	**AL**
2533	2537	2541	2545	2549	2553	

7.5. GREATER MANCHESTER METROLINK

Metrolink was the first modern tramway system in the UK, combining on-street running with longer distance running over former BR lines. The system opened in 1992 from Bury to Altrincham through the streets of Manchester, with a spur to Piccadilly station. A second line opened in 2000 from Cornbrook to Eccles extending the total route mileage to 23 miles.

Further extensions ("Phase 3a") have now been authorised to Rochdale via Oldham to the north of Manchester (involving converting a National Rail line to light rail use), Droylsden to the east (on a line which will eventually reach Ashton-under-Lyne) and St. Werburgh's Road, Chorlton to the south (on a line which will eventually reach Manchester Airport).

When approved "Phase 3b" will consist of Oldham and Rochdale town centre sections, and the extension of above lines to Ashton-under-Lyne and Manchester Airport and East Didsbury.

The system is operated by Serco Metrolink.

System: 750 V DC overhead.
Depot & Workshops: Queens Road, Manchester.

SIX-AXLE ARTICULATED CARS   Bo–2–Bo

Built: 1991–1992 by Firema, Italy. Chopper control.
Traction Motors: Four GEC of 130 kW.
Seats: 82 + 4 tip-up.
Dimensions: 29.00 x 2.65 m.
Couplers: Scharfenberg.
Doors: Sliding.
Weight: 45 t.
Braking: Rheostatic, regenerative, disc and emergency track.
Max. Speed: 50 m.p.h.

Livery: White, dark grey and blue.

Notes: r – refurbished. Light blue doors and cantrail stripe.

* Fitted with front valances, retractable couplers and controllable magnetic track brakes for running to Eccles.

1001	r	
1002	r	VIRGIN MEGASTORES
1003	r	
1004	r	THE ROBERT OWEN
1005	r*	THE RAILWAY MISSION
1006	r	
1007	r	SONY CENTRE ARNDALE
1008	r	
1009	r	VIRGIN MEGASTORES
1010	r*	
1011	r	VIRGIN MEGASTORES

1012	r	VIRGIN MEGASTORES
1013	r	THE GRENADIER GUARDSMAN
1014	r	THE GREAT MANCHESTER RUNNER
1015	r*	BURMA STAR
1016	r	VIRGIN MEGASTORES
1017	r	BURY HOSPICE
1018	r	ELECTRA
1019		
1020	r	LANCASHIRE FUSILIER
1021		STARLIGHT EXPRESS
1022	r	THE POPPY APPEAL
1023		
1024		THE JOHN GREENWOOD
1025	r	
1026	r	THE POWER

SIX-AXLE ARTICULATED CARS   Bo–2–Bo

Built: 1999 by Ansaldo, Italy. Chopper control. Fitted with front valances, retractable couplers and controllable magnetic track brakes for running to Eccles. Can also be used on the Bury–Altrincham route.
Traction Motors: Four GEC of 130 kW.
Seats: 82 + 4 tip-up.
Dimensions: 29.00 x 2.65 m.
Couplers: Scharfenberg.
Doors: Sliding.
Weight: 45 t.
Braking: Rheostatic, regenerative, disc and magnetic track.
Max. Speed: 50 m.p.h.

Livery: White, dark grey and blue with light blue doors.

2001	THE JOE CLARKE OBE
2002	
2003	TRAVELLER 2000
2004	SALFORD LADS' CLUB
2005	WHSMITH WEST ONE
2006	SONY CENTRE ARNDALE

7.6. NOTTINGHAM EXPRESS TRANSIT

This is the newest light rail system in the UK, opened in 2004. Line 1 runs for 8¾ miles from Station Street, Nottingham (alongside Nottingham station) to Hucknall, including a short spur to Phoenix Park. There is around three miles of on-street running through Nottingham. Extensions are planned to Clifton (Line 2) to the south of Nottingham and Chilwell via Beeston to the west (line 3).

The system is operated by the Arrow Light Rail Ltd. consortium (Transdev, Nottingham City Transport, Carillion, Bombardier, Innsfree and Galaxy).

System: 750 V DC overhead.
Depot & Workshops: Wilkinson Street.

SIX AXLE ARTICULATED CARS

Built: 2002–2003 by Bombardier, Derby Litchurch Lane Works. Branded "Bombardier Incentros".
Traction Motors: 8 Asynchronous.
Seats: 54 + 4 tip-up   **Dimensions:** 33.0 x 2.4 m
Couplers: Not equipped.   **Doors:** Sliding plug.
Weight: 36.7 t.   **Max. Speed:** 50 m.p.h.
Braking: Disc, regenerative and magnetic track for emergency use.

Standard livery: Black, silver and green unless stated.
AL Advertising liveries:

201 – Powergen (blue).
209 – Westbury Homes (blue).
213 – Powergen (blue).

201	**AL**	Torvill and Dean	209	**AL**	Sydney Standard
202		DH Lawrence	210		Sir Jesse Boot
203		Bendigo Thompson	211		Robin Hood
204		Erica Beardsmore	212		William Booth
205		Lord Byron	213	**AL**	Mary Potter
206		Angela Alcock	214		Dennis McCarthy
207		Mavis Worthington	215		Brian Clough
208		Dinah Minton			

7.7. MIDLAND METRO

This system opened in 1999 and has one 12½ mile line from Birmingham
Snow Hill to Wolverhampton along the former GWR line to Wolverhampton
Low Level. On the approach to Wolverhampton it deviates from the former
railway alignment to run on-street to the St. George's terminus. It is operated
by Travel West Midlands Ltd. Extensions are proposed from Snow Hill through
Birmingham to Five Ways and from Wednesbury to Brierley Hill and Dudley.

System: 750 V DC overhead.   **Depot & Workshops:** Wednesbury.

SIX AXLE ARTICULATED CARS   Bo–2–Bo

Built: 1998–1999 by Ansaldo Transporti, Italy.
Traction Motors: Four.   **Seats:** 52 + 4 tip-up.
Dimensions: 24.00 x 2.65 m.   **Couplers:** Not equipped.
Doors: Sliding plug.   **Weight:** 35.6 t.
Braking: Rheostatic, regenerative, disc and magnetic track.
Max. Speed: 43 m.p.h.

Livery: Dark blue & light grey with green stripe, yellow doors & red front end.
Note: 07 is currently stored out of use and used for spares.

01	SIR FRANK WHITTLE	09	JEFF ASTLE
02		10	JOHN STANLEY WEBB
03	RAY LEWIS	11	THERESA STEWART
04		12	
05	SISTER DORA	13	ANTHONY NOLAN
06	ALAN GARNER	14	JIM EAMES
07	(S)	15	AGENORIA
08	JOSEPH CHAMBERLAIN	16	GERWYN JOHN

7.8. TYNE & WEAR METRO

The Tyne & Wear Metro system covers 48 route miles and can be described
as the UK's first modern light rail system. However it is not a true light rail
system, but more of a hybrid system, with elements of light rail, underground metro and outer suburban heavy rail operations.

The initial network opened between 1980 and 1984 consisting of a line from
South Shields via Gateshead and Newcastle Central station to Bank Foot (later
extended to Newcastle Airport in 1991) and the North Tyneside loop (over
former BR lines) serving North Shields, Tynemouth and Whitley Bay with a
terminus at St. James in Newcastle city centre. A more recent extension came
from Pelaw to Sunderland and South Hylton in 2002, making use of existing
heavy rail infrastructure between Heworth and Sunderland.

The system is owned and operated by Nexus – the Tyne & Wear PTE.

Metro cars are currently being "refreshed" at South Gosforth depot with minor
livery variations such as yellow doors and new brandings.

System: 1500 V DC overhead.   **Depot & Workshops:** South Gosforth.

SIX-AXLE ARTICULATED UNITS B–2–B

Built: 1978–1981 by Metropolitan Cammell, Birmingham (Prototype cars 4001 and 4002 were built by Metropolitan Cammell in 1976 and rebuilt 1984–1987 by Hunslet TPL, Leeds).
Traction Motors: Two Siemens of 187 kW each.
Seats: 68. **Dimensions:** 27.80 x 2.65 m.
Couplers: BSI. **Doors:** Sliding plug.
Weight: 39.0 t. **Maximum Speed:** 50 m.p.h.

Standard livery: Red & yellow unless otherwise indicated.
B Blue & yellow
G Green & yellow.
O (4001) Original 1975 Tyne & Wear Metro livery of yellow & cream.
O (4027) Original North Eastern Railway style (red & white).
AL Advertising liveries:

4002 – Tyne & Wear Metro (orange & black).
4020 – Modern Apprenticeships (white, red & black).
4038 – Talktofrank.com (white).
4040 – Cut your CO2 day (blue & white).
4042 – Metro Radio (blue & pink).
4045 – Newcastle Racecourse (green).
4048 – Great North Forest (various).
4049 – Kidd & Spoor Harper Solicitors (blue).
4055 – European Regional Development Fund (blue & yellow).
4080 – Tyne & Wear Challenge Project (white & red).

4001	O	4019		4037		4055	AL	4073	
4002	AL	4020	AL	4038	AL	4056		4074	
4003		4021		4039	B	4057		4075	B
4004	G	4022		4040	AL	4058	B	4076	B
4005		4023	G	4041		4059		4077	
4006		4024	B	4042	AL	4060		4078	
4007		4025	G	4043		4061		4079	
4008		4026		4044		4062	G	4080	AL
4009		4027	O	4045	AL	4063		4081	B
4010		4028		4046		4064		4082	
4011		4029	B	4047	B	4065		4083	B
4012		4030		4048	AL	4066	B	4084	
4013		4031	B	4049	AL	4067		4085	
4014		4032		4050		4068		4086	
4015		4033		4051	G	4069		4087	
4016	B	4034		4052		4070		4088	
4017		4035	B	4053	B	4071		4089	
4018	G	4036	G	4054	B	4072	B	4090	

Names:

4026	George Stephenson	4065	Dame Catherine Cookson
4041	HARRY COWANS	4077	Robert Stephenson
4060	Thomas Bewick	4078	ELLEN WILKINSON
4064	Michael Campbell		

Subscription order form

To subscribe, please complete the form below (or a copy) and return it with your remittance to:

Today's Railways UK (Dept. LCS), 3 Wyvern House, Sark Road, SHEFFIELD, S2 4HG, ENGLAND.

BLOCK CAPITALS PLEASE

(All prices include postage and packing.)

Today's Railways UK: Subscription (12 issues)

☐ **UK £43.20 (post free);**   ☐ **Overseas Airmail £52.80.**

JAN   FEB   MAR   APR   MAY   JUN   JUL   AUG   SEP   OCT   NOV   DEC

Please circle start issue required

Name: ....

Address: ....

....

.... **Postcode:** ....

Daytime Tel. No: ....

E-mail: ....

I enclose my cheque/UK postal order for £ ....

made payable to **'PLATFORM 5 PUBLISHING LTD.'**

Please debit my Visa/Mastercard/Maestro

Card No: .... **Expiry Date:** ....

Card Issue No./Date (Maestro only): .... **Security No.:** ....

for £ .... **Date:** ....

Signature: ....

---

or if ordering by debit/credit card, telephone our subscription department on the numbers opposite.

Special note: Subscriptions may begin with the current issue or the next to be published. Subscriptions cannot be backdated.

8. CODES

8.1. LIVERY CODES

Livery codes are used to denote the various liveries carried. It is impossible to list every livery variation which currently exists. In particular items ignored for this publication include:

- Minor colour variations.
- Omission of logos.
- All numbering, lettering and brandings.

Descriptions quoted are thus a general guide only. Logos as appropriate for each livery are normally deemed to be carried.

The colour of the lower half of the bodyside is stated first. Minor variations to these liveries are ignored.

Coaches are in **IC** livery as standard (i.e. a blank livery code space means that vehicle is in **IC** livery).

Code Description

1	"One" (metallic grey with a broad black bodyside stripe. Pink, yellow, grey, pale green and light blue stripes at the unit/vehicle ends).
1S	One Stansted Express (metallic grey with a broad black bodyside stripe. Orange stripes at unit ends).
ACT	ACTS (Netherlands) (Deep blue with a broad yellow stripe).
AL	Advertising/promotional livery (see class heading for details).
AN	Anglia Railways Class 170s (white & turquoise with blue vignette).
AR	Anglia Railways (turquoise blue with a white stripe).
AV	Arriva Trains (turquoise blue with white doors & a cream "swish").
AW	Revised Arriva Trains {Class 175} (turquoise blue with white vignette & two yellow stripes).
B	BR blue.
BG	BR blue & grey lined out in white.
BI	"Visit Bristol" promotional livery (deep blue with various images).
BL	BR Revised blue with yellow cabs, grey roof, large numbers & logo.
BP	Blue Pullman ("Nanking" blue & white (all over blue for locos)).
BR	BR blue with a red solebar stripe.
C2	c2c Rail (blue with metallic grey doors & pink c2c branding).
CC	New Central Trains {Class 150} (light green with a broad blue lower bodyside band & blue cab end sections).
CD	Cotswold Rail (silver with blue & red logo).
CE	BR Civil Engineers (yellow & grey with black cab doors & window surrounds).
CH	BR Western Region/GWR (chocolate & cream lined out in gold).
CI	BR Carmine & Cream.
CO	Centro (grey & green with light blue, white & yellow stripes).
CM	Revised old Midland Mainline (Midland Mainline teal green with white Central logos).
CN	Revised Connex South Eastern/Southeastern (white with yellow doors, black window surrounds & grey lower band).

CR	Chiltern Railways (blue & white with a thin red stripe).
CS	ScotRail Caledonian Sleepers (two-tone purple with a silver stripe).
CT	Central Trains (two-tone green with yellow doors. Blue flash & red stripe at vehicle ends).
CU	Corus (silver with red logos).
CX	Connex (white with yellow lower body & blue solebar).
DC	Scenic lines of Devon & Cornwall promotional livery (black with gold cantrail stripe).
DG	BR Departmental (dark grey with black cab doors & window surrounds).
DR	Direct Rail Services (dark blue with light blue or dark grey roof).
DS	Revised Direct Rail Services (dark blue, light blue & green).
E	English Welsh & Scottish Railway (maroon bodyside & roof with a broad gold bodyside band).
EB	Eurotunnel (two-tone grey with a broad blue stripe).
ECR	Euro Cargo Rail {France} (light grey).
EG	"EWS grey" (As F but with large yellow & red EWS logo).
EP	European Passenger Services (two-tone grey with dark blue roof).
EU	Eurostar (white with dark blue & yellow stripes).
F	BR Trainload Freight (two-tone grey with black cab doors & window surrounds. Various logos).
FA	Fastline Freight (grey & black with white & orange stripes).
FB	First Group plain dark blue.
FD	First Group "Dynamic Lines" {First Great Western} (all over dark blue with thin multi-coloured lines on the lower bodyside).
FE	Railfreight Distribution International (two tone-grey with black cab doors & dark blue roof).
FER	Fertis (light grey with a dark grey roof & solebar).
FF	Freightliner grey (two-tone grey with black cab doors & window surrounds. Freightliner logo).
FG	First Group corporate Inter-City (indigo blue with a white roof & gold, pink & white stripes).
FI	First Group "Local Lines" (varying blue with local visitor attractions applied to the lower bodyside).
FL	Freightliner (dark green with yellow cabs).
FM	FM Rail (all over black with FM Rail logo).
FO	BR Railfreight (grey bodysides, yellow cabs & large BR double arrow).
FP	Old First Great Western (green & ivory with thin green & broad gold stripes).
FR	Fragonset Railways (black with silver roof & a red bodyside band lined out in white).
FS	First Group corporate regional/suburban (indigo blue with pink & white stripes).
FT	First Group "Dynamic Lines" {Trans-Pennine Express and pilot First Great Western} (varying blue with thin multi-coloured lines on the lower bodyside).
FU	First Group "Urban Lights" (varying blue with pink, white and blue markings on the lower bodyside).
FY	Foster Yeoman (blue & silver. Cast numberplates).
G¹	BR Green (plain green, with white stripe on main line locomotives).
G²	BR Southern Region/SR or BR DMU green.
GB	GB Railfreight (blue with orange cantrail & solebar stripes, orange cabs).

GC   British racing green & cream lined out in gold.
GE   First Great Eastern (grey, green, blue & white).
GF   GB Railfreight {First Group style} (All over blue with pink and white stripes at the cab ends).
GG   BR green (two-tone green).
GIF GIF (Spain) light blue with dark blue band.
GL   First Great Western locos/Motorail vans (green with a gold stripe).
GN   Great North Eastern Railway (dark blue with a red stripe).
GS   Royal Scotsman/Great Scottish & Western Railway (maroon).
GW   Great Western Railway (green, lined out in black & orange. Cast numberplates).
GX   Gatwick Express InterCity (dark grey/white/burgundy/white).
GY   Eurotunnel (grey & yellow).
HA   Hanson Quarry Products (dark blue & silver).
HB   HSBC Rail (Oxford blue & white).
HC   Heathrow Connect (grey with a broad deep blue bodyside band & orange doors).
HE   Heathrow Express (grey & indigo blue with black window surrounds).
HN   Harry Needle Railroad Company (orange & grey, lined out in black).
HW   Heart of Wales Line promotional livery (orange with yellow doors).
HT   Hull Trains (dark green & silver with two gold stripes).
IC   BR InterCity (dark grey/white/red/white).
IL   Island Line (light blue, with illustrations featuring dinosaurs etc).
IM   BR InterCity Mainline (dark grey/white/red/light grey & yellow lower cabsides except shunters).
K   Black.
LH   BR Loadhaul (black with orange cabsides).
LM   Original London Transport maroon & cream.
LN   LNER Tourist (green & cream).
LW   LNWR black with grey & red lining.
M   BR maroon (maroon lined out in straw & black).
MA   Maintrain (blue).
ME   Merseyrail Electrics (metallic silver with yellow doors).
ML   BR Mainline Freight (Aircraft blue with a silver stripe).
MM   Old Midland Mainline (Teal green with grey lower body sides & three tangerine stripes).
MN   New Midland Mainline (Thin tangerine stripe on the lower bodyside, ocean blue, grey & white).
MT   GBRf Metronet (blue with orange cabsides).
MY   Merseytravel (yellow & white with a grey stripe).
N   BR Network South East (white & blue with red lower bodyside stripe, grey solebar & cab ends).
NO   Northern (deep blue, lilac & white).
NR   Network Rail (blue with a red stripe).
NS   Northern Spirit (turquoise blue with a lime green "N").
NT   BR Network SouthEast (white & blue with red lower bodyside & cantrail stripes).
NW   North Western Trains (blue with gold cantrail stripe & star).
O   Non standard livery (see class heading for details).
P   Porterbrook Leasing Company (white or grey & purple).
PC   Pullman Car Company (umber & cream with gold lettering lined out in gold).

PS	Provincial Services (dark blue & grey with light blue & white stripes).
R	Plain red.
RE	Provincial Services/Regional Railways Express (light grey/buff/dark grey with white, dark blue & light blue stripes).
RG	BR Parcels (dark grey & red).
RK	New Railtrack (green & blue).
RM	Royal Mail (red with yellow stripes above solebar).
RN	North West Regional Railways (dark blue & grey with green & white stripes).
RO	Old Railtrack (orange with white & grey stripes).
RP	Royal Train (claret, lined out in red & black).
RR	Regional Railways (dark blue & grey with light blue & white stripes, three narrow dark blue stripes at vehicle ends).
RT	RT Rail (black, lined out in red).
RV	Riviera Trains (Oxford blue & cream lined out in gold {blue only for locos}).
RX	Rail Express Systems (dark grey & red with or without blue markings).
RZ	Royal Train revised (plain claret, no lining).
S	Old Strathclyde PTE (orange & black lined out in white).
SB	Serco Railtest blue (deep blue with white Serco brandings).
SC	New Strathclyde PTE (carmine & cream lined out in black & gold).
SD	South West Trains {Class 450 style} (deep blue with red doors & orange & red cab sides).
SCO	Seco-Rail (orange with a broad yellow bodyside band).
SL	Silverlink (indigo blue with white stripe, green lower body & yellow doors).
SP	New Strathclyde PTE {Class 334 style} (carmine & cream, with a turquoise stripe).
SN	Southern (white & dark green with light green semi-circles at one end of each vehicle. Light grey band at solebar level).
SO	Serco Railtest (red & grey).
SR	ScotRail (white, terracotta, purple & aquamarine).
SS	South West Trains inner suburban {Class 455 style} (red with blue & orange flashes at unit ends).
ST	Stagecoach (white & blue with orange & red stripes).
SU	Revised Stansted Express (light blue with a dark blue lower bodyside stripe & light grey doors).
SW	South West Trains {long-distance stock} (white & dark blue with black window surrounds, red doors & red panel with orange stripe at unit ends).
SX	Stansted Express (two-tone metallic blue with grey doors).
TL	New Thameslink (silver with blue window surrounds & ends).
TP	First Trans-Pennine Express (Plum with a yellow "N" and First Group indigo blue lower bodyside band).
TR	Thameslink Rail (dark blue with a broad orange stripe & two narrower white bodyside stripes plus white cantrail stripe).
TSO	TSO (all over yellow with a blue solebar).
TT	Thames Trains (blue & white with lime green doors).
TW	Modified Thameslink (as **TR** but with the yellow band replaced by a white band).
U	Plain white or grey undercoat.
V	Virgin Trains (red with black doors extending into bodysides, three white lower bodysides stripes).

VP   Virgin Trains shunters (black with a large black & white chequered flag on the bodyside).

VN   Venice Simplon Orient Express "Northern Belle" (crimson lake & cream).

VT   New Virgin Trains (silver, with black window surrounds, white cantrail stripe & red roof. Red swept down at unit ends. Black & white striped doors on units).

WA   Wabtec Rail (black).

WB   Wales & Borders Alphaline (metallic silver with blue doors).

WC   Old West Coast Railway Company (all over maroon with a black bodyside stripe).

WD   West Coast Main Line Desiro (grey with a broad blue bodyside band).

WE   Wessex Trains Alphaline promotional livery (metallic silver with various images, pink doors).

WN   Old West Anglia Great Northern (white with blue, grey & orange stripes).

WP   New West Anglia Great Northern (deep purple with white or light purple doors).

WR   Waterman Railways (maroon with cream stripes).

WS   West Coast Railway Company maroon.

WT   Wessex Trains Alphaline (metallic silver with maroon or pink doors).

WX   Heart of Wessex Line promotional livery (cerise pink with various images).

WY   Old West Yorkshire PTE (red/cream with thin yellow stripe).

WZ   Wessex Trains claret promotional livery with various images.

Y   Network Rail or Eurotunnel plain yellow.

YN   West Yorkshire PTE {Class 333 style} (red with light grey "N").

YR   New West Yorkshire PTE {Class 321 style} (red, lilac & grey).

YP   New West Yorkshire PTE {DMUs} (red with grey semi-circles).

8.2. OWNER CODES

The following codes are used to define the ownership details of the locomotives or rolling stock listed in this book. Codes shown indicate either the legal owner or "responsible custodian" of each vehicle.

Code   Owner

24	6024 Preservation Society
40	The Class 40 Preservation Society
50	Class 50 Alliance
62	The Princess Royal Locomotive Trust
73	The Class 73 Locomotive Preservation Society
92	City of Wells Supporters Association
A	Angel Trains
AC	The AC Locomotive Group
AE	AEA Technology Rail
AM	Alstom
AW	Arriva Trains Wales
B1	Thompson B1 Locomotive Society
BB	Balfour Beatty Rail Plant
BC	Bridgend County Borough Council/Rhondda Cynon Taff District Council
BE	Bert Hitchins
BK	The Scottish Railway Preservation Society
BS	Bressingham Steam Museum
BT	Bombardier Transportation
CA	Carillion Rail Plant
CC	Cardiff City Council
CD	Cotswold Rail Engineering
CM	Cambrian Trains
CR	Chiltern Railways
DC	Dorset County Council
DG	Duke of Gloucester Steam Locomotive Trust
DM	Dartmoor Railways
DR	Direct Rail Services
DT	The Diesel Traction Group
E	English Welsh & Scottish Railway
ES	Eurailscout GB
ET	Eurotunnel
EU	Eurostar (UK)
FG	First Group
FL	Freightliner
FM	FM Rail *(in administration)*
FY	Foster Yeoman
GB	GB Railfreight
GD	Garsdale Railtours
GS	The Great Scottish & Western Railway Company
GW	The Great Western Society
H	HSBC Rail (UK)
HA	The Hanson Group
HD	Hastings Diesels

HE	British Airports Authority
HJ	Howard Johnston Engineering
HN	Harry Needle Railroad Company
HX	Halifax Bank of Scotland
IR	Ian Riley Engineering
J	Fastline (Jarvis Rail)
JH	Jeremy Hosking
LW	London & North Western Railway Company
MA	Maintrain
MH	Mid-Hants Railway
MN	Merchant Navy Locomotive Preservation Society
MW	Martin Walker (Beaver Sports)
NE	North Eastern Locomotive Preservation Group
NM	National Railway Museum
NR	Network Rail
P	Porterbrook Leasing Company
PO	Other private owner
RA	Railfilms
RE	Railway Vehicle Engineering
RI	Rail Assets Investments
RM	Royal Mail
RP	Rampart Carriage & Wagon Services
RT	RT Rail Tours
RV	Riviera Trains
SB	SNCB/NMBS (Société Nationale des Chemins de fer Belges/ Nationale Maatschappij der Belgische Spoorwegen)
SF	SNCF (Société Nationale des Chemins de fer Français)
SH	Scottish Highland Railway Company
SM	Siemens Transportation
SN	Southern
SO	Serco Railtest
SV	Severn Valley Railway
SW	South West Trains
TT	Type Three Traction Group
VI	Victa Westlink Rail
VS	Venice-Simplon Orient Express
VT	Vintage Trains
VW	Virgin West Coast
WA	Wabtec Rail
WC	West Coast Railway Company
WF	Western Falcon Rail (Alan and Tracy Lear)
WT	Wessex Trains
X	Sold for scrap/further use and awaiting collection or owner unknown

Keep right up to date with....

Today's Railways

EUROPE

The only UK railway magazine exclusively devoted to events on Mainland Europe's railways.

Every issue is packed with the latest news, informative articles and comprehensive features, plus useful travel information, heritage news, light rail news, diary of events, readers letters and much much more!

On sale 4th Monday of EVERY MONTH

Subscribe to Today's Railways Europe TODAY!

Subscription order form

To subscribe, please complete the form below (or a copy) and return it with your remittance to:

Today's Railways Europe (Dept. LCS), 3 Wyvern House, Sark Road, SHEFFIELD, S2 4HG, ENGLAND.

BLOCK CAPITALS PLEASE

(All prices include postage and packing.)

Today's Railways Europe: Subscription (12 issues)

☐ UK £43.20 (post free);   ☐ Overseas Airmail £52.80.

JAN   FEB   MAR   APR   MAY   JUN   JUL   AUG   SEP   OCT   NOV   DEC

Please circle start issue required

Name: ....

Address: ....

....

.... **Postcode:** ....

Daytime Tel. No: ....

E-mail: ....

I enclose my cheque/UK postal order for £ ....

made payable to **'PLATFORM 5 PUBLISHING LTD.'**

Please debit my Visa/Mastercard/Maestro

Card No: .... **Expiry Date:** ....

Card Issue No./Date (Maestro only): .... **Security No.:** ....

for £ .... **Date:** ....

Signature: ....

---

or if ordering by debit/credit card, telephone our subscription department on the numbers opposite.

Special note: Subscriptions may begin with the current issue or the next to be published. Subscriptions cannot be backdated.

8.3. LOCOMOTIVE POOL CODES

Locomotives are split into operational groups ("pools") for diagramming and maintenance purposes. The official codes used to denote these pools are shown in this publication.

Code	Pool
ACAC	AC Locomotive Group operational locomotives.
ACXX	AC Locomotive Group locomotives under repair.
ARZH	Alstom Class 08 (Glasgow Springburn).
ARZN	Alstom Class 08 (Wolverton).
ATLO	Alstom Class 08.
ATTB	Alstom Class 57.
ATXX	Alstom locos for long-term repair.
CDJD	Serco Railtest Class 08.
CFOL	Class 50 Operations Ltd.
CREL	Cotswold Rail operational locomotives – contract hire.
CROL	Cotswold Rail stored locomotives.
CRRH	Cotswold Rail operational locomotives – spot-hire contracts.
CRUR	Cotswold Rail stored locomotives – undergoing restoration.
CSPC	The Class 73 Preservation Society loco.
DFGC	Freightliner Intermodal Class 86/5.
DFGM	Freightliner Intermodal Class 66.
DFHG	Freightliner Heavy Haul modified Class 66 (general).
DFHH	Freightliner Heavy Haul Class 66.
DFIM	Freightliner Intermodal modified Class 66.
DFLC	Freightliner Intermodal Class 90.
DFLH	Freightliner Heavy Haul Class 47.
DFLS	Freightliner Class 08.
DFNC	Freightliner Intermodal Class 86/6.
DFNR	Freightliner Heavy Haul modified Class 66. Infrastructure services.
DFRT	Freightliner Heavy Haul Class 66. Infrastructure services.
DFTZ	Freightliner Intermodal Class 57.
DHLT	Freightliner locomotives awaiting maintenance/repair/disposal.
EFOO	First Great Western Class 57.
EFPC	First Great Western Class 43.
EFSH	First Great Western Class 08.
ELRD	East Lancashire Railway-based main line registered locos.
GBAC	GB Railfreight Class 87.
GBCM	GB Railfreight Class 66. Railfreight contracts.
GBED	GB Railfreight Class 73.
GBRT	GB Railfreight Class 66. Network Rail contracts.
GBZZ	GB Railfreight. Stored pool.
GPSN	Eurostar (UK) Class 73.
GPSS	Eurostar (UK) Class 08.
GPSV	Eurostar (UK) Class 37.
HBSH	Wabtec hire shunting locomotives.
HGSS	Maintrain Class 08 (Tyseley/Soho)
HISE	Maintrain Class 08 (Derby).
HISL	Maintrain Class 08 (Neville Hill).

HNRL	Harry Needle Railroad Company hire locomotives.
HNRS	Harry Needle Railroad Company stored locomotives.
HWSU	Southern Class 09.
HYWD	South West Trains Class 73 (standby locomotives).
IANA	"One" Class 90.
IECA	Great North Eastern Railway Class 91.
IECP	Great North Eastern Railway Class 43.
IMLP	Midland Mainline Class 43.
IVGA	Gatwick Express Class 73 (stored).
KCSI	Bombardier Class 08 (Ilford).
KDSD	Bombardier Class 08 (Doncaster).
MBDL	Non TOC-owned diesel locomotives.
MOLO	RT Rail Tours locomotives.
MOLS	RT Rail Tours stored locomotives.
QACL	Network Rail Class 86.
QADD	Network Rail Class 31.
QAED	Network Rail Class 73.
QCAR	Network Rail New Measurement Train Class 43.
QETS	Network Rail stored locomotives.
RCJA	Fastline (Jarvis Rail) locomotives.
RFSH	Wabtec hire fleet.
RTLO	Riviera Trains operational fleet.
RTLS	Riviera Trains stored locomotives.
RTSO	Riviera Trains shunting locomotive.
RVLO	Rail Vehicle Engineering operational locomotives.
SAXL	HSBC Rail (UK) off-lease locomotives.
SBXL	Porterbrook Leasing Company off-lease locomotives.
SDED	FM Rail Class 73.
SDFL	FM Rail locomotives (freight traffic).
SDFR	FM Rail locomotives (general).
SDPP	FM Rail operational locomotives (push-pull capability).
SDMS	FM Rail museum locomotive.
SDXL	FM Rail stored locomotives.
TTTC	Type Three Traction Group Class 37.
WAAN	EWS Network Class 67.
WABN	EWS Network Class 67. RETB fitted.
WBAI	EWS Industrial Class 66.
WBAK	EWS Construction Class 66.
WBAM	EWS Energy Class 66.
WBAN	EWS Network Class 66.
WBBK	EWS Construction Class 66. RETB fitted.
WBBM	EWS Energy Class 66. RETB fitted.
WBBN	EWS Network Class 66. RETB fitted.
WBEN	EWS Class 66 for Euro Cargo Rail, France.
WBLI	EWS Industrial Class 66. Dedicated locos for Lickey Incline banking duties. Fitted with additional lights and drawgear.
WCAI	EWS Industrial Class 60. Standard fuel tanks.
WCAK	EWS Construction Class 60. Standard fuel tanks.
WCAM	EWS Energy Class 60. Standard fuel tanks.
WCAN	EWS Network Class 60. Standard fuel tanks.
WCBI	EWS Industrial Class 60. Extended-range fuel tanks.

WCBK	EWS Construction Class 60. Extended-range fuel tanks.
WCBM	EWS Energy Class 60. Extended-range fuel tanks.
WDAK	EWS Construction Class 59.
WEFE	EWS Network Class 90.
WKBN	EWS Network Class 37. RETB fitted.
WKCN	EWS Network Class 37.
WNSO	EWS main line locomotives – sold awaiting collection.
WNSS	EWS main line locomotives – stored serviceable.
WNTA	EWS locomotives – stored Sandite locos.
WNTR	EWS locomotives – tactical reserve.
WNTS	EWS locomotives – tactical stored serviceable.
WNWX	EWS main line locomotives – for major repairs.
WNXX	EWS locomotives – stored unserviceable.
WNYX	EWS locomotives – authorised for component recovery.
WREM	EWS shunting locomotives (Eastern and East Midlands – contract hire).
WRLN	EWS shunting locomotives (North London – contract hire).
WRLS	EWS shunting locomotives (South London – contract hire).
WRSC	EWS shunting locomotives (Scotland & Carlisle area – contract hire).
WRWM	EWS shunting locomotives (West Midlands and North West – contract hire).
WRWR	EWS shunting locomotives (Western Region – contract hire).
WSAW	EWS shunting locomotives (South Wales, on hire to Celsa).
WSEM	EWS shunting locomotives (Eastern and East Midlands).
WSGW	EWS shunting locomotives (Great Western and South Wales).
WSLN	EWS shunting locomotives (North London).
WSLS	EWS shunting locomotives (South London).
WSNE	EWS shunting locomotives (North East).
WSSC	EWS shunting locomotives (Scotland and Carlisle area).
WSWM	EWS shunting locomotives (West Midlands and North West).
WSWR	EWS shunting locomotives (Western Region).
WSXX	EWS shunting locomotives – internal/depot use.
WTAE	EWS Network Class 92.
WZFF	EWS Class 58 – former hire locomotives France (stored).
WZFH	EWS Class 58 – hire locomotives The Netherlands.
WZFS	EWS Class 58 – hire locomotives Spain.
WZGF	EWS Class 56 – former hire locomotives France (stored).
WZKF	EWS Class 37 – possible hire locomotives France (stored).
WZKS	EWS Class 37 – hire locomotives Spain.
WZTS	EWS locomotives – tactical stored.
XHIM	Direct Rail Services locomotives – Intermodal traffic.
XHMW	Direct Rail Services locomotives undergoing long-term repairs.
XHNC	Direct Rail Services locomotives – General.
XHSH	Direct Rail Services shunting locomotives.
XHSS	Direct Rail Services stored locomotives.
XYPA	Mendip Rail Class 59/1.
XYPO	Mendip Rail Class 59/0.

PLATFORM 5 MAIL ORDER

The Platform 5 European Railway Handbooks are the most comprehensive guides to the rolling stock    of selected European railway administrations available. Each book lists all locomotives and railcars of the country concerned, giving details of number carried and depot    allocation, together with a wealth of technical data for each class of vehicle. Each book is A5 size, thread sewn and includes 32 pages of colour illustrations. The Benelux book also contain details of hauled coaching stock.

Dates of publication are shown.

No. 1	Benelux Railways (2000)	£14.50
No. 2A	German Railways Part 1: DB Locomotives & Multiple Units (2004)	£16.95
No. 2B	German Railways Part 2: Private Operators, Preserved & Museums (2004)	£16.95
No. 3	Austrian Railways (2005)	£17.50
No. 4	French Railways (1999)	£14.50

Please add postage: 10% UK, 20% Europe, 30% Rest of World.

Telephone, fax or send your order to the Platform 5 Mail Order Department. See page 384 of this book for details.

8.4. OPERATOR CODES

Operator codes are used to denote the organisation that facilitates the use of that vehicle, and may not be the actual Train Operating Company which runs the train. Where no operator code is shown, vehicles are currently not in use.

Code	Operator
62	The Princess Royal Locomotive Trust
1	"One"
AW	Arriva Trains Wales
BB	Balfour Beatty Rail Plant
BK	The Scottish Railway Preservation Society
C2	c2c Rail
CA	Carillion Rail Plant
CD	Cotswold Rail Engineering
CR	Chiltern Railways
CT	Central Trains
DR	Direct Rail Services
E	English Welsh & Scottish Railway
EU	Eurostar (UK)
FC	First Capital Connect
FL	Freightliner
GB	GB Railfreight
GN	Great North Eastern Raiway
GS	The Great Scottish & Western Railway Company
GW	First Great Western
GX	Gatwick Express
HC	Heathrow Connect
HD	Hastings Diesels
HE	Heathrow Express
HT	Hull Trains
LS	Locomotive support coach
ME	Merseyrail Electrics
MH	Mid-Hants Railway
MM	Midland Mainline
NO	Northern
RA	Railfilms
RP	Royal Train
RV	Riviera Trains
SE	Southeastern
SF	SNCF (French Railways)
SH	Scottish Highland Railway Company
SL	Silverlink
SN	Southern
SO	Serco Railtest
SR	First ScotRail
SW	South West Trains
TP	Trans-Pennine Express
VI	Victa Westlink Rail
VS	Venice-Simplon Orient Express

VT	Vintage Trains
VW	Virgin West Coast
VX	Virgin Cross-Country
WC	West Coast Railway Company
WT	Wessex Trains

8.5. ALLOCATION & LOCATION CODES

Allocation codes are used in this publication to denote the normal maintenance base ("depots") of each operational locomotive, multiple unit or coach. However, maintenance may be carried out at other locations and may also be carried out by mobile maintenance teams.

Location codes are used to denote common storage locations whilst the full place name is used for other locations. The designation (S) denotes stored. However, when a locomotive pool code denotes that a loco is stored anyway then the (S) is not shown.

Code	Depot	Operator
AC	Aberdeen Clayhills	*Storage location only*
AF	Ashford Chart Leacon Works (Kent)	Bombardier Transportation
AK	Ardwick (Manchester)	Siemens/Trans-Pennine Express
AL	Aylesbury	Chiltern Railways
AN	Allerton (Liverpool)	EWS
AP*	Ashford Rail Plant	Balfour Beatty Rail Plant
AS*	Alley's, Studley (Warwickshire)	*Storage location only*
AY	Ayr	EWS
BA	Basford Hall Yard (Crewe)	*Storage location only*
BD	Birkenhead North	Merseyrail Electrics
BH	Barrow Hill (Chesterfield)	Barrow Hill Engine Shed Society
BF	Bedford Cauldwell Walk	First Capital Connect
BI	Brighton Lovers Walk	Southern
BK	Bristol Barton Hill	EWS
BM	Bournemouth	South West Trains
BN	Bounds Green (London)	GNER
BR*	MoD DSDC Bicester	Ministry of Defence
BQ	Bury (Greater Manchester)	East Lancashire Railway
BS	Bescot (Walsall)	EWS
BT	Bo'ness (West Lothian)	Bo'ness & Kinneil Railway
BY	Bletchley	Silverlink
BZ	St. Blazey (Par)	EWS
CD	Crewe Diesel	EWS
CE	Crewe International Electric	EWS
CF	Cardiff Canton	Arriva Trains Wales/Pullman Rail
CH	Chester	Alstom/Arriva Trains Wales
CJ	Clapham Yard (London)	South West Trains
CK	Corkerhill (Glasgow)	First ScotRail
CO	Cranmore (Somerset)	East Somerset Railway
CP	Crewe Carriage	LNWR
CS	Carnforth	West Coast Railway Company
CT*	MoD Caerwent AFD (Caldicot)	Ministry of Defence
CU	Carlisle Currock	*Storage location only*
CV	Coalville Mantle Lane	Victa Westlink Rail
CZ	Central Rivers (Burton)	Bombardier Transportation
DC*	Didcot Yard	EWS
DF	Derby	Railway Vehicle Engineering
DI	Didcot Railway Centre	Great Western Society

DM*	Dollands Moor Yard	EWS
DP*	Devonport, Plymouth	DML
DR	Doncaster	EWS
DY	Derby Etches Park	Maintrain/Midland Mainline
DW*	Doncaster West Yard	*Storage location only*
EC	Edinburgh Craigentinny	GNER
EH	Eastleigh	EWS
EM	East Ham (London)	c2c
EN	Euston Downside (London)	*Storage location only*
ER*	Exeter Riverside Yard	*Storage location only*
ES*	On hire to GIF, Spain	GIF
EU*	Coquelles Eurotunnel (France)	Eurotunnel
FB	Ferrybridge	EWS
FD	Freightliner diesels nationwide	Freightliner
FE	Freightliner electrics nationwide	Freightliner
FF*	Forest (Brussels)	SNCB/NMBS
FN*	Locos in use in France	Euro Cargo Rail (EWS)
GI	Gillingham (Kent)	Southeastern
GL	Gloucester Horton Road	Cotswold Rail
GW	Shields Road (Glasgow)	First ScotRail
HA	Haymarket (Edinburgh)	First ScotRail
HE	Hornsey (London)	First Capital Connect
HG	Hither Green (London)	EWS
HM	Healey Mills (Wakefield)	EWS
HT	Heaton (Newcastle)	Northern
IM	Immingham	EWS
IL	Ilford (London)	"One"
IP	Ipswich stabling point	Freightliner
IR*	Immingham Railfreight Terminal	*Storage location only*
IS	Inverness	First ScotRail
KM	Carlisle Kingmoor	Direct Rail Services
KR	Kidderminster	Severn Valley Railway
KT	MoD Kineton (Warwickshire)	Ministry of Defence
LA	Laira (Plymouth)	First Great Western
LB	Loughborough Works	Brush Traction
LD	Leeds Midland Road	LNWR/Freightliner
LE	Landore (Swansea)	First Great Western
LG	Longsight (Manchester)	Northern
LL	Edge Hill (Liverpool)	West Coast Traincare
LM	MoD Long Marston (Warwickshire)	Ministry of Defence
LU*	MoD Ludgershall	Ministry of Defence
LY*	Le Landy (Paris)	SNCF
MA	Manchester Longsight	West Coast Traincare
MD	Merehead	Mendip Rail
MG	Margam (Port Talbot)	EWS
MH	Millerhill	EWS
ML	Motherwell (Glasgow)	EWS
MO*	Mossend Yard	EWS
MQ*	Meldon Quarry (Okehampton)	Dartmoor Railways
MY*	Whitemoor Yard (March)	GBRf
NC	Norwich Crown Point	"One"

NH	Newton Heath (Manchester)	Northern
NL	Neville Hill (Leeds)	Maintrain/Northern
NN	Northampton King's Heath	Siemens/Silverlink
NP	North Pole International (London)	Eurostar (UK)
NT	Northam (Southampton)	Siemens/South West Trains
NW*	Brunner Mond Works, Northwich (Cheshire)	Brunner Mond
NY	Grosmont (North Yorkshire)	North Yorkshire Moors Railway
OC	Old Oak Common locomotive (London)	EWS
OH	Old Oak Common Heathrow	Heathrow Express
OO	Old Oak Common HST	First Great Western
OM	Old Oak Common carriage	Riviera Trains/EWS
OY	Oxley (Wolverhampton)	West Coast Traincare
PB	Peterborough Yards	EWS/GBRf
PM	St. Philip's Marsh (Bristol)	First Great Western
PZ	Penzance	First Great Western
RG	Reading	First Great Western
RL	Ropley (Hampshire)	Mid-Hants Railway
RM	Ramsgate	Southeastern
RR	Doncaster Robert's Road	Fastline
RU	Rugby Rail Plant	Carillion Rail Plant
RY	Ryde (Isle of Wight)	Island Line
SA	Salisbury	South West Trains
SB*	Sandbach Works	Albion Chemicals
SD*	Stoke Gifford Yard (Bristol Parkway)	*Storage location only*
SE	St. Leonards (Hastings)	St. Leonards Railway Engineering
SG	Slade Green (London)	Southeastern
SI	Soho (Birmingham)	Maintrain/Central Trains
SJ*	Severn Tunnel Junction	EWS
SK	Swanwick Junction (Derbyshire)	Midland Railway-Butterley
SL	Stewarts Lane (London)	Gatwick Express/VSOE
SM*	Swansea Maliphant Sidings	*Storage location only*
SN*	MoD Shoeburyness	Ministry of Defence
SO*	Southall (Greater London)	Flying Scotsman Railways
SP	Springs Branch CRDC (Wigan)	EWS
SU	Selhurst (Croydon)	Southern
SY	Saltley (Birmingham)	EWS
SZ	Southampton Maritime	Freightliner
TB*	Tilburg (Netherlands)	NedTrain
TD	Temple Mills (London) *(closed)*	EWS
TE	Thornaby (Middlesbrough)	EWS
TH*	Pershore Airfield, Throckmorton, Worcs.	*Storage location only*
TJ*	Tavistock Junction Yard (Plymouth)	*Storage location only*
TM	Tyseley Locomotive Works	Birmingham Railway Mueseum
TN*	Tonbridge West Yard	GBRf
TO	Toton (Nottinghamshire)	EWS
TS	Tyseley (Birmingham)	Maintrain/Central Trains
TT*	Toton Training School Compound (Notts.)	*Storage location only*
TY	Tyne Yard (Newcastle)	EWS
WB	Wembley (London)	Alstom/EWS
WD	Wimbledon (London)	South West Trains
WE	Willesden Brent sidings	*Storage location only*

WI	Wilton, Teesside	SembCorp Utilities
WN	Willesden (London)	West Coast Traincare
WR	West Ruislip LUL	London Underground
WY	Westbury Yard	EWS
XW	Crofton (Wakefield)	Bombardier Transportation
YK	National Railway Museum (York)	Science Museum
ZA	RTC Business Park (Derby)	Serco Railtest/AEA Technology
ZB	Doncaster Works	Wabtec
ZC	Crewe Works	Bombardier Transportation
ZD	Derby, Litchurch Lane Works	Bombardier Transportation
ZF	Doncaster Works	Bombardier Transportation
ZG	Eastleigh Works	*Storage location only*
ZH	Springburn Works, Glasgow	Railcare
ZI	Ilford Works	Bombardier Transportation
ZJ	Marcroft, Stoke	Turners
ZK	Kilmarnock Works	Hunslet-Barclay
ZR	York (former Thrall Works)	Network Rail
ZN	Wolverton Works	Railcare

* unofficial code.

8.6. ABBREVIATIONS

The following general abbreviations are used in this book:

AC	Alternating Current (i.e. Overhead supply).
AFD	Air Force Department
BR	British Railways.
BSI	Bergische Stahl Industrie.
CRDC	Component Recovery & Disposal Centre
C&W	Carriage & Wagon
DC	Direct Current (i.e. Third Rail).
DEMU	Diesel Electric Multiple Unit.
DERA	Defence Evaluation & Research Agency
Dia.	Diagram number.
DMU	Diesel Multiple Unit (general term).
DSDC	Defence Storage & Distribution CentreEMU Electric Multiple Unit.
GNER	Great North Eastern Railway
GWR	Great Western Railway.
H-B	Hunslet-Barclay.
h.p.	horse power.
HNRC	Harry Needle Railroad Company
Hz	Hertz.
kN	kilonewtons.
km/h	kilometres per hour.
kW	kilowatts.
lbf	pounds force.
LT	London Transport.
LUL	London Underground Limited.
m.	metres.
mm.	millimetres.
m.p.h.	miles per hour.
RCH	Railway Clearing House.
r.p.m.	revolutions per minute.
RR	Rolls Royce.
RSL	Rolling Stock Library.
SR	BR Southern Region.
t.	tonnes.
T	Toilets.
TD	Toilets suitable for disabled passengers.
TDM	Time Division Multiplex.
V	volts.
w	wheelchair spaces.

8.7 BUILDERS

These are shown in class headings. The workshops of British Railways and the pre-nationalisation and pre-grouping companies were first transferred to a wholly-owned subsidiary called "British Rail Engineering Ltd.", abbreviated to BREL. These workshops were later privatised, BREL then becoming "BREL Ltd.". Some of the works were then taken over by ABB, which was later merged with Daimler-Benz Transportation to become "Adtranz". This company has now been taken over by Bombardier Transportation, which had taken over Procor at Horbury previously. Bombardier also builds vehicles for the British market in Brugge, Belgium.

Other workshops were the subject of separate sales, Springburn, Glasgow and Wolverton becoming "Railcare" and Eastleigh becoming "Wessex Traincare". All three were sold to GEC-Alsthom (now Alstom) but Eastleigh Works closed in Spring 2006, although the site is now used as a storage location.

Part of Doncaster works was sold to RFS Engineering, which became insolvent and was bought out and renamed RFS Industries. This is now Wabtec.

The builder details in the class headings show the owner at the time of vehicle construction followed by the works as follows:

Ashford	Ashford Works (Note that this is not the same as the current Bombardier Ashford depot which is at Chart Leacon).
Birmingham	The former Metro-Cammel works at Saltley, Birmingham.
Cowlairs	Cowlairs Works, Glasgow.
Derby	Derby Carriage Works (also known as Litchurch Lane).
Doncaster	Doncaster Works.
Eastleigh	Eastleigh Works
Swindon	Swindon Works.
Wolverton	Wolverton Works.
York	York Carriage Works.

Other builders are:

Alexander	Walter Alexander, Falkirk.
Barclay	Andrew Barclay, Caledonia Works, Kilmarnock (now Hunslet-Barclay).
BRCW	Birmingham Railway Carriage & Wagon, Smethwick.
CAF	Construcciones y Auxiliar de Ferrocarriles, Zaragosa, Spain.
Cravens	Cravens, Sheffield.
Gloucester	Gloucester Railway Carriage & Wagon, Gloucester.
Hunslet-Barclay	Hunslet-Barclay, Caledonia Works, Kilmarnock.
Hunslet TPL	Hunslet Transportation Projects, Leeds.
Lancing	SR, Lancing Works.
Leyland Bus	Leyland Bus, Workington.
Metro-Cammell	Metropolitan-Cammell, Saltley, Birmingham
Pressed Steel	Pressed Steel, Linwood.
Charles Roberts	Charles Roberts, Horbury Junction, Wakefield.
SGP	Simmering-Graz-Pauker, Austria (now owned by Siemens).
Siemens	Siemens Transportation Systems (various works in Germany and Austria).
SRP	Specialist Rail Products Ltd (A subsidiary of RFS).

NOTES

NOTES

Leasing trains and traction across Continental Europe